Practising
Education, Training and Development
in South African Organisations

Practising
Education, Training and Development
in South African Organisations

Melinde Coetzee (editor)

with
Jo-Anne Botha
Jerome Kiley
Kiru Truman

JUTA

Practising Education, Training and Development in South Africa

First published 2007
Reprinted 2009
Reprinted November 2009

© Juta & Company Ltd/The authors
PO Box 24309
Lansdowne 7779
Cape Town, South Africa

ISBN 978 0 7021 7694 4

Project Manager: Sarah O'Neill
Editor: Ian Parsons
Proofreader: Alexandra Le Feuvre
Typesetter: Christopher Davis
Cover and text design: Christopher Davis
Illustrator: Bronwen Lusted

Printed and bound in South Africa by Mills Litho, Maitland, Cape Town

Typeset in 9.5/12 pt ITC Garamond Std

Contents

About the authors   viii
Preface   x
List of abbreviations and acronyms   xii

Chapter 1/ETD in the South African context   **2**
Kiru Truman & Melinde Coetzee
The ETD challenge in South Africa   4
Raising the skills profile of the labour market   5
The importance of uplifting people's skills   6
The National Skills Development Strategy   7
Skills Development Legislation   14
Learnerships   39
Key terms   43
Review and discussion questions   44
Suggested reading   44
Summary   45

Chapter 2/The psychology of learning   **46**
Jo-Anne Botha & Melinde Coetzee
ETD, learning and performance   48
The nature of learning   50
Learner characteristics   54
Theories of learning   56
Other approaches to learning   60
Principles of learning   65
Accelerated learning   66
Key terms   73
Review and discussion questions   73
Suggested reading   74
Summary   74

Chapter 3/Conducting an ETD needs analysis   **76**
Jo-Anne Botha & Melinde Coetzee
Purposes of ETD needs analysis   80
Levels of ETD needs analysis   85
Methods of ETD needs analysis   102
The ETD needs analysis process   105
Key terms   116
Review and discussion questions   116
Suggested reading   116
Summary   116

Chapter 4/Outcomes-based learning programme design 118
Jo-Anne Botha & Melinde Coetzee
A learner-centered approach 121
Learning programme curriculum design 122
Designing learning activities 144
Choosing training methods 147
Designing learning support materials 149
The facilitator/trainer guide 152
Review and discussion questions 162
Suggested reading 162
Summary 163

Chapter 5/Delivering learning programmes 164
Jerome Kiley & Melinde Coetzee
Training delivery methods 166
Blended learning methods 173
The trainer as learning facilitator 176
Delivering classroom training 180
The learning facilitation process 188
Creating a conducive learning environment 196
Principles of classroom training 202
Transfer of learning 206
Managing classroom training 207
Key terms 210
Review and discussion questions 210
Suggested reading 210
Summary 211

Chapter 6/Assessment and moderation in ETD 212
Kiru Truman
Purposes of assessment 214
Role players in assessment 215
Types of assessment 218
Assessment methods and instruments 223
The assessment process 228
Moderation of assessment 242
Key terms 245
Review and discussion questions 245
Suggested reading 245
Summary 246

Chapter 7/Evaluating ETD effectiveness 248
Jerome Kiley
ETD evaluation 251
Stakeholders in ETD evaluation 254
Compliance evaluation 257
Value-added evaluation 262
Evaluation models 269

The ETD evaluation process 273
Factors that discourage evaluation 282
Key terms 284
Review and discussion questions 285
Suggested reading 285
Summary 286

Chapter 8/Managing ETD in the workplace **288**
Melinde Coetzee
ETD management in the 21st century workplace 290
The learning organisation 292
The ETD value proposition 296
Strategic human resource development 299
The ETD management process 303
The ETD management functions 307
Managing quality in ETD 313
Key terms 324
Review and discussion questions 324
Suggested reading 325
Summary 325

Chapter 9/Profession and practice of ETD **326**
Melinde Coetzee
Roles of the ETD practitioner 328
Characteristics of the professional ETD practitioner 331
A competency profile of effective ETD practitioners 333
Education and training of ETD practitioners 335
Continuous professional development 342
Ethical issues in ETD 345
Challenges for the ETD profession 347
Key terms 347
Review and discussion questions 348
Suggested reading 348
Useful learning and development resources 348
Summary 348

Conclusion **349**
Appendix 1: Example of a SAQA unit standard 350
Appendix 2: Example of an ATR/WSP (Employers with
    50 or more employees) 358
Appendix 3: Example of an ATR/SMME Grant Application 384
Appendix 4: National scarce skills by occupational category 395
Glossary of terms 396
References 405
Index 411

About the authors

Melinde Coetzee (Editor)

Melinde Coetzee (DLitt et Phil) is a professionally registered Industrial Psychologist and an associate professor in the Department of Industrial and Organisational Psychology at the University of South Africa. She has 14 years experience in organisational development, skills development and HRD management in the corporate environment. Since 2000, she has been lecturing subjects such as Personnel, Career, Organisational and Managerial Psychology at undergraduate, honours and masters levels. She also presents workshops in skills development facilitation through Unisa's Centre for Industrial and Organisational Psychology. Melinde is author of *Getting and keeping your accreditation: A quality assurance and assessment guide for ETD providers*; *Empowering the skills development facilitator*; *Planning quality outcomes-based learning programmes*; *Learner support: Toward learning and development*; and *Career planning in the 21st century*. She is also co-author of *Emotional intelligence in the classroom: The secret of happy teachers*; *Career counselling and guidance in the workplace: A manual for career practitioners*; and *Careers: An organisational perspective*.

Contact details
Cell: 083 500 8621 / 012 429 8204
E-mail: coetzm1@unisa.ac.za

Jo-Anne Botha

Jo-Anne Botha (BCom Hons) is a lecturer in the Department of Human Resource Management at the University of South Africa. She has 18 years experience in the Education, Training and Development (ETD) field. Since 2002 she has been designing and presenting courses on various topics in the business world such as: training supervisors, middle and senior managers; team building; communication skills; time management; strategic planning; training management and HRD. Jo-Anne is co-author of various study guides relating to human resource management and industrial and organisational psychology.

Contact details
Phone: 012 429 4318
E-mail: bothaj1@unisa.ac.za

Jerome Kiley

Jerome Kiley (MA, BA Hons HRD) is registered as a Masters Personnel Practitioner (Human Resource Development) with the South African Board for Personnel Practice. He is currently a lecturer in the Department of Human Resource Development at the Cape Peninsula University of Technology. Jerome runs the first-year Industrial Psychology Programme at the University of the Western Cape and lectures in the Honours Programme in Human Resource Development at the University of Johannesburg. He has extensive experience in the field of skills development and HRD management both in the public and private sectors. Jerome is a registered Assessor and Moderator and serves in this capacity for a number of institutions, including Tshwane University of Technology and Umalusi. Jerome is resident in the Western Cape and, besides the field of HRD, has a number of passions including animals, travelling, cycling, sea kayaking and restoring old houses.

Contact details
Phone: 021 959 6350
E-mail: kileyj@cput.ac.za

Kiru Truman

Kiru Truman (BA Hons, TLSD, LTCL, ATCL) has lectured at various higher education institutions in the Eastern Cape, KwaZulu-Natal, Gauteng and Western Cape. In Gauteng, Kiru worked for the former Technikon South Africa, now the University of South Africa. She continued her work with the University of South Africa when she moved to the Western Cape. Kiru is a qualified Verifier, Skills Development Facilitator, Moderator, Assessor and Curriculum Designer. She has facilitated various programmes, such as Assessment of Outcomes-Based Learning, Moderation of Assessment, Training Methodologies, Developing Learning Programmes, Assessment Design, Evaluating Learning Programmes, Skills Development Facilitation, Business Writing Skills and Business Acumen in the ETD and corporate fields. She is a Sector Skills Specialist for the W&R SETA and is co-author of *Pathways to Language: NVC L2* (Heinemann), *Life Orientation: L2* (Juta), *Pathways to Language: NVC L3* (Heinemann), and *Life Orientation: L3* (Juta).

Contact details
Cell: 082 787 7716
E-mail: kiru@trumanconsulting.co.za

Preface

We have come to believe that an effective ETD practitioner is an artist. Helping adults develop their skills in the 21st century workplace requires dedication and creativity; the medium of this great art is the human mind and spirit. THE AUTHORS

The field of ETD is a well-established field of study, which continues to evolve as the needs of society, generations and workplaces change along with technological developments in highly competitive business environments. As a new generation of ETD practitioners enters the field, we believe that it is time to review what we have learnt and to determine what we need to learn. In this book, an eclectic group of experienced ETD practitioners share their experience and wisdom by offering insights on practicing ETD in the 21st century workplace from a sound theoretical base, blended with practical applications.

In the context of skills shortages, high unemployment levels and, in turn, high labour turnover, South African organisations increasingly realise the importance of investing in the education, training and development of their employees as a means to remain viable. Given how expensive and important ETD initiatives are, it is important for ETD practitioners to use a systematic approach in the design and delivery of their ETD interventions. This book aims to guide ETD practitioners through the Training Cycle in offering practical guidelines for the planning, design, delivery and evaluation of learning programmes in the South African workplace. In addition, it aims to provide clarity on the outcomes-based approach to ETD in the context of the National Skills Development Strategy and its supporting legislative framework. Issues such as the assessment and moderation of learners' achievements and quality assurance of ETD design, delivery and management are also addressed. Finally, in exploring ETD as a profession and practice, ETD practitioners are guided towards continuing their professional development as lifelong learners.

Chapter 1, *ETD in the South African context*, introduces the national landscape of ETD in South Africa. The national perspective on skills development gives direction and guides all ETD efforts in both the formal and informal business sectors. In particular, skills development is viewed as an important vehicle through which the human capital and performance capability of people in organisations can be enhanced.

Chapter 2, *The psychology of learning*, explores the concept and principles of learning that form the foundation of effective learning programme design and delivery. In particular, it examines the characteristics of the adult learner and how the principles and theories of learning can be applied to enhance not only the design and delivery of learning programmes, but also individual and organisational learning and performance.

Chapter 3, *Conducting ETD needs analysis*, introduces the first phase of the Training Cycle by exploring the concept, process and methodology of conducting an ETD needs analysis as it applies to the planning, design and delivery of learning programmes as a critical component of broader strategic ETD initiatives.

Chapter 4, *Outcomes-based learning programme design*, explores the second phase in the Training Cycle, namely using the results of an ETD needs analysis to inform the design of quality outcomes-based learning programmes. It also outlines the principles and process of designing learner-centred outcomes-based learning programmes.

Chapter 5, *Delivering learning programmes*, focuses on the third phase of the Training Cycle: the effective delivery of training in the workplace. It explores training delivery methods and the dynamics of the learning facilitation process. Practices in applying training principles to enable transfer of learning to the workplace are also discussed.

Chapter 6, *Assessment and moderation in ETD*, addresses the fourth phase of the Training Cycle by outlining the national requirements for outcomes-based ETD assessment and moderation. The functions, principles, types and methodology of assessment are discussed in light of the importance of shaping learners' competence through the learning and assessment process.

Chapter 7, *Evaluating ETD effectiveness*, discusses the fifth and final phase of the Training Cycle by clarifying what evaluation means in ETD. It also describes the various stakeholders involved in ETD evaluation. In addition, the various types, criteria and models of ETD evaluation relevant to the workplace are discussed. This chapter also explores the evaluation process, examines data collection tools and discusses factors that discourage ETD evaluation.

Chapter 8, *Managing ETD in the workplace*, explores the context and approach to managing ETD in the 21st century workplace. The ETD value proposition, management process and functions are discussed to demonstrate how these contribute to the overall human resource development strategy of an organisation. Specific attention is also given to quality assurance as a critical aspect of managing outcomes-based ETD in the South African workplace.

Chapter 9, *Profession and practice of ETD*, reviews the role, personal characteristics and competency profile of the professional ETD practitioner; training and credentialing issues; professional ethics, and continuing development in line with the national unit standards for occupation-directed ETD practitioners in the South African workplace.

A final word: just as concepts and practices of ETD have evolved over time, our understanding of ETD has been shaped by many friends, colleagues, clients and students in the South African and international multicultural workplace contexts. We are truly grateful for these wonderful people who have shared their practices, wisdom and insights with us in person and through the professional literature.

We trust that this first edition of *Practising Education, Training and Development in South African Organisations* will provide the ETD and HRD fraternity and students new to the field with the foundation needed for independent practice in the challenging and exciting arena of quality outcomes-based ETD provision in the 21st century workplace.

May 2007

MELINDE COETZEE (EDITOR)
JO-ANNE BOTHA
JEROME KILEY
KIRU TRUMAN

List of abbreviations and acronyms

Throughout this book, we continually refer to certain institutions and terms. We found it easier to use these abbreviations and acronyms. Until you are familiar with all the meanings, you may need to refer to this page for clarification.

ABET   Adult basic education and training
ASTD   American Society for Training and Development
BBBEE   Broad-based black economic empowerment
BEE   Black economic empowerment
CBO   Community-based Organisation
CCFOs   Critical cross-field outcomes
DoE   Department of Education
DoL   Department of Labour
EE   Employment equity
EPWP   Extended Public Works Programmes
ETD   Education, training and development
ETQA   Education and training quality assurance bodies
FET   Further education and training
GET   General Education and Training
HET   Higher Education and Training
HR   Human resources
HRD   Human resource development
HRDS   Human resource development strategy
ISOE   Institute of Sectoral or Occupational Excellence
IPM   Institute for People Management
IT   Information technology
KSAO   Knowledge, Skills, Attitudes and Other behaviour
NGO   Non-governmental Organisation
NLRD   National Learner Record Database
NQF   National Qualifications Framework
NSA   National Skills Authority
NSB   National Standards Body
NSF   National Skills Fund
NSP   National Skills Plan
NSDS   National Skills Development Strategy
OBET   Outcomes-based education and training
PPP   Public Private Partnership
QA   Quality assurance
QMS   Quality management system
ROI   Return on Investment
RPL   Recognition of prior learning
SABPP   South African Board for Personnel Practice
SABS   South African Bureau of Standards
SAQA   South African Qualifications Authority

SARS	South African Revenue Services
SDA	Skills Development Act
SDF	Skills Development Facilitation
SDLA	Skills Development Levies Act
SETA	Sectoral Education and Training Authority
SGB	Standards generating body
WSDC	Workplace Skills Development Committee
WSP	Workplace Skills Plan

CHAPTER 1

KIRU TRUMAN • MELINDE COETZEE

Education, training and development (ETD) in the South African context

A skilled and well-developed workforce is at the heart of global competitiveness. Education, training and development is therefore seen as an important factor in meeting the country's economic and the employer's strategic, business and operational goals.

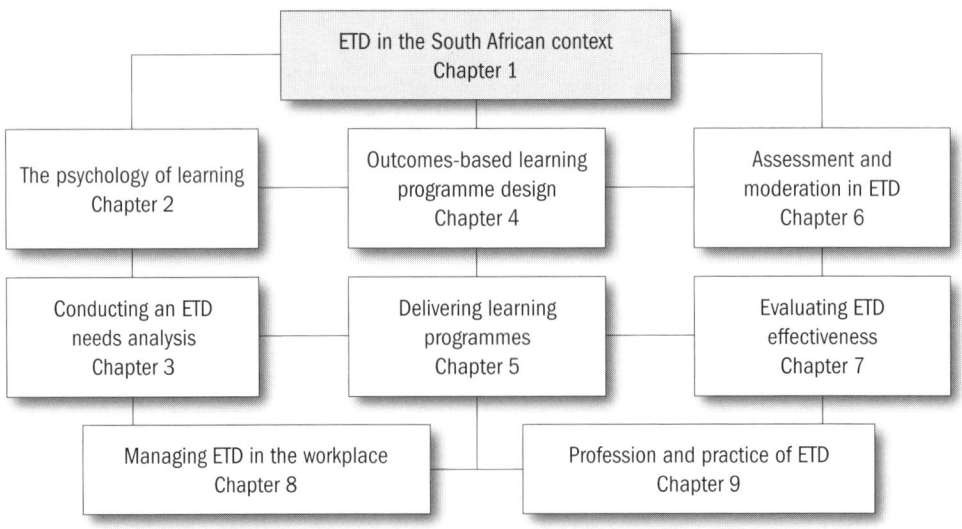

Key points of ETD in the South African context

- ETD is an important factor in meeting the country's economic goals and the employer's strategic, business and operational goals.
- The skills development acts introduce new structures, programmes and funding policies designed to increase investment in skills development and to improve the quality and relevance of ETD to the economy.
- The skills development acts and regulations represent a vision of an integrated ETD system that promotes economic and employment growth and social development.
- The National Skills Development Strategy sees vigorous skills training through learnerships as an important tool for addressing the skills deficit in South Africa.
- All ETD practices, programmes and methodologies must comply with the requirements for quality outcomes-based education and training.

After studying this chapter, you should be able to:

- Discuss the extent of the ETD challenge on a national level and how this impacts on ETD initiatives in South African organisations.
- Explain government initiatives to raise the skills profile of the labour market.
- Evaluate the importance of uplifting people's skills in an organisational context.
- Explain the purpose and objectives of the National Skills Development Strategy.
- Explain the aims of the national skills development legislation, and the governance structures put in place by this legislation and show how these impact on ETD efforts in South African organisations.
- Differentiate between learning programmes, skills programmes and short courses.
- Describe the categories and models for provider accreditation and recognition.
- Discuss learnerships as a skills development initiative.

In the knowledge-based economy of the 21st century, it is not equipment or technology that differentiates organisations. The difference lies in an organisation's workforce and the processes by which that workforce is established, used and maintained (ASTD, 2006). Organisations need talented, skilled and knowledgeable workers, regardless of economic conditions or levels of job growth. A highly knowledgeable, multi-skilled workforce is the most important competitive resource available to organisations. In the past, the economy was built on mass production. But recently, the economy has become dominated by technology and service industries that require innovation, speed, cross-functionality, and strong customer relations. This puts a premium not only on the technological skills of workers, but also on their ability to communicate effectively, access and apply knowledge, synthesise information, solve problems, adapt to fast-moving work environments, and work across the organisation in teams (ASTD, 2006). Organisations that invest in the education, training and development of their workforce are rewarded with improved performance and productivity.

This chapter introduces the national context for education, training and development (ETD) in South Africa. The national perspective on skills development gives direction and guides all ETD efforts in both the formal and informal business sectors. In particular, skills development is viewed as an important way to enhance the performance capability of people in organisations. By understanding the purpose and challenges of people development efforts on a national level, managers and ETD practitioners will be able to determine skills development objectives and targets that will help to improve the performance capabilities of their organisation and its employees.

The ETD challenge in South Africa

The South African labour market is characterised by an oversupply of unskilled workers and a shortage of skilled workers. Population growth exceeds the growth in jobs. This situation is made worse by the constant loss of jobs in the formal sector as the country's economy moves away from labour-intensive to capital-intensive operations that require highly skilled human resources (Department of Labour, 2005). This situation is known as the ETD challenge.

South Africa is faced with skills gaps, an ageing but highly skilled workforce, increasingly complex technology and rising consumer expectations from service providers.The demand for quality outcomes-based education and training, and competent and qualified ETD practitioners, increases as people's needs to acquire the skills necessary for employment grow (Department of Labour, 2005). Policies such as Broad-Based Black Economic Empowerment (BBBEE), Industrial and Sectoral Charters, the Human Resource Development Strategy, the National Skills Development Strategy (including the scarce skills approach) and skills development legislation offer opportunities for improving skills, or upskilling. These policies ensure that different industries enter value-added markets to stimulate demand for skills, employers act in their long-term interest, and there are incentives for organisations to develop both high-level and basic skills.

However, the scale of the ETD challenge is still daunting to most employers and the task of appropriate skills development awaits all South African workplaces (Telela, 2004).

Raising the skills profile of the labour market

The South African government has committed itself to raise the skills profile of the labour market. Short-term measures will address immediate shortages, and longer-term solutions are put in place to address structural imbalances in the labour market. Important decisions taken by government in this regard include:

- facilitating the placement of new entrants in the labour market through learnerships, apprenticeships, bursaries, internships and new venture creation initiatives;
- facilitating the recruitment of skilled foreign workers in fields with critical skills shortages;
- ensuring the development of South Africans in fields with critical skills shortages;
- providing career guidance and counselling to school leavers to assist them to pursue further studies in fields that meet the needs of the economy; and
- speeding up the implementation of the National Human Resource Development (HRD) Strategy by all government departments.

Labour market indicators

The labour market indicators, as reported in 2005 by the Department of Labour, show that:

- Unemployment remains the biggest challenge for transforming the South African labour market. Providing training to historically disadvantaged unemployed youth especially, could give them a better chance of entering the labour market. Such a training programme can also promote social cohesion and build a skills base.
- There is a large number of black workers with relatively low educational levels (up to and including Grade 12). Attempts to link skills development and employment equity should focus on solving this problem.
- There are not enough black workers in certain high-skill occupations. This should also be addressed in attempts to link skills development and employment equity. Training can assist the promotion and growth of black workers.
- Workers with disabilities are mostly excluded from the South African labour market.

Another important labour market indicator is the trend to change occupations. Researchers often use occupations to measure the demand for skills. By tracing occupations over time, it is possible to identify which occupations are growing and, therefore, where demand exists for certain skills. In South Africa, there has been a significant shift in occupations. There has been a growth in employment opportunities in especially middle-level occupations, such as technical and associate professionals, clerical workers and craft workers. Labour market indicators also show that skilled and semi-skilled occupations dominate the make-up of the South African workforce.

Internationally, service industries are the most versatile and flexible when it comes to generating employment, particularly through the establishment of small and medium enterprises (SMMEs). In South Africa, the service sector is taking on an increasingly important role as more and more organisations outsource some of their non-core functions. Business services is the fastest growing industry; it has overtaken manufacturing in its contribution to South Africa's Gross Domestic Product (GDP). Crime has also led to a significant growth in industries such as private security and insurance services. Globalisation is placing a greater demand on some industries (such as banking and other financial services) to align themselves to international standards and practices.

These changes demand a flexible and sophisticated workforce that can quickly adapt to changes in the working environment (Department of Labour, 2003).

The importance of uplifting people's skills

Skills upliftment is the enhancement of employees' applied competence in their jobs by improving their knowledge, skills, abilities and attitudes through formal education, skills training and continuous development. A skilled workforce is at the heart of global competitiveness. According to the Department of Labour, for a developing country such as South Africa, a skilled workforce also means improved living standards for all its people (Department of Labour, 2005). ETD is therefore seen as an important factor in meeting the country's economic goals and the employer's strategic, business and operational goals. International competition, corporate restructuring and technological advances, along with social and economic pressures, increase the importance of employee education, training and development.

There are ten important reasons why managers develop people (Cascio, 2003; Grobler *et al*, 2006):

1. Improve employee performance. Employees who perform poorly because of a deficiency in skills are good candidates for skills training. Although training cannot solve all problems of poor performance, a sound training and development programme can reduce these problems.
2. Update employees' skills. Technological change means that jobs change. Employees' skills must be updated so that technological advances can be successfully integrated into the organisation.
3. Avoid managerial, professional and critical or scarce technical skill obsolescence. Rapidly changing technical, legal and social environments affect the way managers, professionals and technical experts perform their jobs, and the skills of employees who fail to adapt to these changes become out of date and ineffective.
4. Orient new employees. Sometimes a new or newly promoted employee does not possess the skills and abilities required for the job. New workers may undergo training to give them the skills they need to fulfil their roles in the organisation.
5. Prepare for promotion and managerial succession. ETD enables an employee to acquire the skills needed for a promotion, and it eases the transition from the employee's present job to one involving greater responsibilities.
6. Satisfy personal growth needs. Education, training and continuous professional development can play a double role by providing activities and opportunities that result in greater organisational effectiveness and increased personal growth for all employees.
7. Solve organisational problems. Education, training and development can solve organisational problems such as absenteeism, ineffective and inefficient performance, low productivity, high employee turnover, disputes and poor service delivery.
8. Promote employability and sustainable livelihoods. South Africa has a high unemployment rate, worsening social issues such as poverty and crime. The government provides financial support to companies, non-governmental organisations (NGOs) and community-based organisations (CBOs) to run skills development initiatives. All skills development initiatives include strategies for the placement of individuals in employment, self-employment or social development programmes, or engagement in further educational studies.

9. Enhance employability of designated groups. The National Skills Development Strategy (April 2005 to March 2010) emphasises the need to assist unemployed people from designated groups to participate in skills upliftment programmes. Through these programmes, unemployed people can acquire the skills they need to enter the labour market or start their own small businesses. These programmes include learnerships, apprenticeships, internships, bursaries and new venture creation initiatives.

10. Promote and accelerate employment equity. To address the inequalities in the educational and equity profile of South Africa's workforce, skills development legislation makes provision for levy grants for employers who promote the development of blacks, coloureds and Indians, women and the disabled. Workplace skills plans and annual training reports must therefore support and reflect the employment equity targets of the company to qualify for levy grants. Appendix 2 on page 358 provides an example of how employment equity targets should be reflected in the workplace skills plan and annual training report.

The National Skills Development Strategy

The National Skills Development Strategy (NSDS) seeks to develop the skills of the South African workforce, to utilise the workplace as an active learning environment, to promote self-employment, and to secure work opportunities for new entrants into the labour market (Department of Labour, 2005). The NSDS maintains that, for all South Africans to participate in economic and social development and their own advancement, they must possess general capabilities (for example, reading and writing), and also be able to participate in the international market with its complex technologies and requirements for higher skill. This requires rising levels of applied competence. The government's Adult Basic Education and Training (ABET) initiative is an example of how illiterate and semi-literate adults are helped to develop basic numeracy, reading and writing skills, which in turn will enhance their employability.

The aim of Adult Basic Education and Training (ABET)

The aim of ABET is to prepare adults who have very little or no formal education (in other words, adults who do not possess the equivalent of a school-leaving certificate) for learning experiences and opportunities. It does this by bringing their educational level on a par with students who have completed Grade 9.

ABET prepares learners to participate in and influence the South African democratic society through:
- developing learners' full potential by participation in life-long learning experiences;
- participating effectively in the world of work;
- developing communication skills;
- developing mathematical skills;
- participating in the shaping and development of economic policies;
- developing a critical understanding of their society;
- enhancing job creation schemes;
- participating in and utilising development initiatives; and
- understanding science and technology and how it influences their world.

ABET forms an integral part of the National Qualifications Framework (see Table 1.3 on page 16). ABET level 4 (the highest ABET level) is equivalent to Grade 9.

ABET can be offered formally by schools and non-formally by occupation-directed and workplace-based schemes, community programmes, private providers, unions and other accredited ABET providers (such as the University of South Africa).

ACTIVITY

Review the workplace skills plan and annual training report in Appendix 2. Discuss the following questions with a colleague:
- In which section of the document should a company describe its ABET plan?
- What information should be included in the ABET plan?

The first NSDS (2001-2005) was launched in February 2001. The five objectives of the NSDS (2001-2005) were the following:
1. Develop a culture of high-quality, life-long learning.
2. Foster skills development in the formal economy for productivity and employability.
3. Stimulate and support skills development in small businesses.
4. Promote skills development for employability and sustainable livelihoods through social development initiatives.
5. Assist new entrants into employment.

The NSDS (2001-2005) achieved the following targets (as reported by the Minister of Labour):
- 41 753 workers more than the target of 1 398 033 completed their programmes successfully.
- 53% of firms (compared to the target of 40%) employing between 50 and 150 workers received skills development grants.
- 37% of new and existing registered small businesses (compared to the target of 20%) were supported by and benefited from skills development initiatives.
- 666 new learnerships were registered with the Department of Labour.
- 81% of the social development training funds allocated under the National Skills Fund had already been spent by March 2004. A job placement rate of 71% was achieved and equity targets were met.
- 69 000 learners below the age of 35 were registered in learnerships and apprenticeship programmes by the end of March 2004. By October 2004, this number had increased to 85 753 (compared to the target of 80 000).

According to the Department of Labour's (2005) Labour Market Review Report, in 2002/2003, the training rate among permanent workers in private enterprises was 25% (this is good in terms of international standards). This means that one in four workers in South African enterprises received some form of training in the 2002/2003 financial year. The training rate for medium enterprises was slightly higher than for large enterprises. Training rates across occupations were highest for service and sales workers (33%) and lowest for professionals (18%). The training rates for technicians (20%) and craft and skilled trades workers (23%) were considered to be too low. The distribution of training by gender seems to favour men. Overall, 28% of men but only 22% of women received some form of training in 2002/2003. In terms of race, black workers received significantly more opportunities for training than other groups. This suggests that equity considerations are influential, particularly in large enterprises. In addition, the HR and Industry Report (ASTD, 2007) indicates that South African companies spend on average 3,11% of payroll on training, 1% above the skills levy and more than the United States of America. Induction, information technology, leadership and Aids training seem to be the highest priority training programmes in South Africa.

The NSDS (2005-2010) seeks to build on the foundation of the NSDS (2001-2005).

Table 1.1 *Vision, mission and principles of the NSDS (2005-2010)*

Vision	Skills for sustainable growth, development and equity
Mission	The National Skills Development Strategy contributes to sustainable development of skills growth, development and equity of skills development institutions by aligning its work and resources to the skills needs for effective delivery and implementation.
Strategic Indicator	Government and its social partners assess the contribution of the NSDA (National Skills Development Act) institutions and resources to the nationally agreed strategies for growth, development and equity.
Principles	1. Support economic growth for employment creation and poverty eradication. 2. Promote productive citizenship for all by aligning skills development with national strategies for growth and development. 3. Accelerate BBBEE and employment equity. 4. Learners with disabilities should be reasonably accommodated to enable them to have access to and participate in skills development. 5. Support, monitor and evaluate the delivery and quality assurance systems necessary for the implementation of the NSDS. 6. Advance the culture of excellence in skills development and lifelong learning.

Table 1.2 Objectives and success indicators of the NSDS (2005-2010)

Objectives	Success Indicators	Lever
OBJECTIVE 1 Prioritising and communicating critical skills for sustainable growth, development and equity	Skills development supports national and sectoral growth development and equity priorities. Information on critical skills widely available to learners (rising, entry, completion, placement).	SETAs use discretionary funds to identify critical skills in sector (DoL / NSA Guidelines) (Critical skills (entry / intermediate / advanced levels aligned with national growth, development, equity strategy drivers and timeframes DoL consolidates SETA inputs – National Guide on occupational, employment trends, etc. Stakeholder utilisation of info and report back to DoL NSF Critical Skills Support Funding Window fund guide and training of career guidance counselors SETAs use discretionary funds to fund development of guides and training of SDFs/Sector specialists to use info in sector
OBJECTIVE 2 Promoting and accelerating quality training for all in the workplace	By March 2010 skills development in at least 40% of small levy paying firms supported and the impact of the support measured.	All Workplace Skills Plans (WSPs) to be submitted no later than 30 September for 2005 and thereafter 30 June each year. Newly registered skills levy-payers submit WSPs within six months from establishment. WSP to be judged against three criteria in 2005: (1) Timeframe (submitted in time) and (2) WSP meets EE + BBBEE and charter compliance criteria, (3) Stakeholder signoff From 2006 onwards the WSP will be judged by an additional criterion, i.e. a report on the performance against the previous year's WSP. If the WSP successfully meets set criteria then full 50% grant paid in quarterly tranches. Firms failing to meet the set criteria will automatically forfeit the WSP grant for the given financial year. Forfeited grants will be transferred directly into SETA discretionary funds.

Objectives	Success Indicators	Lever
OBJECTIVE 2 Promoting and accelerating quality training for all in the workplace	By March 2010 at least 80% of government departments spend at least 1% of personnel budget on training and impact of training on service delivery measured and reported.	Government budgetary process used to ensure that national and provincial departments spend at least 1% of personnel budget on training.
	By March 2010, at least 500 enterprises achieve a national standard of good practice in skills development approved by the Minister of Labour.	Firms achieving a national standard of good practice in skills development approved by the Minister will automatically get 50% of levy paid and for period standard is maintained. SETAs will secure agreement on information required from such firms based on regulation.
	Annually increasing number of small BEE firms and BEE co-operatives supported by skills development. Progress measured through an annual survey of BEE firms and BEE co-operatives within the sector from the second year onwards. Impact of support measured.	SETA discretionary BEE grants
	From April 2005 to March 2010 there is an annually increasing number of people who benefit from incentivised training for employment or re-employment in new investments and expansion initiatives. Training equity targets achieved. Of number trained, 100% to be South African citizens.	NSF – Industry Support Programme grants. The Department of Labour must provide an annual report on progress made in respect of employment or re-employment generated, linked to new investment initiatives and expansions.
	By March 2010 at least 700 000 workers have achieved at least ABET level 4.	SETAs use discretionary funds and may with the agreement of their boards include the provision of ABET as a criteria for the release of WSP grants. Total sum of all SETA targets to be at least 700 000 workers.
	By March 2010, at least 125 000 workers assisted to enter and at least 50% successfully complete programmes, including learnerships and apprenticeships, leading to basic entry, intermediate and high level scarce skills. Impact of assistance measured.	SETA discretionary grants to include 18(1) grants for learnerships, bursary grants, internship grants and study support to learners acquiring basic entry, intermediate and high level scarce skills identified as scarce in their sectors.

Objectives	Success Indicators	Lever
OBJECTIVE 3 Promoting employability and sustainable livelihoods through skills development	By March 2010, at least 450 000 unemployed people are trained. This training should incrementally be quality assured and by March 2010 no less than 25% of the people trained undergo accredited training. Of those trained at least 70% should be placed in employment, self-employment or social development programmes including Extended Public Works Programmes (EPWP), or should be engaged in further studies. Placement categories each to be defined, measured, reported and sustainability assessed.	NSF Social Development Initiatives Funding Window including EPWP grants.
	By March 2010, at least 2 000 non-levy paying enterprises, Non-governmental Organisations (NGOs), Community-Based Organisations (CBOs), and community-based co-operatives supported by skills development. Impact of support on sustainability measured with a targeted 75% success rate.	20% SETA discretionary funds and 80% NSF Informal Sector Support Funding Window.
	By March 2010, at least 100 000 unemployed people have participated in ABET level programmes of which at least 70% have achieved ABET level 4.	NSF ABET funding window to top up Department of Education (DoE) funding of Adult Learning Centres and funding to other public providers, as well as private and donor funding to other ABET initiatives.
OBJECTIVE 4 Assisting designated groups, including new entrants to participate in accredited work, integrated learning and work-based programmes to acquire critical skills to enter the labour market and self-employment	By March 2010 at least 125 000 unemployed people assisted to enter and at least 50% successfully complete programmes, including learnerships and apprenticeships, leading to basic entry, intermediate and high level scarce skills. Impact of assistance measured.	SETA discretionary grants to include grants for learnerships, bursary grants, internship grants and study support to learners acquiring basic entry, intermediate and high level scarce skills identified as scarce in their sectors. The NSF Critical Skills Support Funding Window provides funding.
	100% of learners in critical skills programmes covered by sector agreements from Further Education and Training (FET) and Higher Education and Training (HET) institutions assisted to gain work experience locally or abroad, of whom at least 70% find placement in employment or self-employment.	SETA provides Work Experience Grants, as per agreement, to levy paying and non-levy paying employers in their sector that will provide work experience opportunities to students/graduates in sector-relevant programmes.
	By March 2010, at least 10 000 young people trained and mentored to form sustainable new ventures and at least 70% of new ventures in operation 12 months after completion of programme.	SETA Discretionary New Venture Creation grants plus NSF Informal Sector Support Funding Window top-up.

Objectives	Success Indicators	Lever
OBJECTIVE 5 Improving the quality and relevance of provision	By March 2010 each SETA recognises and supports at least five Institutes of Sectoral or Occupational Excellence (ISOE) within public or private institutions and through Public Private Partnerships (PPPs) where appropriate, spread as widely as possible geographically for the development of people to attain identified critical occupational skills, whose excellence is measured in the number of learners successfully placed in the sector and employer satisfaction ratings of their training.	SETA Institute of Sectoral or Occupational Excellence Grant. This Grant to cover any or all of the following – and may be used to upgrade a facility in order that it can achieve the status of excellent: • Infrastructural Development • Educator/Trainer up-skilling • Curriculum and materials development • Learner support initiatives • Upgrading of satellite institutions (e.g. emerging providers in partnership with excellence institution) Other – by mutual agreement
	By March 2010, each province has at least two provider institutions accredited to manage the delivery of the new venture creation qualification. 70% of new ventures still operating after 12 months will be used as a measure of the institutions' success.	SETA discretionary grants plus National Skills Fund New Venture Creation Delivery Grant from the Informal Sector Support Funding Window.
	By March 2010 there are measurable improvements in the quality of the services delivered by skills development institutions and those institutions responsible for the implementation of the National Qualifications Framework (NQF) in support of the NSDS.	SETA discretionary grants and specific NSF grants from the Provisioning Support Funding Window approved after advice by the NSA.
	By March 2010, there is an NSA constituency-based assessment of an improvement in stakeholder capacity and commitment to the National Skills Development Strategy.	SETA discretionary funds and NSF Constituency Capacity Building and Advocacy Funding Window.

Skills development legislation

Skills development in the organisational context is governed by the National Qualifications Framework and the following three laws:
- the South African Qualifications Authority Act, Act 58 of 1995;
- the Skills Development Act, Act 97 of 1998; and
- the Skills Development Levies Act, Act 9 of 1999.

The South African Qualifications Authority Act

The South African Qualifications Authority Act (SAQA Act) established a special institution, the South African Qualifications Authority (SAQA). It is in charge of the National Qualifications Framework (NQF). The tasks of SAQA are to register qualifications and standards on the National Qualifications Framework, and to ensure that education and training programmes help learners to reach these qualifications and standards. The Ministers of Labour and Education appoint the 29 members of SAQA who represent all the different stakeholders (including businesses, non-government organisations, unions and ETD providers). The Department of Education is involved in maintaining the structures of SAQA and the NQF. SAQA and the NQF cannot exist without the foundation of the Department of Education. The Department of Education's functions are set out by the SAQA Act and the National Education Policy Act, Act 27 of 1996. The functions of the Department of Education include:
- overseeing the policies that guide SAQA and the NQF;
- upholding the structures of the NQF;
- registering ETD providers; and
- accrediting ETD providers and their learning programmes through ETQAs (Education and Training Quality Assurance body).

The SAQA Act put in place a new framework for education and training in South Africa by:
- creating a single, unified system of education and training qualifications; and
- creating the institutions to ensure that these qualifications are of a high quality.

The SAQA Act tries to unify education and training. In the past, school leavers with Grade 12 could continue their education at universities, or at technikons and colleges. The learning at universities and the theoretical courses at technikons and colleges were thought of as 'education'. The practical learning at technikons and within companies was thought of as 'training'. University education had more status than technikon or college training. As part of the initiative to end this artificial division between education and training, the technikons and universities merged. For example, the former Technikon of Southern Africa and the University of South Africa merged to form one comprehensive institution.

The SAQA Act states that both education and training are recognised forms of learning. Both forms must share important characteristics if they are to be useful to people. This means education is not only about academic theory, and training is not only about practical skills. The SAQA Act states that people must be able to move freely in the education and training system; they must not be stuck on either side of an education–training divide. They must be able to use the learning that they have acquired on one side to move forward on the other side.

Structures created by the SAQA Act

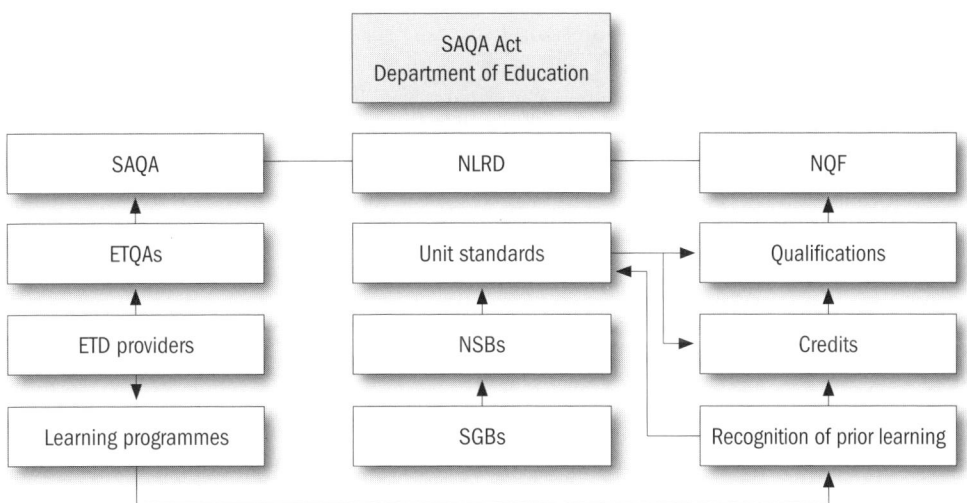

Figure 1.1 *Structures created by the SAQA Act*

The National Qualifications Framework

As shown in Figure 1.1, the SAQA Act brought the NQF into being. It is a framework, or set of principles and guidelines, that provides a vision and structure for the construction of a national qualifications system. The NQF is a national effort of integrating education and training into a unified structure of recognised qualifications. Education and training are brought together into a single, coordinated system designed to encourage lifelong learning. Learners' achievements are captured on the National Learner Record Database (NLRD). In this way, the acquired skills and knowledge of all learners are recognised. All qualifications and competencies are registered on the NQF according to their field of learning and level of progression.

The current framework (as shown in Table 1.3) is made up of eight levels of learning and pathways for learning specialisations (such as communications or engineering), with varying degrees of complexity of skills and knowledge. The new proposed framework (as shown in Table 1.4), developed particularly for the higher education band, consists of ten levels. The new proposed framework still awaits SAQA's formal approval. Different qualifications fit into the framework according to their focus and difficulty. The level of a qualification is based on the exit level; in other words, on what people will know and be able to do when they complete a qualification. This new way of recognising learners' achievements applies to all qualifications, giving education and training the same status. It measures what people know and can do, rather than where and how they acquired their skills and knowledge.

The NQF has three bands that describe the different levels of training and education in South Africa:
- General Education and Training (GET) comprises Level 1, which accommodates the Adult Basic Education and Training (ABET) levels and school up to Grade 9.
- Further Education and Training (FET) comprises Levels 2 to 4. These levels are

equivalent to Grades 10, 11 and 12.
- Higher Education and Training (HET) comprises Levels 5 to 8. In terms of the new proposed NQF, the HET band will comprise Levels 5 to 10.

Table 1.3 *The current National Qualifications Framework*

Higher education and training degrees, diplomas and certificates			
NQF level	Band	Qualifications	Education and training institutions
8 7 6 5	Higher education and training	Post-doctoral research degree Doctorates Master's degrees Professional qualifications Honours degrees National first degrees Higher diplomas National diplomas National certificates	Universities Universities of Technology Colleges
Further education and training certificates			
NQF level	Band	Certificates	Education and training institutions
4 3 2	Further education and training (FET)	School College Trade certificates	Private schools Some nursing Government schools Private schools Technical Labour market schemes Community Unions Some police Workplaces
General education and training certificates			
NQF level	Band	ABET certificates	Education and training institutions
1	Std 7/Grade 9 (10 years)	ABET level 4	Formal schools, urban, rural, farm, special schools Work-based training Labour market schemes Upliftment programmes Community programmes NGOs Churches Night schools Private ABET programmes Unions Workplaces
	Std 5/Grade 7 (8 years)	ABET level 4	
	Std 3/Grade 5 (6 years)	ABET level 2	
	Std 1/Grade 3 (4 years)	ABET level 1	
	1 year reception		

Table 1.4 Proposed new National Qualifications Framework for Higher Education

NQF level	HE Sub level	Cumulative min totals & min credits per qualification	General Vertical articulation	Articulation Horizontal and diagonal articulation	Career focused Vertical articulation
10	PG4	(1020) 360	Doctor of Philosophy (360 @ PG4)		Doctor of Philosophy, Professional Doctorate (360 @ PG4)
9	PG3	(660) 180	Research Masters Degree (120 @ PG3) / Structured Masters Degree (60 @ PG3)		Research Masters Degree (120 @ PG3) / Structured Masters Degree (60 @ PG3)
9	PG2	(600) 180/120	Masters Diploma (120 @ PG2)	Masters Certificate (72 @ PG2) (articulation credits)	Masters Diploma (120 @ PG2) / Professional Masters Degree (180 @ PG2)
8	PG1	480 480/120	Bachelors Honours Degree (120 @ PG1) / General Post-Graduate Diploma (120 @ PG2)	Postgraduate Certificate (72 @ PG1) (articulation credits)	Advanced Career-focused Bachelors Degree (e.g. BTech) (120 @ PG1) / Career-focused Postgraduate Diploma (120 @ PG1)
7		(360) 360/120	General Bachelors Degree (120 @ 7)	Postgraduate Certificate (72 @ 7) (articulation credits)	Career-focused Bachelors Degree (120 @ 7)
6		(240) 240	General Diploma (90 @ 6)	(articulation credits)	Career-focused Diploma (90 @ 6)
5		(120) 120		Foundation Certificate (72 @ 5)	Career-focused Certificate (72 @ 5)
4		(120) 120	FETC (72 @ 4)	Bridging Certificate (72 @ 4)	FETC (72 @ 4)

As shown in Table 1.5, level descriptors define the level of complexity of a unit standard or learning programme and the level of achievement expected from an individual at each of the levels. These level descriptors are not standards of achievement or assessment criteria, but rather indications of the level of learning required at each level.

Table 1.5 NQF level descriptors (Prinsloo, 2007)

Competence	NQF 5 (First year higher education)	NQF 6 (Second year higher education)	NQF 7 (Third year higher education)	NQF 8 (Honours/ post-graduate)
What should the learners know about the subject? (Foundational competence)	A fundamental knowledge base in the main areas of one or more fields. An informed understanding of the important terms, rules, concepts and principles. An understanding of the organisation or operating environment as a system within a wider context and in relation to society.	A solid knowledge base in at least one field/discipline. A sound understanding of one or more discipline/field's key terms, rules, concepts, principles and theories, and how it relates to other areas.	A well-rounded and systematic knowledge base in one or more fields/disciplines and a detailed knowledge of some specialist areas. A coherent and critical understanding of one or more discipline/ field's key terms, rules, concepts, principles and theories, and how it relates to other areas. Ability to map new knowledge onto a given body of theory, an acceptance of the possibility of many right answers.	A comprehensive and systematic knowledge base in a discipline/ field and a depth of knowledge in some area of specialisation. An ability to critique current research and advanced scholarship in an area of specialisation An ability to make sound theoretical judgments based on evidence and an ability to think epistemologically (think critically about theory).
What types of problem should the learner be able to solve? (Practical competence)	An ability to use knowledge to solve well-defined problems both routine and unfamiliar within a familiar context.	An ability to solve well-defined but unfamiliar problems using correct procedures and appropriate evidence.	An ability to deal with unfamiliar, concrete and abstract problems and issues using evidence-based solutions and theory-driven arguments.	An ability to identify, analyse, and deal with complex and/or real-world problems and issues using evidence-based solutions and theory-driven arguments.
How should learners gather information and how should they interact with it? (Practical competence)	An ability to interpret, convert and evaluate text (manuals, written instructions) and operational symbols and representations. Efficient information gathering, analysis and synthesis, and evaluation skills.	A critical analysis and synthesis of information. Presentation of information using basic information technology.	Well-developed information retrieval skills. Critical analysis and synthesis of quantitative and qualitative data. Presentation skills following prescribed formats, using IT skills appropriately.	An ability to engage with current research and scholarly or professional literature in a discipline/ field.

Competence	NQF 5 (First year higher education)	NQF 6 (Second year higher education)	NQF 7 (Third year higher education)	NQF 8 (Honours/ post-graduate)
How should learners be able to communicate? (Practical competence)	Presentation skills using appropriate technologies Ability to communicate information. coherently using basic conventions of an academic/professional discourse reliably in writing and verbally.	Ability to communicate information coherently using basic conventions of an academic/professional discourse reliably.	An ability to present and communicate information and own ideas and opinions in well-structured arguments, showing an awareness of audience and using the academic/professional discourse appropriately.	An ability to present and communicate academic professional work effectively, catering for a range of audiences by using a range of different genres appropriate to the context
How independent should learners be in their learning? (Reflexive competence)	A capacity to take responsibility for own learning within a supervised environment. Take decisions about and responsibility for own actions. Evaluate own performance against given criteria.	Capacity to evaluate own learning and identify learning needs within a structured learning environment. Capacity to assist others with identifying learning needs.	A capacity to operate in variable and unfamiliar learning contexts, requiring responsibility and initiative. A capacity to accurately self-evaluate, identify and address own learning needs. An ability to effectively interact in a learning group.	A capacity to operate effectively in complex, poorly defined contexts. A capacity to self-evaluate, exercising responsibility and initiative. A capacity to manage learning tasks autonomously, professionally and ethically. A capacity to continue to learn independently for continuing academic/professional development.

Table 1.6 *Principles of the NQF (SAQA, 2000)*

Principle	Definition: Education and training should ...
Integration	Form part of the system of human resource development, which provides for the establishment of a unifying approach to education and training (including practice and theory).
Articulation	Provide for learners, on successful completion of accredited prerequisites, to move between different parts of the education delivery system.
Flexibility	Allow for multiple pathways to achieve the same learning.
Access	Provide ease of entry to appropriate levels of education and training for all prospective learners, in a manner which facilitates progression.
Progression	Ensure that the qualifications framework permits individuals to move through the levels of qualifications through different appropriate combinations of the parts of the education delivery system.
Coherence	Work within a consistent framework of principles and certification.
Portability	Enable learners to transfer their qualifications from one learning institution and/or employer to another.

Principle	Definition: Education and training should ...
Recognition of prior learning	Through assessment, give credit to learning which has already been acquired in different ways (for example, through life experience).
Guidance of learners	Provide for the counselling of learners by trained individuals, to help learners to understand and make decisions about their entry into and progression through the education and training system.
Equality of opportunity	Provide the same standards for entry and progression for all learners.
Relevance	Be responsive to personal, social, economic and political development needs.
Quality	Be expressed in standards, in terms of a nationally agreed framework and internationally acceptable outcomes.
Credibility	Have national and international value and acceptance.
Legitimacy	Provide for the participation of all national stakeholders in the planning and coordination of standards and qualifications.
Democratic participation	Achieve legitimacy through democratic participation.

Outcomes-based training and development

Outcomes-based training focuses on what learners need to achieve at the end of the learning process. The word 'outcomes' is used broadly to refer to everything that is learnt, including social and personal skills, the activities of learning, how to learn, and concepts, knowledge, methodologies, values and attitudes. In addition, seven critical outcomes and five lifelong learning developmental outcomes were adopted as the basis for the design of all learning programmes. These 12 learning outcomes are known as critical cross-field outcomes (CCFOs).

The South African government established the NQF as a broad outcomes-based and assessment-led strategy (read more about this in Chapter 6) to transform education and training in South Africa. According to this approach, SAQA (as the central authority) decides on detailed criteria that any learner should meet before being issued a qualification. These criteria are formulated as unit standards, which include a description of the knowledge, skills, attitudes and values a qualified learner should be able to demonstrate in the future.

ACTIVITY
Study the unit standard in Appendix 1 on page 350.
Identify the knowledge, skills and values that learners have to demonstrate.

Critical cross-field outcomes

Critical cross-field outcomes (CCFOs) are relevant to your whole life, not only to employment and further learning. The seven critical outcomes are:
- problem-solving skills;
- team member skills;
- self-responsibility skills;

- research skills;
- communication skills;
- technological and environmental literacy; and
- the ability to understand the world as a set of related systems.

The five developmental outcomes are:
- learning skills;
- responsible citizenship;
- cultural and aesthetic understanding;
- employment-seeking skills; and
- entrepreneurship.

ACTIVITY

Study the critical outcomes below and then rate your ability (in your role as ETD practitioner) to demonstrate these behaviours. Rate yourself as follows:

3 Outstanding performance
2 Standard performance
1 Unacceptable performance

Identify and solve problems using critical and creative thinking. Examples: insight, problem-solving.	
Work effectively with others as a member of a team or group. Examples: working with other staff members to get information.	
Organise and manage yourself and your activities responsibly and effectively. Examples: punctuality, working independently, planning.	
Collect, analyse and critically evaluate information. Examples: obtaining relevant information, displaying the ability to analyse information, suggesting improvements.	
Communicate effectively using visual, mathematical and/or language skills in oral and written communication. Examples: writing skills, discussing issues, doing presentations.	
Use science and technology effectively and critically, showing responsibility towards the environment and the health of others. Examples: adopting a professional and scientific approach to ETD practices, safety awareness, using technology such as computers to plan, design and deliver learning programmes.	
Explore various learning and development strategies, apply the most appropriate one and evaluate the effectiveness of the learning and development strategy applied. Example: continued professional development strategies.	
Demonstrate employment-seeking skills for entry into the field of ETD, using all of the theoretical principles and reflecting on the effectiveness of such applications.	
Apply your occupational competence within the organisation and local community, showing an understanding of and sensitivity for diversity.	

Applied competence

The term 'outcomes' also refers to the applied competence that learners should demonstrate when they complete a learning programme. As shown in Table 1.7, applied competence is the combination of a learner's foundational, practical and reflexive competence (SAQA, 2005). These competencies are also reflected in the NQF level descriptors, as shown in Table 1.5.

Table 1.7 Elements of applied competence

Foundational competence	• Demonstrating an understanding of the knowledge and thinking which underpin the actions taken.
Practical competence	• Demonstrating the ability to consider a range of practical actions and make a decision about which action to do. • Demonstrating skills based on acquired knowledge.
Reflexive competence	• Demonstrating whether one is able to integrate knowledge and skills with understanding. • Demonstrating an ability to apply knowledge and skills in different contexts, and to adapt to change in unforeseen circumstances.

Qualifications, unit standards, credits and recognition of prior learning

The SAQA Act stipulates that:

- All skills must be written as learning outcomes. These outcomes should set out what learners will know and be able to do when they are declared competent. These outcomes will be recognised through national unit standards and qualifications.
- A qualification is made up of unit standards, each of which carries a number of smaller parts called credits. Each credit is equal to about ten hours of learning.
- People can earn their credits without formally attending a learning programme if they can show that they already have the skills and knowledge required. This *recognition of prior learning* (RPL) means that people's skills must be recognised. It does not matter whether someone has acquired these skills through experience or through a formal course. RPL is an acknowledgement of the learner's previous learning and work experience that is relevant to the content and level of a learning programme. Previous learning can take the form of a formal course (for example a degree), years of work experience, or a training course done through the workplace or a private training provider. Learning acquired from a tertiary institution such as a university can lead towards some kind of formal qualification.

According to Meyer *et al* (2004), there are four steps in the recognition of prior learning process:

1. Identify what learners can do and what knowledge underlies their ability to do something.
2. Compare this knowledge and skill with what is required in the unit standard.
3. Assess whether learners have achieved the outcomes of the learning programme by evaluating evidence of their performance against the standard.
4. Give the learner the appropriate credits if his/her knowledge and skill meet the required standard.

By bringing together all forms of education and training, the SAQA Act provides the basis for lifelong learning. Lifelong learning means that people have the opportunity to continue learning throughout their lives, whether through schools, colleges, universities of technology, universities, at work or elsewhere.

According to the SAQA Act, unit standards must be agreed upon in a democratic way. In this way, everyone will recognise the unit standards, and they will be transferable from one workplace to another and from one ETD provider to another. It is also important that standards are the same across the country so that everyone knows what a particular standard means. That is why every unit standard must be registered on the National Qualifications Framework.

A *unit standard* is a registered statement of education and training outcomes and their associated assessment criteria, together with administrative and other information as specified by SAQA regulations. It describes the scope and context within which the learner's competence is assessed. The results of the learning, not the processes, are described in unit standards. The national unit standards are available from the SAQA website. Appendix 1 on page 350 also provides an example of a unit standard.

ACTIVITY

Study the unit standard provided in Appendix 1 on page 350.
- Review the various elements of a unit standard as shown in Table 1.8.
- Identify the various elements of the unit standard.

Table 1.8 Elements of a national unit standard

Element	Description
Title	The title of a unit standard is unique. No title registered on the NQF will be identical.
Registration number	This registration number identifies the unit standard and is used for administration and identification purposes.
Level	This indicates the level of complexity required to achieve the unit standard, according to the eight levels described on the NQF.
Credit value	The credit value refers to the notional hours, which indicate the amount of time a learner will need to complete the learning programme. One credit equals ten notional hours.
Field and subfield	This indicates to which learning field and subfield the unit standard belongs.
Issue date	This is the date on which SAQA registered the unit standard.
Review date	Unit standards have a lifespan of three years. This date indicates when the unit standard will need to be reviewed again.
Purpose	This describes for whom the unit standard is intended and why it was written. It also describes the general skills that a learner will have acquired upon completion and states the reasons for the development of the standard.
Learning assumed to be in place	The learning assumed to be in place is the knowledge and skills that the learner is expected to have before starting the unit standard.

Element	Description
Specific outcomes	Specific outcomes are outcomes that focus on learning and performance. They capture a specific skill, knowledge and attitude that a learner must demonstrate in the unit standard. These are the outcomes that the learner aims to achieve.
Assessment criteria	Assessment criteria set out the evidence required to declare the learner competent in each specific outcome. An assessor will assess the learner's achievements (competencies) against the assessment criteria and determine whether the learner is competent in the required skills and knowledge.
Critical cross-field outcomes	These are generic outcomes that apply to all unit standards. These outcomes assess the life skills a learner needs to be a responsible member of the community and workforce. There are 12 critical cross-field outcomes. Not all of these are included in a unit standard; only those necessary at the appropriate level of the unit standard.
Range statements	The range states the scope, context and level of the unit standard. It also describes the situations and circumstances in which the learner is expected to perform.
Accreditation process	The accreditation process describes what the quality assurance and regulatory bodies must do to assess and approve the quality of the learning programme.
Essential embedded knowledge	Essential embedded knowledge is the knowledge that the learner needs in order to show competence in the unit standard. It is all the knowledge the learner will gain during the learning programme.
Supplementary information	This refers to any additional information in the unit standard. This may include definition of terms, legislation and regulations, and general information that may be of value to the assessor.

SAQA defines a *qualification* as a planned combination of learning outcomes with a defined purpose or purposes, which is intended to provide learners with applied competence and a basis for further learning. National qualifications can be based on unit standards, but not all of them are. Qualifications based on unit standards consist of a cluster of unit standards that are combined according to the rules of combination prescribed by SAQA. Qualifications that are not based on unit standards consist of clusters of learning outcomes combined as learning units. The learner has to progress through these units to complete the qualification. As shown in Table 1.4, a qualification is made up of a minimum of 120 credits.

Credits indicate the approximate time it would take a learner to complete a particular learning programme (1 credit = 10 notional hours). This is an estimate of the time the average learner would take to master the learning outcomes of the learning programme, the unit standard or qualification. Notional hours take into consideration learners' formal training, homework, assignments, preparation and assessments.

Table 1.9 The three components of qualifications

Fundamentals	The fundamental component forms the basis of the qualification. It includes units such as communication, maths and literacy, and life skills.
Core components	This is the compulsory learning that contextualises the qualification. For example, in the BCom degree in Human Resource Management, the core would consist of subjects related to the field of human resource management.
Electives	The electives enhance the qualification. These are additional units that a learner may choose to add value to the qualification. For example, in the BCom degree in Human Resource Management, learners can choose to take a subject such as Labour Relations Management or Training Management.

Learning programmes and short courses

SAQA (2004) differentiates between programmes, learning programmes, short learning programmes and courses. In SAQA terms, the term 'course' refers to the content of a programme.

- A programme is a coherent set of courses which lead to a certain qualification.
- A learning programme is the sequential learning activities that lead to the achievement of a particular qualification or part of a qualification.
- A short learning programme describes all short programmes, whether credits are awarded or not. These include skills programmes, credit-bearing short courses (courses containing less than 120 credits) and non-credit-bearing short courses.
- A short course is a type of short learning programme through which a learner may or may not be awarded credits, depending on the purpose of the programme.

According to SAQA (2004), short courses have a particular place in the new education and training system, and have an important role to play in the development of human resources. Short courses are being offered at all levels and in most fields of learning of the NQF. These range from courses for continuing professional development to skills-based courses. The provision of short courses assists workplaces in developing meaningful career and learning pathways for their employees in an accessible manner. To ensure an integrated and coherent approach to the provision of short courses, SAQA (2005) urges designers of short courses to include a focus on the teaching and learning assumptions and the proposed approaches, in the interest of the learner. Designers should also ensure that credits achieved through short courses are recognised in terms of registered qualifications and unit standards. This approach may lead to improved workplace practice and to the improved employability and mobility of employees.

Standards generating bodies

The SAQA Act requires that standards must be agreed upon in a democratic way. People with a direct interest in developing a standard meet as a standards generating body (SGB) to agree on the content of that standard. The SGB sends the agreed upon qualifications and standards to their national standards body for registration on the NQF. The national standards bodies are made up of representatives of government, organised business, organised labour, education and training providers, community and learner organisations, and other groups. National standard bodies (NSBs) ensure that all standards and qualifications fit into the NQF. The NSBs meet regularly to keep qualifications and unit standards up to date. There are 12 NSBs, each covering a different area of learning. They are:

NSB 01   Agriculture and nature conservation
NSB 02   Culture and arts
NSB 03   Business, commerce and management studies
NSB 04   Communication studies and language
NSB 05   Education, training and development
NSB 06   Manufacturing, engineering and technology
NSB 07   Human and social studies
NSB 08   Law, military science and security
NSB 09   Health science and social services
NSB 10   Physical, mathematical, computer and life sciences
NSB 11   Services
NSB 12   Physical planning and construction

All 12 areas of learning are important for the social, economic and political development of South Africa.

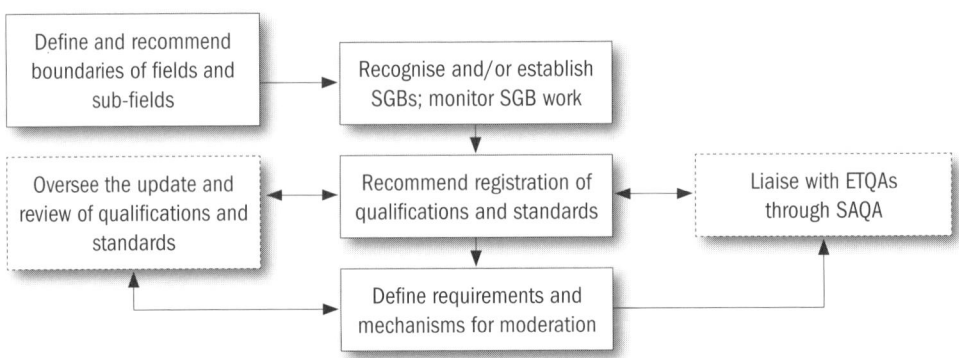

Figure 1.2 Functions of the NSBs (SAQA, 2000)

The NSBs recommend qualifications and standards to SAQA for registration. The NSBs check that all qualifications recognise prior learning. The rules for the qualifications must say what the person must know and be able to do to get the qualification, not how they must get the knowledge and skills.

Education and training quality assurance bodies

Education and training quality assurance bodies (ETQAs) are established by SAQA. In terms of the SAQA Act, ETQAs are moderating bodies with specific functions related to the monitoring and auditing of national standards and qualifications. ETQAs are appointed to ensure that the process of assessment is fair, reliable and valid. An ETQA may not be an ETD provider. Its primary function is to assure the quality and proper assessment of registered standards and qualifications.

The functions of ETQAs are to:
- accredit providers for specific qualifications and standards registered on the NQF;
- evaluate the assessment and facilitation of moderation among providers;
- register assessors and award certificates to successful learners;
- cooperate with relevant bodies appointed to moderate across ETQAs;
- monitor the quality of the provision of education and training;
- recommend new standards or improvements to standards to the NSB;
- maintain a database of records and submit reports to SAQA; and
- promote quality provision of education and training.

Accreditation of ETD providers

In terms of the SAQA Act, ETD providers are organisations that deliver and manage the assessment of learning programmes that form part of unit standards or qualifications. An ETQA may accredit a provider that meets the specified criteria when an application is received. Accreditation also depends on whether the provider:
- is registered in terms of applicable legislation;
- has the same primary focus as the ETQA;
- has a quality management system with the necessary:
  - financial, administrative and physical resources;
  - policies and procedures for staff selection, appraisal and development;
  - policies and procedures for learner entry, guidance and support;
  - policies and procedures for the management of off-site practical or work components;
  - policies and procedures for the management of assessment, moderation, RPL and appeals;
  - reporting procedures; and
  - ability to use available resources and procedures considered by the ETQA;
- is able to develop, deliver and evaluate learning programmes that lead to specified registered qualifications and standards; and
- has not already been granted accreditation by or applied for accreditation to another ETQA.

The benefits of becoming an accredited ETD provider are as follows:
- Clients prefer to use accredited providers.
- Employees know what is expected of them in the workplace, because they know which criteria are used to measure quality.
- ETQAs promote accredited providers to prospective learners by publishing lists of accredited providers.
- Clients are assured that the programmes they include in their workplace skills plans and annual training reports meet the quality requirements of the Sector Education and Training Authorities (SETAs).
- Grant payments from skills levies will be increasingly linked to organisations that use accredited training providers.

- All relevant stakeholders are assured that the qualifications or learning programmes offered by an accredited provider meet the national quality requirements.
- Employees are assured of the portability of their skills and qualifications obtained from an accredited ETD provider.

Applying for accreditation as a provider of education and training

Applying for accreditation can be a long process. These are the steps an ETD provider should follow when applying for accreditation:

- Appoint someone to take responsibility for the accreditation process.
- Before making contact, read about the relevant SETA and its ETQA on the SAQA website. Familiarise yourself with the expectations and requirements of the SETA.
- Contact the relevant SETA, indicating your interest in becoming an accredited provider.
- Submit a letter of intent to the SETA.
- Complete the accreditation forms and self-evaluation forms supplied by the ETQA.
- Identify a team of employees to help with the quality management process required for accreditation.
- Develop a quality management system for the provider organisation. Use the criteria and quality checklists provided by the ETQA.
- Obtain the approval and commitment of top management.
- Submit the necessary documents and evidence to the ETQA for accreditation.
- Study the response from the ETQA and make adjustments accordingly until accreditation is achieved.
- Continuously monitor and revise documents and systems to ensure sustainable quality assurance.

ETD providers, regardless of the sector in which they work, can be accredited by only one ETQA. It is the responsibility of the constituent ETQA to draw up agreements with other ETQAs if its providers offer programmes that fall outside the primary focus of that ETQA (SAQA, 2001). ETD providers can seek accreditation from an ETQA in one of the sectors listed in Table 1.10.

Table 1.10 ETQA sectors

Economic sector	Education and training sector	Social sector
There are two types of ETQA in the economic sector: • SETAs; and • Professional statutory bodies (such as the Pharmacists' Council and the South African Board for Personnel Practices).	There are two types of ETQA in the education and training sector, namely: • the Higher Education Quality Committee within the Council on Higher Education; and • Umalusi, which is the quality assurance committee for general and further education.	ETQAs in the social sector take the form of organisations representing a specific group or profession, for example the South African Council for Theological Education.

Table 1.11 Categories of provider accreditation (SAQA, 2001)

Category 1	Category 2	Category 3
• ETD providers who only deliver learning, but not summative assessments. • Providers who only deliver summative assessment, not formative and/or diagnostic assessment. • Providers who deliver learning and manage the assessment thereof. (The topic of assessment is discussed in Chapter 6)	• Multi-purpose ETD providers offering a wide range of programmes covering a variety of learning areas and fields. Examples: public and private higher education universities, universities of technology and further education and training institutions. • Single-purpose ETD providers including providers focusing on one field of learning (and related fields). Examples: large and small providers and consultancies offering, for example, computer-related training, and in-house and work-based learning.	• ETD providers that offer full, credit-bearing qualifications and short learning programmes based on unit standards and/or qualifications not based on unit standards for which they are accredited. • ETD providers that offer credit-bearing short learning programmes only, based on parts of qualifications (which may or may not be based on unit standards) for which they are accredited. • ETD providers that offer only non-credit-bearing short learning programmes that are not based on unit standards or qualifications. • ETD providers that offer a combination or all of the above options.

Models of provider accreditation

Based on the categories of provider accreditation shown in Table 1.11, SAQA (2001) differentiates between two models of provider accreditation, namely for:
- providers that offer credit-bearing, full qualifications and short learning programmes, which may or may not be based on unit standards; and
- providers that offer only credit-bearing short learning programmes, based on parts of qualifications, which may or may not be based on unit standards.

Recognition of providers

SAQA (2001) also makes provision for the approval or recognition of providers whose programmes are not aligned with the NQF. This group of ETD providers generally offers only short learning programmes that are not based on unit standards or qualifications. These may include providers that offer product-specific or equipment-specific training, or an entire range of other short learning programmes that fall outside of unit standards. These programmes are non-credit bearing in relation to unit standards and qualifications, but integral to effective workplace practice.

Although it is not necessary to regulate and accredit providers offering short learning programmes that are not aligned with the NQF, ETQAs in a particular sector may want to quality assure the provision of these programmes within their sectors. The ETQA will establish criteria whereby approval or recognition is granted. In practice, it is up to the client (individuals, organisations or employers with specific training needs) to decide whether a particular provider's services are needed or not.

Structures created by the Skills Development Act

The Department of Labour implemented the Skills Development Act and the Skills Development Levies Act to improve the skills of the South African workforce by encouraging learners to participate in learnerships and other learning programmes. Various incentives were offered to learners and employers in terms of the Skills Development Levies Act. The Department of Labour's responsibilities include:

- registering learnerships and skills programmes;
- assisting with the formulation of the National Skills Development Strategy, as well as sector skills development plans;
- directing funds to SETAs; and
- developing skills development legislation and regulations.

The aim of the Skills Development Act is to improve the working skills of South Africans so that the economy can grow and all South Africans can live a better life. The Skills Development Act fits into and builds on the SAQA Act. The Skills Development Act made many changes to traditional skills development. In support of the National Skills Development Strategy, the Skills Development Act created new structures for training in workplaces, new funding incentives to encourage more training, new forms of learning programmes and proposed new ways of assisting all people to get skills and jobs.

The Skills Development Act changes the old ways of vocational training, or on-the-job training, by introducing learnerships and skills programmes. Learnerships and skills programmes are meant for people who are already employed and people who want to enter the workplace. The Skills Development Act created the following structures:

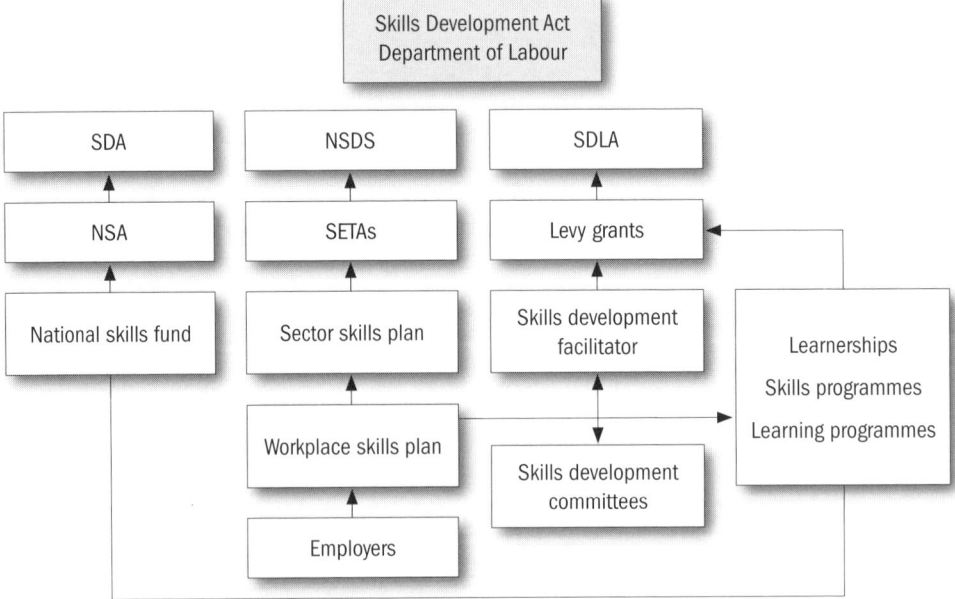

Figure 1.3 Structures created by the Skills Development Act

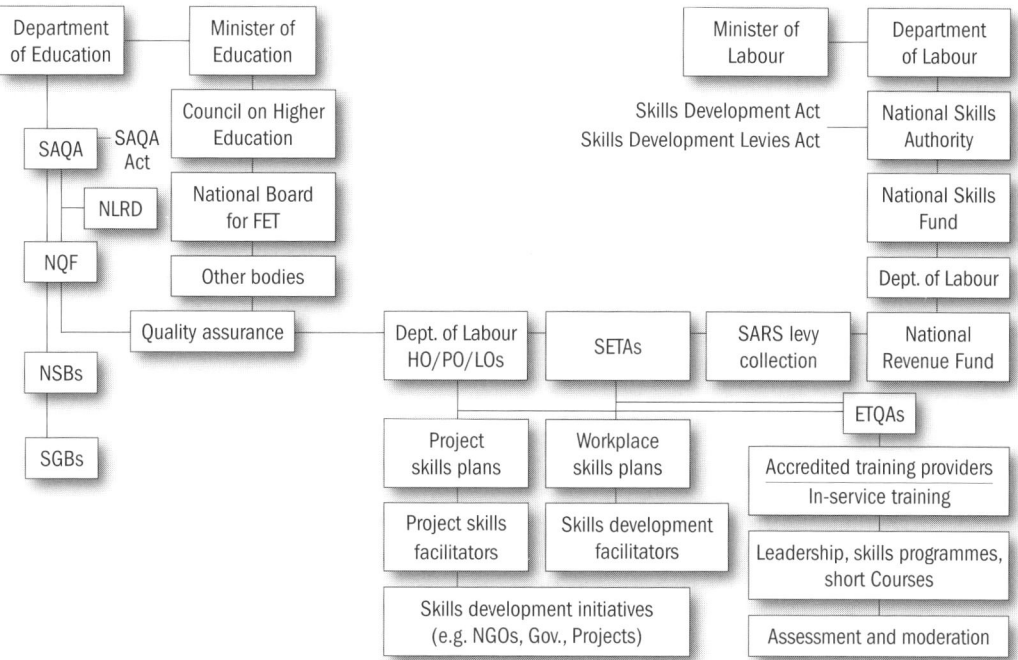

Figure 1.4 *National Institutional Framework (Department of Labour, 2003)*

The National Skills Authority

The National Skills Authority (NSA) was set up to advise the Minister of Labour on policies and strategies for the new skills-building system. The members of the NSA represent organised labour, organised business, the community, government, ETD providers, experts on employment services, and SAQA. The community representatives include people who represent women, youth, general public, rural groups and people with disabilities. The NSA works closely with the Department of Labour.

Sector Education and Training Authorities

There are two important organisations responsible for implementing skills development and identifying priorities for skills development. The first is the Department of Labour, which works mostly through its provincial offices and local labour centres. The other is all the Sector Education and Training Authorities (SETAs). The SETAs cover every industry and occupation.

The Minister of Labour established 25 SETAs on 20 March 2000. These were revised in March 2005, as shown on page 32. Each SETA serves a specific sector of the economy. A sector covers a group of linked and related economic activities. For example, there is a SETA for construction, another for wholesalers and retail activities, and another for the whole of the transport sector. The number of SETAs is currently under review and may change in the future.

Functions of SETAs

The Skills Development Act defines the functions of SETAs and states that each SETA must:

- Develop a sector skills plan and implement this through learnerships, encourage employers to compile workplace skills plans, allocate grants to employers to encourage education and training, and monitor education and training in the sector.
- Approve, register and promote learnerships.
- Oversee quality assurance of training and accredit ETD providers by means of the SETAs ETQA.
- Administer the levy grant system by paying grants to employers.
- Inform the National Skills Authority about their progress, and report to the Director-General.
- Provide information on job opportunities to both the employment services of the Department of Labour and education and training providers.

The SETA governing board

Each SETA has a governing board or council. This is made up of equal numbers of representatives from organised labour and organised employers. Government departments are also represented on SETA boards and (with the Minister of Labour's approval) relevant professional bodies and bargaining councils. SETAs may establish chambers to concentrate on the skills development needs of subcontractors. Each SETA must make a definite contribution to skills development that must be approved by the Minister. SETAs employ their own staff. The administrative and operational costs of the SETAs are limited by regulation to a maximum of 10% of the levy payments collected in that sector (read the sections on levy payments and levy grants on pages 35 to 37). If a SETA fails to work properly, or mismanages money, or fails to represents its sector properly, the Minister can, after consulting with the NSA, ask the Director-General to take over the administration of the SETA. The Minister may suspend the SETA and take any actions that are needed to get it working again.

From July 2001, each SETA has to sign a memorandum of understanding with the Director-General of the Department of Labour. The memorandum of understanding defines the responsibilities and obligations of the Department of Labour and each SETA, outlines what each SETA plans to achieve during the year, and how it will report to the Department of Labour.

Functions of a SETA

A SETA's main function is to contribute to the development of skills. SETAs aim to develop the skills of people employed (or who want to be employed) in their sector. They do this by ensuring that people learn skills that employers and communities need.

SETAs approved by the Minister of Labour in March 2005

The following 21 SETAs were approved by the Minister of Labour in March 2005:

- Financial and Accounting Services (FASSET)
- Banking Sector Education and Training Authority (BANKSETA)
- Chemical Industries Education and Training Authority (CHIETA)
- Clothing, Textiles, Footwear and Leather Education and Training Authority (CTFLSETA).
- Construction Education and Training Authority (CETA)
- Education, Training and Development Practices Sector Education and Training Authority (ETDPSETA)

- Energy Sector Education and Training Authority (ESETA)
- Food and Beverages Manufacturing Industry Sector Education and Training Authority (FOODBEVSETA)
- Forest Industries Sector Education and Training Authority (FIETA)
- Health and Welfare Sector Education and Training Authority (HWSETA)
- Information Systems, Electronics and Telecommunication Technologies (ISETT)
- Insurance Sector Education and Training Authority (INSETA)
- Local Government Sector Education and Training Authority (LGSETA)
- Media, Advertising, Publishing, Printing and Packaging Education and Training Authority (MAPPPSETA)
- Mining Qualifications Authority (MQA)
- Manufacturing, Engineering and Related Services Education and Training Authority (MERSETA)
- Public Service Education and Training Authority (PSETA)
- Services Sector Education and Training Authority (SERVICES)
- Tourism and Hospitality Education and Training Authority (THETA)
- Transport Education and Training Authority (TETA)
- Wholesale and Retail Sector Education and Training Authority (W&RSETA)

The following SETAs combined to form new SETAs in July 2005:

- The Diplomacy, Intelligence, Defense and Trade and Industry Sector Education and Training Authority (DIDTETA) and the Police, Private Security, Legal and Correctional Services Sector Education and Training Authority (POSLECSETA) combined to form the Police, Security, Legal and Correctional Services Education and Training Authority (POSLEC).
- The Primary Agriculture Education and Training Authority (PAETA) and the Secondary Agriculture Sector Education and Training Authority (SETASA) combined to form the Agriculture Sector Education and Training Authority (AGRI-SETA).

Sector skills plans

The SETA sector skills plan must cover the whole sector, from the biggest to the smallest business. Sector skills plans are necessary to ensure that SETAs know their sector, understand how it is changing and what skills are needed to support growth. The Department of Labour's guide to sector skills plans suggests that the plan should include:

- a profile (description) of the sector, which should include a description of current education and training happening in the sector;
- factors that might bring about future changes in the sector;
- employment and skills needs based on an analysis of the current situation and expected changes, including a list of scarce and critical skills in the sector;
- a vision of where the sector hopes to be in a few years, how the SETA plans to get there, and how it will measure success; and
- a budget and methods for monitoring, reporting and evaluating progress and successes.

The Skills Development Act states that SETAs can implement their skills plans through setting up learnerships, approving the skills plans from workplaces in the sector, allocating grants to employers, providers and workers, and monitoring education and training in the sector.

Workplace skills plans

A sector consists of many workplaces. Workplace skills plans are similar to sector skills plans, but they are compiled for one workplace instead of a whole sector. Like a sector skills plan, a workplace skills plan describes what skills are needed, who needs the skills, how employees will get the skills, and how much it will cost. However, the workplace skills plan goes into much more detail about all these things.

Workplace skills plans provide SETAs with the information they need to compile a meaningful sector skills plan, especially for scarce and critical skills. To draw up a workplace skills plan, the business requirements and the skills needs of staff are determined. The workplace skills plan then defines the skills priorities that the workplace will pursue for a particular year (generally from 1 April to 31 March in the following year), the training programmes that are required to meet and deliver those priorities, and the staff who will be targeted for training (also called the beneficiaries of the training) (SAQA, 2001). Appendices 2 and 3 show an example of a workplace skills plan and the information that must be captured to complete such a plan.

Regulations under the Skills Development Act state that workers and employers should work together to draw up a workplace skills plan. Towards the end of each financial year, every organisation that submitted a workplace skills plan must also submit an annual training report to report on the previous year's workplace skills plan. The annual training report reflects the ETD activities that the organisation implemented in the previous year. Companies must explain any differences between the workplace skills plan and the annual training report. Records of all ETD activities should be available to confirm the information in the report.

When the organisation submits a completed workplace skills plan and annual training report before the submission deadline of 30 June, a mandatory grant amounting to 50% of the levy is paid to the company. The mandatory grant includes amounts due for both the annual training report and the workplace skills plan. The organisation can utilise these funds to implement training. If the organisation does not submit its annual training report, the SETA transfers the 50% grant that would have been allocated to the discretionary grant fund. The organisation will then have to wait for the next financial year to claim the mandatory grant.

ACTIVITY

Study the examples of a workplace skills plan and annual training report in Appendices 2 and 3. Review each section of the documents.

- What information does the organisation need to supply to comply with the SETA's grant requirements?
- How does the workplace skills plan and annual training report for levy-paying companies with more than 50 employees differ from the annual training report, or grant application form for SMMEs (levy-paying companies with less than 50 employees)?

The Skills Development Levies Act

One of the reasons for poor skills development in the past was that not enough money was spent on training. The Skills Development Act provides regulations to control how the skills development strategy will be funded. The Skills Development Levies Act describes how money will be collected through levies paid by employers. All employers who pay R500 000 or more in monthly wages and salaries and who pay income tax, must pay the levy. All levy-paying employers who use a skills development facilitator, compile a workplace skills plan and report on skills development on an annual basis can claim money back. This is an incentive, or reward, to encourage employers to provide training for their employees. Employers who do not provide training for employees also benefit, because there are more people with skills in the labour market. Furthermore, an incentive for employers who take part in learnerships or skills programmes was established in April 2001.

Levy payments

- The levy payment is regarded as fair, because it is based on payroll. Payroll is a measure of the number and skills levels of workers, and it is workers who must be trained.
- The levy was only 0.5% of the monthly payroll until March 2001. From then on, the levy was 1% of the payroll. This is such a small cost that employers will not employ fewer workers to reduce costs.
- Although public service departments do not pay a levy, they are required to budget 1% of payroll for training purposes. They should report on the usage of that 1% when they submit their workplace skills plans and annual training reports to their SETA.

As shown in Figure 1.5 below, employers pay the levy to the South African Revenue Services (SARS) each month. SARS then sends the money to the Department of Labour. The Department of Labour puts 20% of the total income in the National

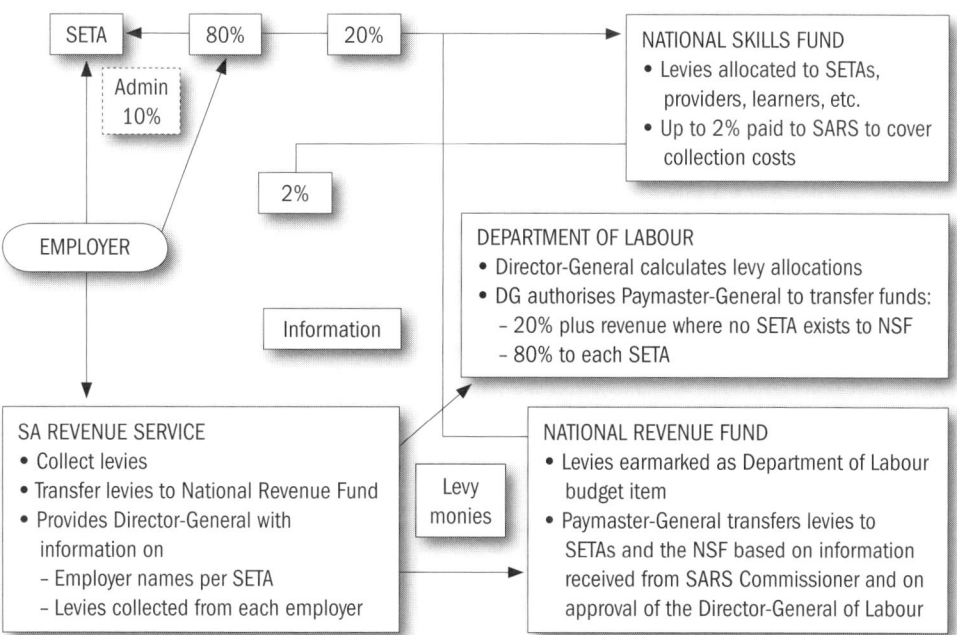

Figure 1.5 Flow of funds and information in the levy finance system (Coetzee, 2006)

Skills Fund and divides the other 80% between the SETAs. The money is divided between the SETAs according to the amounts paid by the organisations that make up the SETA. In other words, SETAs receive 80% of the money collected from employers in their sector. The remaining 20% goes into the National Skills Fund (SARS receives 2% of this 20% as payment for its services). Up to 10% of the money that goes to the SETAs can be used to cover the SETAs' administration and running costs. The rest of the money from the levies is used to pay grants to employers and to encourage employers to train their staff.

Levy grants

Levy grants are only available to employers who pay the levy. These grants fall into two main groups, namely mandatory grants and discretionary grants.

- Mandatory grants are linked to levy payments. There are large business mandatory grants for employers who employ 50 or more employees, and SMME mandatory grants for employers who employ fewer than 50 employees.
- Discretionary grants are available to employers, ETD providers, workers and the unemployed who apply for the funding of ETD programmes or projects that support the National Skills Development Strategy, the SETA priorities and, where specified, sector-specific needs. Discretionary grants are cash grants that a SETA may pay out to an employer. There are three types of discretionary grant:
  - learnerships;
  - skills programmes; and
  - ETD interventions aimed at meeting sector-specific needs determined by the SETA.

If an employer meets certain conditions (such as being up to date with its levy payments, producing a workplace skills plan and reporting on progress through an annual training report), the SETA will pay 50% of the levy back to the employer in the form of a grant. Employers need to apply for this grant before their SETA's deadline. Mandatory levy grants are paid out to qualifying organisations on a quarterly basis (July, October, January and March). Organisations need to provide the SETA with up-to-date levy payment information for verification purposes. The SETAs provide employers with the application forms and deadlines to claim this grant.

ACTIVITY

Study the annual training report, or SMME grant application form, provided by the W&RSETA for organisations with fewer than 50 employees (Appendix 3 on page 384).
- What are the SETA's requirements for SMMEs who want to claim levy grants?
- How do these requirements differ from companies with 50 or more employees?

In 2001/2002, employers could claim back 50% of their levies if they compiled and implemented a workplace skills plan. In 2002/2003, this dropped to 45%. As shown in Table 1.12, from 2006 to 2010, the mandatory levy grant will be 50% if all requirements are met. Up to 20% of the employer's levy payments are paid out to levy-paying companies in discretionary grants. That means 70% of an organisation's levy payment could be returned in the form of mandatory and discretionary grants, if it complies with the grant requirements.

The way in which SETAs award grants are determined by the skills development levies regulations. These regulations are available on the Department of Labour website at http://www.labour.gov.za.

Table 1.12 Levy grants: 2006 to 2010

	% Levy	Criteria/conditions
Mandatory levies	50%	• Skills development facilitator • Workplace skills plan for full financial year (for example, 1 April 2008 to 31 March 2009) • Submitted by 30 June every year from 2006 to 2010 • Employment equity/BBBEE/critical and scarce skills • Stakeholder compliance • Implementation and annual training report • ABET (if identified as a priority)
	50% Only identified enterprises	• Compliance with national standard of good practice • Maintain good practice for agreed period of time • Approved by Minister of Labour

Sector discretionary (cash) grants
• ABET • Learnerships/bursaries/internships • Study support • Work experience programmes • New venture creation assistance and mentoring • Sectoral and occupational provision excellence • BBBEE

NSF top-up funding
• Employment and re-employment support • New venture creation delivery • ABET • Critical skills guidelines support • Constituency capacity building and advocacy

Addressing employment equity

In principle, skills development and employment equity are both concerned with the development of people. Both approaches help people to find ways to progress at work. The Employment Equity Act says clearly that skills development is one of the ways in which black people, women and people with disabilities can be helped to grow and develop. The regulations for workplace skills plans and annual training reports require that employers must state how many black people and people with disabilities will benefit from training. The Skills Development Act and the Employment Equity Act apply to levy-paying companies with 50 or more employees. Both acts state that employers must consult with workers when they make plans to implement training, and that employers should have a formally appointed officer assisting with the compilation, implementation and reporting of these plans. The Skills Development Act states that the workplace skills plans must help companies to reach their employment equity targets. In this way, the Employment Equity Act and the Skills Development Act work together to develop skills where they are needed most.

Skills development committees

Every workplace with more than 50 workers must have a skills development committee, also called a workplace skills development committee or a training committee. This committee includes representatives from the various departments in a company. If there is a union, the union must also be represented on this committee. The skills development committee takes part in discussions about the workplace skills plan, annual training report and other ETD initiatives.

Skills development facilitator

The person who advises on and helps to plan skills development for a workplace is called a skills development facilitator. In terms of the Skills Development Act, an employer must appoint a skills development facilitator. The skills development facilitator's details must be sent to the relevant SETA. Some organisations (particularly smaller ones) may appoint someone from outside the organisation to be their skills development facilitator. Some organisations with similar needs may agree to club together and appoint one person to act as skills development facilitator for all of the organisations. Other organisations will ask one of their existing employees to do the job. Some employers may decide to fulfil the role themselves. SETAs will accept any of these ways of choosing a skills development facilitator, if the employer thinks that the person has the ability to do the job.

ACTIVITY

Study the example of a workplace skills plan and annual training report in Appendix B. What information about the skills development facilitator needs to be captured on the form?

The role of the skills development facilitator

The role of the skills development facilitator needs to be understood against the background of the new legislation driving training and development. Skills development facilitators are required to:

- Assist the employer and employees to develop a workplace skills plan for the financial year that complies with specific requirements, guidelines and set timetables.
- Submit the workplace skills plan to the relevant SETA.
- Advise the employer on the implementation of the workplace skills plan and ensure that the training specified in the workplace skills plan is implemented.
- Assist the employer to draft an annual training report, based on training as implemented according to the workplace skills plan. The report must be accompanied by appropriate training records and submitted on deadline. The utilisation of all levy funds must also be set out in this report.
- Advise the employer on learning provision quality assurance requirements as determined by the SETA and ETQA.
- Act as liaison between the employer and the SETA.
- Monitor and audit the achievement of training goals as set out in the workplace skills plan.
- Monitor administration costs, operational costs, exceptional SETA costs and training levy schemes as described in the regulations of the Skills Development Act.

- Act as liaison with training boards (these boards still deal with apprenticeships, but they have largely been replaced by SETAs).
- Determine and meet the criteria for successful grant applications.
- Serve as a resource with regard to criteria required for accreditation, skills programmes, or learnership development, and any matter that an employer may need for skills development.

ACTIVITY

Review the role of the skills development facilitator. Then study the roles of ETD practitioners, as discussed in Chapter 9. How do the roles of ETD practitioners and skills development facilitators differ and how do they complement one another?

Role of the skills development facilitator	Role of the ETD practitioner	Difference in roles	The roles of ETD practitioners and skills development facilitators complement one another as follows:

Project skills plans

Community development projects can help people in the long term if they provide skills as well as temporary jobs. So, for the community development sector, there are project skills plans to develop skills at community level. As with workplace skills plans, the project skills plan must identify opportunities, and then determine which skills are needed. People can get help in drawing up a project skills plan from project skills facilitators. Project skills facilitators have a community development focus, and they are employed by the Department of Labour. They can ask the provincial Department of Labour for money from the National Skills Fund to help with the plan and to implement the plan. The government member of the relevant SETA can also help with project skills plans, and the SETA must check that the plan meets the sector standards and qualifications.

Learnerships

The National Skills Development Strategy sees vigorous skills training through learnerships as an important tool for addressing the skills deficit in South Africa (Hattingh, 2003). Learnerships are regarded as a way to align ETD initiatives more closely with labour market needs. They establish a relationship between structured learning provided by ETD providers and structured work experience. The result is that learners are equipped with the competencies that are required in the labour market (Hattingh, 2003).

A learnership is therefore described as a structured learning programme that leads to a qualification recognised by the NQF. It is an integrated, occupation-directed programme that combines learning at a training institution with practical, on-site experience and learning at a workplace. Learnerships must be related to a specific occupation and be registered by the relevant SETA with the Department of Labour. Learnerships play an important role in career planning, because they prepare learners to perform effectively in occupations for which there is a clear demand.

Chapter 4 of the Skills Development Act states that a learnership may be established if:
- the learnership consists of a structured learning component;
- the learnership includes practical work experience of a specified nature and duration;
- the learnership would lead to a qualification registered by SAQA;
- the learnership is related to an occupation; and
- the learnership is registered with the Director-General in the prescribed manner.

Every learner that enters the organisation on a learnership must be registered on the National Learner Record Database. Learners must receive a certificate when they complete a learnership. A national certificate of competence is awarded to learners who prove that they have the skill and knowledge as set out in the unit standards of the qualification. Learnerships are designed to serve a wide range of learners. Learnerships especially benefit:
- Unemployed learners who start on a learnership not initiated by the employer that is party to the learnership agreement. The aim is to build the skills and knowledge of these learners so that they can seek employment.
- Employed learners whose employers are party to the learnership agreement. These learners follow learnerships for job advancement and/or further learning.

Learnership agreements are formed between the following three parties for a specified period of time:
- a learner who must be employed by the employer for a specified period and attend the specified education and training interventions;
- an employer who must employ the learner for a specified time, provide the learner with practical work experience and allow the learner time to attend the training interventions; and
- an accredited ETD provider who must provide the specified education, training and learner support.

In an organisational context, learnerships form part of an integrated human resource development system focusing on education, training and employment. Learnerships replace the old apprenticeship system. The learnership system combines structured learning and work experience into qualifications registered on the NQF. These qualifications will reliably signify work readiness. The system must meet current and future economic and social needs, and it must be accessible to people in formal employment, as well as target groups outside formal employment. Through learnerships, education and training can be integrated and organised for accreditation on the NQF in a way that provides both vertical and horizontal movement within the qualification framework, and produces meaningful competencies for productive work. Apprenticeship qualifications should be seen as a subset of the learnership system.

Table 1.13 *Learnership requirements*

Learnership requirements	Evidence required for registering a learnership with a SETA
• Consists of a structured learning component and a practical work experience component • Leads to a qualification registered with SAQA • Guarantees that the successful candidate is competent for the specified occupation (the practicality of this requirement is questionable: it places a severe burden on training providers, and unless 'guarantee' is defined in a way acceptable to providers, it could lead to liability claims by learners against providers)	• Accredited outcomes-based and/or NQF-aligned training • Qualified ETD practitioners and relevant training and development of staff • Qualified and registered assessors and internal moderators • A quality assurance system in terms of processes and policies • A records management system • Compliance with other government regulatory requirements

Learnerships are similar to the old apprenticeship system: both are work-based routes for learning and gaining qualifications. However, learnerships are different from apprenticeships in a number of ways:
- Learnerships aim to integrate theoretical education and skills training in both the learning programme and in assessment.
- Learnerships are future-orientated. They prepare learners not only for current work, but also for lifelong learning, by including abilities and skills that are important in any occupation.
- Learnerships prepare learners to participate in changing the culture of their occupation.
- Learnerships specialise in a work-related area, but also promote employability across occupational fields wherever possible.

The main characteristics of learnerships
1. Learnerships are led by demand.
   Learnerships are often established in response to a social or economic need. These needs are not limited to the needs of the formal economic sector only.
2. Learnerships are more diverse then apprenticeships.
   Apprenticeships tended to focus on manual trades, whereas learnerships cover any occupations in which work-based learning paths are viable.
3. Learnerships take place in a wider variety of contexts.
   An apprentice tended to be registered under a single employer for the duration of the apprenticeship, whereas learnerships might involve partnerships and cooperation between different employers to provide learners with the necessary spectrum of work experience.
4. Learnerships differ from apprenticeships in that:
   - they are intended for a broader group of learners (that is, beyond the manual trades) in a broader range of economic sectors and occupations;
   - they aim to promote access to employment and education and training opportunities (rather than consolidate a worker's ability in his/her current trade);

- the learner's primary role is that of learner, rather than that of employee or helper; and
- they are focused interventions in the labour market.

5. By integrating education (theory) with training (workplace experience), learnerships are intended to transform the way in which ETD is done.

Learnerships and skills programmes

The Skills Development Act introduced the concept of skills programmes as a new ETD initiative. Chapter 5 of the Skills Development Act focuses on the importance of skills programmes in the provision of education and training. Skills programmes are specific to occupations and make use of accredited ETD providers to train learners. On completion of a skills programme, learners obtain credits towards a qualification registered with SAQA.

ETD providers that are accredited by an ETQA or comply with accreditation regulations may be used to deliver the skills programmes that make up a learnership qualification. As shown in Figure 1.6, a skills programme can comprise a single learning outcome or unit standard, or form part of a cluster of learning outcomes or unit standards. Skills programmes can form part of a learnership qualification or exist as a single learning intervention.

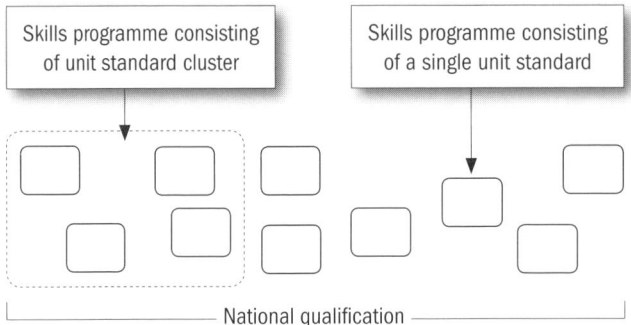

Figure 1.6 *Skills programmes as components of a national qualification*

Many ETD providers call their existing short courses skills programmes. These courses range from self-management courses, mentorship programmes and computer skills training, to programmes aimed at building cross-cultural understanding. However, these examples are in fact short learning programmes and not skills programmes as described by the Skills Development Act (Hattingh, 2003). The Skills Development Act describes the characteristics of skills programmes as follows:

- It is occupation-based.
- When completed, it will constitute a credit towards a qualification registered on the NQF.
- Accredited ETD providers are used.
- Any person that has developed a skills programme may apply for a grant from a SETA, or for a subsidy from the Department of Labour.

- The SETA or Department of Labour may fund the skills programme if it complies with the requirements stipulated in the Skills Development Act; is in accordance with the SETA's sector skills plan, or is in accordance with the National Skills Development Strategy.

Table 1.14 *Differences between learnerships and skills programmes*

Skills programme	Learnership
Learners are awarded credits, which can lead to a full qualification	A full qualification on the NQF with a minimum of 120 credits
Registered or recorded with the SETA	Registered with the Department of Labour through the SETA
Needs to comply with set outcomes or unit standards that are registered on the NQF	Based on a set curriculum built on the NQF
Can comprise one unit standard, or a cluster of unit standards or learning outcomes	Comprises a number of unit standards
No fixed duration	Takes about 12 months to complete, depending on the competencies of the learner (120 credits = 1 200 notional hours of learning)
Learners are awarded a certificate to declare competence.	A nationally recognised qualification is awarded to the learner on completion
No formal agreement between learner, provider and employer	Formal agreement reached between learner, employer and provider
Core, fundamental, and elective components might be assessed in a cluster or individually, depending on the programme.	Core, fundamental and elective components are assessed
Integrated workplace learning (skills) and foundational learning are clearly defined.	Integrated workplace learning and foundational learning are not necessarily a requirement or clearly defined

Organisations can gain more from learnerships than simply getting money back from skills levies. Organisations should use learnerships and other ETD initiatives to build the competence required to meet current and projected business goals (Hattingh, 2003).

Key terms

- Annual training report
- Learnerships
- Learning programmes
- Levy grants
- National Skills Development Strategy
- Outcomes-based education and training
- Project skills plan
- Provider accreditation

- Quality assurance
- Short courses
- Skills development facilitator
- Skills profile
- Skills programme
- Unit standards
- Workplace skills plan

Review and discussion questions

1. How does the ETD challenge impact ETD initiatives in South African organisations? What can organisations, managers and ETD practitioners do to address the South African skills development challenges?
2. How will the various skills development initiatives of the government assist in raising the skills profile of the labour market?
3. Why is it important for organisations to implement ETD initiatives that contribute to the upliftment of their employees' skills?
4. How do the purpose and objectives of the National Skills Development Strategy influence ETD initiatives in the workplace? What can managers and ETD practitioners do to ensure that the organisation's ETD initiatives contribute to the objectives of the National Skills Development Strategy?
5. What are the aims and governance structures of the national skills development legislation? How do these impact ETD efforts in South African organisations?
6. How does SAQA describe learning programmes? What are the differences between learning programmes and short courses?
7. How do the learning programmes offered by providers with accreditation status differ from providers with approval or recognition status?

Suggested reading

Bellis, I. (2001). *Skills Development – A practitioner's guide to SAQA, the NQF and the Skills Development Acts*. Johannesburg: Knowres.

Department of Labour, (2005). *Labour Market Review Report 2005*. Pretoria: Government Printer.

Employment Equity Act, Act 55 of 1998.

Ensuring quality in education and training – the role of Education and Training Quality Assurance Bodies (ETQAs). (2001). Pretoria: Department of Labour.

Further Education and Training Act, Act 98 of 1998.

Gultig, L., Lubisi, C., Parker, B. & Wedekind, V. (1999). *Understand outcomes-based education, teaching and assessment in South Africa*. Cape Town: SA Institute for Distance Education and Oxford University Press.

Hattingh, S. (2003). *Learnerships: A tool for improving workplace performance*. Johannesburg: Knowres.

Hattingh, S. & Smit, S. (2004). *Building learning organisations to enhance competitiveness*. Johannesburg: Knowres.

Telela, P. (2004). In McGrath, S., Badroodien, A., Krrak, A. & Unwin, L. (Eds.). *Shifting understanding of skills in South Africa: Overcoming the historical imprint of a low skills regime*. Department of Labour, Pretoria.

The National Skills Development Strategy. (2001). Pretoria: Department of Labour.

www.labour.gov.za

www.saqa.org.za (Information about SAQA, its regulatory bodies and unit standards are constantly updated. You can keep your knowledge current by subscribing to the free SAQA Alert mailing list.)

www.polity.org.za (This website contains all the acts referred to in this chapter. It is worthwhile visiting this site to stay up to date with changes in policies and legislation.)

Summary

The South African government recognises skills development as a crucial tool in enabling the South African economy to change and grow in line with global trends. This chapter explored how the National Skills Development Strategy, the skills development acts and governance structures represent a vision of an integrated ETD system, promoting economic and employment growth and social development. The various acts introduced new structures, programmes, requirements and funding policies for ETD initiatives in South African organisations. These are designed to increase investment in skills development and to improve the quality and relevance of education and training to the economy. ETD providers contribute to the vision of integrated skills development by ensuring that their ETD programmes, methodologies and practices comply with the quality requirements for outcomes-based education and training. Quality outcomes-based ETD practices and methodologies are the focus of the chapters that follow.

> *Developing people's skills should be done in such a way*
> *that it is perceived as a valuable gift, not a duty.*

CHAPTER 2

JO-ANNE BOTHA • MELINDE COETZEE

The psychology of learning

*The ways in which people learn and how they acquire competencies for
effective job performance are important considerations for the design,
delivery and evaluation of effective learning programmes.*

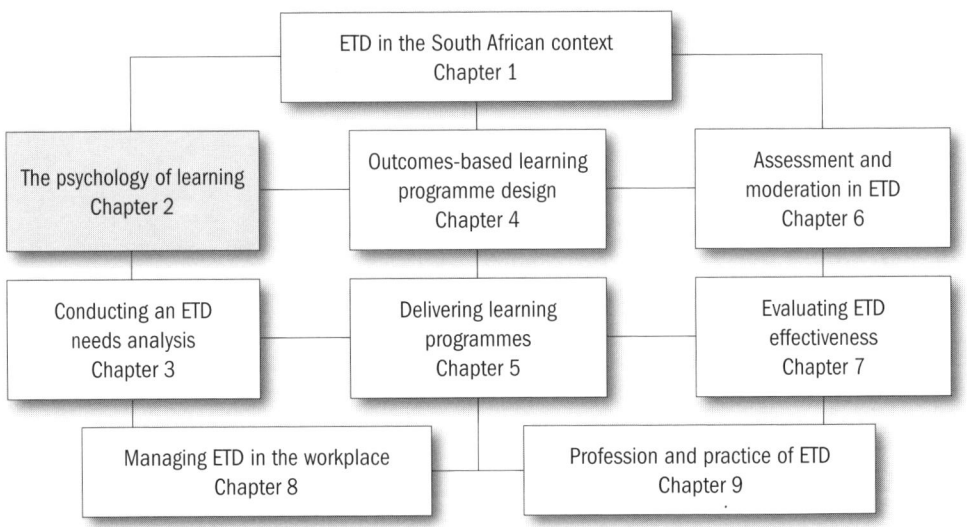

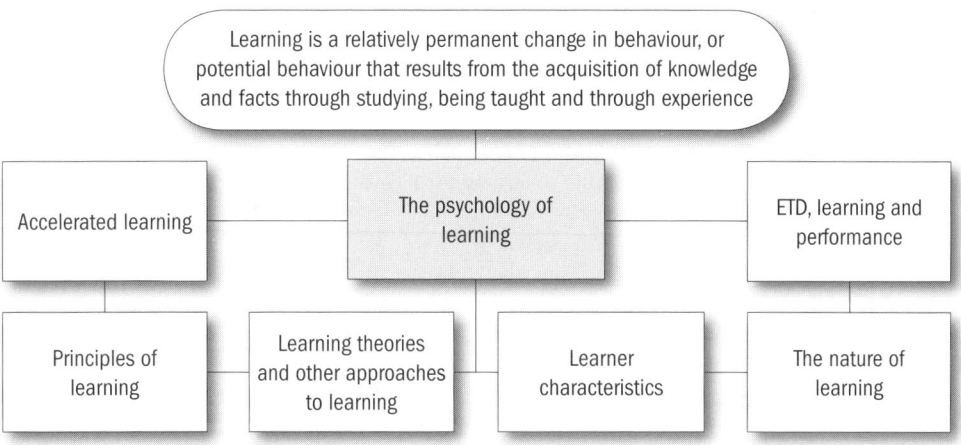

> Learning is a relatively permanent change in behaviour, or potential behaviour that results from the acquisition of knowledge and facts through studying, being taught and through experience

- Accelerated learning
- The psychology of learning
- ETD, learning and performance
- Principles of learning
- Learning theories and other approaches to learning
- Learner characteristics
- The nature of learning

Key points of the psychology of learning

- In an organisational context, learning occurs through ETD and organisational learning processes.
- ETD design begins with an understanding of how learning occurs. Adult learners' characteristics (readiness to learn, motivation to learn) and training design characteristics (principles of learning, objectives) affect the learning process and learning outcomes.
- ETD practitioners use principles from learning theories and approaches to design learning programmes and to enhance learning processes during training.
- Learning at an individual level strongly influences organisational learning processes.

After studying this chapter, you should be able to:

- Describe the link between ETD and learning in an organisational context.
- Explain how the characteristics of adult learners influence the learning process and the design of learning programmes.
- Differentiate between the various theories and approaches of learning.
- Explain how ETD practitioners can apply the principles of learning theories and approaches to the design and delivery of training.
- Explain how multiple intelligences influence adult learning.

Within an organisational setting, learning most frequently occurs through education, training and development. Organisations increasingly realise the importance of investing in the education, training and development of their employees as a means to remain viable. In South Africa, the combination of skills shortages and high unemployment levels creates a high turnover of labour. In this context, learning through education, training and development has an important role to play in helping organisations to retain valuable, talented staff.

Given how expensive and important ETD initiatives are, it is important for ETD practitioners to use a systematic approach to the design and delivery of their ETD interventions (such as learning programmes). A systematic approach includes assessing and analysing the organisation's and employees' ETD needs, incorporating principles of learning in training delivery, considering transfer of learning to the workplace, assessing learners' achievements and evaluating the effectiveness of the ETD programme. Chapters 3 to 7 will discuss this scientific approach (also called the Training Cycle), particularly as it applies to the design, delivery and evaluation of learning programmes, and the assessment and moderation of learners' achievements. In this chapter, the concept and principles of learning that form the foundation of effective learning programme design and delivery will be explored.

ETD, learning and performance

In the South African organisational context, the central focus of ETD is the human resource development (HRD) component of the human resources management process. HRD consists of education, training and development and is defined as organised learning experiences provided by employers within a specified period of time to bring about the possibility of performance improvement, personal growth and enhancement of employees' employability orientation, to satisfy the current and future needs of the organisation (Rothwell, Sullivan & McLean, 1995; Van Dam, 2004).

Training

Training is a specific way to facilitate learning in an organisation. Learning by means of formal training in the workplace forms the basic foundation for learning programmes. Training is regarded as a planned, short-term change effort to modify competencies, attitudes and beliefs, knowledge or skill behaviour through learning experiences (such as formal learning programmes). The goal is to sustain employees' employability by helping them to achieve effective performance in an activity or range of activities (Rothwell *et al*, 1995; Robinson, 2006).

Competencies

Competencies are typical behaviours (including attitudes and beliefs, knowledge and skills) that individuals demonstrate when undertaking tasks to produce job-related outcomes within a given organisational context. Competencies relate to specific descriptions of work tasks or job outputs that have to be achieved to demonstrate satisfactory job performance. Competency frameworks are used to define the dimensions of a job, and provide criteria by which the effectiveness of performance can be evaluated (Robinson, 2006). The outcomes-based ETD approach supports the notion of competency development by focusing on developing individuals' ability to apply their newly acquired competencies at work.

Attitudes and beliefs

Shaping or changing attitudes and beliefs through training might involve raising aware-ness of prejudices to modify behaviour; developing flexibility and cooperation in team work; or cultivating a culture of courtesy and sensitivity when dealing with customers. Attitudes and beliefs are regarded as the affective outcomes of learning programmes (Landy & Conte, 2004).

Knowledge

Knowledge is regarded as the cognitive outcome of a learning programme. Knowledge relates to the way in which people process information and attach sense and mean-ing to it. A distinction can be made between explicit knowledge (which is quantifiable and easily transferred and reproduced) and tacit knowledge (which is concerned with understanding and application). Tacit knowledge is often combined with experience and interpretation. It is therefore more difficult to capture tacit knowledge in a learn-ing programme (Robinson, 2006).

Skills

Skills are those aspects of behaviour that need to be performed to an acceptable level to ensure effective job performance. Skills-based outcomes of learning programmes are the procedural knowledge component of individuals' set of competencies (Landy & Conte, 2004). Skills include a range of abilities, such as:
- manual or technical skills;
- the application of specific competencies, knowledge and skills to perform a task;
- interpersonal skills such as the ability to work in a team;
- analytical and problem-solving skills involved in making sense of complex situ-ations, applying judgement and making decisions (Marchington & Wilkinson, 2005).

Education

Education is a medium-term change effort intended to prepare individuals for promo-tions (upward career progression) or for enhanced technical abilities in their current jobs (horizontal career progression). Education is broader in scope than training. It aims to develop individuals' knowledge, social understanding and skill, and intellec-tual capacity.

Development

Development is a long-term change effort intended to broaden individuals through experience and to give them new insights about themselves and their organisation. Development focuses on the longer-term growth and development of individuals in a way that fulfils their potential (Rothwell et al, 1995). Buckingham (1999) suggests that successful managers and ETD practitioners (as facilitators of learning) seek to build on the innate talents that individuals possess rather than simply to develop attitudes, com-petencies, knowledge and skills. ETD efforts (and in particular learning programmes) should therefore be designed and delivered in a manner that encourages individuals to use and apply their innate talents.

In the broader context of ETD, learning is defined as a relatively permanent change in behaviour or potential behaviour. It results from the acquisition of knowledge and facts through studying, being taught and even through experience (Lee-Davies, 2007; Rollinson, 2006). In other words, the individual is affected in some way or another as a result of exposure to ETD activities or interventions in the workplace. Learning therefore implies sustained change, as it is expected to increase job performance. Anything that produces only a short-term effect is not regarded as true learning. For example, a student who crams as much information as possible into her head before an examination, and forgets most of it after the examination, has not learned anything (Martin, 2005). Learning therefore also excludes changes in behaviour that result purely from growing older. Whereas performance can be directly observed, learning can only be inferred from behaviour or performance.

The nature of learning

How people learn and how they acquire skills for effective job performance are important considerations for the design, delivery and management of effective learning programmes. Knowing how people learn can help managers and ETD practitioners to diagnose performance problems, assess ETD needs and identify development strategies (Robinson, 2006). Research indicates that people generally learn in two ways, namely through implicit learning and explicit learning (Stevenson & Palmer, 1994).

Implicit learning

Implicit learning refers to the implicit knowledge that people use daily. They use this knowledge in most of what they do, but they cannot describe it. For example, people learn their mother tongue through implicit learning. They are not always consciously aware of the knowledge they gain from implicit learning, but they can still apply that knowledge when the situation requires it. People cannot always explain why they understand and are able to respond to what their parents ask or tell them to do. They cannot necessarily describe the relevant knowledge, unless they are taught the rules of the language (such as grammar and syntax). Implicit learning is therefore described as noticing regularities in the world and responding to them in consistent ways. Implicit learning is automatic; it occurs without our conscious control and leads to implicit knowledge (Stevenson & Palmer, 1994).

Explicit learning

Explicit learning requires conscious and deliberate thought and effort. Educational institutions facilitate explicit learning. They help learners to think deliberately and consciously about the meaning of things, how to solve problems and how to remember things. Explicit learning can be roughly divided into three activities: memorising, problem solving and understanding (Stevenson & Palmer, 1994).

Memorising

Learners who focus only on memorising and problem solving have a shallow approach to their own learning. They only want to reproduce the subject matter in some way, for example by answering assignment questions. When learners and facilitators of learning concentrate on understanding, they take a much deeper approach. They think about what they are learning and they try to understand the material so that they can use it to develop and change their pre-existing ideas (Stevenson & Palmer, 1994).

Explicit learning is a conscious action. Therefore, it requires deliberate effort and the use of memory. Memory serves as a storage facility for everything we have learnt about the world (all the knowledge we have acquired in our lives so far) and provides a facility where conscious thinking can occur. The long-term memory is our storage facility. The short-term memory is the workspace where we consciously think. For this reason, it is also called the working memory. The working memory has a storage function as well: it stores the ideas we are thinking about while we are thinking about them. The working memory has a limited capacity; it can hold between five and nine ideas at one time. People can usually only think about one idea at a time. A computer works in a similar way. The hard drive is the computer's long-term memory; the RAM (random-access memory) is the computer's working memory, and this is where the processing of data takes place.

The limited capacity of the short-term memory gives some explanation of why explicit learning is difficult. If the demands made by explicit learning exceed the capacity of the working memory, learning will not occur or will only occur to a limited extent. But when learners practise what they have learnt through explicit learning, it becomes implicit (automatic), and the information or knowledge is stored in the long-term memory. This frees up space in the working memory.

When do you use memorising?

Memorising happens when we read or listen to material because we want to memorise it. How do you prepare for examinations? Do you read through the work, summarise the sections you think are important and then repeatedly read through your summaries until you feel that you remember enough of the work to pass an examination?

We memorise by rehearsing or repeating information, and sometimes by integrating the new material with existing knowledge. When we memorise information, we are accumulating the information in our memories. We can either combine the new information with our existing knowledge, or add it to our memories without linking it to existing knowledge.

Memorising does not change the new or existing knowledge in any way. The emphasis is only on the accumulation of knowledge. Research has shown that repetition alone is not a good technique for memorising facts. Memory (and thus learning) improves when learners organise the learning material in a way that is logical to them, and integrate the material with pre-existing knowledge.

Problem solving

A problem can be described as a goal that seems to be out of the reach of a person, either because of lack of information or lack of resources (Stevenson & Palmer, 1994). When the person does something that leads to achieving the goal, the problem is solved. When the goal is achieved, the person learns something new about that situation or problem. So, when a learner finds a solution to a problem, he/she learns something new. When the learner applies the solution so often that the behaviour becomes automatic, further learning occurs. In this way, the learner frees up working memory for more complex or difficult problems or situations. For example, when we learn to multiply, we learn that 2 x 2 = 4. At first, this is a difficult problem for us. But when we apply what we have learnt from the problem to different problems, the calculation becomes automatic.

Problem solving does not require the use and explicit awareness of prior knowledge. This is why learners are not afraid to get involved in problem-solving situations.

The danger is that learners may only use problem solving and memorising when they learn, while neglecting true understanding. The ability to solve problems as described in the example above is limited to situations where the learner must know that 2 x 2 = 4. The knowledge gained cannot be used in new situations, unless it is similar to the one described. For the learner to use the generalised knowledge that is gained through understanding, he/she must be able to understand the conceptual principles that underlie a range of problems that seem different from each other (Stevenson & Palmer, 1994). For example, if learners only know how to multiply with a pocket calculator, they may find the solution to a problem, but they will not be able to apply the solution in any situation where they do not have a calculator. For them to do the calculation without the calculator, they must understand the mathematical concepts behind the solution, or the steps that will lead to the solution (Stevenson & Palmer, 1994).

Understanding

Understanding not only requires the use of the working memory, but also the ability to think about and deliberately control knowledge and thought processes. This is a high-level cognitive (thinking) activity; it takes years to develop this ability (Stevenson & Palmer, 1994). Most people find this type of learning difficult, and many avoid trying to use it. To grasp the concept of understanding more clearly, try to think of it in terms of your new knowledge and your existing knowledge. When understanding occurs, there is interaction between your existing knowledge and the new knowledge that you are processing.

Existing knowledge is used to make sense of the new knowledge. At the same time, the new knowledge may lead to a change in our existing knowledge. Learners often do not achieve understanding because they fail to evaluate their existing knowledge by using information from the new material they are studying. Learners who attempt to understand new work deliberately use their prior knowledge to help them to make sense of the new information. They also try to modify their existing knowledge with the new information (Stevenson & Palmer, 1994).

The kind of knowledge that is enhanced and modified through the activity of understanding is called conceptual knowledge. This knowledge describes the world around us. One of the important reasons why we should learn through understanding is that it assists us to understand and change our understanding of the world. Why was Alexander Graham Bell the one to 'discover' the telephone? Why was Galileo Galilei the person who found that the earth revolves around the sun? They used understanding to evaluate their existing knowledge and incorporate new information into the existing knowledge. In this way, they created new knowledge.

Although all learning does not result in better performance, careful attention to training design, principles of implicit and explicit learning and work environment characteristics can greatly increase the likelihood that learning will result in improved job performance (Landy & Conte, 2004). Training increases the probability of learning, and learning increases the probability of better performance. However, for learning to be effective, it must take account of the factors that accelerate, enable and hinder the learning process. Table 2.1 below provides an overview of typical barriers to learning.

ACTIVITY

Read through the following descriptions. Determine whether implicit or explicit learning is taking place

Description	Implicit/Explicit
Nomsa is learning how to behave at the dinner table.	
Pieter has started working at his new job, and he is still getting used to the new ideas of acceptable and unacceptable behaviour.	
Jonathan is studying for an examination and is memorising the names of the different learning theories and their characteristics.	
Siviwe is participating in a group exercise where he is learning to apply interviewing skills.	
Seshni has to apply the interpersonal communication principles she learned on a supervisor's training course in her work situation.	
Alice is doing a case study where she has to solve the planning problems of a production manager.	

Table 2.1 Barriers to learning (Lee-Davies, 2007; Martin, 2005)

External factors	
Physical	Inappropriate time or place
Specific environment	Unsupportive colleagues or superiors Pressure to undergo learning
Internal factors	
Perceptual	Inability to see that there is a problem
Personality	Learning style and preferences Demographics (including race, gender, age and cultural background) Habits
Cultural	Conditioning about the way things are done currently
Emotional	Mood, anxiety
Motivational	A lack of willingness to take risks
Cognitive	Previous bad learning experiences
Intellectual	Limited ability Memory limitations
Expressive	Ineffective communication skills
Learning experience	
Situational	A lack of opportunity Poorly designed learning event

Learner characteristics

In the workplace, ETD activities and interventions are developed for adult learners. While children learn because they are curious or simply for the sake of learning, adults are more orientated towards learning for application in the near future. Several characteristics of adult learners affect the learning process and outcomes. These are learners':

- motivation or need to know;
- readiness to learn;
- performance orientation;
- mastery orientation; and
- experience level (Landy & Conte, 2004).

The 'need to know' aspect is the perceived value of the knowledge to learners, and learners' interest in attending a learning programme, learning from the training and transferring the competencies acquired in training back to the job. 'Readiness to learn' is the amount of prerequisite knowledge the learners possess and the learners' subjective opinion of their ability to learn the material. It also includes learners' general mental ability, goal orientation, and experience level. For example, in a group of learners with widely different mental abilities, high-ability learners will be bored, while low-ability learners will have trouble keeping up with their peers. In a group of learners with similar abilities, learning facilitators can proceed through material at a pace appropriate to the backgrounds of the participants (Landy & Conte, 2004).

Learners with a *performance orientation* are concerned about doing well in training and being evaluated positively. They perceive their abilities as somewhat fixed, and they are generally not open to learning environments in which errors and mistakes are encouraged. They direct their energy towards performing well on tasks, often at the expense of learning. Performance-orientated learners are often sensitive to feedback. To avoid criticism, they might reduce their efforts and goals in challenging situations. In contrast, individuals with a *mastery orientation* are concerned with increasing their competence for the task at hand, and they view errors and mistakes as part of the learning process. Mastery-orientated individuals are flexible and adaptable in learning situations, which is particularly important when learning dynamic tasks and making complex decisions (Landy & Conte, 2004). Compared to performance-orientated learners, individuals with a mastery orientation are more motivated to learn, more actively engaged in the training task, more prepared to acquire new skills in training, and more effective at transferring their new skills to the job (Towler & Dipboye, 2001).

ACTIVITY
- When learning new information in your studies or on the job, do you tend to have a mastery orientation or a performance orientation?
- Does this orientation help or hinder what you learn, and how you later apply that information when you take a test or perform on the job?
(Landy & Conte, 2004)

An additional characteristic of adult learners that influences the learning process is *experience* level. Inexperienced learners with lower levels of competency generally benefit more from longer and more structured learning programmes (Gully, Payne, Koles & Whiteman, 2002). In contrast, experienced learners with high levels of competency thrive in shorter, less structured learning programmes. All of these characteristics of adult learners must be addressed for learners to feel capable of learning and willing to engage in the learning experience (Camp, Blanchard & Huszczo, 1986). ETD practitioners must therefore evaluate the relevance of the learning material and process to the learners' goals, values, needs, readiness for and orientation to learning, and experience level. The role of the learning facilitator or trainer should always be to support and enhance the adult learners' natural energies and talents for learning.

Adults prefer *self-directed learning strategies*. It seems that adults want to set their own pace, establish their own structure, and keep open the option to revise their learning strategy. Adults walk into learning situations with a fairly well-defined cognitive map. This map is based on their experiences of the world, and the older they are, the more detailed their map is likely to be. This means that ETD practitioners must consider the differences between members of a training group in terms of their learning strategies and needs. Differences in experience should also be regarded as a valuable learning resource. ETD practitioners (in their role as learning facilitators) must be skilled in guiding learners to share those experiences in a non-threatening manner. Learning approaches that emphasise an individualised and self-directed learning strategy, and makes use of other group members as resources for learning, will be most likely to succeed with adult learners (Camp *et al*, 1986; Knowles, 1972).

CASE STUDY

Lorna McKee, Area HR Manager, Hilton Hotel Belfast

"We can't train everyone to do everything. The emphasis is on getting people to learn within the environment where they work, and getting them to adapt and apply that knowledge. Every customer has different expectations. There is no way we can train for every eventuality. We want our staff to be spontaneous and react and respond to guest expectations".

Source: Sloman (cited in Robinson, 2006).

Questions
- How would you describe the link between education, training, development and learning?
- How is this link illustrated in the case study?
- What actions do you take to ensure that you learn as much as possible from your work environment?
- How can individuals, managers and ETD practitioners help people to adapt to changes in the work environment and apply their knowledge to the advantage of themselves and the organisation?

Adult learners are regarded as lifelong learners who have critical insight, independent thought and the ability of reflective analysis. They can make judgements about different theories or arguments (Brookfield, cited in Tennant, 2006; Merriam, 2004). These learners can manage their own learning because they act out of their own free will and initiate the learning themselves. According to Knowles (cited in Tennant, 2006), the *lifelong learner* has the ability to:
- develop and be in touch with curiosities;
- formulate questions that can be answered through enquiry (finding out the facts);
- identify the information required to answer different kinds of questions;
- locate the most relevant and reliable sources of information;

- select and use the most efficient methods for collecting the required information from the appropriate sources;
- organise, analyse and evaluate the information to get valid answers; and
- generalise, apply and communicate answers.

ETD practitioners can nurture and develop these abilities of adult learners by adopting the principles of *andragogy* (adult learning) in their ETD practices and processes. The andragogical approach is based on the following assumptions about adult learners:

- The learners need to know why they need to learn something before the learning event takes place.
- The learners need to be treated as people capable of self-direction.
- The learners have accumulated prior experiences that can be used fruitfully in the learning environment.
- The learners' readiness to learn is influenced by the need to solve a problem or fill a gap.
- The learners have a problem-centred orientation to learning and learn best when learning places them in real-life situations.
- The learners are driven more by internal motivators than by external motivators (Bash, 2003; Dooley et al, 2005; Knowles cited in Tennant, 2006).

ETD practitioners who adopt an andragogical approach to training are regarded as true facilitators of learning. Learning becomes a participative process in which the learner shares the responsibility for the learning with the facilitator. Mutual respect, trust and supportiveness are evident in the relationship between the facilitator and the learners. An *effective facilitator of learning* typically possesses the following characteristics:

- *Realness.* The facilitator enters into a relationship with the learner without presenting a mask.
- *Acceptance and trust.* The facilitator accepts the learner as a unique person with his/her own views, feelings and ideas. The facilitator also believes that the learner is trustworthy.
- *Empathic understanding.* The facilitator is aware of the learner's view of the learning process (Rogers cited in Tennant, 2006).

ETD practitioners and managers should strive to develop an environment that facilitates learning and training. The learning experience can be enhanced by using principles from several learning theories and various approaches to learning.

Theories of learning

Theories of learning have their roots in the study of psychology. Initial theories were developed from research into animal behaviour and learning. From these early studies, different perspectives were developed, which provide insights into the nature of individual learning (Robinson, 2006). Four main approaches have emerged over time, namely the behaviourist theories, cognitive theories, social learning theories and humanist perspectives on learning. Each one of these adds to the understanding of the learning process by building on top of the earlier approaches and making sense of different learning experiences. ETD practitioners have to think critically about how learners learn and what they can do to assist learners. Learning theories help learning facilitators to understand the learning process. By incorporating the principles behind the learning theories into the design and development of learning materials, ETD practitioners can enhance the learning process.

Behaviourist perspectives on the learning process

The behaviourist approach has been influential in highlighting specific elements in the learning process that need to be considered when designing or facilitating learning events. This approach demonstrates how behaviour can be shaped through appropriate reinforcement techniques (Robinson, 2006). The behaviourist approach explains learning in terms of what happens in the world around us. We learn because someone praises us when we do something right. Mental processes are not taken into account. The basic principle of the behaviourist approach to learning is that we form associations between a stimulus (a mother praises a baby who takes a step) and a response (the baby takes a step) (Schunk, 2004; Erasmus, Loedolff, Mda & Nel, 2006). Learning occurs when desired behaviour is praised (enforced) and this increases the likelihood of the person repeating that behaviour in the future. For example, a mother repeatedly encourages her baby to take a step and praises the baby warmly when the baby does take a step. The baby learns that, when he takes a step, his mother will praise him, so he takes another step. The behaviour is reinforced and the probability that the behaviour will be repeated in the future increases (Dooley *et al*, 2005).

The behaviour that the mother wants to see (the baby walking on his own) can be caused by repeated practise. This means that the relationship between the behaviour and the reinforcement is important, as long as the reinforcement (reward) is given immediately after the behaviour. The more the mother praises the baby's efforts, the more the baby will try to repeat those efforts, but only if the mother praises him while the effort is being made, or immediately afterwards. The rewards each of us find important, or reinforcing, are unique. We cannot assume that everyone's behaviour will be reinforced using the same rewards.

Cognitive approaches to learning

Cognitive approaches to learning build on the work of Kohler (1925), who researched how animals solved problems and Piaget (1926), whose work was focused on child development. Cognitive theories focus on how individuals process and interpret information, while acknowledging that humans do not always learn by performing a task and receiving direct reinforcement. Instead, humans can use memory, judgement, problem solving, reasoning and understanding to make connections between what they observe and how they should behave or perform in situations (including work situations). For example, a young woman touches a red-hot coal. It burns her fingers and she pulls away her hand. When this woman sees a red-hot coal again, she will not touch it, because she knows that it will burn her fingers. According to the theory of cognitive information processing, the woman received information from the environment (the coal is hot!). She processed the information (don't touch, it is hot!) and stored this information in her memory. This stored information is expressed in her behaviour when she is in a similar situation.

How do we process information?

Every day, we all receive information through our senses, but we only process the information that we pay attention to. This is called selective attention (Dooley *et al*, 2005). Think of a time that you were engrossed in a conversation with someone, and then clearly heard your name mentioned by someone else in the same room. This is an example of selective attention. Another example is when you start thinking of buying a car or cell phone. Have you noticed how often you see the same model of car or cell phone that you want to buy? You probably saw that model of car or cell phone just as often before you made your decision, but you did not pay attention to it at the time.

Sometimes, behaviours become automatic. We do not have to pay as much attention to these behaviours as we had to when we first started doing them. Think about making a cup of coffee. How much attention do you pay to all the tasks involved in making the coffee? And yet, how often do you burn yourself with hot water or forget to add sugar? This is called automaticity (Dooley *et al*, 2005). You have made coffee so often that it has become automatic. You can make a good cup of coffee without consciously thinking about it.

Pattern recognition is another important concept in cognitive information processing. When we receive new information, we try to fit it into a pattern that is already established in our memories. Pattern recognition enhances the transfer of new stimuli (information people receive through their senses) from the environment to our working memories. There is no conscious thought involved in pattern recognition (Dooley *et al*, 2005).

Cognitive information processing relies on the following processes: the senses must pass on information; the individual must pay sufficient attention to the information; and an appropriate pattern must exist in the sensory memory for pattern recognition to occur. When all three of these processes are completed, new information can enter the working memory. Conscious processing can then start to take place: information is retrieved from the long-term memory and used in the processing of the new information (Dooley *et al*, 2005).

ACTIVITY

The seven wonders of the short-term memory

The short-term (working) memory of most people seems to have a capacity of roughly seven bits of information. It can be described as a closet with seven hangers. The wonderful thing is that, although there are only seven hangers in a person's closet, what they hang on each of them is almost unlimited (Dooley *et al*, 2005). People can deal with more than seven pieces of information by dividing information into chunks.

Look at the following 15 letters:

SAASACPANCSANDF

- Try to memorise them. (Difficult, isn't it?)
- Now chunk the letters into something that makes sense:
  SAA   SACP   ANC   SANDF

You can increase the capacity of your short-term memory by creating larger and larger chunks of information. If we want to remember something for longer than the 15 to 30 seconds that it remains in the working memory, we must repeat the information and then encode it. We encode information by relating new information and concepts to information already present in our long-term memory. If we arrange information in some kind of logical order (for example, chronologically, or according to size, colour or importance), it helps us to remember more information for longer periods. Research has found that the best way to remember is to use meaningful connections to things we already know. One way to do this is to compare or contrast new information to old information. For example, compare your beliefs about how learning occurs to the information you have gained in this chapter (Dooley *et al*, 2005).

According to the cognitive information processing model, learning materials must be well organised to help learners process and encode information. Learners must also be allowed to practise what they have learned. In this way, certain skills become automatic, and this frees up learners' attention for more learning. ETD practitioners must include graphic material such as mind maps, diagrams and pictures in the learning material to help learners process and encode the information more efficiently. Lastly, learners must be encouraged to notice, think about and experiment with how they learn so that they can improve their own learning (Dooley et al, 2005).

Social learning

Social learning theory, or observational learning, is a refinement of behaviourist and cognitive approaches (Stewart, 2002). According to social learning theories, people learn from observing other people. By observing, they acquire knowledge, beliefs and attitudes and learn rules, skills and beliefs (Schunk, 2004). For example, consider how children learn to clean a room or to dress themselves. They do so by watching others and trying to copy them. Social learning helps us to observe the consequences of certain behaviours of others in a social setting (Erasmus *et al*, 2006).

Social learning theory introduces the concept of role model. It suggests that individuals will seek to model themselves on others who they perceive to be successful. In other words, they will try to imitate the behaviour of their role models (Stewart, 2002). A technique called behaviour modelling is often used to apply principles of social leaning theory to the development of interpersonal skills. Behaviour modelling works by observing employees (or recordings of employees) that demonstrate positive modelling behaviours, rehearsing the behaviour using a role-playing technique, receiving feedback on the rehearsal and finally, trying out the behaviour on the job. Role modelling also underpins mentoring initiatives within organisations (Landy & Conte, 2004).

Social learning theory is not concerned with the cognitive processes and conceptual structures involved in learning. It focuses on the social environments and relationships that will provide the correct context for learning (Dooley *et al*, 2005). In the context of training, learners participate in a framework with structure (the organisational environment); at the same time, they contribute to that structure (their own behaviours influence the organisation). Learners learn by practising the required behaviours in a group. In the context of training, learners, practice, learning, participation and the group context are connected; they cannot be isolated from each other. This means that the whole group is affected by the learning that takes place in each participant.

Social learning can often be unintentional: learners master certain situations or behaviours as a result of their participation in the group. Social learning does not require mastery of specific knowledge but rather full engagement (participation) in the specific situation or group (Tennant, 2006). The focus is on the group, not the individual. The situation and the group provide information about probable consequences of behaviours, and motivate the participants to act in certain ways. ETD practitioners should remember that learning is a social process. The learner, learning and the social environment are all interconnected. When designing learning processes, ETD practitioners should apply this knowledge by making provision for group work and social interaction.

Humanist perspectives on learning

The humanist perspective views knowledge as a personal, subjective issue, not an external commodity waiting to be internalised through the absorption of content (Reynolds, Caley & Mason, 2002). Based on the work of Carl Rogers (1969), the humanist perspective says that individuals have a natural aptitude for learning and have control over their own learning processes and outcomes. All training should therefore take a learner-centred approach. The role of the ETD practitioner shifts to that of learning facilitator, while the responsibility for learning rests firmly with the learner (Robinson, 2006).

Facilitation involves creating an environment in which people are motivated to think, contribute ideas, listen to others, share perspectives and experiences as adult learners and evaluate their learning and contribution. Humanist approaches thus emphasise a shift from traditional, instructor-led, content-based ETD interventions to self-directed, work-based learning processes. Humanist approaches also thrive in an organisational culture that encourages individual and collective learning and embraces change (Robinson, 2006). The humanist perspective on learning is applicable to the South African outcomes-based approach to ETD practices.

ACTIVITY

From the following examples, identify which learning theory is being described. Explain how you identified the learning theory.

Description	Learning theory
People learn because they are offered a reward for doing specific things.	
People are concerned with the thinking processes involved in learning. People's long- and short-term memories and the attention they pay to the information they receive from the world, influence the way they learn.	
People learn through social situations. They are influenced by the situation, but they also influence the situation.	

Other approaches to learning

Experiential learning

A theme of cognitive learning theory is that learning does not just occur in formal, structured situations: learning can be informal and spontaneous. The experiential learning approach sees learning as a cyclical, dynamic and continuous process. It also emphasises that learning is an active process. Learners are not passive recipients of training, but actively seek out opportunities to apply their behaviour in new situations (Robinson, 2006). The dynamic, continuous and cyclical nature of learning is best described with Kolb's (1985) famous learning cycle. According to this model, effective learning results from progression through four stages, which are repeated all the time as learning progresses (Lee-Davies, 2007):

- *Reflective observation* (watching). Reflecting upon previous experiences and feelings occurs in this stage. Watching, listening and actively thinking through issues ensure that careful consideration is made before taking action.
- *Abstract conceptualisation and generalisation* (thinking). In this stage, theories for the future are developed. Using reflections, information is analysed and conceptualised in an abstract form. That is, the learner thinks through the possible repercussions of ideas and applies previous learning to increase the success of the idea. Logical thought and modelling (brainstorming) give rise to new things to try out.
- *Active experimentation/testing* implications of concepts in new situations (acting/doing). This involves learning through doing. Previous thoughts and ideas are applied in a practical situation. Trial and error give rise to further thoughts and ideas, which can be followed through the whole cycle.
- *Concrete experiences* (feeling). Following active experimentation, the learner gains concrete experience in terms of the development of feelings. These feelings are used as a reference point for future actions.

Kolb's model sees learning as goal-directed. As individual goals may vary, individuals will pay more attention to different stages of the cycle (Stewart, 2002).

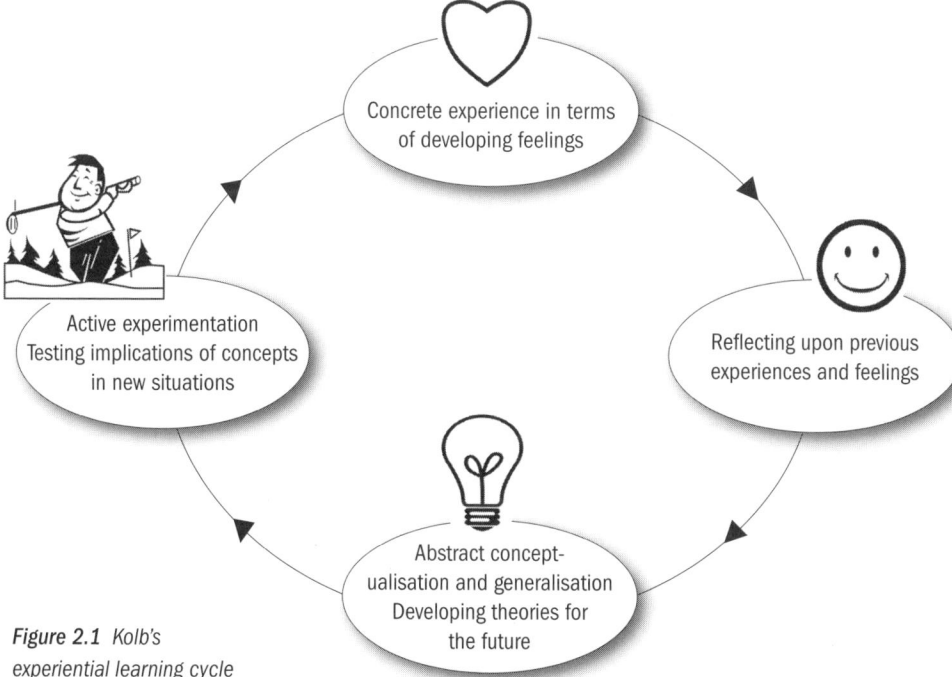

Figure 2.1 Kolb's experiential learning cycle

Learning styles

An important question about learning is why everyone is not equally successful at the learning to which they are exposed. For example, not everyone achieves the same marks in an examination, even though they study the same course, with the guidance of the same lecturer. Some individuals learn to drive a car quickly, while others need many lessons before they pass the driving test (Martin, 2005). According to Kolb (1985), individuals have a preference for one of the four stages in the learning cycle. This is known as the individual's preferred learning style.

The Kolb and Fry learning style inventory

Table 2.2 Kolb and Fry's four learning styles (Tennant, 2006)

The converger uses abstract conceptualisation and active experimentation abilities to learn.	• Can apply ideas in practical ways • Performs well when there is a single correct answer • Uses hypothetical, deductive reasoning to solve specific problems • Not emotional; would rather deal with objects than with people • Usually specialises in physical sciences
The diverger uses concrete experience and reflective observation abilities to learn.	• Well developed imaginative ability • Sees situations and problems from different perspectives • Good at generating ideas • Finds people interesting and has broad cultural interests • Usually specialises in arts
The assimilator uses abstract conceptualisation and reflective observation abilities to learn.	• Good at creating theoretical models • Very good at inductive reasoning • Concerned with abstract concepts; does not worry about the practical use of theories • Not overly concerned with people • Usually specialises in basic science and mathematics
The accommodator uses concrete experience and active experimentation abilities to learn.	• Good at doing things (application) • Does not shy away from taking risks • Can adapt quickly to changing circumstances • Solves problems intuitively • Gets information from other people • Prefers action-oriented jobs

Kolb and Fry (1975) argue that individuals prefer using different stages in the learning cycle. Most individuals prefer to use one stage – the one with which they are most at ease – most of the time. While a person's style can be modified over time with a great deal of persistence and effort, people have a natural inclination to use their dominant style in preference to others. Trying to learn in another style is difficult, stressful or even unpleasant (Rollinson, 2005). The learning style inventory (Kolb cited in Tennant, 2006:88) developed by Kolb and Fry can be used to identify an individual's dominant learning style. Table 2.2 gives an overview of the four learning styles (converger, diverger, assimilator, accommodator) within Kolb's learning cycle (Tennant, 2006).

Gregorc's learning styles

Gregorc (cited in Gregory, 2005) bases his learning theory on two variables: how people order the world (random or sequential) and how people view the world (abstract or concrete). This creates four learning styles, each with its own preferences in learning activities and learning environments. Table 2.3 gives an overview of these four learning styles.

Table 2.3 Gregorc's learning styles (Gregory, 2005)

Preferences	Learning style	Characteristics
• Concrete • Prefers practical situations • Uses models to learn • Can see the big picture • Prefers to use trial and error	**Concrete/random**	• Random • Divergent thinkers • Can make intuitive leaps in reasoning • Wants choices • Seeks alternatives
• Concrete • Makes lists • Prefers hands-on activities • Enjoys learning	**Concrete/sequential**	• Sequential • Likes details • Prefers procedures • Encourages timeliness • Prefers order
• Abstract • Enjoys feelings and emotions • Prefers a supportive environment • May know the answer but cannot always explain how it was reached	**Abstract/random**	• Random • Is flexible and spontaneous • Prefers variety • Well developed visual imagination
• Abstract • Must be given time to process new information • Uses analytical strategies to solve problems • Prefers to investigate and analyse	**Abstract/sequential**	• Sequential • Prefers order • Reasoning is rational and logical • Enjoys personal connections with others

McCarthy's 4MAT model

McCarthy's 4MAT model (Gregory, 2005) identifies four types of learner: the imaginative learner; the analytical learner; the common sense learner and the dynamic learner. Table 2.4 on the following page summarises the characteristics and preferred learning styles of each of these types.

Table 2.4 McCarthy's 4MAT model (Gregory, 2005)

The imaginative learner learns through experiencing and asks "why"? • Wants to know why something must be learned • Asks questions • Says "what if?" • Questions content and purposes • Wants to understand • Seeks alternative solutions	The analytical learner learns by conceptualising and asks "what?" • Wants facts and information • Works systematically • Work must be organised • Must have purpose, directions and expectations • Must be able to think and reflect before taking action
The common sense learner learns through applying and asks "how?" or "how to?" • Work must be practical and learner must be able to use it • Content should be applicable to life and experience • Compares and contrasts new information to old to make sense of it	The dynamic learner learns by creating and asks "what can this become?" or "what can this be used for?" • Uses knowledge and skills to create something • Must be allowed the freedom to take risks and enjoy new ways of thinking • Thinks creatively and in unusual ways • Prefers working alone but will work with others • Dislikes routine • Likes applying ideas

One of the most important implications of learning styles is that they influence how people prefer to learn. This may have a big impact on how well learners interact with each other. Knowledge of learners' preferred learning styles is therefore important for ETD practitioners. Learning facilitators should avoid designing learning programmes from the perspective of their own learning style, as they may ignore the preferences of their learners and lose them in the learning process.

ACTIVITY
What is your learning style preference?
Think back to a mathematics, science or language class when you were at school. Some of the learners always understood what the teacher was trying to explain, while others were completely lost. This has to do with learning style and intelligence, not only with intelligence.

How many of you were good at mathematics and science, but poor at languages? And for whom was it the other way around? Did you do well in a test when the subject matter was easy to memorise (such as Business Management), or did you perform better when you were required to understand and apply (such as science or languages)?

Mentoring and coaching

Mentoring and coaching are growing in popularity as learner-centred development tools (Robinson, 2006). Mentoring refers to a relationship where a senior, experienced individual provides support, advice and friendship to a younger, less experienced member of staff. Mentoring can be formal or informal, and it can take different forms. For example, some organisations use mentoring arrangements for new employees and people from historically disadvantaged groups as a strategy to accelerate the development of potential.

The concept of coaching is used to describe a one-to-one relationship between a manager and an individual employee. The aim is to develop or enhance the employee's on-the-job performance. This form of learning relies on one individual (manager or supervisor) teaching a particular skill to the employee through demonstration. The employee literally sits next to the coach to watch and practice under his/her guidance.

Action learning

Action learning is a form of organisational and individual learning. It is also cyclical and experiential in nature. In action learning, individuals and the organisation learn how to deal with problems and situations by developing an understanding of problems, and then creating change. Change is followed by reassessment and further adaptation as necessary, based on the new learning achieved. In practice, it is learning through action, a form of continuous development. In individual learning terms, action learning follows the same experiential learning process described by Kolb (Martin, 2005).

Principles of learning

A thorough knowledge of learning principles helps ETD practitioners in their role as learning facilitators. These principles include practise and overlearning, physical and psychological fidelity, whole versus part learning and massed versus distributed practice (Landy & Conte, 2004).

Practice and overlearning

Practice is critical to retain newly learned skills. That is why many learning programmes emphasise active practice. For example, musicians actively practise scales on their instruments. They cannot retain and develop their skills by passively watching someone else. Overlearning is the practice of presenting learners with several extra learning opportunities even after they have demonstrated mastery of a task. Overlearning tends to lead to automaticity (the ability to perform a task with limited attention) and thus adequate, long-term task performance (Landy & Conte, 2004).

Physical and psychological fidelity

Fidelity is the extent to which the task in the training situation is similar to the task required on the job. It is important that training tasks have fidelity; it means that training can directly benefit performance on the job. Physical fidelity refers to the extent to which the training task mirrors the physical features of the actual task. For example, aircraft simulator tasks possess physical fidelity if they accurately represent the layout of the cockpit and the motion that occurs in actual aircraft (Landy & Conte, 2004). Psychological fidelity refers to the extent to which the training task helps learners to develop the competencies (attitudes, knowledge, skills and abilities) and other characteristics that are necessary to perform the job. For example, lieutenant candidates in a fire department are trained (and assessed) in a simulated setting where they have to respond to a fire by actually speaking the directions and orders they would give. This setting highlights their communication and decision-making skills and possesses psychological fidelity (Landy & Conte, 2004).

Whole versus part learning

Another important consideration in training is the size of the learning tasks. Whole learning occurs when the entire task is practised at once. Part learning occurs when subtasks are practised separately and later combined. ETD practitioners should consider the task's difficulty level (task complexity) and the extent to which the subtasks are interrelated (task organisation) to determine the usefulness of whole and part learning (Landy & Conte, 2004). For example, developing the skills to land an aircraft involves a number of complex tasks. An example of part learning is the way actors rehearse various parts of a play (such as dance steps, fight scenes and pieces of dialogue) separately.

ACTIVITY
- Describe how learning to drive involves part learning.
- Next, describe whether you think the learning sequence is likely to be different for learning to drive a car with an automatic transmission compared to one with a manual transmission. (Landy & Conte, 2004)

Massed versus distributed practice

Massed practice conditions are conditions in which learners practise a task continuously and without rest. Distributed practice gives learners rest intervals between practice sessions, which are spaced over a longer period of time. In general, distributed practice results in more efficient learning and retention than massed practice, because the rest periods reduce fatigue and allow time to strengthen learned associations. For tasks with high complexity (such as air traffic control), longer rest periods between practice sessions are more beneficial for learning and skill acquisition (Landy & Conte, 2004).

Accelerated learning

Accelerated learning is the process of creating and maintaining a positive learning state by enhancing people's self-esteem and encouraging confidence in their ability to learn and perform. The positive learning state reduces mental barriers to learning and improves performance (Clement, 1992). Accelerated learning is a well-researched learner-centred approach. It uses learners' natural talents to give them the best opportunity to maximise their learning, retention, and performance. Accelerated learning technology accomplishes this by creating a stress-free, positive, joyful, and psychologically and physically healthy environment that enhances self-esteem and focuses on the needs of learners.

To understand accelerated learning approaches, we must first understand how our brains work. Research in neurosciences has led to the development of the following brain models.

Split-brain theory

The split-brain model stems from work done by Sperry (1974) and Ornstein (1977). According to the left/right brain hemisphere model, the left brain is verbal, logical, and sequential and can generally do only one thing at a time. Most traditional ETD programmes present information in a manner that appeals to the left brain. The right brain, by contrast, is creative, visual, and holistic. Apparently, it has direct access to people's enormous memory banks. The right brain can absorb huge amounts of information with little effort. Its visual memory is essentially perfect and, with memory techniques that link lists of data to visual images, most memorisation activities become rapid and easy. Given the analytical capabilities of the left brain and the visualisation ability of the right brain, cooperation between the two hemispheres leads to optimal learning and performance outcomes. This is called whole-brain learning (Clement, 1992).

Accelerated learning technology involves the entire person (mind, brain, and body) in the learning process. All efforts (from needs assessment and initial learning material development to delivery and follow-up) focus on maximising the abilities and success of the learner. An important task of accelerated learning is to engage the right brain in cooperation with the left brain. The left brain wants step-by-step information (to analyse), while the right brain wants rich information (to synthesise). Balancing the involvement of the left and right brains requires that we use the logical and the emotional, the sequential and the global, and the linguistic and the musical in more or less equal proportions. Both hemispheres are involved in activities such as exercises and games that evoke the playful part of the learner, provide an overview, and draw on analytical resources to integrate details. Processes that involve both hemispheres imprint subject matter deeply into memory (Clement, 1992).

Regenerative brain theory

Diamond's (1984) regenerative brain theory teaches that a rich emotional classroom environment stimulates brain cell activity in certain parts of the brain. Sensory stimuli with emotional content cause the brain to release opiate-like neurotransmitters in the brain, which produce a sense of well-being and a state of heightened awareness. So, elements of accelerated learning such as relaxation, music, games, art, and storytelling trigger a powerful learning state that enhances long-term memory. The pleasurable feelings induced by the natural opiates released in the brain make the learning experience desirable (Clement, 1992).

Triune brain theory

Triune brain theory (MacLean, 1973) divides the evolutionary development of the brain into three phases: the reptilian brain, the old mammalian brain (limbic system) and the neomammalian brain (neocortex). Each of these parts of the brain has its own special functions, and each part is important to learning. The neocortex surrounds the limbic system, which in turn surrounds the reptilian brain. All three parts of the brain are interconnected.

The *reptilian brain* automatically handles our basic physical needs (such as heart rate, breathing and hunger). It contains the reticular activating system which, like a computer, runs our stored mental 'programmes' without judgement. Many people have internal programmes that negatively influence their learning ability. For example, these programmes might cause an inner voice to say, "I can't learn this", or "I'm a slow learner" (Clement, 1992). The *limbic system* is the seat of our emotions and feelings. It also contains the hippocampus, which is essential to long-term memory. The neocortex contains our higher-level thinking skills. It is this part of the brain that separates people from other animals. The *neocortex* performs its function effectively only when the other parts of the brain have processed the information according to their specific functions. Long-term memory depends on all three parts of the triune brain (Clement, 1992).

Multiple intelligences

Gardner (1983) identified and tested seven distinct intelligences, and proposed an eighth form of intelligence. These intelligences are divided into three categories: communication, relating to objects and relating to the self. Table 2.5 gives an overview of the eight intelligences and how they apply to individual learning.

Table 2.5 *Gardner's eight intelligences (Gardner, 1983)*

Category	Intelligence	Application in learning
Communication	Verbal/ Linguistic	• Uses words as communication and thinking skills • Becomes involved in debates, storytelling and poetry • Uses metaphors, puns, analogies and similes • Can read for long periods • Chooses to listen, speak, read and write
	Musical/ Rhythmic	• Can recognise and produce melody, rhythm and rhyme • Is conscious of the impact of music • Likes music • Responds to music and rhythm sources • Responds to sounds
Relating to objects	Visual/ Spatial	• Attuned to pictures, symbols and drawings • Can see detail • Enjoys graphs, charts and representations that explain ideas • Thinks in pictures
	Bodily/ Kinaesthetic	• Keen sense of the tactile and aware of own body • Prefers manipulating and handling materials to make sense of information • Learning should involve some kind of activity, such as walking, building or role play
	Logical/ Mathematical	• Enjoys numbers and reasoning • Can identify patterns, and recognise cause and effect and sequencing • Likes solving problems and posing and answering questions • Wants to analyse, assess and organise information and use spreadsheets
	Naturalist	• In touch with the natural world (animals and plants) • Enjoys geography, landscapes and the weather • Wants to be outdoors • Can see details in nature and recognise patterns and characteristics • Uses patterns and attributes to classify information • Appreciates the environment

Category	Intelligence	Application in learning
Relating to the self	Interpersonal	• Interacts well with others • Social beings, sensitive and intuitive to other people's moods and feelings • Often friendly and extroverted, in touch with others' temperaments • Valuable members of a team
	Intrapersonal	• High degree of self-awareness • Knows and can manage own emotions and feelings and can use this knowledge to manage own behaviour • Self-reflection and goal setting are important • Acts on a strong awareness of own strengths and needs

Sternberg's three intelligences

Robert Sternberg (cited in Gregory, 2005) identified three intelligences: practical, analytical and creative intelligence.

- *Practical intelligence.* This kind of intelligence applies new information practically. It asks, "what can I do with this?" Information is used to solve problems and make decisions to apply to real-world situations.
- *Analytical intelligence.* This kind of intelligence identifies problems, creates different solutions, decides on an optimal solution and applies the solution in practice. Information is used to judge situations critically.
- *Creative intelligence.* This kind of intelligence challenges existing assumptions and concentrates on new ways of doing things. It involves using cognitive processes to create questions, problems and projects that internalise new learning.

According to Sternberg, intelligent people can use knowledge combined with these intelligences to make sense of information. In other words, information must be used intelligently to be of any value.

Emotional intelligence

The term emotional intelligence was originally coined by Salovey and Mayer (1990) to complement the traditional view of general intelligence by emphasising behaviour that requires emotional and behavioural control in social situations (Kanfer & Kantrowitz, 2002). Emotional intelligence is distinct from but related to other intelligences. More specifically, it is intelligence (the ability to grasp abstractions) applied to emotions. Emotional intelligence differs from person to person (some people have more emotional intelligence than others). This form of intelligence develops over a person's lifespan and can be enhanced through training. Emotional intelligence involves particular abilities to reason intelligently about emotions, including identifying and perceiving emotion (in self and others). It also provides the skills to understand and manage those emotions successfully (Ashkanasy & Daus 2005; Locke 2005; Mayer, Caruso & Salovey 1999).

The literature distinguishes between ability models and mixed models of emotional intelligence (Mandell & Pherwani 2003). The ability model defines emotional intelligence as a set of abilities that involves perceiving and reasoning abstractly, using information that emerges from feelings (Mayer *et al*, 1999). The mixed model incorporates the underlying abilities identified by the ability model. It further defines emotional intelligence as a set of abilities that includes social behaviours, traits and competencies such as:

- Self-awareness is an awareness of and appreciation of one's own emotions.
- Managing one's emotions means allowing the situation to determine appropriate ways of expressing emotions.
- Motivation refers to the ability to focus on a task despite obstacles and challenges.
- Empathy means being sensitive to and responding appropriately to others' emotions and feelings.
- Social skills are skills to manage the emotions of other people and deal with their emotions and feelings (Goleman, 2001).

People who are self-aware can put names to their feelings. They can recognise their emotions and ask others for support by giving voice to their emotions. These people also have strategies to cope with their emotions and can change them when they feel the need.

ACTIVITY
Review the statements in the table opposite, and answer the following questions.
- Identify your preferred emotional style.
- How does your preferred style influence your interpersonal relations and your ability to learn on your own and in a group?
(Source: Wechsler cited in Wolmarans, 2004)

When we manage our emotions, we are guided by a situation; we can adapt our emotions to the demands of the situation. This means that we can calm our emotions when we know that they are not appropriate, or that we will gain nothing by expressing or feeling our emotions in the situation. Some of the strategies we can use to calm ourselves are to count slowly to ten (or more if we need to), take several deep breaths, go for a walk, or look inwards to get in touch with our feelings at that moment.

When we are able to keep going even when things are not going according to plan (or seem to be working against us), we are behaving in a motivated way. Our ability to use intrinsic, or internal motivation to persist at a task is enhanced when we receive ongoing feedback on our progress, when we are sure that we are up to the challenge and when we have a sense of control over our progress.

When we are sensitive to other people's feelings and respond to them appropriately, we show empathy. We learn this ability in an environment of mutual respect and concern for other people's problems and emotions. When we use our own social skills to positively and constructively deal with other people and their emotions, we are using our social skills. This means that we are attuned to other people's body language signals, their needs and behaviours. By using our social skills we can respond appropriately.

Friendly Helper	Strong Achiever	Logical Thinker
Rejects strong emotions Hostility, animosity, aggression	Rejects tender emotions Love, affection, endearment, compassion	Uncomfortable with all emotions Blocks out emotions
Accepts tender emotions	Accepts strong emotions	Displaces emotions with logic, data, facts and figures
√ which is true of you	√ which is true of you	√ which is true of you
☐ Prefers warmth, harmony and cooperation ☐ Peacemaker, non-assertive ☐ Attempts to minimise tension ☐ Praises others, looks for common ground, does favours to others ☐ Fears conflict and emotional hurt ☐ Reaction to stress – dependence or depression ☐ Needs to learn: – to assert themselves – to ask for what they want – to be critical and evaluative of ideas	☐ Task-orientated, initiates action, coordinates, pushes for results ☐ Prefers to be in command ☐ Assertive and readily accepts aggressive qualities in themselves and others ☐ Influences by giving orders, threatening, withholding rewards or challenging others ☐ Fears being perceived as soft and sentimental or losing control ☐ Reaction to stress – domination or impulsive over activity ☐ Needs to learn: – patience – how to support others	☐ Prefers information gathering and clarification of words and ideas ☐ Replaces emotion with logic, accuracy and self-reliance ☐ Rejects strong and tender emotions ☐ Fears confusion, loss of structure or being wrong ☐ Dislikes being obligated to others or being overpowered by emotions and impulse ☐ Influences by logic, fact and clever arguments and their knowledge of rules and regulations ☐ Reaction to stress – withdrawal or rule bound ☐ Needs to learn: – awareness of own feelings – acceptance of closeness and intimacy – expression of emotion

What are the implications for ETD? In addition to taking into account different learning styles of learners, ETD practitioners also have to consider the principles of accelerated learning and the various kinds of intelligence when they design learning programmes. They should attempt to involve as many different kinds of intelligence as possible in the learning process and think of ways to develop the different aspects of emotional intelligence in all learners.

Table 2.6 Stimulation of intelligences (based on Clement, 1992)

Intelligence	Stimulus to accelerate learning and performance
Linguistic	Reading and writing. Encourage learners to speak to each other in a topic-specific manner. Use dyads, or pairs of learners, to allow learners to discuss what they have just learnt. Use plays.
Logical/ Mathematical	Play games and puzzles. Exercises that are different from the traditional to entice those who are weak in these areas.
Musical	Listen to songs, raps, background music, concert readings, and so on. Keep a variety of music at hand to create different moods.
Visual/Spatial	Use colourful models, patterns, pictures and symbols. Draw simple posters to describe key points, using colourful markers, and post them around the room. Encourage the use of mind maps. Replace words with icons. Use guided imagery to introduce a subject and review it.
Bodily/ Kinaesthetic	Exercise, walk and dance. Make models of what you are teaching. Let learners touch objects pertinent to the subject. Include stretching exercises and educational kinaesthetic exercises. Use ball tossing to stimulate memory exercises. Use role play and mind maps.
Interpersonal	Dyads or small groups. Converse about the subject matter and have learners actively listen to others. Get learners to share how they feel about the subject.
Intrapersonal	Keep a journal of feelings, discovered blocks, and assets. Teach relaxation procedures to help learners let go and reflect.
Practical	Ask learners to demonstrate learning by designing models. Give workplace assignments such as conducting interviews or collecting evidence for a portfolio to demonstrate workplace application.
Analytical	Give puzzles to solve. Ask learners to provide solutions to problematic situations by means of case studies and brainstorming.
Creative	Give learners challenging projects such as researching real issues of concern in the workplace and coming up with solutions and recommendations for improvement.
Emotional intelligence	Ask learners to identify their own mood and emotional state before starting a workshop. Create a positive mood by means of music and relaxation exercises. Use dyads to help learners find creative solutions for identifying and dealing with their anxiety and concerns. Use small groups to guide learners in expressing their concerns and finding creative solutions for dealing with them.

Key terms

- Accelerated learning
- Action learning
- Adult learners
- Behaviourist perspective
- Coaching
- Cognitive information processing
- Competencies
- Development
- Education
- Emotional intelligence
- Experiential learning
- Humanist perspective
- Intelligence
- Learning
- Learning styles
- Mentoring
- Social learning theory
- Training

Review and discussion questions

- What is the link between ETD and learning in the organisational context? Why is it important to understand the principles that influence adult learning? Give reasons for your answer.
- How do the characteristics of adult learners influence the learning process and design of training? How can ETD practitioners improve their training design by incorporating the needs of adult learners?
- How would you explain the difference between implicit and explicit learning to a group of learners?
- How do the various theories of learning support the design and delivery of effective learning programmes? Describe the important principles of each learning theory as they apply to adult learning.
- Why is it important for ETD practitioners to incorporate the principles of learning in the design and delivery of learning programmes?
- Why is it important for ETD practitioners to have a sound knowledge and understanding of learning styles, multiple intelligences and emotional intelligence? How would you, as a learning facilitator, develop the emotional intelligence of your learners?

Suggested reading

Bash, L. (2003). *Adult learners in the academy.* Bolton, MA: Anker Publishing.

Cranton, P. (2006). *Understanding and promoting transformative learning: A guide for educators of adults.* Second edition. 2006. San Francisco, CA: John Wiley & Sons.

Dooley, K.E., Lindner, J.R. & Dooley, L.M. (2005). *Advanced methods in distance education.* (2005). Hershey, PA: Information Science Publishing.

Erasmus, B.J., Loedolff, P.v.Z., Mda, J. & Nel, P.S. (2006). *Managing training and development in South Africa.* Fourth edition. Cape Town: Oxford University Press, South Africa.

Gregory, G.H. (2005). *Differentiating instruction with style.* Thousand Oaks, California: Corwin Press.

Merriam, S.B. (2004). The changing landscape of adult learning theory. *Review of adult learning and literacy*, 4, 199-220.

Reid, G. (2005). *Learning styles and inclusion*. London: Paul Chapman Publishing.

Schunk, D.H. (2004). *Learning theories: an educational perspective*. Fourth edition. Upper Saddle River, New Jersey: Pearson Prentice Hall.

Stevenson, R.J. & Palmer, J.A. (1994). *Learning: Principles, processes and practices*. New York: Cassell Educational Limited.

Tennant, M. (2006). *Psychology and adult learning*. Third edition. New York: Routledge.

Summary

In this chapter we explored the characteristics of the adult learner. We saw how the principles and theories of learning can be applied to enhance not only the design and delivery of learning programmes, but also to optimise individual and organisational learning and performance. A solid understanding of the psychology of learning is critical to create a learning environment that motivates adult learners in the workplace to engage in continued ETD initiatives.

It is important for ETD practitioners to use a systematic approach to training that assesses training needs, incorporates principles of learning in the design and delivery of training, assesses learner achievements and evaluates the effectiveness of learning programmes. Chapters 3 to 7 will discuss this scientific approach (also called the Training Cycle). Chapter 3 introduces the first phase in effective learning programme design, namely analysing an organisation's and employees' ETD needs.

No one can be a great facilitator of learning unless they see their learners as unique and capable individuals, and have a genuine desire to impart to learners what they believe to be of value.

CHAPTER 3

Jo-Anne Botha • Melinde Coetzee

Conducting an ETD needs analysis

The extent to which ETD decisions are rationally justifiable is dependent on the extent to which a rigorous ETD needs analysis has been performed, and whether training is, in fact, the best solution for the performance problem or development need.

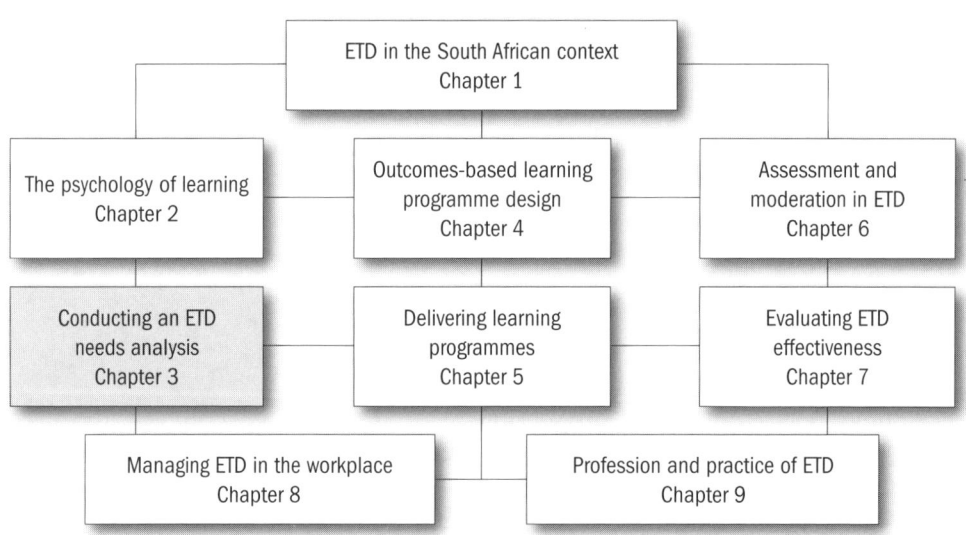

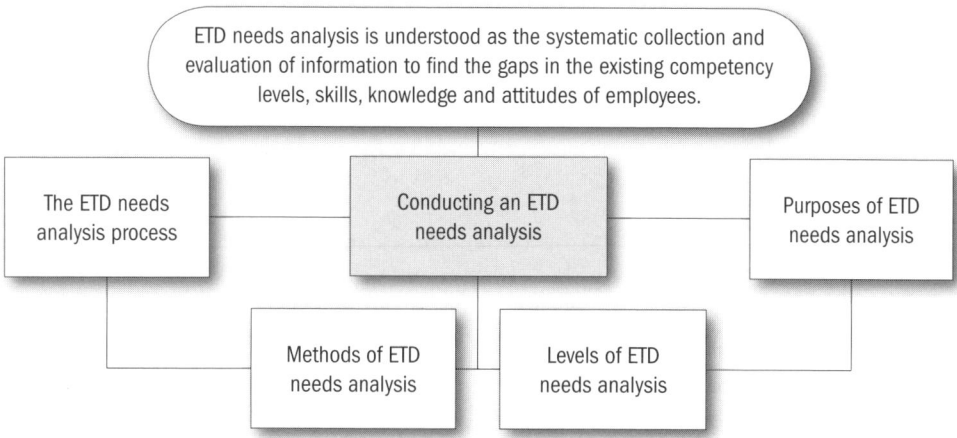

ETD needs analysis is understood as the systematic collection and evaluation of information to find the gaps in the existing competency levels, skills, knowledge and attitudes of employees.

The ETD needs analysis process

Conducting an ETD needs analysis

Purposes of ETD needs analysis

Methods of ETD needs analysis

Levels of ETD needs analysis

Key points of conducting an ETD needs analysis
- ETD needs analysis is the first step in the planning, design and delivery of any ETD initiative. It involves gathering and evaluating data about existing employees' capabilities and the organisation's demands for skills.
- Before learning programme design issues are considered, a careful needs analysis is required to develop a systematic understanding of where training is needed, what needs to be taught or trained, and who needs to be trained.
- An ETD needs analysis typically occurs on four interrelated levels, namely sectoral, organisational, task and person analysis.
- ETD needs analysis models and employs a systematic process and technology for improving human performance capability.

After studying this chapter, you should be able to:
- Explain the various phases of the Training Cycle.
- Evaluate the importance of ETD needs analysis in the Training Cycle.
- Discuss the purposes of ETD needs analysis.
- Explain the methods an ETD practitioner can employ to gather data for an ETD needs analysis.
- Evaluate the appropriateness of needs analysis methods for the four levels of analysis.
- Explain the steps involved in conducting an ETD needs analysis.
- Describe how the information gathered from an ETD needs analysis informs the design of learning programmes.
- Explain the importance of establishing an ETD needs analysis information system.

Right-skilling the workforce has become the main focus of all ETD efforts and initiatives in organisations. As pointed out in Chapter 1, organisations world-wide are finding themselves ill-equipped to compete in the 21st century economy. The reason is that too many workers lack the right skills to help their employers grow and succeed. The connection between human capability and organisational success is even clearer today, as skills shortages threaten the short- and long-term success of businesses and industries throughout the world (ASTD, 2006).

As the global, knowledge-based economy places an ever-growing premium on the talent, creativity and efficiency of the workforce, business leaders talk of a widening gap between the skills their organisations need and the current capabilities of their employees. In South Africa, the skills development acts introduced new structures, programmes and funding policies designed to increase investment in skills development and to improve the quality and relevance of education and training. These acts also introduced a planned approach to developing skills, which integrates skills planning and development at national, provincial, sector and company level (Hattingh, 2003). Working together, individuals, business leaders, ETD providers, practitioners and the government must meet the challenge of right-skilling head-on to bring about future growth and success in a global economy.

ETD needs analysis is therefore regarded as crucial to the planning, design and delivery of any ETD initiative. In the context of ETD, needs analysis is understood as the systematic collection and evaluation of information to find the gaps in the existing competency levels, skills, knowledge and attitudes of employees. It involves gathering and analysing data about existing employees' capabilities and the organisation's demands for skills, and analysing the implications that new and changed roles have for changes in capability (CIPD, 2007). The information obtained from an analysis of the assessed needs provides the foundation for ETD as a profession and a practice. In reality, organisations will always face some type of skills gap. This may be caused by shifting market conditions, evolving industries or changing customer needs. The extent to which ETD decisions are rationally justifiable is dependent on the extent to which a rigorous ETD needs analysis has been performed (to explain the actual why and how to carry out ETD activities), and whether training is, in fact, the best solution for the performance problem or development need.

ETD needs analysis is the first phase in the Training Cycle. A training cycle is a reiterative, or repeating process comprising five phases:
1. ETD needs analysis;
2. learning programme design;
3. training delivery;
4. assessment and moderation of learners' achievements; and
5. evaluation of programme effectiveness.

The focus of the Training Cycle is the continuous improvement of learning programmes and learners' performance in the workplace. As organisations' and learners' ETD needs change, so the design and delivery of learning programmes should be adapted. The design and delivery of learning programmes in turn influence assessment and moderation methods. Learning programme evaluation ensures the continuous improvement and enhancement of learning programme design and delivery, and assessment and moderation practices. Often, new needs arise from the assessment and evaluation results. The Training Cycle also emphasises that ETD in the workplace is a process of continuous learning and development. Learners' behaviours and values change or are modified by learning programmes and other ETD efforts. Therefore, their needs change and evolve during the course of their working lives. The various phases of the Training Cycle are discussed in chapters 3 to 7.

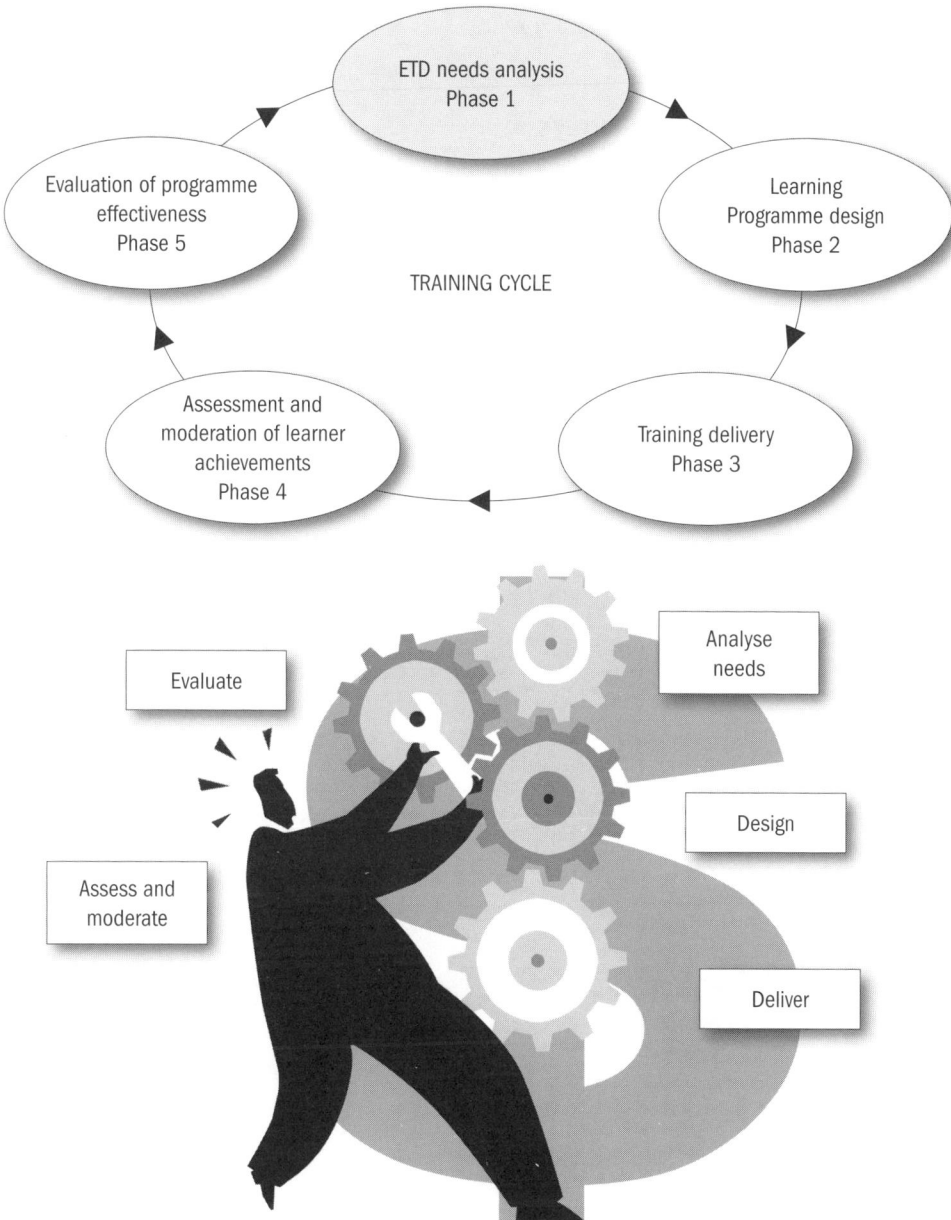

Like cogs in a machine, every phase in the Training Cycle contributes to the eventual success of a learning programme. All phases are equally important.

Figure 3.1 *The Training Cycle*

This chapter explores the concept, process and methodology of conducting an ETD needs analysis as it applies to the planning, design and delivery of learning programmes. All ETD provision should be designed to meet identified learning and development needs; in this way, ETD provision is cost-effective and adds value. If an initial assessment based on correct assumptions identifies ETD needs, it is likely that effective ETD provision will build the motivation and performance capability of the workforce (CIPD, 2007).

Purposes of ETD needs analysis

ETD needs analysis serves several purposes in ETD planning, design and delivery. It provides a means to evaluate an organisation and individual's current situation by gathering, assessing and disseminating information about optimal and actual performance, the causes of performance problems and possible solutions. With the gathered information and data, an assessment of the gap between desired performance and current performance is conducted. From this, the causes of existing performance-related problems and their possible future consequences can be identified.

Proactive and reactive needs analysis

Needs analysis can be proactive or reactive (Blanchard & Thacker, 2004). The focus of a *proactive needs analysis* is on the future. Performance problems that may occur in the future are identified now. Employees are exposed to training programmes that address identified needs before they can cause performance problems. This is a good approach to use if an organisation plans to go into a new venture that requires different knowledge, skills and competencies from its employees. *Reactive needs analysis* focuses on the present. It identifies a current performance problem that should be addressed now.

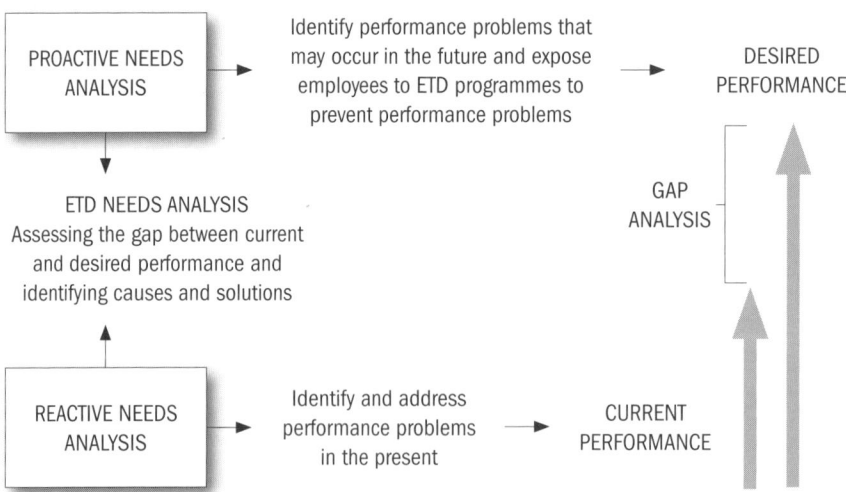

Figure 3.2 Purpose of ETD needs analysis

Identify causes of performance problems

ETD needs analysis uses a systematic process and technology to improve human performance capability. A systematic analysis is orderly and consistent. Most importantly, the output of each analysis activity serves as the input for subsequent efforts and decisions. Once the ETD practitioner has identified the cause of the performance problem, ETD interventions focus on solving the performance problem. This might mean that some ETD interventions are eliminated (Rossett, 1992). Especially critical to a needs analysis is an ETD practitioner's ability to identify the root causes of performance problems, not just their observable symptoms. When causes can be distinguished from symptoms, ETD practitioners can begin to correct problems at their sources (Rothwell *et al*, 1995). Table 3.1 gives a few guidelines in this regard. It is important to identify the causes of performance problems, because recommended solutions are based on identified causes. For example, training interventions and job support tools can be extended to enhance motivation and to increase skills and knowledge. Problems caused by improper environments and incentives are usually handled through a broader strategy, which often involves management and organisational redesign (Rossett, 1992).

Table 3.1 Performance problems and solutions (adapted from Blanchard, et al, 2004)

	System problems	Remove system problems
	Lack of or inadequate feedback	Provide adequate and timely feedback
Needs analysis	Incongruence in rewards or punishments of behaviour	Change punishment/reward systems of organisation
	Gaps in knowledge, skills and attitudes	• Provide on-the-job assistance • Give employee time to practise new skills and knowledge • Change the nature of the job • Transfer employee to another job • Terminate employment • Provide required training in knowledge, skills or attitudes

System problems are caused by the environment in which employees must work. Here is an example of a systems problem: the organisation's mission is to improve innovation, but employees must seek permission before they can try something innovative. In this case, training in innovative behaviour is not the answer; a change in policy is needed. System problems that prevent the achievement of organisational goals must be removed before employees can perform. Some of these changes require support from senior management.

Lack of or inadequate feedback on work performance is an important need. Supervisors may be afraid to give negative feedback, so poorly performing employees often think that they are performing well. In this case, training the employee will not solve the problem. Instead, the supervisor should be trained to give appropriate feedback (Blanchard & Thacker, 2004).

Managers should consider the messages they send out with the reward system. Does the employee who works hard receive the same increase as the employee whose work is only adequate or even mediocre? When hard-working employees suddenly start underperforming, a new look at the reward system should be taken before considering training as an option. Peer pressure also plays a role. For example, a group of employees set a production standard. It is easy to spot employees who do not meet this standard, so when one of the employees fails to meet the standard, the other employees 'punish' him/her through ridicule or exclusion. Training these employees is not the answer to the performance problem. Rather, the reward system and ways to avoid the possibility of punishment should be considered as solutions (Blanchard & Thacker, 2004).

Sometimes, training is not the best solution, even when there are deficiencies in knowledge, skills and attitudes. Alternatives such as the following could rather be considered (Blanchard & Thacker, 2004):

- Provide on-the-job assistance. Give the employee time to practise new skills and knowledge. When tasks are performed infrequently, employees may become less proficient at performing them. Providing adequate practise opportunities may prevent performance gaps. For example, police officers are required to practise at a shooting range a specific number of times every year.
- Change the nature of the job. When a specific part of a job requires a skill or knowledge that is difficult to acquire, the job may be changed to exclude the difficult parts. For example, call-centre staff can deal with routine enquiries, but any unusual enquiry is referred to the call centre manager or technical staff.
- Transfer the employee to another job. Sometimes, employees may possess the knowledge and skills required to do a job well, but they do not like the job. Reasons might be that they do not find the job stimulating, or they find the environment intimidating or unsupportive. It may solve the problem if the employee is transferred to another job.
- Terminate employment. If the employee has received a lot of training, time to practise, support and so on, and still refuses to perform to the required standard, his/her employment may be terminated.

When a lack of knowledge, skills and attitudes is the cause of a performance problem, and if the alternatives above have been considered, training is the most obvious solution. ETD practitioners can then proceed to list and describe the knowledge, skills and attitudes that are lacking. These will form the basis for the development of training objectives and learning outcomes.

Is training the solution for a performance deficiency? (based on Swanepoel, Erasmus, Van Wyk & Schenk, 2003)

Quick reference checklist
What is the performance discrepancy?
- What is the difference between what is being done and what should be done?
- What is the evidence, and is it reliable?

Is the discrepancy important?
- What does it cost?
- Will the problem grow?
- Is it worth fixing?

Is it a lack of skill/knowledge/attitude?
- Could they do it if their lives depended on it?

Did they know how to do it in the past?
- Have they forgotten?
- Is the skill used often?
- Do they get regular feedback on how they are doing?

Is there a simpler way?
- Can the job be simplified?
- Could job aids be used?
- Can they learn by being shown instead of through training?

Do they have the potential to do the job well?
- Are they physically fit?
- Do they have the mental potential?
- Are they overqualified or underqualified?

Is the correct performance being punished?
- Do they think that correct performance will be penalised?
- Is not doing the job rewarding?
- Is there some reward for non-performance (less work, worry, tiredness, more attention)?

Does correct performance really matter?
- Is there a favourable outcome for performance?
- Is there any status or job satisfaction connected with the job?
- Are there any obstacles to performing?
- Are the resources available (time, equipment, tools, space, support)?
- Are there any other barriers (policy, work environment, culture, motivation, systems, improper incentives, authority or conflicting time demands)?

What is the best solution?
- Are there any solutions that are unacceptable to the organisation?
- Are the solutions beyond the resources of the organisation?

ETD needs analysis aims to involve main stakeholders and meet their requirements. Every ETD intervention (including those developed on request from management) must be seen as an opportunity to sell products and services and provide information about these products and services. It is also an opportunity to collect data and perspectives that will ensure that ETD interventions add value for stakeholders and contribute to the organisation's bottom line. The consulted sources influence the nature and richness of the proposed ETD solutions.

Provide information for ETD interventions

Needs analysis provides the background information needed to plan, design and deliver an ETD intervention or learning programme. An ETD needs analysis identifies the following:
- the gap between desired performance and current performance;
- the cause of the gap; and
- the specific target group.

ETD solutions are then chosen from a wide range of possibilities, which flow from the causes of the problem. The needs of the target group are identified, and these needs determine the objective of the learning programme and the appropriate learning outcomes (read more about learning outcomes in Chapter 4). For example, ETD practitioners will source the correct unit standards from the SAQA website when they intend to design a learning programme based on unit standards.

A needs analysis helps ETD practitioners to learn more about their learners before they design their learning materials. The learners bring unique needs and expectations to the learning experience. They know where they want to go and what it will take to get them there. They also know their own strengths and weaknesses, and they often want to improve their job performance. Learners have many differences: they come from different backgrounds, speak different languages, are from different age groups and live in different circumstances. These factors all influence learners' willingness to participate in the learning. An effective needs analysis will capture these details of the target learner group. As discussed in Chapter 2, learners learn in different ways. But they also differ in terms of the following:

- *Education levels.* Some of the people attending a learning programme may have qualifications relevant to the learning programme, while for others, all the information will be new.
- *Work experience.* Some participants may be fresh from university, while others may have years of working experience.
- *Age.* Different generations prefer to learn in different ways. The New Millennium generation prefers electronic media and talking. The Baby Boomers (older generation) are quite comfortable with the written word; they may prefer lectures and opportunities to read through material. This topic is also discussed in Chapters 4 and 5.
- *Socio-economic background.* Learners' socio-economic backgrounds may affect how they learn, what they understand and how they assimilate data. It also influences learners' ability and willingness to participate in group discussions if their experiences are vastly different from the rest of the group.
- *Cultural background.* Cultural differences can lead to many challenges in the training process. These include language barriers, the kinds of examples that participants will be able to identify with, the kinds of activities that people will feel comfortable with, and the interpretation of body language.
- *Differences in knowledge, skills and attitudes.* When ETD practitioners know that the participants in a learning programme have varying capabilities, they should ensure everyone's participation by devising different activities or opportunities for participation.
- *Motivation to learn.* To ensure effective learning, learners must be ready emotionally, physically and psychologically. However, not everyone participating in the learning programme will experience the same degree of readiness.
- *Belief in one's ability to master the learning material and participate meaningfully in the learning process.* Self-belief has a great influence on success and unfortunately, the reverse is also true. Learners who do not believe in their ability to master the material and contribute to the learning process may start out unmotivated. They may be unwilling to participate and expose themselves in group learning activities.
- *Recognition of prior learning (RPL).* As discussed in Chapter 1, RPL is an acknowledgement of the learner's previous learning and work experience that is relevant

to the content and level of a learning programme. RPL can give learners access to learning opportunities that may otherwise have been closed to them. By conducting an effective RPL, ETD practitioners can establish where learners are in the learning process. They can then advise them on appropriate ways to continue with their learning.

ETD needs analysis provides a basis for feedback, for tracking change and evaluating the outcomes of an ETD intervention. When results are positive, the information can be used to ensure that the ETD initiative continues. When results are negative, the ETD practitioner can decide to take corrective action or stop the ETD intervention. The ETD practitioner's decision should be based on evaluation results, not on his/her or the learner's intuitive impressions of what is happening (Rothwell *et al*, 1995). It is valuable to give stakeholders and employees feedback about the results of the ETD needs analysis and intervention evaluation. Feedback can give ETD interventions momentum and lead to action as managers and individuals gain a better understanding of the performance problems they face.

Levels of ETD needs analysis

An ETD needs analysis typically occurs on four levels, including sectoral, organisational, task and person analysis. It is important to note that these four levels of analysis are interrelated and often conducted at the same time. Data from one analysis is often used to ensure that the data for another analysis is complete. Take the workplace skills plan as an example. Information on individual and departmental needs are needed to compile a workplace skills plan. Information gathered in job analysis is also needed to identify training needs at the individual level. So, while we can identify four levels of ETD analysis, they must never be considered in isolation.

Table 3.2 Levels of ETD needs analysis (Coetzee, 2006)

Level	Description
National and sectoral analysis	• Identify key skills shortages and assess relative importance of identified shortages in the sector. • Feed skills gap information into the national skills plan by means of the sector skills plan.
Organisational analysis	• Examine company-wide goals and problems to determine where training is needed by means of a formal skills audit. • Feed skills gap information into the sector skills plan by means of the workplace skills plan.
Task analysis (job analysis)	• Examine tasks performed and competencies required to determine what employees must do to perform successfully. • Feed skills gap information into the workplace skills plan by means of the department/section plan.
Person analysis	• Examine competencies, current performance and career development needs to determine who needs training. • Feed skills gap information into the workplace skills plan by means of the personal development plans and department/section plan.

Sectoral analysis

A sectoral needs analysis identifies key skills shortages and assesses the relative impor-tance of the identified shortages in the sector as they relate to the national skills plan. Sectoral skills shortages are shortages that seriously endanger the successful opera-tion of an important economic and/or social activity. These shortages are regarded as training priorities for the sector. In the public sector, for example, the human resource development strategy for the public service and the Batho Pele principles describe the typical skills and values that need to be developed in the public sector (the PSETA skills plan and the national guide on scarce and critical skills will also show which skills and occupation categories are regarded as scarce and critical to the sector). Skills and learning programmes in any sector will typically be designed to address scarce and critical skills.

ACTIVITY

Study the list of scarce skills across the various occupations provided in Appendix 4 on page 395. Which of these skills are applicable to the company where you work or where you intend to work?

Strategic objectives of the Public Service Human Resource Development Strategy (HRDS)

1. Improving the foundations for human development
2. Improving the supply of high-quality skills (particularly scarce skills), which are more responsive to societal and economic need
3. Increasing employer participation in lifelong learning
4. Supporting employment growth through industrial policies, innovations, research and development
5. Ensuring that the four pillars of the HRDS are linked

Batho Pele principles

'Batho Pele' is Sesotho, meaning People First. It is the name of the government's programme for transforming its public service delivery from an inefficient bureaucracy with a focus on rules to a culture of customer care, in which the needs of all the citizens of South Africa are truly served irrespective of their race, gender or creed. This programme is set out in the White Paper on Transforming Public Service Delivery (Government Gazette 18340, 01 October 1997). A guiding principle of the public service in South Africa will be that of service to the people. Batho Pele seeks to do this by calling on Public Sector organisations to deliver responsive, quality services according to eight national principles referred to as the Batho Pele principles.

These principles are:

1. Consultation. Citizens should be consulted about the level and quality of the public service they receive and wherever possible should be given a choice about the services that are offered.
2. Service standards. Citizens should be told what level and quality of public services they will receive so that they are aware of what to expect.
3. Access. All citizens should have equal access to the services to which they are entitled.
4. Courtesy. Citizens should be treated with courtesy and consideration.
5. Information. Citizens should be given full, accurate information about the public services that they are entitled to receive.

6. Openness and transparency. Citizens should be told how national and provincial departments are run, how much they cost, and who is in charge.
7. Redress. If the promised standard of service is not delivered, citizens should be offered an apology, a full explanation, and a speedy and effective remedy. When complaints are made, citizens should receive a sympathetic, positive response.
8. Value for money. Public services should be provided economically and efficiently in order to give citizens the best possible value for money.

Organisational analysis

An organisational needs analysis examines organisational goals (such as those described in the HRD strategy for the company), available resources, and the organisational environment to determine where ETD interventions should be directed. As shown in Table 3.2, ETD needs analysis at the organisational level is often referred to as a skills audit. Its aim is to identify critical and scarce skills, and to compare these to the skills required by the organisation now and in the future. With this information, the shortfall or surplus of key skills can be determined and addressed (Folscher & Chonco, 2006). The National Scarce Skills Guide (Appendix 4) gives an outline of these skills in the South African context. For example, managerial and ETD practitioner skills are scarce skills in South Africa.

ACTIVITY

Study Section 3.5 of the workplace skills plan and annual training report provided in Appendix 2. Identify the scarce skills applicable to the wholesale and retail sector.

Table 3.3 *Skills analysis for talent pool development (based on Palmer, 2002)*

Skills analysis area	Description
Skills shortages	Examine where current shortages exist within the organisation and review how these can be met from within.
Scarce skills	Examine the National Scarce Skills Guide (Appendix 4) and sector-specific scarce skills list. Review how these apply to the organisation's list of scarce skills and develop strategies for increasing these skills. These must also be reflected in the workplace skills plan and annual training report.
Core competencies	These are the skills, knowledge and attributes that the organisation deems to be critical for employees and managers. Competency frameworks are a great place to start for identifying skills that are currently in great demand or will be needed in greater numbers in the future.
Core skills	Examine whether there are adequate supplies of talent at managerial, professional, technical, craft or clerical levels. Seek out groups requiring the same common skills. The talent pool becomes particularly important where larger groupings of a skill are needed.

Skills analysis area	Description
Generic skills	Examine skills that are common to a number of jobs, for example IT skills, presentation skills, problem solving and team working. Some of these may appear in the core competency lists.
	Generic skills are a pool of skills that many will use in the organisation and for which there will be a steady demand. Training in this area is therefore rarely wasted. It also provides the person transferring to another job with some good basic skills.

In an organisational context, a skills gap analysis compares the actual skills of the current workforce with real skills requirements. The skills gap analysis also assesses the ETD needs of different departments or subunits in the organisation. Lastly, the skills gap analysis determines the extent to which managers, peers and technology support the transfer of training, or the workplace application of training. The skills gap analysis is used to draw up the workplace skills plan.

Table 3.4 Steps in completing a workplace skills plan

Steps	Description
Form a workplace skills development committee (WSDC)	• The WSDC should not be too big. A maximum of eight is suggested for small departments and 12 for bigger departments. • Representatives of all stakeholders in the workplace must be included in the WSDC. It is essential that union representatives are included if the workplace is unionised. • The skills development facilitator must be included as a member of the WSDC. • The skills development facilitator should serve as a convener of all meetings of the WSDC, and act as facilitator of the activities of the WSDC. • Once it has been established, the WSDC should develop guidelines and rules to govern the functioning of the WSDC and the expected conduct of its members.
Develop vision, mission, mandate and service delivery targets of the organisation	An important objective of the skills development strategy is to ensure that education and training becomes more strategic in nature. Therefore, there should be a link between training and education identified in the workplace skills plan and the overall strategic direction of the organisation. All workplace skills plans should include the following: • vision statement of the organisation; • mission statement of the organisation; • strategic objectives; and • service delivery priorities and targets for the organisation. The above information provides an explanation of how the strategic priorities of the organisation inform training and education needs outlined in the workplace skills plan. It may also be appropriate to include some explanations of how the strategic direction of the organisation may be changing and the implications of these changes on its ETD priorities.

Steps	Description
Prepare statistical information	The SETA requires some statistical information about employees to update the sector profile. This information also has implications for human resource development in the organisation. From the statistics, the skills development facilitator will be able to see the following: • the gender and race composition of the company (this is important for employment equity, which has strong training implications in South Africa); • the age profile of the company; and • qualifications of employees in the organisation according to population groups. This section also provides a solid foundation of facts from which to develop the workplace skills implementation plan. It is important that this information is provided in the format required by the SETA, as this will assist the SETA to consolidate all the information it receives from organisations. The information collected should be as accurate as possible. Any concerns about the accuracy of this information should be noted in the report and the source of the information acknowledged. The following information is required for this section: • total number of employees according to population group, gender and salary levels; • total number of employees according to occupational groups/class; • total number of employees according to education/skills level in terms of the NQF; • total number of employees according to age (including population group and gender); • number of people in each occupational group (by race and gender) who have received training in the previous financial year; • name, addresses and contact details of training providers your department has used during the last financial year; and • feedback on the adequacy of existing training and education provision.
Develop a skills matrix for the company	This section of the workplace skills plan should outline the process used to develop the skills matrix and provide the following information. • What are the competencies/skills required to meet the organisation's objectives and targets? • What skills are regarded as scarce skills? How do these compare with the sector's scarce skill list? • What competencies/skills are currently available in the organisation? • What are the education and training gaps in the organisation? • What are the interdepartmental training needs of the organisation? • What are the specific training needs in the organisation? • What are the strategic skills development priorities on which the organisation will be spending its 1% of payroll training budget? • Are there vacancies which the organisation is unable to fill? What are the reasons for this inability? • Is the organisation interested in developing or participating in specific skills programmes or learnerships?

Steps	Description
	In outlining the education and training gaps in the organisation, the SETA may ask that a distinction is made between generic and organisation-specific training needs. Generic training needs refer to training needs that are generic to all departments in the organisation. Examples are financial management training, human resource management, driver training and literacy training. Department-specific training refers to training related to the specific and unique activities of a department.
	It is also important to indicate where the organisation sees the need for skills programmes and learnerships that could be registered with the SETA, and whether the organisation plans to participate in any existing learnerships and skills programmes.
Develop the HRD strategy	Finally, the company needs to combine all the above elements into a comprehensive ETD/HRD strategy that addresses the strategic priorities and skills gaps. This strategy should include measurable targets so that the organisation can measure whether it has achieved its objectives at the end of the financial year. This strategy should include a detailed explanation of the following: • training programmes to be offered during the year; • number of people (including gender and race profile) to be trained; • ETD providers (including addresses and contact details) and their accreditation status; • costs of training; • implementation plan (including timelines for implementation); and • quality assurance, monitoring and evaluation of training.
Submit the workplace skills plan	The workplace skills plan must be signed off by all members of the WSDC and the senior manager or director of the organisation.

Table 3.5 Example of data captured on the workplace skills plan form

Section A Administrative detail	It consists of the following tables: Table A.1: Information on company Table A.2: Details concerning the Skills Development Facilitator (SDF) of the company.
Section B Statistical information	Table B.1: Total number of employees according to salary levels and population groups. Table B.2: Employees according to age, population group and gender. Table B.3: Employees' qualifications according to NQF levels.
Section C Training needs analysis/Skills audit	Section C of the WSP Form consists of the following sub-sections: C.1 Vision statement of the department. C.2 Mission statement of the department. C.3 Specific mandates and functions of the department. C.4 Strategic objectives identified by the department. C.5 List of competencies required by the department to enable the department to deliver on its vision, mission, and strategic objectives.

	C.6 Skills Gap Analysis. C.7 Compiling the Training Needs Matrix for the department. Comments: The main thrust in Section C is to determine the organisation's training needs. This section is the "heart" of the Workplace Skills Plan. It requires a comprehensive analysis of the organisation. In order to perform this analysis efficiently and effectively, SDFs should have expertise in research in general, organisational analysis techniques and training needs analysis/audit skills.
Section D **Training needs** **matrices**	D.1 Total number of employees requiring training – according to occupational groups. D.2 Number of Africans according to training needs and occupations. D.3 Number of Asians according to training needs and occupations. D.4 Number of coloureds according to training needs and occupations. D.5 Number of whites according to training needs and occupations.
Section E **Prioritisation matrix**	This section has only one table. Table E.1: Training programmes planned for e.g. 2008/2009. Comments: It is important to prioritise. It may not be possible to satisfy all training needs identified in the previous section in one financial year. In this section, enter only those ETD interventions, which will be undertaken during the current financial year.
Section F **Training interventions** **for lower level workers** **(salary levels 1–4)**	There are two tables in Section F: Table F.1: ABET. Table F.2: Other training interventions. Comments: Lower level workers are often marginalised in many organisations. This situation has to be corrected very urgently. Some of the employees in this category have enormous potential. Companies are encouraged to make resources available to unlock potential in lower level workers. The information required in this section is straightforward.
Section G **Implementation**	The implementation of workplace skills plans for 2008/2009 commences on 01 April 2008 and ends on 31 March 2009. The implementation plan should reflect what will be achieved during this period.
Section H **Promoting skills** **development for** **employability and** **sustainable livelihoods**	This section centres around the issue of Social Development Initiatives/Plans. The purpose is to assist employees who aspire to participate in the SMME sector or to acquire alternative skills.
Section I **Stakeholder support** **(meaningful** **influencing) and** **authorisation**	Throughout the development of the WSP, the SDF works through the Workplace Skills Development Committee (WSDC) and reports regularly to the top management of the company. At the end of the process the members of the WSDC must indicate their support by signing against their names in table 1.1. Likewise the head of the company and the HRD/ETD practitioner must append their signatures in sub-section 1.2. The SDF must also sign in this sub-section.

Table 3.6 Example of a skills matrix

Training & Education Band	Type of Qualification	NQF Level	Male				Female				Total
			African	Asian	Coloured	White	African	Asian	Coloured	White	
GET	ABET 3 and lower										
	Gr 9 (Std 7) and lower ABET 4	1									
FET	Gr 10 (Std 8) or Technical N1	2									
	Gr 11 (Std 9) or Technical N2	3									
	Gr 12 (Std 10) or Technical N3	4									
HET	Career Certificates	5									
	General/Career-focused Diplomas	6									
	General Bachelor's/Career-focused Degree	7									
	Post-Graduate Degrees (Honours, Master, Doctorate/Professional)	8									
Total											

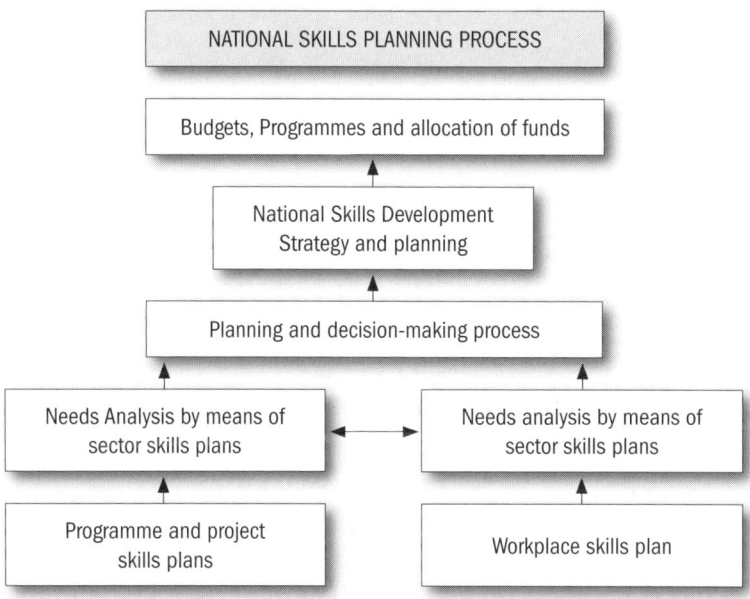

Figure 3.3 *Skills planning at national, sectoral and organisational level (Coetzee, 2006)*

Table 3.7 *Planning a skills audit (based on CIPD, 2007)*

Type of data	What to include
Business objectives	• Requirements in terms of outputs, levels of customer service and interactions with other parts of the organisation. • How are these measured? • What is going to change?
National and sectoral requirements	• What are the national and sectoral requirements regarding scarce and critical skills? • How are these linked to the company's scarce and critical skills categories? • How does the company perform in terms of equity requirements?
Technology and organisation of work	• How are jobs done now in terms of organisation and resources available? • What technologies do people use, and how might this change? • Changes may be planned in terms of numbers of people to carry out the targeted performance or in terms of the way they are supervised or managed.
Employee demographics	• Who is currently employed in the area you are analysing? • Who is joining and leaving the organisation? • What categories of employees are included?
Education	• Basic education, vocational or academic qualifications. • Link education to assumptions about people's expectations around ETD provision, cognitive or thinking abilities, and their level of current skills and knowledge.

Type of data	What to include
Past experience	• What previous knowledge, skills and behaviours have been expected in the past and are required currently? • This may be linked to the organisation's competence framework. • Experience of past ETD interventions.
Job roles and responsibilities	• What are individuals doing at the moment? • What implications will any changes have for their roles?
Current competence	• Current performance levels of individuals and teams and any areas where competence needs to increase. • This can be measured against both current and changed roles.
Employee status	• Are people employed permanently or part-time, on a fixed or short-term contract?
Location	• The physical location of employees and their access to ETD provision.
Length of time in job	• The length of time people have spent in their current role might have an effect on their training needs and the forms of training they require.
Employee attitudes and culture	• How do employees feel about changes; do they see the changes as opportunities or threats? • How will this affect their willingness to learn and acquire new skills? • Does the organisation want to change attitudes or focus on particular performance standards?

Figure 3.4 Strategic skills planning at organisational level (Coetzee, 2006)

Task analysis

Task analysis examines what employees must do to perform their jobs properly. In so doing, task analysis helps to determine the content of a learning programme. A job analysis identifies and describes the tasks performed by employees and the knowledge, skills, attitudes and other behaviours needed for successful job performance. If available, the results of a job analysis are helpful in determining training needs. Task analysis generally consists of:

- developing task statements;
- determining homogeneous task clusters, which are more usable and manageable than individual task statements; and
- identifying competencies, or knowledge, skills, attitudes and other behaviours (KSAOs) required for the job (Landy & Conte, 2004).

The links between task clusters and KSAOs can be used to develop training programmes that enhance the most important KSAOs. Table 3.8 shows the task clusters derived from a task analysis conducted on the job of a train operator. As an example, the results of this task analysis can be used to design training on the steps train operators must follow in emergency situations.

Table 3.8 Task clusters for train operators (Landy & Conte, 2004)

Task cluster	Description
Pre-operation responsibilities	Prepare for operating the train for a given shift. This includes reporting for duty in a state of preparedness with proper equipment, and getting information from the bulletin board and/or dispatcher.
Pre-operation equipment inspection	Check the train for defects and safety. Check the brake system, gauges, and track under the train.
Train operations	Operate the train in a safe and timely manner. This includes controlling the train in the yard or on the road, considering conditions (such as weather, curves and grades, and speed restrictions) and interpreting warnings and signals.
Maintain schedule	Perform activities associated with timely operations, including adhering to the timetable and communicating with personnel to prevent disruption of service.
Emergency situation activities	Identify and react to emergency situations. Keep customers safe, communicate with the control centre, and troubleshoot mechanical difficulties.

ACTIVITY

Review Table 3.8, then read the case study at the end of this chapter.
- Identify the five main task clusters for a customer care consultant.
- Give a description of the tasks involved in each of the identified task clusters.
- Based on the task analysis, give examples of the typical training needs of customer care consultants.

Job: customer care consultant	
Main task clusters	Description of tasks
1.	
2.	
3.	
4.	
5.	

ACTIVITY

- Select a job profile or job description of a job with which you are familiar.
- Identify one job performance area.
- List three main tasks to be performed in the job.
- Using the graph below, analyse the main tasks in terms of:
  - frequency of use (scale: 0% to 100%); and
  - importance (criticality) to organisation (scale: 1 to 10).

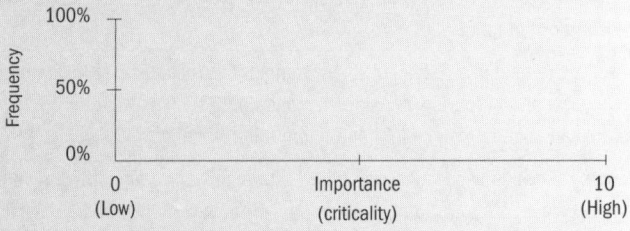

- Analyse one main task in terms of KSAOs required to complete the task successfully.
- Complete a competency matrix.

Description of main task	Knowledge required	Skills required	Attitudes and values required	Other behaviours required

- Using the following graph, analyse the competencies (knowledge, skills, attitudes/values and other behaviours) in terms of:
  - frequency of use (scale: 0% to 100%)
  - importance (criticality) to organisation (scale: 1 to 10)

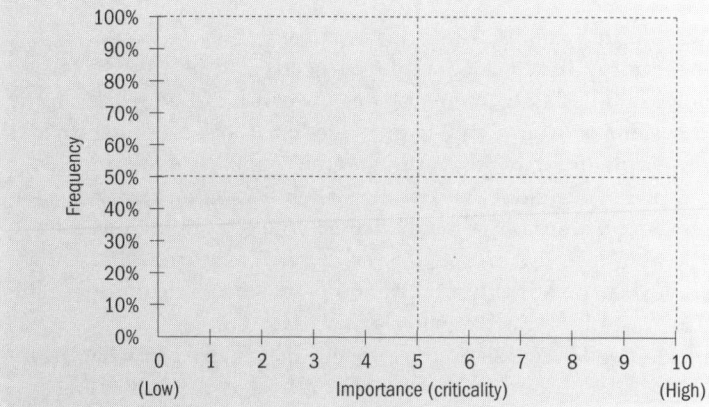

- Analyse the results and identify the most important competencies to be addressed.
- Review Table 3.3 on pages 87-88. Are the identified competencies:
  - skills shortages;
  - scarce skills;
  - core competencies;
  - core skills; or
  - generic skills?

As discussed in Chapter 1, SAQA distinguishes between three types of competency:
- *Foundational competence* is the knowledge, underpinning theory and principles that learners must acquire and apply in their lives and work.
- *Practical competence* is the skills that learners must be able to demonstrate in their lives and work.
- *Reflexive competence* is the ability of learners to reflect on their own learning and growth, and the ability to reflect on how the acquired knowledge and skills could be applied in different social contexts.

The combination of these competencies is referred to as applied competence – the core focus of outcomes-based learning programmes. The ETD needs analysis is an important part of identifying and developing applied competencies.

ACTIVITY

Study the three types of competency described above, then read the case study at the end of this chapter.
- Identify these competencies for a customer care consultant using the following sentences as starting points:
  - A customer care consultant requires foundational competence in ...
  - A customer care consultant requires practical competence in ...
  - A customer care consultant requires reflexive competence in ...

Person analysis

Person analysis identifies the individuals within an organisation that should receive training, and the kind of training they need. Employee needs can be assessed using a variety of methods. For example, assessments of KSAOs can be obtained from the performance evaluation system or from a 360-degree feedback system that provides input for training and development activities. A 360-degree feedback system includes feedback from managers, peers, customers and other stakeholders; and a self-evaluation. Objective data on accidents and job performance are often examined as part of the needs analysis, and written tests are used to assess employees' current job knowledge. Assessments of employees' personality, ability, and prior learning experience are increasingly being used as part of the needs analysis process.

At a personal level, ETD needs analysis is the process of finding out what an individual is supposed to do (the desired performance) and what the individual can actually do (the actual performance, or what an individual is doing incorrectly, inadequately or not at all). Individuals' learning and development needs may be personal, performance-related or career-related. Individual learning and development needs include the following:

- updating knowledge, skills and job-related competencies;
- increasing job satisfaction and fulfilling personal goals;
- making decisions about career choices;
- identifying personal strengths and growth areas;
- identifying and achieving personal work values and work targets;
- developing communication, personal effectiveness and life skills;
- improving qualifications;
- facilitating individual learning and self-development; and
- building self-awareness, self-confidence and motivation.

Any job requires a person to meet certain standards. Standards are levels of expertise, skills or performance that a person needs to comply with to do a job properly. Training might be necessary if an employee does not meet the required standards . Training based on such a need (or needs) will aim to address that need by giving the employee the skills to do the job properly.

Organisations use personal development plans to identify the needs of staff and possible ways to meet those needs. Personal development plans are evaluated within the context of the individual's overall career progression, and within the context of the organisation or department's objectives. By using personal development plans, organisations show that all staff are entitled to meaningful training and education opportunities. Personal development plans identify the following:

- the current competencies of staff (which will help to form the basis for an effective skills audit);
- the work values of staff (for example career progression, helping others, creativity, being skilled and respected in one's work);
- the work and career targets of staff;
- the competencies that need to be developed to enable staff to meet their work and career targets; and
- an individually tailored programme of development, training, education and support (including learnerships where appropriate), designed to enable staff to acquire the relevant competencies to meet their work targets and personal and career objectives.

Personal development plans are negotiated between the line manager or supervisor and the individual staff member. These plans are reviewed regularly. Managers and ETD practitioners try to find a balance between individual and organisational needs (because of budgetary constraints, this is not always possible). Conflicts may arise between the needs of different individuals, between different organisational needs, and between individual and organisational needs. To resolve such conflicts, ETD practitioners should prioritise organisational and individual ETD needs according to budgetary constraints, national priorities for transformation, priorities for a specific SETA, local circumstances and strategic planning priorities. Decisions in this regard should be transparent, and should be taken in consultation with training committees, staff members, unions and other relevant stakeholders.

ACTIVITY

Prepare for a development conversation with your manager. Follow the guidelines provided below.

Personal development discussion planner

Name:
Date of discussion:
Manager/supervisor:

My expectations of the session with my manager/supervisor:

Issues to discuss
Career plan
Internship/learnership programme
ETD goals and needs
Development opportunities
Further education opportunities
Work performance
Personal problems

What is important to me?
• What have I achieved, and to what standard or level?
• What evidence do I have (portfolio of evidence) of my achievements?
• Whose evidence is this (own work, correspondence, references or commendations from customers, colleagues)?
• What have I learned during the development process? How did I learn this?
• What am I satisfied with? What do I want to develop further?

Talk about yourself in the areas of skills, working style, interests, and values.

Skills: What do I do really well?

What is my working style and personal style?

How do others see me?

What feedback have I received from others?

- Supervisors
- Coworkers
- Interactions with others

Interests: What ideas/activities do I find fulfilling? Use the interest sort below.

Interest sort:

High interest and high competence *High satisfaction area*	High interest and low competence *Development opportunity areas*
Low interest and high competence *Burnout areas*	Low interest and low competence *Red flag areas*

Values: What ideas do I cherish about my career (for example challenges, clear-cut procedures, creativity, flexibility, independence, mental stimulation, teamwork, stability)?

What specific feedback do I need?

What information do I need in terms of trends?

Identify the future trends in your industry, organisation, and profession and understand the implications for making career decisions.

- Organisational structure
- Environment
- Norms and culture of organisation
- ETD opportunities

Which two options are the most appealing?

Set multiple career directions and determine the resources critical for success.

Multiple options

- Vertical (seeking promotion and more responsibility on current path)
- Lateral (moving to new duties or areas, but at the same level)
- Enrichment (enhancing present skills and duties; adding new challenges)
- Realignment (starting over or returning to a position with less status)
- Exploratory (testing changes without permanent commitment; researching options)
- Relocation (looking outside the organisation for a better career fit)

Future thinking

Keeping in touch with mentor and other sources on new developments.

Enrichment

Identify activities/projects related to your present opportunities that will provide a greater challenge.

Education, training and development opportunities (NQF aligned)

Identify further development opportunities related to your current ETD needs and career path.

What two development activities are most important?

Conversation tips
- Take some time to think before your first meeting.
- Be candid, constructive and to the point.
- Keep an open mind. Your first task is to explore, brainstorm, and build on ideas about options and how to accomplish them. Do not get locked into one goal, one development area, or one strategy too early.
- Create a comfortable climate so your mentor does not feel defensive.
- Share your own experiences, thoughts and feelings.
- Agree on next steps and schedule another meeting.
- Identify the subject of your discussions ahead of time.

ACTIVITY
- Reflect on your current job, then work through the items below.
- Draw up your personal development plan. If you do not have a job profile, use your ultimate career goal and your current competency profile to determine your development gaps and ETD needs.

Your personal development plan	
Employee name: Position:	Date captured: Date updated:
Actions	**Responsibility**
1. Do a self-assessment of how your current competencies compare with those required in your job. Do this by looking at your current competencies, job profile, competency profile and the ultimate career development plan you have chosen.	You
2. Identify areas where you need to improve your competence.	You
3. Complete your personal development plan: • List the competency gaps that prevent you from achieving your job outputs. • Identify where learning and development are required. • Describe your future career aspirations.	You
4. Discuss your personal development plan with your manager: • Discuss your performance in terms of the gaps that have been identified. • Agree on a suitable learning solution. • Prioritise learning needs. • Draw up a timeline that indicates when you plan to complete training.	You and your manager
5. • Implement ETD solutions by integrating the learning outcomes of the learning programmes you intend to complete into your career pathway.	You, your manager and the organisation

Example of a needs analysis questionnaire with selected questions (based on Grobler *et al*, 2006)
Please read the list of training areas carefully before answering. Circle √ if you believe you need training in that skill, either to use in your current job or to prepare for promotion to a better position. Circle ? if you are uncertain. Circle X if you feel no need for training in that area.

In column A, rate the skills necessary for the employee to perform the job. Use the following ratings:
1 = not important
2 = moderately important
3 = very important

In column B, rate the employee's need for training for each skill area that received a rating of 2 or 3 in column A. Use the following ratings:
1 = no need for training
2 = moderate need for training
3 = immediate, critical need for training

		A How important is the skill?	B Employee's need for training?
1. How to manage my time more effectively	√ X ?		
2. How to handle stress on the job	√ X ?		
3. How to improve my written communication skills	√ X ?		
4. How to improve my oral communication skills	√ X ?		
5. How to improve my listening skills	√ X ?		
6. How to improve my customer relations	√ X ?		
7. How to improve my service to customers	√ X ?		
8. How to deal with customer complaints	√ X ?		
9. How to improve my personal productivity	√ X ?		
10. How to improve my problem-solving skills	√ X ?		

Methods of ETD needs analysis

Various methods can be used to gather data from employees and employers in an organisation. The most common methods include questionnaires, observation, skills and knowledge tests, personal development plans, performance appraisal data and critical incidents. According to the HR and Industry Report (ASTD, 2007) question-naires (82%), interviews (65%) and performance appraisal data (66%) are regarded as important methods for identifying ETD needs in South African organisations.

Questionnaires

Questionnaires are used widely as a method of gathering data. Usually, a survey is done on a sample, or representative group of the organisation (for example, a number of randomly picked employees and managers each complete a questionnaire). But sometimes a whole department or the entire organisation is involved in the survey.

A questionnaire is an inexpensive way to gather data, and a large number of people can be reached in a short time. Respondents also get the opportunity to give their opinions without fear of recrimination or embarrassment. The data gained from ques-tionnaires can be summarised and reported easily.

Questions must be clear and unambiguous. Questioners should avoid asking two (or more) questions in one. Questionnaires cannot always identify the causes of problems, and they do not allow for free expression or responses other than the options provided. Often, not many employees complete and send back the questionnaire. Only literate employees can take part in surveys (Landy & Conte, 2004).

Observation

During observation and work sampling, employees are observed doing their jobs or specific parts of their jobs. The biggest advantage of this method is that it does not interrupt the work of a person or department. Observation requires a highly skilled person who has a good understanding of the job being observed and the process of observing.

Employees may sometimes react negatively and feel that the observer is spying on them. Observation is a more subjective technique than questionnaires, but it provides information on the employee's behaviour and the results of that behaviour. The effectiveness of the technique is influenced by the type of job being observed.

Individual interviews

The individual interview is a popular and versatile way to gather information. Managers and employees accept this as a valid method for gathering information, because they can contribute their own views to the information. Some kinds of information can only be obtained through the personal interaction of an interview. Respondents can explain their views in their own terms and, because the interview is a discussion, respondents may gain insight into their own situations. Literacy is not a requirement when the interview method is used. When in-depth questions are used, participants may reveal their feelings and explore causes of problems and possible solutions. Other advantages of the interview method are that all the questions of the survey are answered and a higher response rate is achieved.

The information obtained from an interview may be biased or distorted. Sometimes, important information is lost because the interview is a stressful situation for some respondents. It is also a time-intensive and expensive way to gather information. The confidentiality of the information cannot always be ensured and the results may be difficult to analyse and quantify (Erasmus *et al*, 2006).

Skill and knowledge tests

Tests can be designed for a specific job, or standardised. Well constructed tests will determine employees' abilities to perform certain aspects of a job to a certain standard. The test should measure job-related qualities. The scoring mechanism should be developed by a trained person to ensure validity and reliability. Cognitive tests measure levels of knowledge in a specific area, while behavioural tests measure skills. Tests can usually be scored easily and can be administered to a large group of employees at once.

However, tests are time consuming and expensive to develop. There are relatively few tests available to determine training needs, so organisations would need to construct their own tests (Aamodt, 2007).

Personal development plans

A personal development plan sets out an employee's future ETD opportunities to achieve long-term career goals, and the ETD opportunities that he/she has already been exposed to by the organisation. A personal development plan assists the employee and employer to keep the employee's long-term career goals in mind when ETD needs are discussed. It provides an opportunity to identify areas where knowledge and skills should be improved, in the current job and as preparation for future positions. The personal development plan lists the employee's knowledge and skills that must be developed, how and when these will be developed and the person who will be responsible for ensuring that the development is implemented. Read more about personal development plans on page 98.

Performance appraisal data

Performance appraisal data can be relevant in the needs analysis process, if the performance appraisal system allows for the identification of employee training needs. Strengths and weaknesses in past performance are identified. Action plans and goals are developed to address the weaknesses and build on the strengths. Training and development can often solve performance problems (Grobler *et al*, 2006). As part of the performance appraisal, the personal development plan can be used to plan the employee's future development and identify development opportunities. Performance appraisals must be conducted regularly for the information to be useful in the needs analysis process. Supervisor bias and misuse of the system may invalidate the information gained from performance appraisals (Brown, 2002). To ensure that performance appraisal information is relevant, reliable and valid for needs assessment, the following principles should apply:

- The appraisal system should be relevant to the job and acceptable to both parties.
- The manager who does the appraisal must have regular contact with the employee to ensure that the manager has access to performance-relevant information.
- The appraisal should be for developmental purposes only.
- The employee should understand the benefits (in the form of development and training) he or she will derive from the appraisal.

Critical incidents

The critical incident, or samples of behaviour method is a relatively easy method to use, especially if a proper job description is available. To use this method for ETD needs assessment, critical incidents are sorted into dimensions (based on the job description) and separated into examples of good and poor performance. Dimensions with many examples of poor performance indicate areas in which many employees are performing poorly. Additional training is required for these areas (Aamodt, 2007).

When deciding which method to use to collect data for needs assessment, the following should be considered:

- the involvement of employees and management;
- the time available to do the analysis;
- the costs involved with each method and the available budget for the needs analysis;
- the type of data required; and
- the geographical distribution of the respondents.

Choosing the appropriate method to gather data is only one of the steps in the needs analysis process. After sufficient data has been gathered, an evaluation or assessment of the data must be conducted to determine which (if any) conclusions can be drawn from the data. Only then can ETD practitioners make any recommendations about existing ETD needs. We now look at the ETD needs analysis process in more detail.

The ETD needs analysis process

A completed ETD needs analysis expresses the:
- ETD programmes required to address the ETD needs (including the contents of such learning programmes);
- ETD priorities;
- assumptions behind the identified needs and priorities;
- resources required;
- timing and implementation; and
- expected rate of progress and returns.

The needs analysis process as shown in Figure 3.5 includes the following seven phases: plan the needs analysis system; develop data-gathering methods and procedures; develop data-gathering cycle; implementation; data analysis and development planning; evaluation and feedback; and establishing the HRD information system.

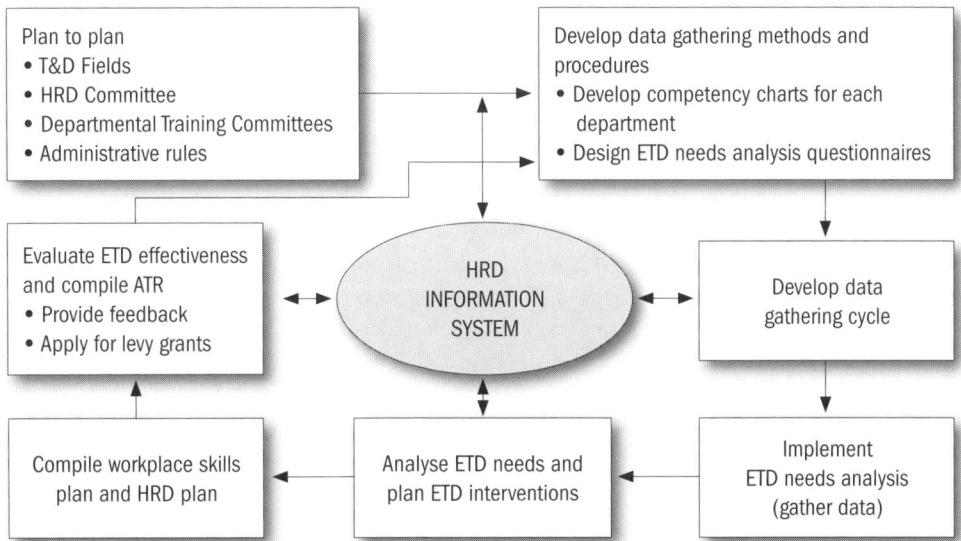

Figure 3.5 *ETD needs analysis process (based on Castley, 1996)*

Plan the needs analysis system

The first phase in ETD needs analysis is planning an ETD needs analysis system. This system should consist of the various elements of the ETD needs analysis process. Without a detailed plan, the ETD needs analysis will provide inaccurate information. Three main activities are essential when planning the ETD needs analysis system: establish training and development fields, form committees and establish administrative policies and procedures.

Establish training and development fields (T&DFs)

Establish the training and development fields according to an approximation of jobs found in the various departments of the organisation. Under each field, training and development programmes and activities are then designed and offered (refer to Table 3.9 for an example). Organisations are established with different purposes and functions. These functions are related to various bodies of knowledge and disciplines. For example, an organisation that deals in automobile production is mainly concerned with the body of knowledge related to the science of electrical and mechanical engineering. Financial organisations, on the other hand, are primarily concerned with the financial field of enquiry.

Form committees

The next step is to form a Human Resource Development (HRD) committee in the HRD department of the organisation. In addition, training committees (as required by the Skills Development Act) are formed in each department. As shown in Figure 3.6, the HRD committee includes HRD practitioners and a representative from each department's training committee. Representatives from the various job levels and various race and gender groups form the training committee of a department.

The HRD department (through the HRD committee) advises the departments on how to conduct an ETD needs analysis. Each department is responsible for its own ETD needs analysis, ETD planning and implementation process. The HRD practitioners provide administrative support, technical expertise on processes, tools and methods of ETD needs analysis, planning and development. HRD practitioners also complete the workplace skills plan and annual training report (as discussed in Chapter 1). The HRD department also manages the HRD information system.

The main objective of training committees is to enrich the activities related to the assessment of the ETD needs of the department. The HRD committee represents the various departments in the organisation in all training and development matters (setting institutional ETD objectives, developing curricula and programme outlines for ETD programmes, recommending ETD providers and participating as a trainer). The HRD committee is informed by the training committees. These committees are the backbone of the entire ETD needs analysis system. Members of the committees bring direct information related to employees' job performance and development needs. In this way, the committees help to identify needs and evaluate the effectiveness of ETD outcomes.

Establish administrative policies and procedures

The last step of planning is to establish administrative policies and procedures to manage the activities of the HRD committee and training committees. Some of the most important matters that should be described in policies and procedures are:

- the number of meetings each year;
- the duration of each meeting and dates, if possible;
- general objectives of each meeting;
- general guidelines for recording and distributing minutes of meetings.
- the responsibilities of and coordination between the various departments, the departmental training representative, the HRD committee and the HRD department.

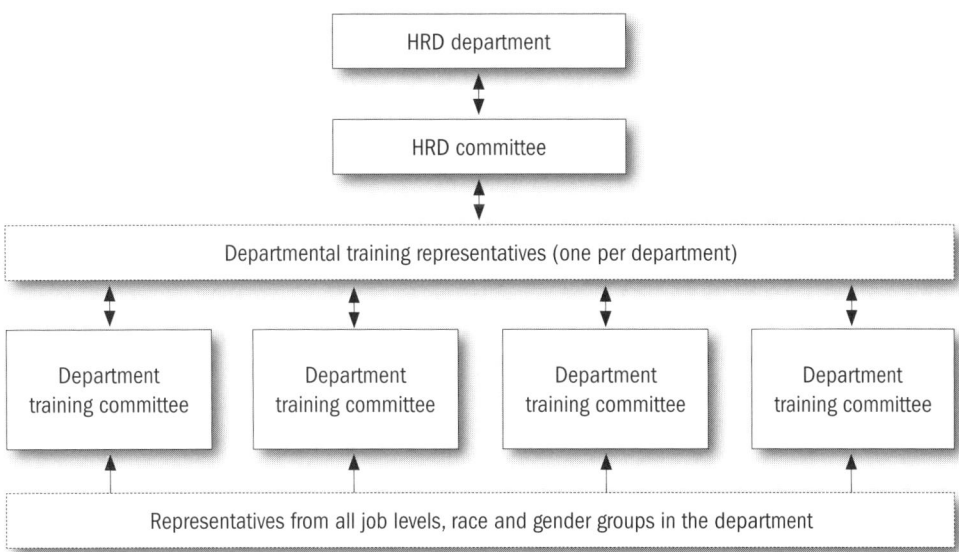

Figure 3.6 *ETD needs analysis committee structure*

ACTIVITY
Read the case study at the end of this chapter.
- Establish an HRD committee for the lifestyle management equipment company.
- Who will you involve in this committee?
- Identify the roles of committee members.

Table 3.9 *Training and development fields of banking and/or financial institutions (Castley, 1996)*

Training and development fields	Examples of training and development programmes
Banking operations	• Letters of credit • Basic banking • Letters of guarantee
Treasury operations	• Foreign exchange and money market • Economic analysis • Portfolios and mutual funds
Credit and loan management	• Financial and credit analysis • Project financing • Real estate management

Training and development fields	Examples of training and development programmes
Management of personal effectiveness	• Supervisory skills • Time management • Creativity
Marketing and business development	• Customer care • Selling skills • Quality assurance
Information technology and audit	• System design and development • Software quality assurance
Banking laws and regulations	• Legal aspects of credit • Introduction to banking laws

ACTIVITY

Review Table 3.9, then read the case study at the end of this chapter.
• Think about the position of a customer care consultant. Identify at least three training and development fields relevant to a customer care consultant.
• Give examples of typical training and development programmes for the identified training and development fields.

Use this table as an example of how to present your information.

Training and development field	Examples of training and development programmes
• Dealing with customer complaints	• Conflict resolution, interpersonal communication

Data-gathering methods and procedures

In this phase, tools and techniques are developed to collect data about the ETD needs of the organisation and its employees. The purpose of gathering data is to identify ETD needs. Since ETD is about improving performance, data gathering in this phase concentrates on the competencies required for the jobs in an organisation.

The various training committees identify the general competencies required in a specific department. Once this is done, the HRD committee develops competency charts and questionnaires to be used in the data-gathering process.

Competency charts

A competency chart is a list of competencies required for an approximation of jobs found in the various departments of an organisation. Competencies include the knowledge, skills, values and other behaviours people require to be successful in their jobs. The aim is not to develop a precise definition of competencies for each job in the organisation, but rather to develop an approximation of the main competencies required for each training and development field.

Table 3.10 Sample of a competency chart for a marketing and business development training and development field (Castley, 1996)

Training and development field	Competency
Product development and management	• Managing the product development process • Evaluating new product ideas and plans • Corrective skills • Time and product entry strategies
Pricing-related competencies	• Costing products and services • Planning and controlling cost of performance • Pricing strategies
Competencies related to marketing strategy	• Negotiation skills • Networking • Methods for competitive marketing strategies • Methods and techniques for analysing the industry • Calculating market share • Market segmentation and product and service positioning
Competencies related to service quality	• Assessment of service gaps • Measuring service quality standards • Managing service quality team

ACTIVITY
Review the competency chart in Table 3.10, then read the case study at the end of this chapter.
• Determine the required competencies for a customer care consultant in this organisation.
• Develop a competency chart for a customer care consultant.

Questionnaire design

Questionnaires can be used to collect data about the actual ETD needs of the staff members in a department. For each training and development field, a questionnaire is designed, based on the training and development field's competency chart. The questionnaire is divided into four sections: profile data, professional knowledge and skills, cross-functional knowledge and skills, and other competencies. Only the second section (professional knowledge and skills) differs from one departmental training committee to another. This section should reflect the core competencies and skills required in a department (as defined in the training and development fields). The other three sections of the questionnaire are the same for each training committee. Go to page 111 for an example of a questionnaire.

Profile data

The profile data section of the questionnaire collects personal and professional information about respondents, such as name, department, title and years of experience.

Professional knowledge and skills

The professional knowledge and skills section of the questionnaire measures employees' level of knowledge and skills in relation to the technical aspects of their jobs. For example, a credit officer in a bank is usually expected to perform activities related to financial analysis, credit analysis and cash flow analysis.

Cross-functional knowledge and skill

The cross-functional knowledge and skill section of the questionnaire measures employees' understanding of competencies related to non-technical aspects of their jobs. The assumption is that there are various skills that are required in any job, regardless of its area of specialisation. That is why this section is the same for each department in an organisation. For example, credit managers will require a strong background in credit operations (specialised skill). They must also have good leadership and planning skills, marketing skills, computer skills and knowledge of the legal aspects related to their job (generic skills). Each training committee needs to identify the non-technical competencies required for specific training and development fields.

Other competencies

The final section ensures the comprehensiveness of the questionnaire. The respondent is given the opportunity to indicate any other training needs that might not have been identified in the rest of the questionnaire. It is important to differentiate between an employee's training needs and wants. *Training needs* are competencies that the employee needs to perform the job, but that are lacking in the employee. *Training wants* are competencies that an employee believes they need, but these needs are not necessarily related to the job.

Questionnaires should also give managers of a department an opportunity to indicate any skills shortages, and scarce and critical skills relevant to the department. In this way, the HRD committee can identify important areas for talent retention and development.

Questionnaires are often criticised as time consuming, lengthy and complicated. Good questionnaires form questions in a standard way and use a measuring scale. Instruction sheets explaining how to complete and return questionnaires must be attached to the questionnaires. Each section of the questionnaire starts by asking respondents to rate their level of familiarity with the listed competencies. A standard rating scale is used throughout the questionnaire. The questionnaire also includes a 'not applicable' box for each competency. Respondents tick this box if the knowledge and/or skill described does not relate to their job. A well-developed questionnaire minimises response times and errors.

The questionnaire must be reviewed and updated every training year. This task is done in participation with the HRD department, the HRD committee, line management and the various training committees.

Sample questionnaire for a marketing and business development training committee (Castley, 1996)

Profile data

Name:	Current job:
Since:	Supervisor:

Brief summary of job description:

Previous training courses attended:

Rate each competency according to the following scale:
Not familiar (1) – Very familiar (7) or N/A (not applicable)

PROFESSIONAL COMPETENCIES

A. Product development and management	1	2	3	4	5	6	7	N/A
Managing product development process								
Evaluating new product ideas and plans								
Corrective skills								
Time and product entry strategies								
B. Pricing-related competencies	1	2	3	4	5	6	7	N/A
Costing products and services								
Planning and controlling cost performance								
Pricing strategies								
C. Competencies related to marketing strategy	1	2	3	4	5	6	7	N/A
Negotiation skills								
Networking								
Methods of competitive marketing strategies								
Methods and techniques for analysing the industry								
Calculating market share								
Market segmentation and product positioning								
D. Competencies related to service quality	1	2	3	4	5	6	7	N/A
Assessment of service gaps								
Measuring service quality standards								
Managing service quality team								

CROSS-FUNCTIONAL COMPETENCIES

A. General management competencies	1	2	3	4	5	6	7	N/A
Goal setting								
Steps of the planning process								
Setting priorities and scheduling								
Leadership skills								
Creative thinking								
B. Computer skills	1	2	3	4	5	6	7	N/A
Spreadsheet applications								
Word processor applications								
Database applications								
E-mail and Internet								
Others (please specify)								

Other competencies

In the space below, please indicate other training needs that you require (knowledge and skills that were not mentioned above).

Develop data-gathering cycle

The data-gathering cycle is the process of distributing and administering question-naires. As shown in Figure 3.7, the HRD department initiates the ETD needs analysis process, sends the questionnaires to the departmental training representatives, collects the completed questionnaires, analyses the data, prepares the results (with the help of the departmental training representatives) and communicates the outcome to the ETD unit of the HRD department. On the basis of their feedback the HRD depart-ment develops a final HRD plan for approval. The HRD plan comprises the broader HRD strategies to address the ETD needs in the short (a financial year), medium (two to three years) and long term (three to five years). The HRD plan will also include capability-building strategies such as talent pool development, managerial develop-ment and succession development. The short-term strategies are included in the work-place skills plan.

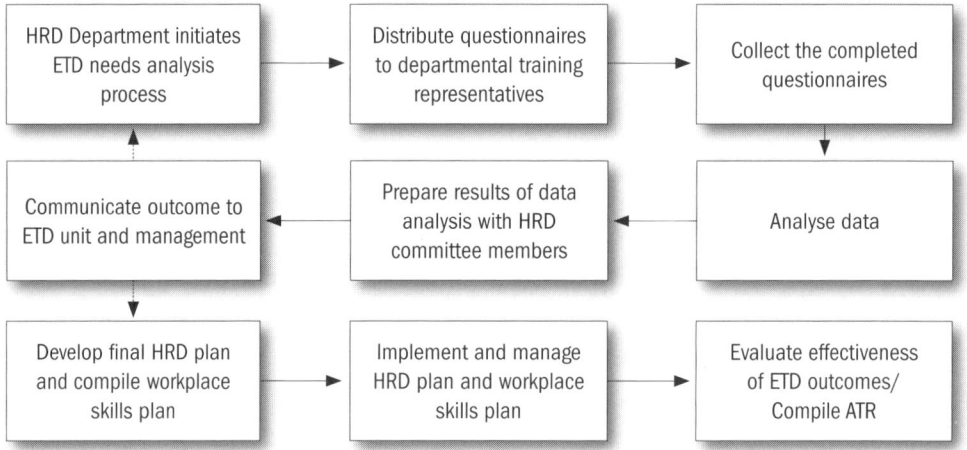

Figure 3.7 The data-gathering cycle

The training representative from each department studies the draft HRD plan and establishes ETD priorities according to the department's business plan and workplace skills plan. The training committee members are involved in each step of the data-gath-ering process. Their duties include explaining the ETD needs analysis process to other managers, supervisors and staff members, helping to administer and collect question-naires, and providing input into the HRD plan. To perform this role, training committee members may need training to acquire skills and knowledge about ETD.

Implementation

During the implementation phase, the ETD needs analysis process is executed. This includes allocating resources, timing the ETD needs analysis and scheduling tasks. The detailed roles and responsibilities of each party involved in the process is defined. In the implementation phase, the efforts of all parties involved must be coordinated to ensure a successful ETD needs analysis. Keep the following in mind during the imple-mentation phase:

- The HRD department must take a leading and central role in the process.
- Enough time should be allowed for implementation, especially if the departments are going through peak times (such as salary weeks or strategic planning exercises) or holidays.
- The implementation phase produces a lot of paper work that needs to be handled carefully.
- Responses and results should be treated with confidentiality.

Ethical concerns in conducting an ETD needs analysis

An ETD needs analysis and/or skills audit collects sensitive information, particularly when individuals' knowledge and skills gaps are identified. Individuals' needs and rights have to be respected. In addition, planned major changes in an organisation may give rise to new ETD needs. Senior management may wish to keep the planned changes secret. In these situations, ETD practitioners may need to convince senior management that they need to gather data to plan timely ETD interventions that will contribute to the success of the initiative. ETD practitioners then have to conduct an ETD needs analysis while maintaining confidentiality (CIPD, 2007).

Data analysis and development planning

In this phase, the questionnaires are analysed using a suitable data analysis technique. The skills and topics that respondents most frequently marked to indicate a low level of familiarity, are identified. These are the skills and topics where employees lack knowledge and skills. These skills and topics are then integrated into formal ETD interventions and activities for the year. As shown in Figures 3.5 and 3.7, data analysis also involves the development of the final HRD plan of the department. This forms the basis of the annual workplace skills plan. The HRD plan includes a list of learning programmes required, the contents and the selection of appropriate curricula, unit standards, target groups and programme durations.

Evaluation and feedback

No ETD needs analysis is complete without an evaluation (this is also the topic of Chapter 7). The main objective in this phase is to find out whether the actual ETD needs (not wants) were identified. It is also an attempt to find weaknesses in the needs analysis system, provide feedback to the concerned parties and suggest corrections. The HRD department should develop an evaluation system to detect shortcomings. For example, at the end of a learning programme, a questionnaire can be used to determine to what extent the learning programme met the needs of the learner. The questionnaire might include questions such as:

- To what extent is the content of the learning programme related to your job?
- Is the content of the learning programme based on an appropriate unit standard?
- To what extent did the learning programme meet your actual ETD needs?
- What topics of the learning programme were irrelevant to your job?
- Were learners assessed in terms of learning outcomes?
- Did learners have the opportunity to apply the skills in the workplace?
- Were learner support structures established?

In addition, informal investigations (in the form of discussions with people involved in implementation) during implementation might reveal shortcomings related to the execution period, the amount of paper work generated, and the clarity of questions.

ETD needs analysis information system

The ETD needs analysis process requires the support of a rigorous HRD information system. This information should help ETD practitioners to:
- integrate the processes into a productive system;
- facilitate a reliable flow of information among involved parties;
- minimise paper work; and
- facilitate follow-up activities.

As shown in Figure 3.5, the HRD information system might easily be integrated with the ETD needs analysis process. With an HRD information system, the organisation (and the HRD department) will be able to track employees' career development. On such a system, employees' records could include ETD programmes they have attended, and current and future ETD needs.

CASE STUDY

Problems in the customer care department

Read the following case study and answer the questions that follow.

Mr Jason Hlongwe is the customer care manager of a large lifestyle management equipment retail outlet. This outlet sells gym equipment, camping gear and sports equipment. The business has been flourishing for the past seven years. Recently, just after the opening of the customer care department, sales figures dropped and customer complaints increased. Customers complain that customer care consultants are untrained, unfriendly and unwilling to help. Mr Hlongwe has asked you, as the training manager, to develop and present a course in basic customer care to the customer care consultants.

During your investigation you gathered the following information:
- Customer care consultants successfully conclude sales, but they find it difficult to deliver at the promised time. Apparently, equipment is often received late from the stores department.
- When the equipment is received, the customers have to wait for up to an hour to collect the equipment from the dispatch department. If they request home delivery, customers often wait for a week or more.
- Customer care consultants are not allowed to contact the stores manager or the dispatch manager to follow up on the receipt and dispatch of equipment, but have to work through Mr Hlongwe's office. He is often in meetings and therefore, difficult to reach. This causes enquiries to pile up in his office.
- Customer care consultants are not allowed to explain to customers why there is a delay in the delivery of equipment. They end up making promises that they cannot keep.
- Customer care consultants are not allowed to refer complaints to Mr Hlongwe's office, unless the customer specifically requests this. It is an unspoken rule that they have to 'keep the customers happy if they want to get their commission'.
- Most of the customer care consultants have little sales and customer care experience, because the employee turnover in the department is so high.
- There is no time to send customer care consultants for intensive training because there is a permanent shortage of staff (also as a result of the high employee turnover).

Questions

1. How would you go about doing an ETD needs analysis? Explain the steps you will follow.
2. Which of the needs that you identify in this case study are training needs? Which needs will have to be addressed in other ways?
3. Identify the levels of the training needs you have identified.
4. Identify the information you will need to compile a workplace skills plan for this organisation.
5. Which method will you use to gather data on individuals' training needs?
6. Which learner differences will you keep in mind when you design the learning material?

Table 3.11 Quality checklist for an ETD needs analysis (Coetzee, 2007)

Standard	Evidence required	In place Yes/No	In progress	Action
1. Are identified ETD needs based on employees' personal development needs, career plans, occupational profiles, performance appraisals, RPL assessments and competence assessments?	Workplace skills plan ETD needs report Business plan/HRD business plan Assessment reports Development plans Career plans Succession plans Occupational profiles			
2. Are identified ETD needs linked to applicable national unit standards (if applicable) and inherent job performance standards/requirements?	Unit standards Performance criteria Occupational profile			
3. Are ETD needs formulated in terms of learning outcomes to be achieved in the learning event (in relation to skills plans, national unit standard outcomes, learning outcomes and learner needs)?	Formulated training/learning outcomes Lesson plan Learning material Assessment methodology and procedures			
4. Do the identified ETD needs address the organisation and the individuals' needs?	Business plans Development plans			
5. Are identified ETD needs prioritised in terms of resource availability, criticality and feasibility?	Management reports Management approval			

Key terms

- Interviews
- Observations
- Organisational needs analysis
- Performance appraisal
- Personal development plan
- Person needs analysis
- Scarce skills
- Sectoral needs analysis
- Skills audit
- Task needs analysis
- Training needs analysis

Review and discussion questions

1. What is a Training Cycle? How do the various phases relate to one another?
2. Why is an ETD needs analysis such an important phase in the Training Cycle? What are the purposes of an ETD needs analysis?
3. What methods can an ETD practitioner employ to gather data for an ETD needs analysis? Which methods would be the most appropriate for the different levels of training needs analysis? Give reasons for your answers.
4. What are the typical steps involved in an ETD needs analysis?
5. Who should be involved in an ETD needs analysis?
6. How does the information gathered from an ETD needs analysis inform the design of learning programmes?
7. Why is it important to establish an ETD needs analysis information system?

Suggested reading

Blanchard, P.N. & Thacker, J.W. (2004). *Effective training. Systems, strategies and practices*. Upper Saddle, River, NJ: Pearson Prentice Hall.

Brown, J. (2002). Training needs assessment: a must for developing an effective training programme. *Public personnel management*, 31(4), 569-578.

Dooley, K.E., Lindner, J.R., Dooley, L.M. (2005). *Advanced methods in distance education. Application and practices for educators, administrators and learners*. Hershey, PA.: Information Science Publishing.

Erasmus, B.J., Loedolff, P.v.Z., Mda, T. & Nel, P.S. (2006). *Managing training and development in South Africa*. Cape Town: Oxford University Press.

Folscher, E. & Chonco, L. (2006). *Skills development practice made easy*. Johannesburg: Knowres.

Gregory, G.H. (2005). *Differentiating instruction with style. Aligning teacher and learner intelligences for maximum achievement*. Thousand Oaks, CA: Corwin Press.

Grobler, P.A., Wärnich, S., Carrell, M.R., Elbert, N.F. & Hatfield, R.D. (2006). *Human resource management in South Africa*. London: Thomson learning.

Meyer, M., Mabaso, J., Lancaster, K. & Nenungwi, L. (2004). *ETD practices in South Africa*. Durban: LexisNexis Butterworths.

Summary

ETD needs analysis is the starting point of the Training Cycle. This chapter explored the importance of performing an ETD needs analysis on various levels to explain the why and how to carry out ETD activities and whether training is, in fact, the best solution for the performance problem or development need. Before learning programme design issues are considered, a careful needs analysis is required to develop a systematic understanding of where training is needed, what needs to be taught or trained, and who will be trained. Chapter 4 explores the next phase in the Training Cycle, namely using the results of an ETD needs analysis to design quality outcomes-based learning programmes.

Employees become increasingly committed to jobs where they can learn new skills, and to jobs they find personally challenging. Allowing employees to customise their growth opportunities provides them with further opportunities to learn and shifts responsibility for that learning to the employees themselves (Ulrich, Zenger & Smallwood cited in Palmer, 2002).

CHAPTER 4

JO-ANNE BOTHA • MELINDE COETZEE

Outcomes-based learning programme design

By creating detailed, measurable learning outcomes, selecting relevant course content, designing supportive and interactive learner guides and incorporating support materials in the learning programme design process, ETD practitioners guide learners to the knowledge, skills, attitudes and behaviour they need to master.

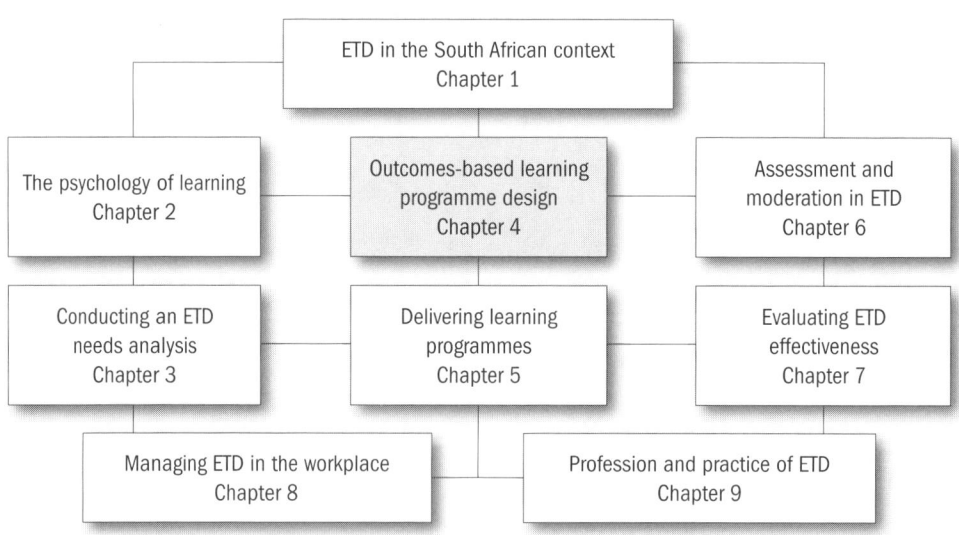

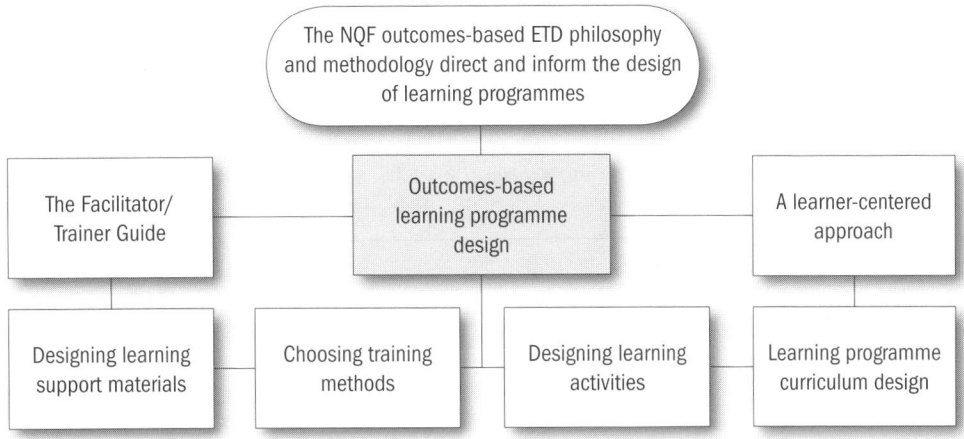

Key points of outcomes-based learning programme design

- Within an outcomes-based ETD system, a learning programme is regarded as a combination of courses, modules or units of learning, learning support materials and methodology by which learners can achieve specified learning outcomes.
- The effective ETD practitioner recognises that few (if any) of the desired outcomes will be reached unless learners are actively involved in the learning process and perceive the learning as valuable to them. This implies moving away from a content-driven approach to a learner-centred approach.
- The effectiveness of the learning process depends on developing learning outcomes that are meaningful and appropriate to the needs of learners.
- The facilitator/trainer guide contains guidelines on how to facilitate quality assurance in respect of learning programme delivery, assessment and the evaluation of value added.

After studying this chapter, you should be able to:

- Evaluate the benefits of adopting a learner-centred approach to learning programme design.
- Explain the 'design down and deliver up' approach to outcomes-based curriculum design.
- Discuss the characteristics and importance of accurate and appropriate learning outcomes.
- Explain how unit standards inform the formulation of learning outcomes.
- Explain the steps involved in designing the curriculum of outcomes-based learning programmes.
- Evaluate how learning taxonomy levels guide ETD practitioners in formulating learning outcomes.
- Develop a course outline for a learning programme.
- Explain the characteristics of well-designed learning activities.
- Discuss the aspects to be considered when choosing training methods.
- Discuss the elements of well-designed outcomes-based learning materials.
- Describe the process of selecting sources of and sequencing learning content.
- Discuss the function and content of the facilitator/trainer guide in outcomes-based learning programme design.

This chapter explores the second phase in the Training Cycle, namely the design of outcomes-based learning programmes. The ETD philosophy and methodology that the ETD practitioner follows direct and inform all training and learning activities. In the past, education and training tended to be content driven. Learning materials and activities were designed around content, which supported the content orientation of curricula and modes of instruction. NQF-aligned, outcomes-based education and training moves beyond content. The reasoning is that content is not studied for its own sake; rather, learners are expected to apply and reflect upon the content.

Figure 4.1 The Training Cycle

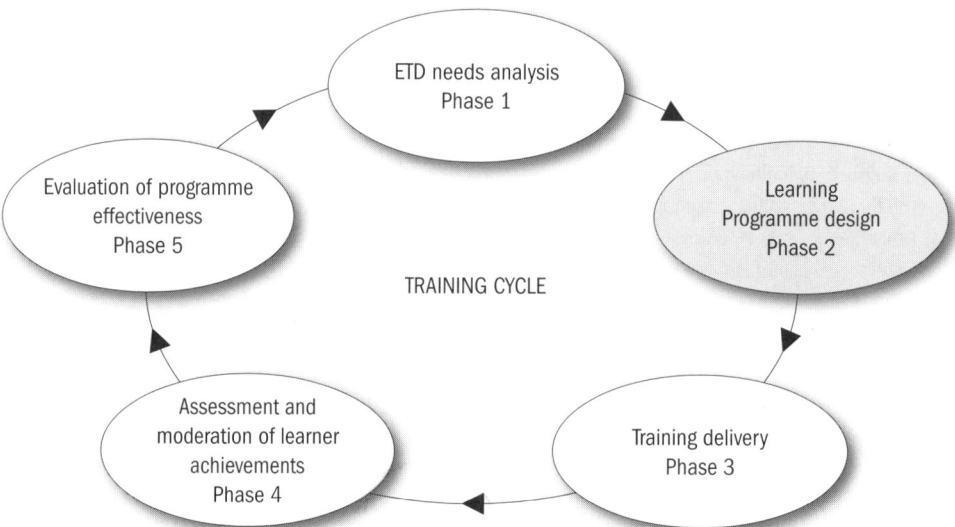

Within an outcomes-based ETD system, a learning programme is regarded as a combination of courses, modules or units of learning, learning support materials and methodology by which learners can achieve specified learning outcomes. As pointed out in Chapter 1, ETD providers can also design and offer short learning programmes that are based on only parts of qualifications (SAQA also recognises short learning programmes that are not based on unit standards). In the workplace, ETD practitioners will often be requested to design short learning programmes; these may or may not be linked to unit standards or qualifications.

The concept learning programme is used in this chapter to refer to short learning programmes based on whole or part unit standards, or not based on a unit standard at all. A short learning programme comprises a series of structured learning activities or events that are intended to equip learners with the applied competence needed to fulfil a particular occupational role (Coetzee, 2007). The effective ETD practitioner recognises that few (if any) of the desired outcomes will be realised unless learners are actively involved in the learning process and perceive the learning as valuable to them. Therefore, determining the ETD needs of the organisation and the learner (as discussed in Chapter 3) is a prerequisite for planning the design of a learning programme.

A learner-centred approach

Outcomes-based ETD revolves around learners, and their ability to achieve the learning outcomes of a learning programme. ETD practitioners should therefore keep the following in mind when designing learning programmes:
- the overall goal or objective of a learning programme;
- the learning outcomes formulated for the programme;
- the goals of the learning process;
- the nature of the learning process;
- the construction of knowledge;
- the context of the learning;
- learners' intrinsic motivation to learn;
- the effect that motivation to learn will have on learners' efforts; and
- individual differences between learners (Dooley, Lindner & Dooley, 2005).

A learner-centred approach attempts to involve learners in the learning process; enable learners to apply their knowledge to emerging issues; and help learners to integrate discipline- or subject-based knowledge in the learning process.

A learner-centred approach generally leads to a more positive attitude towards what is being learned, which improves learners' motivation to learn. It also leads to understanding at a deeper level and therefore, new knowledge is retained better. Learning materials should be clear and understandable, support the ways in which adult learners learn and communicate and engage learners' interests and motivations. By creating detailed, measurable learning outcomes, selecting relevant course content, designing supportive and interactive learner guides and incorporating support materials in the learning programme design process, ETD practitioners guide learners to the knowledge, skills, attitudes and behaviour they need to master. Effective learning programme designers stimulate learners' curiosity and think of ways to improve their motivation. Learners must have direct access to the knowledge base. They should be allowed to work individually and in groups to master the material by solving problems, trying to understand and apply the material, and memorising important concepts.

In the learner-centred approach, the ETD practitioner's role (as learning programme designer) is to develop skills such as critical thinking, problem solving and decision making. This can be achieved by helping learners to access, interpret, organise and apply information to specific situations (Dooley *et al*, 2005). In a learner-centred approach, ETD practitioners are led by learners' characteristics (such as learning pace, learning style and motivation to learn) when they design learning programmes. The learning programme should be flexible to allow learners to master the knowledge at their own pace and to address individual learners' needs.

The learner-centred approach uses specific ways to make knowledge and information available to learners. Training facilitators begin by informing the learners of what they should be able to do at the end of the learning session. These are the learning outcomes they have developed for the learning programme. Learning outcomes help learners to set their own learning goals (the steps they will take to ensure they master the information and knowledge).

Various methods can be used to achieve learning goals. In a learner-centred approach, learners find out which strategies are effective for their own learning. When learners use their own methods and resources to achieve learning goals, they begin to construct their own knowledge.

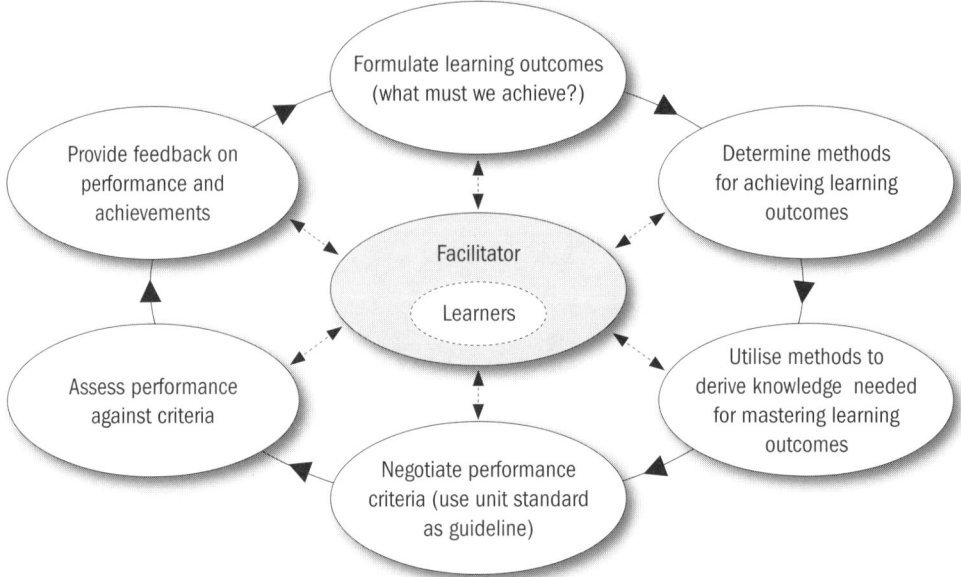

Figure 4.2 A learner-centred approach to learning programme curriculum design

Learning programme curriculum design

SAQA (2005) proposes a design down, deliver up approach to learning programmes. In the design down approach (as shown in Figure 4.3), learning programme designers move from:

- an analysis of the objective, or overall purpose of the learning programme;
- to the purpose of the qualification (if the learning programme is based on a full qualification);
- to the unit standard (if the learning programme is based on a unit standard, parts of unit standards or a combination of unit standards); and finally
- to a close examination of the learning outcomes, its assessment criteria, course content, learning and assessment activities and other relevant information.

The outcomes-based approach means that learners should be involved in a range of learning and assessment experiences during which they acquire knowledge, skills and values and execute specific tasks and activities that help them to achieve specified outcomes. In the case of learning programmes based on unit standards, the purpose of the unit standard should be linked to the overall objective of the learning programme. In the case of full qualifications based on unit standards, learners work to achieve unit standards which build towards the purpose of the qualification as a whole.

Once the design down process is complete, learning programme designers deliver up; that is, they design learning activities to prepare learners for the assessment activities set out in the curriculum. Learning and assessment activities help learners to build up evidence that they have achieved the learning outcomes.

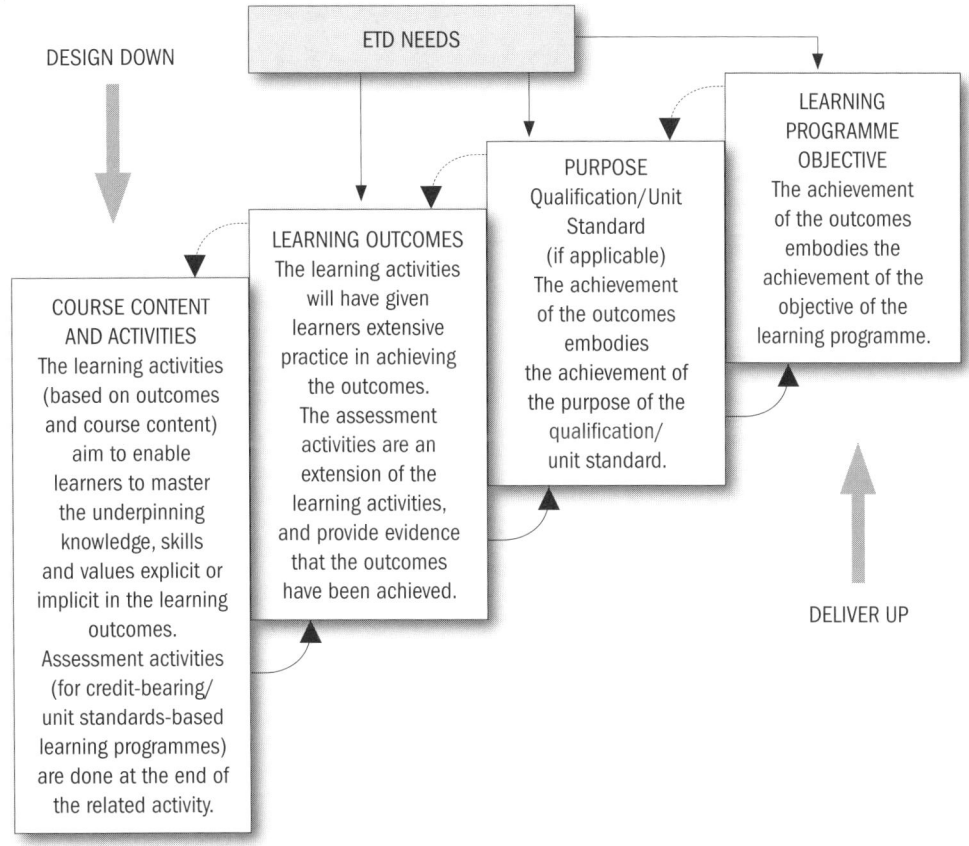

Figure 4.3 *Design down, deliver up approach in outcomes-based learning programme curriculum design (based on SAQA, 2005)*

Modules

Learning programmes often consist of learning units, or modules. The learning programme is structured and ordered according to these modules to help learners progressively achieve the learning outcomes. Learning and assessment activities of the first module build up to the second module and so forth, to help learners master the learning outcomes of the programme as a whole.

Planning the curriculum design

As shown in Figure 4.4, a learning programme is a plan for implementing a curriculum (the specifics regarding the what, when and how of learning and assessment activities), which leads to learners' achievement of the programme's learning outcomes (SAQA, 2005). A *learning programme* is about what happens in the classroom, including learning and assessment activities associated with the learning facilitation process (described in the facilitator/trainer guide). A *learning programme curriculum* deals with the learning programme strategy (the broad plan of action for achieving the learning programme objectives and enabling learners to master the learning outcomes), which includes activities such as:

- determining the learning programme objective based on the ETD needs analysis;
- choosing and analysing unit standards, where applicable;
- formulating learning outcomes;
- grouping learning outcomes into modules;
- choosing and sequencing appropriate and sufficient course content and materials;
- designing learning and assessment activities;
- designing learner support materials;
- designing facilitator/trainer and assessment guides; and
- choosing training delivery and evaluation methods (Coetzee, 2006a).

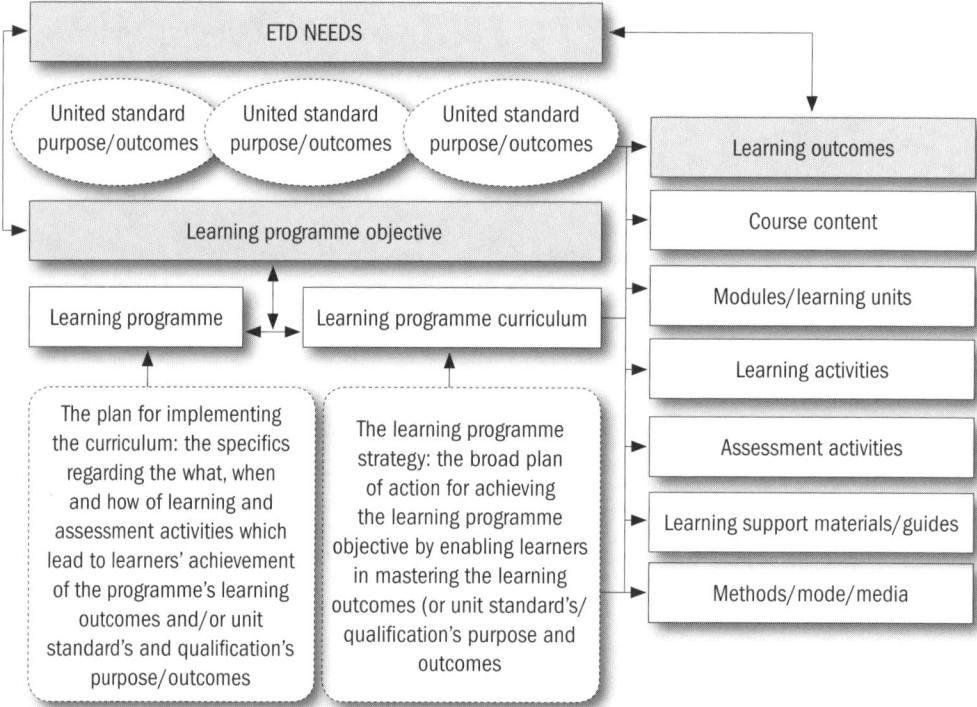

Figure 4.4 *Planning the curriculum design*

In SAQA's terms, curriculum refers to all the teaching, learning and assessment opportunities that take place in the learning institution including: purpose and values of the learning; learning outcomes; content, activities, methods, mode and media; teaching and learning facilitation strategies; forms of assessment and moderation; and the evaluation of delivery. To develop a curriculum, facilitators must follow a sequence of steps:

- Assess learners' ETD needs (read more about learners' needs in Chapter 3).
- Identify the target learner audience.
- Plan the design of a learning programme.
- Determine the learning or course content.
- Develop a learning programme strategy.
- Develop a facilitator/trainer guide.

- Design the learning support materials.
- Pilot the learning programme and adjust the learning programme strategy and materials, if necessary.
- Deliver and evaluate the learning programme.

These steps will be discussed in the section that follows.

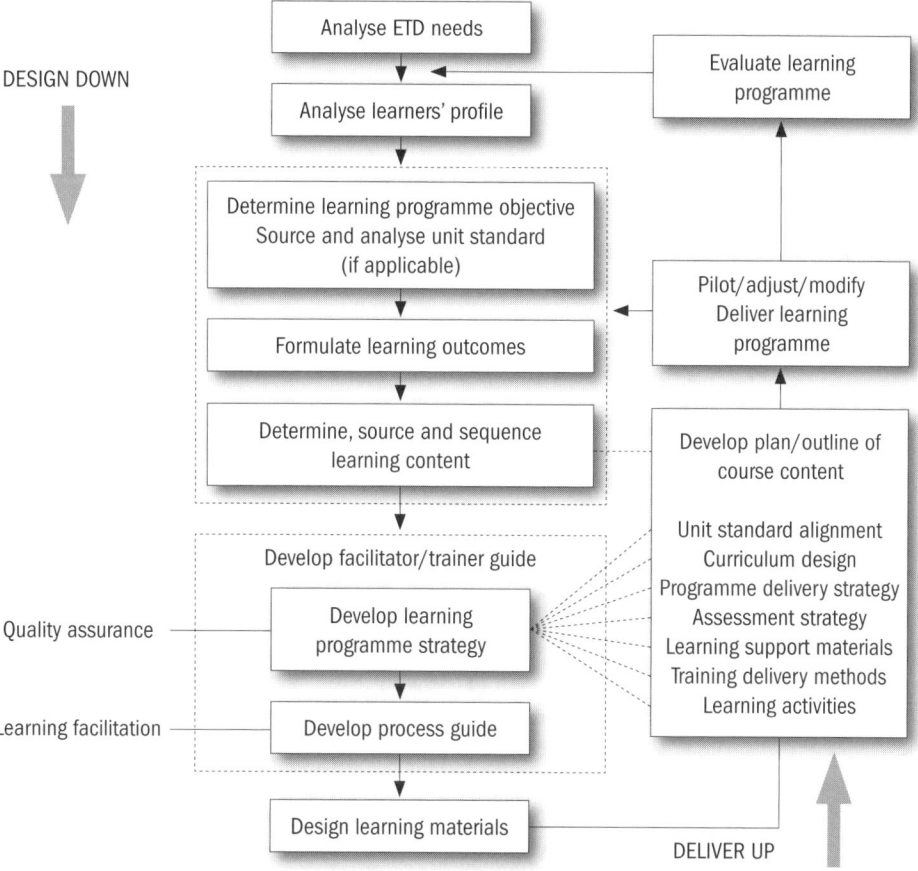

Figure 4.5 *Steps in designing an outcomes-based learning programme (Coetzee, 2006a)*

Analysing the learners' profile

Outcomes-based ETD follows a learner-centred approach. This means that the needs, level and preferences of the targeted learner audience will largely determine the learning content, structure, presentation and language level. Planning and designing learning materials, course content and methodology are dependent on a sound background knowledge of the targeted learning audience. Apart from the aspects listed in the checklist below, ETD practitioners are required by SAQA to record the following information about their learners:

- learner's prior experience;
- gender;
- geographic location;
- socio-economic status;
- cultural background;
- educational background;
- employment status;
- language;
- access to communication technology;
- physical disability; and
- ETD needs and motivation for attending a learning programme.

Quality checklist
Analysing learners' profile (Coetzee, 2007)

Demographic information
- What is the average experience of the learners?
- What is the ratio of male and female learners? Indicate the percentages.
- How many learners are employed?
- In what different fields are the learners employed?
- Where do most of the learners live? In rural or urban areas?
- What is the ratio of the different cultural groups? Indicate the percentages.

Language level
- Are they first language, second language or third language English speakers? Indicate the percentages.

Access to technology
- Do the learners have access to tape recorders, video recorders and/or computers with CD-Rom?

Entry level of the learners
- What is the highest level of education? If applicable, indicate through which education department of the previous government they matriculated?
- What are the prerequisites for each of the subjects?

Motivational information
- Why did the learners enrol for the course?
- How does the learning programme relate to their work?
- What is the learners' attitude towards the learning programme?
- What are the hopes and fears of the learners?

Information on learning
- What previous experience do the learners have of learning by means of a study text?
- How much time do the learners have available to study and master a programme?
- Do the learners have enough time to study?
- Do they have enough resources available for reference purposes, if necessary?

Learning programme information
- What do most learners know about the learning programme?
- Do they have any previous experiences in laboratory work, if applicable?
- What personal interests and experiences relevant to the learning programme do the learners have?

Determining the learning programme objective

Proper planning and design of a learning programme can only be done after a thorough needs analysis (as discussed in Chapter 3). Based on the information obtained from the needs analysis, the next step is to define the learning programme objective. This is a broad goal that explains the overall purpose of the learning programme. Learning programme objectives should therefore begin with a description of the intended purpose of training. The needs analysis should state the desired result of training. However, as shown in Table 4.1, such a description is generally too broad to be of much help in developing a set of procedures and activities that will lead to an effective learning experience. The next step is therefore to formulate learning outcomes. These are more specific and measurable in terms of what learners should be able to do after participating in the learning programme. The following aspects need to be considered when determining the learning programme objective:

- What kind of organisation do we want?
- What are the needs of the organisation?
- What are the organisational and learning contexts? What are the requirements?
- What types of learner will contribute to such an organisation?
- Who are the stakeholders in the organisation?
- Who are the learners?

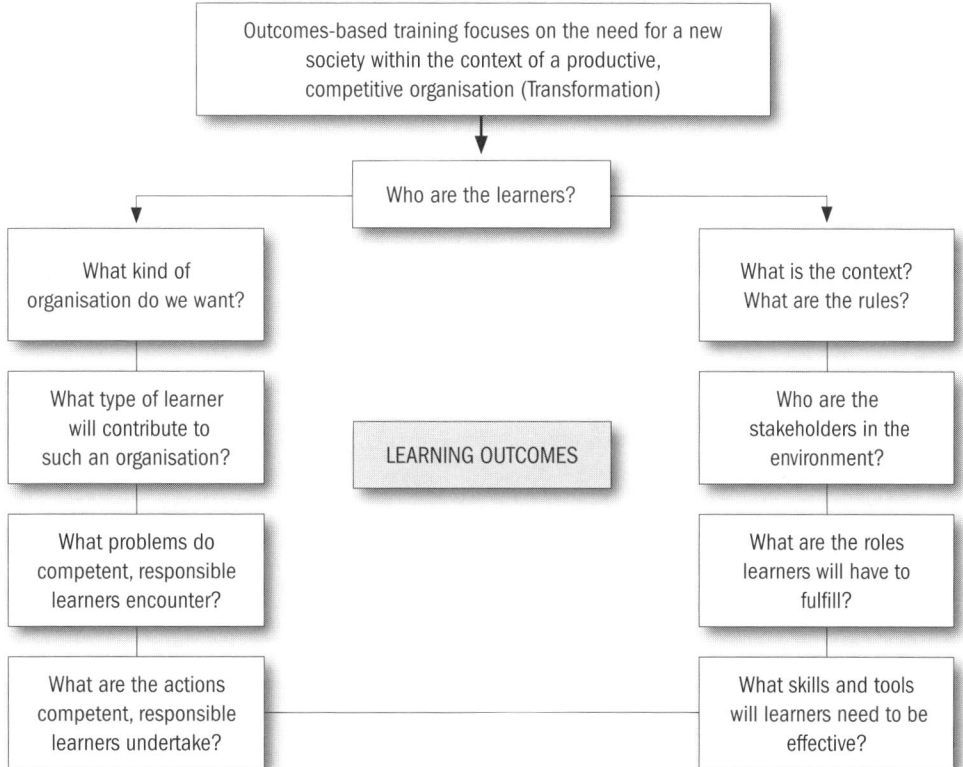

Figure 4.6 *Aspects to consider when determining a learning programme objective (based on Prinsloo, 2007)*

- What are the needs of the learners?
- What are the roles learners will have to fulfil?
- What problems do competent, responsible learners encounter?
- What are the actions competent, responsible learners undertake?
- What skills and tools do learners need to be effective?

Choosing and analysing an applicable unit standard

For learning programmes based on unit standards, the next step in developing a curriculum is to source an applicable unit standard from SAQA's website. A unit standard is applicable when its purpose, specific outcomes and associated assessment criteria show a clear link with the learning programme objective and identified training needs. Learning programmes can be designed using the full unit standard or only parts of the unit standard. When the full unit standard is used, it implies that all of the specific outcomes match the learning programme objective. In some instances, a learning programme consists of more than one unit standard to ensure that all of the identified training needs are addressed. In other instances, only one or two specific outcomes of a unit standard might be applicable to the learning programme. An ETD provider could also develop its own unit standard according to SAQA's guidelines if a unit standard on the subject matter is not available from a standards generating body or on SAQA's website. Table 4.1 gives an example of an accredited short learning programme with a curriculum based on selected specific outcomes of various national unit standards.

Table 4.1 Example of a learning programme based on unit standards

Title of course	Short course in organisational behaviour
Provider details	ABC ETD Provider
Learning programme objective	The learning programme's objective is to refine management skills regarding understanding and managing organisational behaviour on individual, group and organisational level. For this purpose, various unit standards that address competencies on an individual, group, and organisational behaviour level form the basis for the course in organisational behaviour.
Module 1 Unit standard titles	*Introduction to organisational behaviour* • Build teams to meet set goals and objectives • Empower team members through recognising strengths • Encourage participation in decision making and delegating tasks
NQF level	5
Credits	12
SAQA US registration number	15237 15224 115407
National unit standard alignment	
Module 2 Unit standard title	*Managing diversity in the workplace* • Harness diversity and build strengths of a diverse working environment

Title of course	Short course in organisational behaviour
NQF level	5
Credits	3
Field	Business, Commerce and Management Studies
Sub-field	Generic Management
SAQA US registration number	15233
National unit standard alignment	
Module 3 Unit standard title	Managing self • Apply self-management concepts
NQF level	4
Credits	3
Field	Manufacturing, Engineering and Technology
Sub-field	Manufacturing and Assembly
SAQA US registration number	14048

When learning programmes are based on unit standards, learning programme designers need to carefully analyse the unit standard. SAQA (2005) provides the following guidelines for analysing a unit standard:

- What is the purpose of the unit standard? The purpose describes for whom the unit standard is intended and why it is written. It also describes the general skills that a learner will have acquired upon completion of the learning programme and states the reasons for the development of the standard.
- What is the learning assumed to be in place? This refers to the learning that the learner already has (or should have) before participating in the particular learning programme to which the unit standard applies.
- How many outcomes does the unit standard contain? Specific outcomes are competence outcomes that focus on learning and performance. They capture a specific skill, knowledge and attitude that a learner must demonstrate in the unit standard.
- What does the outcome or group of outcomes indicate that learners need to know and be able to do?
- What will need to be assessed according to the assessment criteria for the outcome(s)? Assessment criteria indicate the evidence required to declare the learner competent in each specific outcome. An assessor will assess the learner's achievements by evaluating the evidence provided for this purpose against the assessment criteria. The learner will be declared competent or not yet competent.
- What content/subject matter will the learner need? Study the underpinning, or embedded, knowledge and the content that is implicit in the outcome and range statements.
- What embedded knowledge does the learner need? Embedded knowledge is the knowledge that the learner needs to know to show competence and achievement in the unit standard. It is all the knowledge the learner will gain from the start to

the end of the learning programme.

- If the outcome has a range statement, do the selected activities sufficiently cover the requirements of the range statement? A range statement is a guide that states the scope, context and level for the unit standard. It also describes the situations and circumstances in which the learner is expected to perform.
- How should the activities be ordered?
- What is the duration of each activity?
- How many formative and summative assessment activities would result in the learner producing sufficient evidence to meet the outcomes?
- What resources/materials will learners need to do the learning and assessment activities?
- What activities will enable learners to achieve the outcome and meet the assessment criteria?
- What learning strategies, methods, and approaches will get learners to the point where they can produce the required evidence of learning?

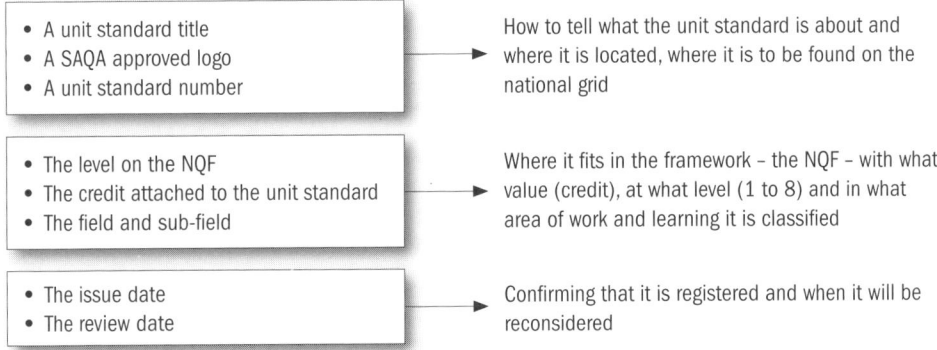

Then a number of issues that really are the heart of the unit standard and, in terms of SAQA's definition, are really the standard.

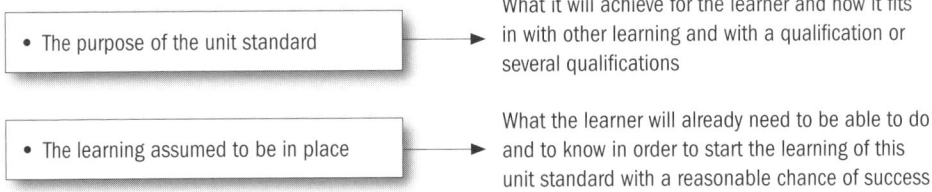

Then possibly the most crucial items or elements of a unit standard

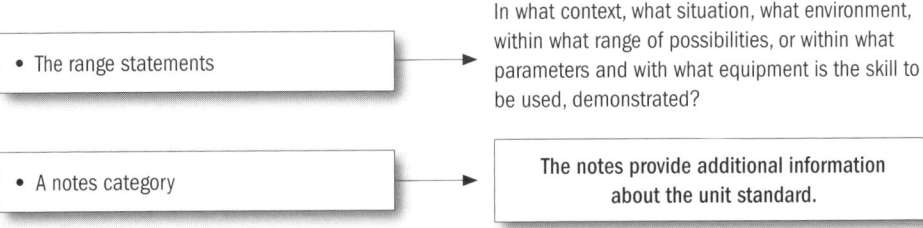

Figure 4.7 Unit standard elements (Grobler et al, 2006)

ACTIVITY
Study the unit standard in Appendix 1 on page 350, then review Figure 4.7.
* Identify the various elements of the unit standard.
* What embedded knowledge does the learner need to master the specific outcomes?

Formulating learning outcomes

Determining the learning outcomes of a learning programme is an important activity, because the whole ETD process that follows depends on developing meaningful and appropriate learning outcomes. Appropriate outcomes are outcomes that comply with the national standards as set out by government bodies such as SAQA and the NQF (the roles and functions of these official bodies are discussed in Chapter 1). Learning outcomes are also regarded as appropriate if they are closely related to the learning programme objective.

The achievement of the learning outcomes leads to the achievement of the learning programme objective. The learning outcomes help programme designers to design learning activities that give learners extensive practice in achieving the outcomes. Furthermore, learning outcomes form the foundation for the design of assessment activities that help learners to build up and provide evidence that the outcomes have been achieved.

Table 4.2 Link between a learning programme objective, unit standard outcomes and learning outcomes (Coetzee, 2006a)

Learning programme objective (the overall purpose of the programme based on the ETD needs analysis) To enable managers and supervisors to analyse the skills development legislation within the context of the public service, and to implement and promote the legislation in a national, provincial and local context.	
Specific outcomes SAQA Unit Standard US ID: 242899	**Learning outcomes** (what learners can do with what they remember, understand, know, and believe)
Demonstrate an understanding of the social contexts and values underpinning skills development.	**Module 1** • Interpret the objectives of the NSDS, HRDS and Batho Pele principles as they apply to the public service. • Explain the challenges regarding people development within the public service and the specific department. • Describe the roles of the various stakeholders in implementing the NSDS, HRDS and Batho Pele principles in the public service. • Explain the principles and values underpinning skills development in the public sector. • Link skills development priorities to labour market opportunities.
Promote legislation that directly supports skills development.	**Module 2** • Interpret the aims of the skills development legislation as they apply to the public service. • Interpret the aims of the NQF as they apply to people development in the public service.

	• Explain the national structure for implementing the skills development legislation. • Describe ways the department can apply the NQF principles and skills development legislation.
Apply the relevant strategies to implement skills development laws.	**Module 3** • Link the department's people development strategies and goals to the organisation's HRD strategies and goals. • Develop a process model for the systematic development of the department's people.
Apply the relevant values, laws and strategies in the workplace.	**Module 4** • Design a process for ensuring the effective development of the department's people. • Design a process for determining the department's and employees' training and development needs. • Compile skills matrices for the department. • Contract learning with the department's employees. **Module 5** • Design a process for managing the development of the department's employees. • Establish quality measures for the management of the department's workplace skills plan. • Evaluate the effectiveness of employees' development progress. • Evaluate the effectiveness of the department's workplace skills plan.

Critical cross-field outcome: Organising

The learner is able to demonstrate an ability to organise and manage his/her own learning activities responsibly and effectively.

Critical cross-field outcome: Collecting

The learner is able to demonstrate an ability to collect, organise and critically evaluate information pertaining to the relevant legislation and strategies.

Critical cross-field outcome: Communicating

The learner is able to demonstrate an ability to communicate effectively when implementing the skills development legislation utilising relevant technical data.

Critical cross-field outcome: Contributing

The learner is able to demonstrate an ability to:

• make responsible decisions in the process of applying the strategies for implementing the skills development legislation; and
• be culturally and aesthetically sensitive in the implementation of the strategies in the workplace.

Critical cross-field outcome: Demonstrating

See the world as a set of related systems in understanding the consequences of non-compliance with legislative and sector requirements and to see the links between the different laws and strategies.

As shown in Table 4.2, learning outcomes are defined as specific, measurable learning results that learners have to demonstrate at the end of each learning experience. Outcomes are things that learners can actually do with what they remember, know, believe and understand. Learning outcomes need to be formulated in such a way that it shows the actions or demonstration process required from the learner. There are three requirements for developing a learning outcome:

- An outcome needs to include a *verb* or 'do' word. This indicates the type of learning activity that will take place. This verb must indicate behaviour that can be observed and measured. Examples of these verbs are: 'develop' (a business plan), 'analyse' (a case study), 'compile' (a budget), 'formulate' (training needs) and 'build' (a wall).
- An outcome also needs to include a *noun*. The noun indicates the object of the verb. For the abovementioned examples, we can use the following nouns: 'business plan', 'case study', 'budget', 'training needs' and 'wall'. In other words, learners need to know what they have to develop, analyse, compile, formulate or build. This is the object linked to the verbs.
- Thirdly, an outcome must also include a *qualifier* that indicates the scope, standard or method of how something is done. Let us take the building of a wall as an example: after completion of the training programme the trainees will be able to build (verb) a wall (noun) according to the relevant municipal regulations (qualifier).

A learning programme designer can add more criteria to these three, for example by indicating how the learning facilitator will assess the outcomes; how the learner will demonstrate the outcomes; and what learning activities and methodology will accompany the learning experience.

ACTIVITY
- Write a learning outcome that contains all three criteria for a module on emotional intelligence.

Here is an example of such a learning outcome:
At the end of this session, the learner will be able to describe the five abilities of the emotionally intelligent person, as identified by Goleman.

Verb: describe
Noun: five abilities (of the emotionally intelligent person)
Qualifier: as identified by Goleman

- Write an outcome for a module on training needs assessment.

Here is an example:
After studying the first phase of the training cycle, that is, ETD needs analysis, the learner must be able to formulate training needs based on the discrepancy or gap experienced in the workplace.

Identify the verb, noun and qualifier from this learning outcome.
Verb:
Noun:
Qualifier:

ACTIVITY

Review the following specific outcomes (SAQA US ID: 117877):

- Prepare for one-on-one training on the job.
- Conduct training sessions.
- Monitor and report on learner progress.
- Review training.

Consider the following questions:

- For whom were these outcomes written?
- What learning is assumed to be in place?
- Identify the verbs in each of these outcomes.

The outcomes are meant for ETD practitioners, or trainers. The verbs are the things you have to know and be able to do or demonstrate after working through, for example this chapter. (Review the learning outcomes of this chapter on page 119.) After you have studied this chapter you should be able to:

- describe (know);
- discuss (know);
- develop (do);
- evaluate (do); and
- explain (know).

In order for you to be able to develop the knowledge and skills implied by the learning outcomes, it is assumed that you already have a qualification or equivalent competence in an occupation in which you will be able to practise the competencies described by the learning outcomes. It is for this reason that learning programmes comprise both theoretical content and activities. Learners gain knowledge by working through theoretical material, but they are also given opportunities to apply new knowledge and consequently, practise new skills.

Classifying learning outcomes

All learning outcomes do not require the same level of knowledge, skills and attitudes to achieve. As discussed in Chapter 1, unit standards are written at the various NQF levels. Some learning outcomes refer to simple ideas, while others refer to more complex issues. This means that learners can learn at different levels of complexity and may be required to demonstrate abilities at different difficulty levels. Learning is therefore not only about identifying information, but also about interacting with the content. Generally, learners interact with or utilise information across three main areas:

- The *cognitive domain* focuses on thinking processes. Learning outcomes for this domain focus on learners' knowledge needs.
- The *affective domain* focuses on feelings and emotions. Learning outcomes for this domain focus on fostering certain values, attitudes and preferences in learners.
- The *psychomotor domain* focuses on physical skills. Athletes and dancers are highly skilled in this domain. Learning outcomes for this domain focus on developing physical skills (such as using a computer keyboard) (Erasmus *et al*, 2006).

These domains of learning are generally classified according to levels of complexity (refer to Table 4.3 and Figures 4.8, 4.9 and 4.10). Such classification systems are referred to as taxonomies. They describe how the different levels build on (and often include) previous levels (Van der Horst & McDonald, 1997).

ACTIVITY

Study the taxonomy of learning outcomes in Table 4.3, then review the unit standard in Appendix 1 on page 350.
- Identify which domains are being addressed by the unit standard's outcomes and assessment criteria.

Table 4.3 Taxonomy of learning outcomes (adapted from Erasmus et al, 2006; Gregory, 2005)

Cognitive domain (thinking) Based on Bloom's taxonomy of learning (Bloom cited in Van der Horst & McDonald, 1997)	Knowledge To know and remember information, but not use or apply it. Knowledge is foundational, learners cannot accomplish other levels if they do not have knowledge.	Words commonly used in outcomes are: name, list, define, label, select, state, and identify.
	Comprehension Remembering and using information, understanding the meaning of learning material.	Words commonly used in outcomes are: describe, convert, illustrate, distinguish, discuss, summarise, and give examples.
	Application Applying material already learned to new, concrete, comprehensive situations. To transfer information when needed and use it in a new context.	Words commonly used in outcomes are: calculate, demonstrate, construct, solve, and apply.
	Analysis Identifying and looking at the different parts of the information, indicating the relationship between the different parts and recognising the principles involved in the organisation of the different parts.	Words commonly used in outcomes are: analyse, classify, categorise, differentiate, and compare.
	Synthesis Using different kinds of information or knowledge in new ways to create something unique to the learner. The end result should show that critical thinking was involved, thus indicating planning.	Words commonly used in outcomes are: plan, adapt, combine, create, compile, compose, construct, model, revise, design, develop, formulate, and organise.
	Evaluation Considering alternatives and making a judgement based on criteria that the learner developed. Being able to defend the decision by substantiating the reasons.	Words commonly used in outcomes are: assess, judge, criticise, rate, argue, justify, recommend, and conclude.

Affective domain (feeling) Based on Krathwohl's taxonomy (Krathwohl cited in Van der Horst & McDonald, 1997:40)	**Receiving or attending** The learner receives information but pays minimal attention to it.	Words commonly used in outcomes are: ask, choose, describe, follow, give, identify, locate, name, select, and use.
	Responding The learner reacts to the information and enjoys reacting to it.	Words commonly used in outcomes are: answer, assist, discuss, help, label, greet, perform, practise, present, select, read, and write.
	Valuing The learner attaches a certain value to an activity or phenomenon and reacts voluntarily to increase participation in the activity.	Words commonly used in outcomes are: complete, demonstrate, differentiate, explain, initiate, invite, join, justify, propose, report, share, and work.
	Organising The learner organises values in a way that is characteristic of the learner.	Words commonly used in outcomes are: arrange, alter, combine, compare, defend, integrate, modify, relate, and synthesise.
	Characterisation The learner conceptualises the value to which he/she is responding by forming characteristics to evaluate a matter.	Words commonly used in outcomes are: act, discriminate, display, influence, listen, perform, qualify, question, revise, solve, and verify.
Psychomotor domain (physical)	The learner receives information; the sense organs guide physical activity.	Words commonly used in outcomes are: detect, differentiate, choose, describe, feel, relate, draw, select, and isolate.
	The learner is physically ready to take action.	Words commonly used in outcomes are: begin, display, explain, move, process, react, show, and volunteer.
	The learner imitates actions from others, and uses trial and error.	Words commonly used in outcomes are: copy, trace, follow, reproduce, respond, and watch.
	The learner can do a task alone in less time and without describing the steps.	Words commonly used in outcomes are: assemble, calibrate, construct, dismantle, display, fix, manipulate, measure, mix, and sketch.
	The learner can do a task without error, is skilful in performing physical acts that involve complex movements, and highly coordinated.	Words commonly used in outcomes are: assemble, calibrate, construct, dismantle, display, fasten, fix, manipulate, measure, mix, and sketch.
	The learner can do a task in a different way. Skills can be modified to respond to special requirements.	Words commonly used in outcomes are: adapt, alter, change, rearrange, reorganise, revise, and vary.
	The learner can do a task in an original way, or create a new pattern to fit a specific situation or problem.	Words commonly used in outcomes are: arrange, build, combine, compose, create, design, and make.

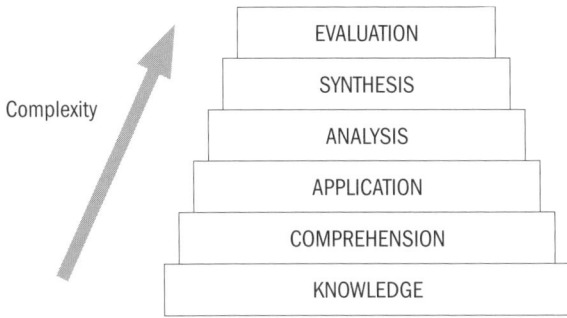

Figure 4.8 *Cognitive domain*

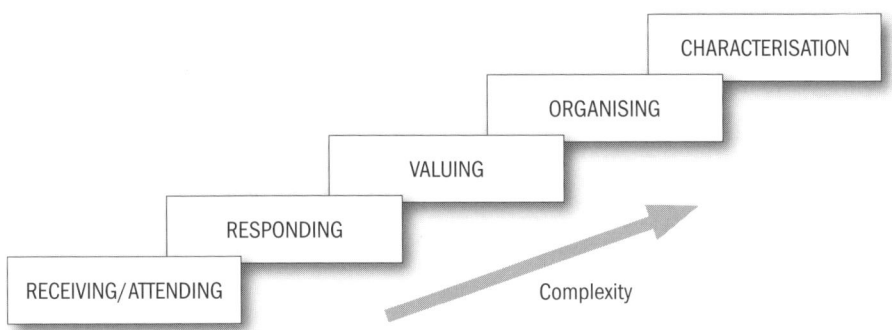

Figure 4.9 *Affective domain*

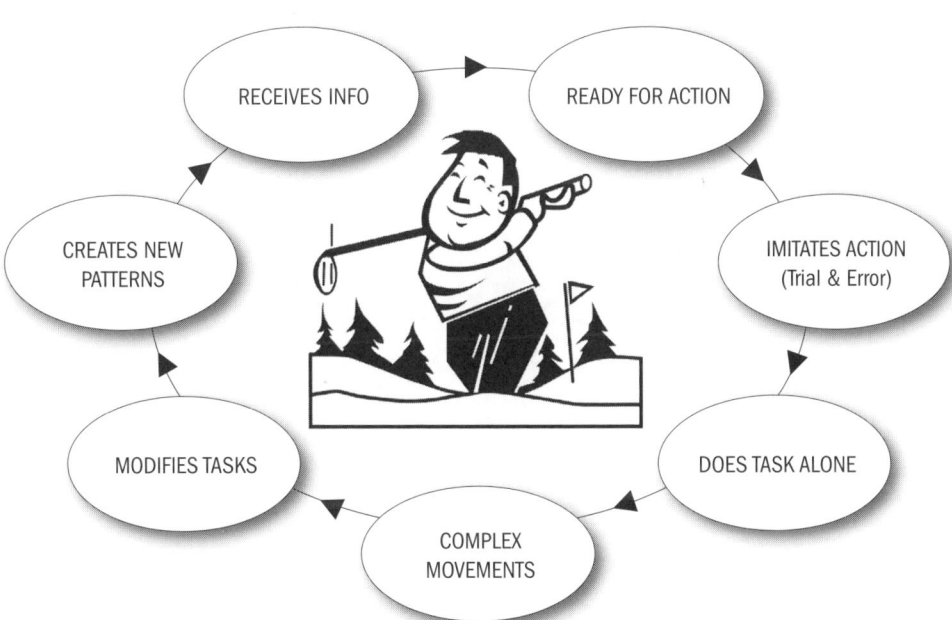

Figure 4.10 *Psychomotor domain*

In Table 4.3, the verbs in the various learning taxonomy levels are guidelines to assist learning programme designers in formulating appropriate learning outcomes. When writing learning outcomes, learning programme designers should attempt to engage all aspects of each domain. For example, if learners are required to demonstrate their ability to differentiate between two theories, they should not only be required to describe those theories. Rather, they should be required to discuss, evaluate and differentiate between the advantages and disadvantages of those theories. Using the various domains as guidelines when writing learning outcomes will also ensure that the learning design accommodates the needs of different learning styles and preferences.

Critical cross-field outcomes

The 12 critical cross-field outcomes (CCFOs) discussed in Chapter 1 are the foundation for developing learning outcomes. CCFOs are general outcomes designed by SAQA; they apply to all the learning areas. The CCFOs are broad statements of intent, and of the learning activities that will lead to the achievement of those goals. These outcomes should serve as broad, basic guidelines when formulating more specific learning outcomes for a learning programme (SAQA, 2005). Unit standards do not include all the CCFOs. However, learners should achieve all the CCFOs during the course of completing a full qualification (or at least the CCFOs relevant to the particular unit standard for a learning programme).

The critical cross-field outcomes (SAQA, 2005)

Learners must be able to:

- identify and solve problems;
- work effectively with others in teams;
- organise themselves effectively;
- collect, analyse, organise and evaluate information;
- communicate well orally or in writing;
- use science and technology responsibly;
- understand that the world is a set of related systems;
- explore strategies to learn more effectively;
- participate as responsible citizens in community life;
- be culturally and aesthetically sensitive;
- explore education and career opportunities; and
- become entrepreneurial.

ACTIVITY

Review the unit standard in Appendix 1 on page 350.
Identify which CCFOs the unit standard addresses.

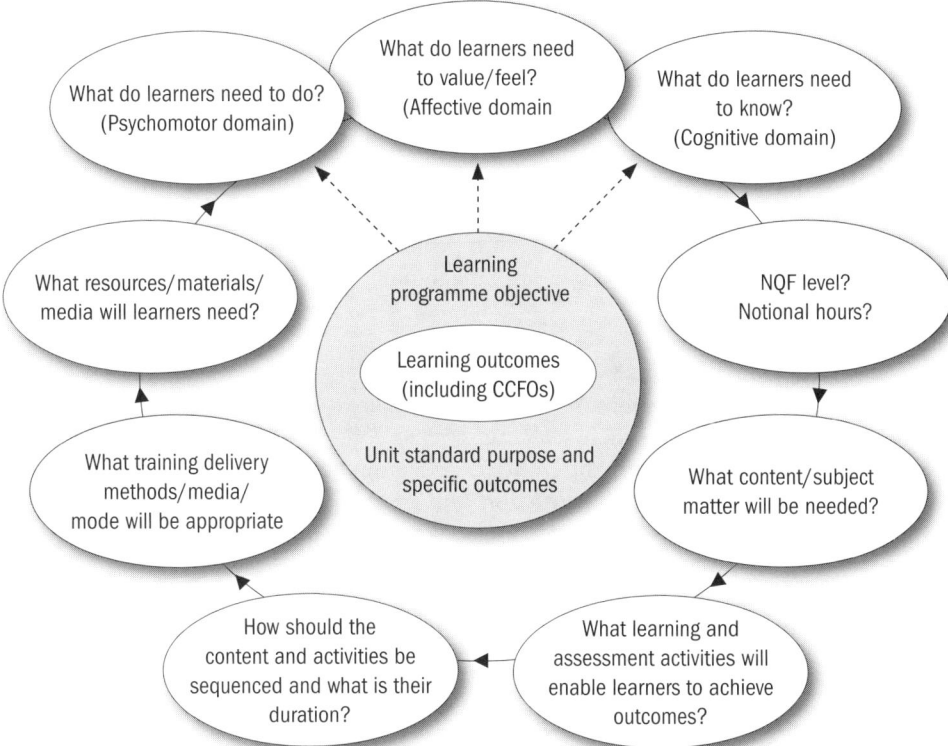

Figure 4.11 Analysing learning outcomes for curriculum design (based on SAQA, 2005)

Determining learning content

Content refers to the underpinning knowledge, skills and values that learners have to master, combined with the different ways in which the learning facilitator will convey it to the learners. In a learner-centred approach, the ETD practitioner does not teach the content, but facilitates a learning experience driven by outcomes. The selection of content for a learning programme is therefore determined by the learning outcomes. A programme designer normally selects course content from several sources. The content must then be arranged in a specific sequence to enable learners to achieve the learning outcomes.

The link between training need, learning outcome and learning content

Training need
A number of employees are not able to make a garment (such as a dress) according to specific measurements taken from a pattern.

Outcome
After training this worker, she will be able to make (verb) garments (noun) from patterns (qualifier).

Content
- Reading material on how to interpret a pattern
- Examples of different types of pattern
- Instructions on how to measure with a measuring tape

A number of factors influence an ETD practitioner's selection of relevant course content. These factors will also influence the way the content is presented to the learners. The factors that influence content selection include the following:

The type of subject presented in the learning programme

Each subject uses specific types of content, whether it is figures (such as in economics) or words (such as in history). The same applies to areas within an organisation, such as sales training (with the emphasis on profit margins), human relations (with the emphasis on interpersonal relations) or management (with the emphasis on processes and structures).

Learners differ from each other

It is impossible to know exactly how each learner learns. However, some aspects of learners can be considered when selecting course content. These aspects include the learners' cultures and cultural differences, and language ability, or learners' ability to understand the language of instruction and express themselves in that language. Learners' learning styles also influence the selection and presentation of content.

The ability of the facilitator

ETD practitioners who are experts in the field of study are the right people to select content for a learning programme. But sometimes, ETD practitioners are not experts in the field in which they have to train employees. They need to consult an expert to help them to select the relevant content.

Sources of content

An ETD practitioner needs to investigate relevant sources to find the content for a learning programme. The primary, or most important source, is job data. Job data include job analysis reports and performance agreements. It is useful to use learners' job descriptions as the point of departure as these consist primarily of a series of job outcomes, that is, what employees need to know and be able to do in their jobs. Other documents that can assist the ETD practitioner to find appropriate content for a learning programme include: technical and operator manuals; standard operating procedures; standard reference books; textbooks in libraries or bookshops; and organisation and function manuals. Use the following questions as a guideline when selecting content. Is the information from this source (or the content that you wish to include in the programme):
- essential (absolutely necessary to reach the outcome);
- helpful (adding some value to the programme, such as examples or case studies);
- peripheral (not really essential or helpful, but nice to have and something that will increase the performance level of trainees, such as a discussion given by some expert in the field); or
- unrelated (no relevance to the learning outcomes)?

Table 4.4 Categories of content (Erasmus et al, 2006.)

Essential content	Helpful content	Peripheral content
Must know	Should know	Nice to know
What the learner must be able to do after the learning programme	Information that supplements the essential information and can be included if time and other constraints permit	Information that is not essential, but may have a bearing on how well a learner masters the learning outcomes

---

Examples of learning resources (Strong & Vorwerk, 2001)
- Books and other printed matter, such as study guides
- Video and audio tapes, CDs and DVDs
- Overhead projector transparencies, slides and photos
- Departmental procedures and checklists
- Sales literature, magazines and newspapers
- Collection of raw data
- Email, newsgroups, chat rooms and list servers
- Subject matter experts and current professionals or practitioners
- User or interest groups
- The work environment
- Museums, art galleries and exhibitions
- Government documentation
- The Internet

Developing a course outline or plan

Before starting to design learning materials, ETD practitioners should:
- understand their learners;
- decide which media they will use to deliver the learning material;
- organise the content of the material;
- select methods that will create the required learning experience for the learners; and
- choose the environment in which learners will be engaging with the material.

In other words, ETD practitioners need an outline or framework (such as shown in Table 4.5 and Figure 4.12) that sets out the different ways to guide the learners in achieving the learning outcomes. Some of the basic principles that apply to the course outline are the following:
- In outcomes-based learning, learning outcomes are the starting point. Learning outcomes always determine the content and design of the learning process. The number of learning outcomes is determined by the content and the curriculum. Include the content that will help the learners to master the basic knowledge, skills and attitudes required at a specific level. If learners are required to delve deeper into some of the information, optional activities or further reading suggestions can be included. It is essential to keep learning focused on the learning outcomes. Learners cannot learn everything there is to know about a certain subject in a single

learning programme.

- It is important to capture learners' attention before presenting the content. This will help learners to be more attuned to the experience of learning.
- Present the contents in a meaningful and understandable way. The learners should not only understand the information, but also its context and meaning. They should also be able to use the information to create their own meaning and understanding in different situations or examples.
- Guide the learners through the material. This helps the learners to understand how the material relates to their needs and helps with long-term memorisation.
- Learners must practise what they have learned. In this way, information is captured in long-term memory. Practice also provides feedback on how well learners are mastering the learning outcomes (facilitators should give feedback on this step so that learners know where they are in the learning process).
- Learners' mastery of the content needs to be assessed.

Table 4.5 *An example of a course outline*

Learning outcomes	At the end of the learning programme, learners should be able to ...			
Capture attention	Ask a question, show a diagram or picture, describe a scenario, give learners a case study or problem to solve, make an argumentative statement, or let them play a game.			
Content		Must know	Should know	Nice to know
	A			
	B			
	C			
	D			
Learner guidance	How will I help learners to understand the material? I can give examples, do a demonstration, let them practise a skill, do a role play, or let them evaluate a situation.			
Practice	Exercises to practise			
Assessment	How will I know that learners have mastered the material and that they are ready to move on?			

Learning outcomes
At the end of the learning programme, learners should be able to...

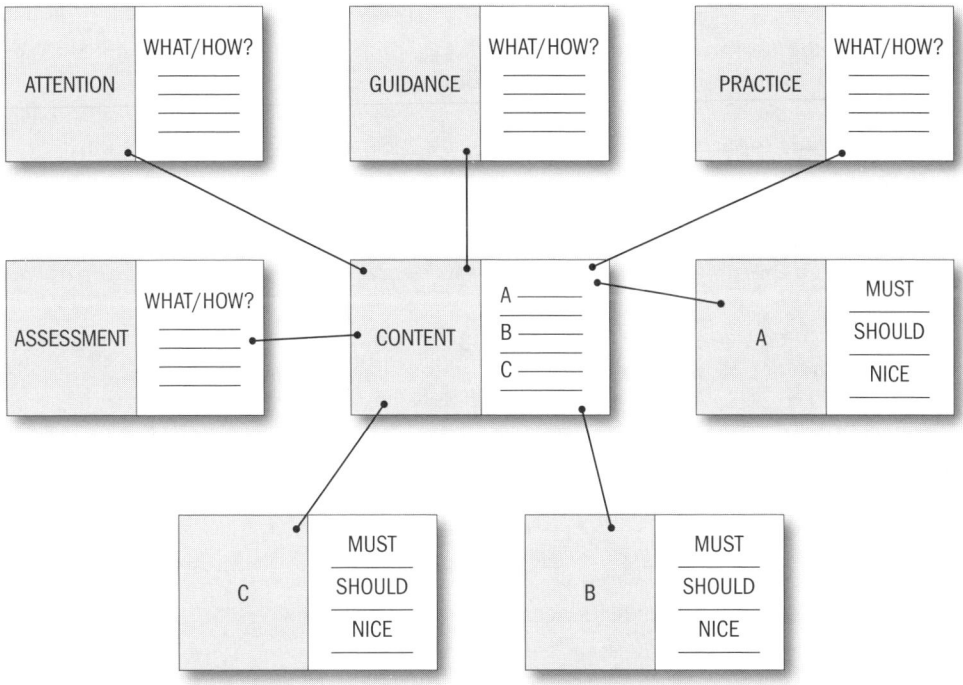

Figure 4.12 *Example of a course mind map*

Sequencing the content of a learning programme

Proper sequencing of content can make a significant difference to the effectiveness of learners' learning experience. There are various ways to sequence learning content and the learning experience as a whole:

- *Chronological sequencing.* The content is arranged according to dates or a series of events, for example from past to present.
- *Step-by-step sequencing.* Learners analyse how a task is performed, and then each step of the process is explained. For example, this sequencing is used in instructions on how to cook a certain dish.
- *Whole-to-part sequencing.* Learners are exposed to a whole model, situation or procedure. Thereafter, the parts of the model, situation or procedure are explained in more detail. This sequencing was used to explain Bloom's taxonomy in this book (Table 4.3).
- *Part-to-whole sequencing.* Learners are exposed to each part of a model, process or situation. The parts are combined into a whole at the end of the learning experience.
- *Known-to-unknown sequencing.* The learning experience starts out with material that is familiar to the learner and then moves on to new material. For example, this

chapter started out with the learner-centred approach that was also discussed in chapter 2, and then moved on to unknown material.

- *Unknown-to-known sequencing.* Learners are exposed to new material at the start of a learning programme or learning session (for example, by asking a question to which the learners will probably not know the answer). Learners are then guided towards the information that they do know. Some facilitators believe that this sequencing creates a motivation to learn more.
- *General-to-specific sequencing.* Learners are given an overview of a topic. Each aspect of the topic is then discussed in detail. This sequencing is often used at conferences. Speakers give an overview of what they will be talking about, and then continue with a more detailed discussion of the content.
- *Specific-to-general sequencing.* This type of sequencing starts with specific topics or information the learner should have, and ends with a general overview of the topic.
- *Concrete-to-abstract sequencing.* This type of sequencing starts with learning experiences that are easy to understand and define. The learner is then guided through a learning experience that becomes gradually more complex, challenging and abstract. For example, a learning experience may start out with a description of a theory (including advantages and disadvantages, and applications of the theory) and end with a debate between learners on the relative merits of two different theories on the same subject (Erasmus *et al*, 2006).

Guidelines on sequencing content (Erasmus *et al*, 2006.)
- Start out with information that is easy to learn.
- Start out with broad terms and technical concepts or cover them as early as possible in the learning experience.
- Practise new concepts immediately after you introduce them.
- Link new knowledge and skills by placing previous knowledge and skills just before the new material.
- If certain knowledge and skills are essential for mastering later parts of the work, allow enough time and opportunity for practice.
- Use sequencing that makes sense to you and will make sense to the learners.
- Complex tasks and tasks that need a lot of new knowledge should be placed later in the sequence.

Designing learning activities

Learning activities are the tools ETD practitioners use to expose learners to the knowledge, skills, attitudes and behaviour they need to master the learning outcomes. In this book, for example, there are various learning activities designed to help you achieve the learning outcomes formulated for each chapter. Activities differ in how information is transmitted, how the learners will practise the knowledge, skills and attitudes and how the practitioner will assess whether learners have enough understanding of the content to move on to the next part of the content. Learning activities are created first, because outcomes-based learning concentrates on the outcomes learners must achieve. Outcomes describe what learners must be able to do with the information they receive and understanding they develop during the learning process. Once learning activities have been developed, ETD practitioners can think about the information the learner will need to be able to complete the activities.

Well-designed activities can help learners to remember information for later recall and use, practise new skills, and provide feedback on their mastery of the information and skills. Learning activities must do the following:

- allow the learner to take information (descriptions, rules, guidelines, advantages and disadvantages, definitions and so on) and apply it to practical situations;
- help learners to practise what they have learnt;
- allow learners to make mistakes, and guide them to deal with or correct them;
- refine knowledge and skills so that learning outcomes can be achieved; and
- allow learners the opportunity to practise new knowledge, skills and attitudes in a safe, non-threatening environment and in different contexts and situations.

Examples of learning activities

- Reading materials independently to prepare for participating in discussions
- Summarising information to extract key points
- Exercises such as listing advantages and disadvantages, or creating definitions
- Problem solving, such as analysing a case study and making suggestions on possible solutions to problems
- Observing and noting what is happening in a role play or on a video
- Making a drawing or other representation
- Conducting a survey
- Simulating a real situation (this method is often used in management games)

Accommodating the needs of various generations

Few ETD practitioners are fortunate enough to work with only one generation in a training session. The hierarchical systems in the workplace that once kept generations separate are breaking down. This means that it is increasingly likely that learners attending a learning programme comprise people from several different generations. The difficult part for ETD practitioners is that each generation has a unique perspective on the world. As shown in Table 4.6, each generation also has different ways of absorbing, organising and applying information and skills. It is important to know how members of each generation prefer information to be organised, the type of learning facilitator that appeals to them, the activities to which they respond best, and learning formats that appeal to them.

Table 4.6 Characteristics of various generations' training preferences (Codrington & Grant-Marshall, 2004)

Silents (born 1920s to 1940s)	
Ideal trainer/learning facilitator	Knowledgeable expert Credible Authority figure Provide a comprehensive CV
Likes	Prefer training on a one-to-one basis, especially when it is related to technology Appreciate the classical, straightforward presentation of information Motivated by training that is linked to the overall good of the company Want information presented logically
Dislikes	Trainers who are informal and too familiar Overly casual dress and manner of speaking Personal anecdotes, examples and stories
Training/learning materials	Print out the course notes Require handouts – they do not want electronic notes or a list of websites Avoid small font sizes and funky fonts
Boomers (born 1940s to 1960s)	
Ideal trainer/learning facilitator	Knowledgeable friend who comes across as an equal/colleague Recognised qualifications (provide CV) Must come across as a facilitator who helps participants to learn rather than a teacher who imparts information
Likes	Love problem solving Motivated and self-driven Challenge everything – enjoy personal challenges (avoid generic examples/case studies, rather make these personal)
Dislikes	Role playing, acting out or interactive industrial theatre Have to be encouraged to practise newly acquired skills but ensure they do not feel foolish as they do so
Training/learning materials	Ensure that any information is readily accessible (for example, a website with an overview of information in an easy-to-scan format) Want the look and feel of any material to be slick and professional
Generation Xers (born 1960s to 1980s)	
Ideal trainer/learning facilitator	A guide rather than a formal trainer Age and experience do not matter, as long as the trainer is clearly an expert in the subject matter Respect has to be earned
Likes	Highly motivated learners who ask lots of questions and want interaction Like to learn by experimenting Love role playing – want to get involved with what they are learning, to experiment with it and then receive feedback Keep imparting of knowledge brief and get back to interactive learning A variety of learning activities/methods

Dislikes	Boredom – love surprises (change pace, process and style constantly)
	Showmanship or hype
Training/learning materials	Do not like to read much
	Use lots of visual stimulation such as headlines, subheads, quotes, graphics and lists
	Give them options for the format of notes such as print, email, CD or web page
Millennials (born 1980s to 2000s)	
Ideal trainer/learning facilitator	An experienced mentor
	Authority figure
	Qualifications and expertise (spell those out to them)
Likes	Explain practical benefits of what they are learning at the start of the session
	Give constant feedback and encouragement
	Allow them to discover information – do not just hand it to them on a platter
	Learning programmes that go beyond teaching simple job functionality
	Want to learn about parenting, marriage, personal financial management, health, wellness
	Enjoy training that teaches them skills they can continue to use long after the course is over
	Mentor programmes
	Multiple tasks
Dislikes	Boredom
	Speaking down to them
Training/learning materials	Keep them lively and varied
	Use multimedia and different techniques to get points across
	Printed materials should have the same focal points as materials targeted at Xers, with one exception: millennials are readers, so include printed articles and written information
	Provide lots of links to web pages

Choosing training methods

Once the learning programme objective, learning outcomes and activities have been established, the next step in developing a learning programme is to choose the most appropriate training method for the objective and learning outcomes. For example, if a learning outcome is to learn an actual skill, some type of hands-on training such as role play or simulation will be necessary. Most learning programmes have a number of learning outcomes, so the best learning programmes use a variety of methods (Aamodt, 2007). The most common training methods are as follows:

- Lectures deliver uniform information to a large group of people in a short time. It is the most common method, but it is not interactive. It does not work to teach behaviours or learn skills.
- Discussions are structured conversations between learners and facilitators. They provide immediate feedback on contributions, creating higher motivation levels and better participation from the learners.

- Case studies are written descriptions of an organisational problem that can be analysed by a group or an individual. Recommendations are presented for further discussion in the larger group.
- Role play is the simulation of organisational problems by learners, followed by a discussion. This is a good method to teach and learn skills such as interpersonal communication, conflict management, interviewing, performance appraisal and assertiveness.
- Management games are simulation exercises that replicate conditions in real organisations. Teams compete against each other, making decisions about planning, organising, financial issues, production and control of a hypothetical organisation.
- In-basket exercises develop problem-solving skills. A manager or trainee manager is given an in-basket filled with the typical problems that a manager should be able to solve. The learner must make an immediate decision on how to solve the problems.
- Demonstrations are actual displays of how to perform a specific task or set of tasks.
- Sensitivity training focuses on feelings and how one person's behaviour affects the feelings, behaviours and attitudes of others.
- Technology-based methods include computer-based methods, web-based training or e-learning, interactive multimedia and virtual reality training (Grobler *et al*, 2006).

Table 4.7 Technology-based training methods

Computer-based methods	Web-based training or e-learning	Interactive multimedia	Virtual reality training
• Learning materials are made available on computer and learners can access the materials when it is convenient for them. • Learners can also set their own pace for the learning.	• These methods offer training opportunities that are accessible wherever the learner can access the Internet. • Learners can develop their skills and knowledge while sitting at their computers, at any time and in any place.	• This method combines text, video, graphics, animation and sound to create a training environment with which the learner can interact.	• With these methods, the learner learns in an artificial three-dimensional environment. • Situations that the learner may experience in the work environment are simulated. • The learner must interact with the environment to accomplish goals.

It is important to note that, while these methods differ in their specific applications, they all have the learning principles discussed in Chapter 2 in common. Learners generally react more positively to integrated learning (learning that uses a wide range of methods). Using a wide range of methods will also require learners to use different learning styles. This ensures that most of the learners get involved. Salas and Cannon-Bowers (2001) (cited in Rothwell, Sullivan & McClean) note that most effective training methods are created around four basic principles:

- They present relevant information and content to be learnt.
- They demonstrate applied competencies (knowledge, skills, abilities, attitudes and behaviour) to be learnt.
- They create opportunities for learners to practise the required skills.
- They provide feedback to learners during and after practice.

When choosing training methods, ETD practitioners should consider the aspects listed in Table 4.8.

Table 4.8 Aspects to consider when choosing training methods (Galbraith, 1990)

The learners	<ul><li>Characteristics</li><li>Differences</li><li>Learning styles</li><li>Generational preferences (see Table 4.6)</li></ul>
The facilitator	<ul><li>Strengths and weaknesses</li><li>Education, training and development philosophy</li><li>Facilitation style</li></ul>
The content	<ul><li>Nature of the content</li><li>Resources that will be needed</li></ul>
The situation	<ul><li>One-to-one</li><li>Classroom-based</li><li>Group work</li><li>Computer-based or online</li></ul>
Other considerations for ETD practitioners	<ul><li>How much time and money do I have?</li><li>Will I have adequate equipment and materials for development?</li><li>Do I possess the required skills?</li><li>Can I create an appropriate learning environment?</li><li>Am I using the appropriate design, given the learning content and the learners?</li><li>How easy will it be to update the material?</li></ul>

ACTIVITY
- Do you think that classroom lectures are an effective outcomes-based training method?
- Think also about the training preferences of the various generations. Which training method would you recommend for each generation? Give reasons for your answer.

Designing learning support materials

Learning support materials is the complete package of learning resources designed to enable the achievement of learning outcomes (for example, learner manuals, handouts, books, slides and posters). Learning support materials must be relevant to the learning area and suitable for the target group. Using a profile of learners, the ETD practitioner designs a framework for the learning support materials, ensuring that support materials are suitable for the learners. The framework needs to include specific details, including the mode of delivery and media to be used; the content; the structure and sequence of learning activities and materials; and training methodology. As with the learning programme, it is advisable to test the learning materials with a representative sample of learners and practitioners, and revise and adapt the materials and methodology, if necessary. Some examples of learning materials are:

- self-study material;
- modules;
- handouts;
- workbooks;
- lesson plans;
- evaluation forms;
- checklists for course planning; and
- report formats and procedures.

Self-study material

Self-study material should be developed if learners need to gain some knowledge before the training session. Learners work through self-study material at their own pace and without trainer assistance to bring all learners to the same level of understanding. Self-study material should meet the following requirements:

- It should explain the aim of the particular study method to learners.
- It should define the objectives clearly and be set out systematically.
- It should ask appropriate questions and provide opportunities for self-evaluation.
- Examples should be relevant and related to actual practice.
- It should provide support if the learner wishes to clear up uncertainties.

Modules

The layout of a module should be neat, user-friendly and should provide a clear indication of the structure of the module. Each module of learning material should consist of three sections:

- An introduction provides learners with a motivational preview of the objectives and material.
- The main section contains explanations of subject matter and includes examples and exercises.
- The conclusion reviews content and helps learners remember and apply new information.

Handouts

Exercise instructions, written case studies or guidelines for role interpretations are a few examples of handouts. Handouts must be relevant to the subject matter. It should have an introduction that sets out the aim, questions and required content clearly and logically.

Workbooks

Workbooks should contain appropriate modules and/or handouts and possibly, checklists, self-evaluation questionnaires and other material. A workbook should be an organised collection of relevant material, and should save learners time.

Evaluation forms

Evaluation forms are used to assess the effectiveness of a learning programme by getting feedback from learners. Evaluation forms should ensure that information is unbiased. The layout should be neat and the results should be quantifiable. A combination of closed and open questions should be used. Closed questions make use of multiple choice questions or rating scales (quantitative information). Open questions provide an opportunity for giving reasons, comments or suggestions (qualitative information).

Checklists for course planning

Drawing up checklists to plan, control and carry out a presentation will ensure that the learning process runs smoothly.

Elements of well-designed outcomes-based learning material (Coetzee, 2007)

- Learning programme title
- Guidance on how to use the material
- Learning route map
- Flowchart showing progression to qualification (qualification, standards and credit guide)
- Personal record book
- Portfolio of evidence examples
- Overview of learning programme
- Purpose and learning outcomes
- Content assumptions
- Structure
- Methodology
- Learning outcomes
- Specific outcomes
- Critical cross-field outcomes
- Assessment criteria
- Evidence requirements
- Discussions or explanations
- Content and theory
- Headings
- Sub-headings
- Numbering system
- Manageable chunks
- Learning experiences and activities
- Portfolio activities and evidence
- Performance self-assessment activities and evidence
- Assessment (formative and summative) process and evidence requirements
- Feedback and evaluation
- Pictures or icons, flow diagrams and mind maps
- Interactive, learner-friendly text
- Summary
- Self-assessment (readiness for assessment/achievement of learning outcomes)
- References
- Glossary

Table 4.9 *Characteristics of effective learning materials (Chang, 1994)*

Characteristic	Description
Stimulating	They involve all the senses.
Understandable	The content is easy to understand and limited in scope. Important words and concepts are highlighted.
Accurate	Information provided is accurate, factual, properly ordered and complete.
Interesting	The layout is attractive and the sequencing makes sense to the learners.
Practical	The programme is practical; learners can easily identify with it.
General guidelines	• Use headings in learning materials. Whether lectures, demonstrations, case studies or computer-based methods are used, learners must be able to determine where they are in the learning experience. • Keep the information short and to the point, real and accessible. • Involve the learners in the learning experience, right through the experience. • Tell a story. Stories are a good way to involve learners' emotions and commit learners to learning. • Be specific, especially when using examples. Link examples to experiences that the learners will be able to relate with.

ACTIVITY

Study the unit standard in Appendix 1 on page 350, then review Figure 4.7.
• Plan the curriculum of a learning programme aimed at training learners in conducting outcomes-based assessment.

The facilitator/trainer guide

In terms of SAQA's requirements for quality outcomes-based learning programme design, ETD practitioners need to demonstrate that the design of their learning programmes comply with the quality requirements for provider accreditation. The facilitator/trainer guide is part of the evidence that the learning programme is aligned with SAQA's requirements for NQF-aligned outcomes-based learning programmes.

Moreover, it facilitates quality assurance in respect of learning programme delivery, and facilitates the evaluation of programme effectiveness. The facilitator/trainer guide is a complete package containing written descriptions of the learning programme strategy, the learning facilitation process and quality assurance aspects related to the programme design and delivery (Coetzee, 2004).

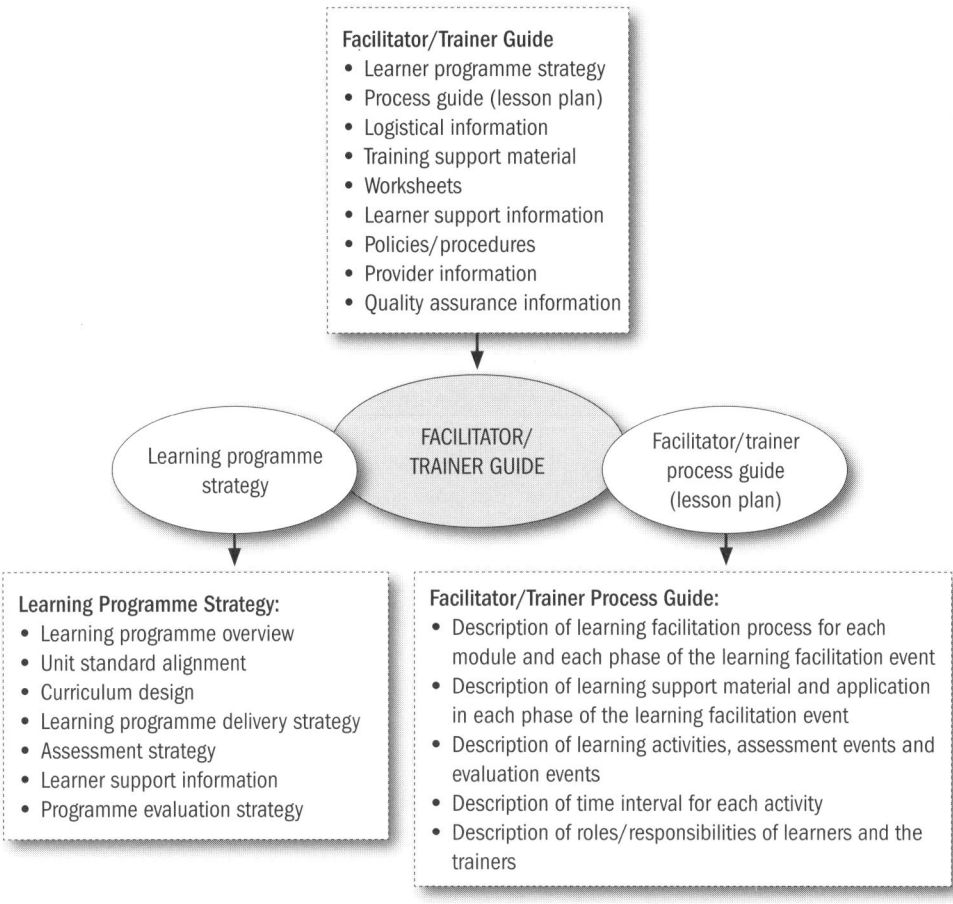

Figure 4.13 *Contents of the Facilitator/Trainer Guide (Coetzee, 2004)*

Learning programme strategy

A learning programme strategy is a broad, detailed plan for achieving the learning programme objective and enabling learners to master the learning outcomes. The strategy includes an outline of the activities that will be undertaken in the design of a learning programme curriculum. These include activities such as developing learning outcomes and learning and assessment activities, choosing and sequencing content, and deciding on training delivery methods. The learning programme strategy outlines the ETD practitioner's intended approach to enable learners to achieve the learning outcomes (Coetzee, 2004). The learning programme strategy includes an overview of the following:

- An overview of the learning programme. This is a brief description of the learning programme, including the title of the programme, the relevant unit standard, the targeted learner audience, the objective of the learning programme, entry level requirements, RPL arrangements and articulation possibilities of the programme (that is, an explanation of how the particular learning programme links with other ETD initiatives in the company).

- Unit standard alignment. This is a description of how the learning outcomes of the programme align with the applicable unit standard. Unit standards provide ETD practitioners with the ability to assess whether their learners' achievements are at the required standard. Alignment with unit standards ensures that the learning programme and assessment strategy are at the appropriate level and based on an acceptable standard. Qualifying learners are thus entitled to a number of credits.
- Curriculum design. This is an outline of how the learning outcomes are linked to the foundational, practical and reflexive competencies that learners are required to master. It includes a description of the prescribed content (embedded knowledge, skills and values as described in the unit standard outcomes and the associated assessment criteria), the formative and summative assessment activities, required learning support materials and the learning programme delivery strategy. The learning programme delivery strategy describes the learning facilitation mode (for example, classroom or distance learning), training methods, learning material, media, resources and equipment that will be used to facilitate the learning programme. Examples of a curriculum design and programme delivery strategy are shown in Tables 4.10 and 4.11 and Figure 4. 14.
- Assessment strategy (this is discussed in more detail in Chapter 6).
- Learner support information. This is a description of the roles of the learning facilitator and learners. It shows how learners will be supported and guided in achieving the learning outcomes (as shown in Table 4.12).
- Programme evaluation strategy (this is discussed in more detail in Chapter 7).

Table 4.11 *Example of a learning programme delivery strategy (Coetzee, 2006a)*

Mode	Method	Media
Pre-course learning Self-study (knowledge assessment on Learning units 1 and 2) **Notional hours: 8 hours**	Pre-course work on the legislation (self-study) Knowledge questionnaire	Pre-course manual Legislative documents
Contact learning in classroom (workshop) Experiential learning facilitation (Learning units 3, 4 and 5) **Notional hours: 18 hours (3 days)**	Group discussions Case studies Lectures	Learning manual Overhead projector Powerpoint slides Flip chart and pens
Workplace application of classroom learning **Notional hours: 10 hours**	Job assignments Skills portfolio	Learning manual Skills portfolio guidelines
Reflexive learning CCFO: Organising CCFO: Collecting CCFO: Communicating CCFO: Contributing Notional hours: 4 hours **Total notional hours: 40 hours**	Self-evaluation report **Learner support** Instruction Guidance and coaching Learning facilitation	Self-evaluation questionnaire

Table 4.11 *Example of a curriculum design and delivery strategy*

Unit standard: Performance improvement coaching							
Specific outcome 1: Demonstrate knowledge and skills in conducting a development discussion and identifying employees with performance problems							
Foundational competence (knowledge)	**Practical competence (Skills)**	**Reflexive competence**	**Formative assessment activities**	**Learning support material and facilitator templates**	**Mode, methods & media**	**Reference materials**	**Time frame (Notional hours)**
• Steps in the Performance management process • Goals of conducting development discussions • Knowledge of interpersonal skills • Definition of a personal development plan	• Applying interpersonal skills to conduct a development discussion • Compile a personal development plan	• Assess own learning points and application in a work context	**Discussion groups:** Activity 1.1 "Exchange viewpoints" Activity 1.3 "Brainstorming" Activity 1.5 "Feedback discussion" **Individual exercises:** Activity 1.2 "Listening" Activity 1.3 "Listening quiz questionnaire" Activity 1.6 "Communication skills" Activity 1.7 "Self-evaluation"	Learning manual Presentation slide show Hand outs Flip charts	**Mode:** Contact 3-day workshop **Method:** Instruction Facilitation Group work Case studies Individual exercises **Media:** Presentation Learning manual Facilitator's manual Handouts	Learner manual	8

Prescribed content/Embedded knowledge
- Principles of Performance management
- Knowledge of Interpersonal skills
- Theories of learning styles
- Knowledge of Coaching technique
- Principles of Development discussions
- Knowledge of Criteria for compiling development plans
- Principles of Coaching
- Principles of Performance review

Resources and equipment
- Training venue
- Data projector
- Flipchart stand
- Coloured Pens
- Laptop computer
- Presentation slide show
- Flipchart paper
- Prestik

Table 4.12 Example of learner support information (Coetzee, 2006a)

Learner role and responsibility	The learner is expected to: • participate in discussions; • form part of small groups; • do self-study; and • complete individual tasks.
Learner support	The learner can expect the following support: • time off from work to attend the workshop; • facilitator guidance and assistance with workshop activities; • references for self-study; • structured information presentation; • opportunities to complete the workplace assignment.

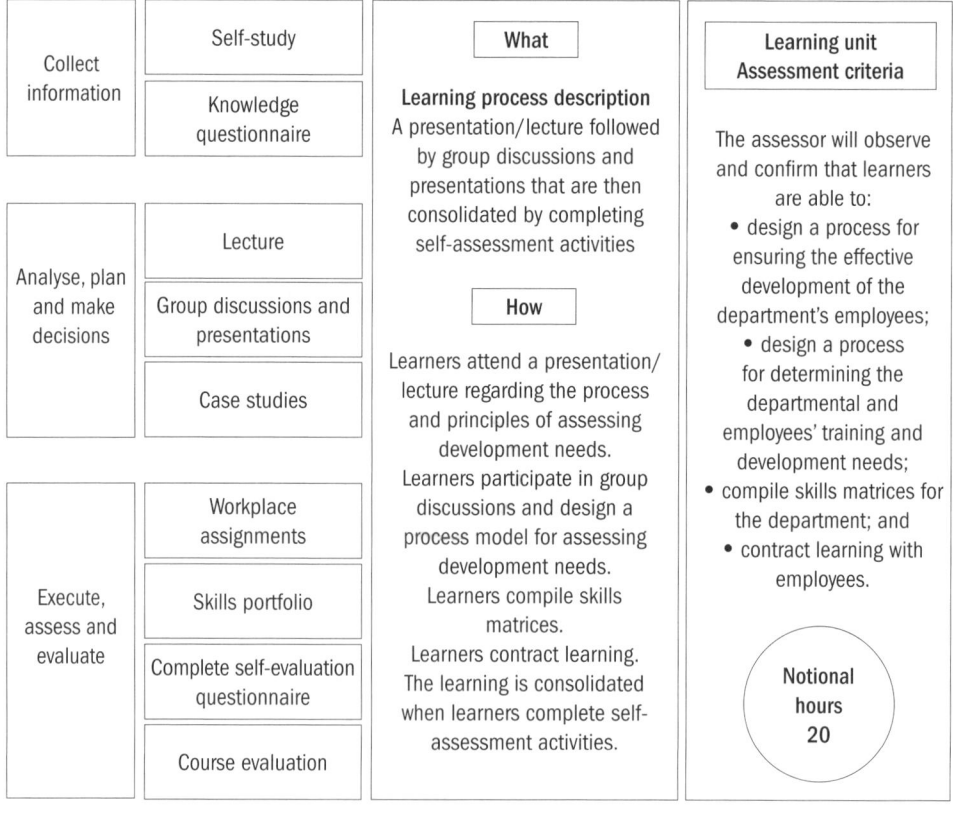

Figure 4.14 Planning the learning programme strategy: example

The facilitator/trainer process guide

The process guide provides a broad outline of the learning facilitation strategy which generally describes how the learning facilitator plans to present, manage and monitor the learning process and environment so that learners can be effectively and productively engaged in learning (Coetzee, 2004). The process guide is a very useful document, not only to guide inexperienced learning facilitators but also to ensure the quality and cost effectiveness of the learning facilitation process. The facilitator/trainer process guide generally includes a description of the following:

- learning outcomes to be achieved during each phase of the learning programme;
- each stage of the experiential or practical learning programme;
- approximate duration of the learning programme;
- when to introduce visual support material, exercises and handouts;
- roles of the learning facilitator and learners;
- formative assessment activities and worksheets;
- detailed questions to be asked to promote learner participation in discussions;
- debriefing or planning activities to ensure that participants put into practice what they have discussed and learnt during the learning programme;
- training venue layout and equipment requirements;
- visual learning support material to prompt and help the learning facilitator/trainer;
- handouts, which provide a record of the learning programme's important messages, and exercises and formative assessment activities such as case studies;
- personal action plans for the participants, so that they may record their commitment to improve in the areas identified during the learning programme;
- portfolio of evidence guidelines for work-based assignments;
- formative and summative assessment worksheets and marking memoranda; and
- RPL processes and procedures for assessing the learning programme.

Process guide (Example 1) Module 5 Managing the development of people	Time
• Explain the learning outcomes for Module 5. • Explain the importance of managing and evaluating the effectiveness of their people development efforts. • Ask participants to discuss in their small groups the management functions and activities of managing the development of their people. • Ask them to complete Activity 5.1 (The management functions and training) on page XX. • Ask them to reflect on the roles and responsibilities described in the HRD strategy for the public service and why people development efforts fail. • Participants can use the learning material in Module 5 as a reference document.	2 hours
• Review the small groups' inputs and viewpoints in the large group. • Ask participants to complete Activity 5.2. In the large group, discuss any issues of concern regarding the HRD strategy for the public service. • Explain the NQF/SAQA principles regarding quality assurance in training and development. • Ask participants to complete Activity 5.3 (HRDS and SAQA quality assurance requirements for training and development).	1 hour

• Review the participants' viewpoints in the large group.	
• Ask the participants to complete Activity 5.4 (The HR information system) with a learning partner.	1 hour
• Discuss any comments or observations regarding the HR information system for the public service in the large group.	
• Explain the importance of evaluation.	2 hours
• Discuss the principles of training and development evaluation.	
• Ask participants to complete Activities 5.5 and 5.6 (Evaluating HRD) in their small groups.	
• Review the groups' viewpoints in the large group.	
• Review the workplace application activities.	30 minutes
• Address any concerns regarding the activity and collection of evidence.	
Module reflection Ask learners to complete the Module reflection activities for Module 5.	30 minutes
Workshop closure Work through the workshop needs and concerns lists to ensure participants' needs and concerns have been addressed.	1 hour
Work through the portfolio guidelines and the summative assessment guidelines with the participants. Address any concerns. Arrange dates for the submission of the skills portfolios. Record any specific needs.	30 minutes
Workshop evaluation Ask participants to complete the workshop evaluation form. Analyse and summarise participants' feedback and compile a report for the HRD department.	Total: 9 hours and 30 minutes

Process guide (example 2)
Workshop 2 Emotions and the classroom atmosphere

Objective
This workshop provides participants with an understanding of how people's thoughts, feelings and emotions create their inner reality and how these influence their interpersonal relationships. Participants will also understand how teachers' emotions and mood influence the general classroom atmosphere.

Embedded knowledge
After completing this workshop, participants should understand that:
1. Happy teachers are in touch with their feelings and know how to move along through the many feelings that life brings.
2. Emotions can be used and regulated to help us create lives and interpersonal relationships that promote our emotional well-being and sense of satisfaction with our lives.
3. Our feelings create our inner reality, and our inner reality creates our outer experience.
4. Teachers' thoughts and emotions have a profound impact on the classroom atmosphere.
5. Positive emotions are more powerful than negative emotions.
6. Teachers who are too self-absorbed have difficulty in sensing the classroom atmosphere. Developing our empathy and compassion helps us to overcome our blind spots and develop healthy connections with learners.

Learning outcomes
1. Explain emotions and feelings, and how they are triggered in our bodies.
2. Explain the reasons human beings have a feeling nature.
3. Describe how emotions influence the classroom atmosphere and explain the role of teachers' emotions.
4. Describe how the primary emotions influence our interactions with others.
5. Identify the blind spots in sensing the classroom atmosphere.
6. Explain the importance of empathy and compassion in the classroom.
7. Identify ways teachers can establish healthy connections with their learners.

Trainer guidance
The activities create opportunities for participants to reflect on their own and others' moods and feelings and how these influence the general classroom atmosphere. You need to promote an atmosphere of openness and trust. This may be particularly difficult where the prevailing culture appears resistant to these qualities.

Your contribution to this process will be enhanced by the following:
• helping participants to understand and apply the skills of being sensitive to their own and others' moods and emotional state;
• assisting people to clearly define the behaviours they wish to modify;
• giving quality attention and support when new behaviours are being practised; and
• encouraging group members to offer support to each other.

The most important point of the activities is to encourage participants to be honest, take a longer-term view and identify behaviours that will help to unlock their potential ability to develop and improve their effectiveness as teachers. Participants may find it difficult to detach themselves from their immediate situation: you may need to encourage them to think of the activities as an investment in their personal growth. Some may be reluctant to share their personal information and others may feel threatened.

As trainer, you are well placed to encourage participants to share their concerns with the group. Participants need to feel safe by knowing that their right to privacy and confidentiality will be respected and honoured at all times.

The activities are complex, so a maximum group size of six to eight is recommended.

Activities
Activity 2.1 Setting the mood
Activity 2.2 Developing my emotional sensitivity
Activity 2.3 Identifying the blocks to an emotionally warm classroom climate
Activity 2.4 Self-assessment and development planning

Example: Activity 2.1 Setting the mood
Method
1. Read the story Sounds of the Forest on Document 2.1 aloud to the group, or ask for a volunteer. Use it to set the mood for participants to think about their relationships with each other in a deeper way. As the story is being read, you might want to further set the mood by playing slow flute music, recordings of bird songs, or music of seagulls and waves lapping at the seashore. If you use music to accompany the reading, ensure that the music is played quietly as background music to the story.
2. Ask participants to think of the workshop activities they did in workshop 1. Ask them if any of their 'unheard' feelings or ideas had or could have had an effect on the outcome of the workshop's process and activities. Prompt them with questioning such as:
• Unspoken thanks?
• Discomfort?

- Feelings of insecurity?
- Sadness?
- Worries?
- Pleasure?
- Enjoyment?

3. Ask participants to discuss their perceptions of the activity and how they could apply the insights to the classroom environment. Explain to them that their learners' 'unheard feelings' also influence the general classroom climate, and their personal unresolved feelings and emotions.

Timing
Total estimated time: 30 minutes

Materials required
1. Sufficient copies of Document 2.1
2. Audiotape of quiet flute music
3. Paper, pens, flip chart

General quality assurance documentation

As discussed in Chapter 1, ETD providers and practitioners are required by SAQA and the relevant ETQA to provide evidence that they manage the quality and relevance of their learning programmes. Compiling a comprehensive facilitator/trainer guide, which describes the learning programme strategy and the learning facilitation process, helps to ensure that ETD practitioners comply with the requirements for quality outcomes-based learning programme design and delivery. In addition, ETD practitioners are required to record and document the following as part of the quality assurance process:

- a learner information form;
- an attendance register form;
- learning facilitator information, such as a curriculum vitae to describe the ETD practitioner's competence, educational background, expertise and experience;
- assessor and moderator information, such as a curriculum vitae to describe the competence, educational background, expertise and experience of the assessors and moderators involved in the learning programme;
- ETD provider information, such as accreditation or recognition status, skills levy number, and contact details;
- an example of the certificate that successful learners receive for achieving the learning outcomes (the certificate of completion) and/or the attendance certificate for learners who participate in the learning programme;
- a learning programme effectiveness evaluation form;
- learner achievement record forms;
- quality assurance checklists;
- self-evaluation forms (quality checklists) for the learning facilitator and improvement/development plan;
- moderator assessment report formats (these are discussed in Chapter 6); and
- company training and development, assessment and moderation procedures, which describe how these are aligned with SAQA/ETQA accreditation requirements.

Quality checklist
Learning programme design (Coetzee, 2007)

Standard	Evidence required	In place: Yes/No	In progress	Action
Are learning experiences designed in accordance with identified training needs or skills development needs?	Skills plan Formulated learning experience outcomes			
Are formulated learning outcomes aligned with the specific outcomes related in relevant unit standards (if applicable) and the learning programme objective?	Unit standards			
Do learning experiences consist of a series of activities that will enable learners to achieve the intended outcomes?	Activities Learning outcomes			
Are reliable and valid assessment methodologies in place to measure the intended outcomes to be achieved by the learner?	Assessment methodologies and procedures			
Are learning support materials in place for each activity? Are these support materials appropriate to the level of learners and the purpose of the activities?	Learner support			
Do the learning materials contain self-assessment activities to enable learners to assess their own progress?	Self-assessment activities			
Are the learning materials designed in a way that will facilitate learner comprehension, retention, and motivation/support to apply the knowledge and skills?	Learning material			
Is the learning material content non-discriminative, unbiased and learner-centred?	Learning material (examples, case studies, tasks, activities, illustrations)			
Are the learning materials evaluated and revised continuously to ensure relevance?	Learning material Evaluation reports Assessment reports			
Are the learning materials customised to ensure that the learner can relate the materials to real-life situations?	Evaluation reports			
Will the learning programme lead to a national qualification, or part of a qualification? Is it clear how learners will progress through the qualification (if applicable)?	Learning design Qualifications description			

Standard	Evidence required	In place: Yes/No	In progress	Action
Is the course outline clear? Is the purpose of the course clear? Are the outcomes, assessment methodology and mode of delivery specified?	Course outline			
Is the learning curriculum clearly defined in terms of learning outcomes?	Curriculum			
Is the assessment framework clearly defined?	Assessment framework Assessment report Assessment plans			

Review and discussion questions

1. What are the benefits of adopting a learner-centred approach to learning programme design?
2. How does the learning programme curriculum guide and inform the design of learning programmes?
3. Why is it important to formulate accurate and appropriate learning outcomes? What are the characteristics of well-formulated learning outcomes? How do unit standards inform the formulation of learning outcomes?
4. What steps can ETD practitioners follow when designing quality, outcomes-based learning programmes?
5. How do learning taxonomy levels guide ETD practitioners in formulating learning outcomes? Give examples of these taxonomy levels.
6. What aspects would you describe in the outline for a learning programme?
7. What are the characteristics of well-designed learning activities?
8. Which aspects do ETD practitioners need to consider when they choose training methods for their learning programmes?
9. What are the elements of well-designed outcomes-based learning materials?
10. What aspects do ETD practitioners need to consider when they select sources for and sequence the learning content of their learning programmes?
11. What are the functions and content of the facilitator/trainer guide in quality, outcomes-based learning programme design?

Suggested reading

Chang, R.Y. (1994). *Creating high-impact training*. London: Kogan Page Limited.

Codrington, G. & Grant-Marshall, S. (2004). *Mind the gap!* Cape Town: Penguin Books.

Coetzee, M (2004). *Planning quality outcomes-based learning programmes*. Johannesburg: Knowres.

Dooley, K.E., Lindner, J.R. & Dooley, M.R. (2005). *Advanced methods in distance education. Applications and practices for educators, administrators and learners*. Hershey, PA: Information Science Publishing.

Erasmus, B.J., Loedolff, P.vZ., Mda, T. & Nel, P.S. (2006). *Managing training and development in South Africa*. Cape Town: Oxford University Press.

Galbraith, M.W. (Editor). (1990). *Adult learning methods. A guide for effective instruction*. Malabar, Florida: Krieger publishing.

Gregory, G.H. (2005). *Differentiating instruction with style. Aligning teacher and learner intelligences for maximum achievement*. Thousand Oaks, CA: Corwin Press.

Grobler, P., Warnich, S., Carrell, M.R., Elbert, N.F. & Hatfield, R.D. (2006). *Human resource management in South Africa*. London, UK: Thomson learning.

Neidorf, R. (2006). *Teach beyond your reach*. Medford, NJ: Information today, Inc.

Summary

This chapter examined how the outcomes-based ETD philosophy directs and informs the design of learning programmes. Within the NQF's outcomes-based ETD system, learning programmes are regarded as the combination of courses, modules, learning materials and methodology by which learners can achieve the learning outcomes of a unit standard or qualification. ETD practitioners, in their role as learning programme designers, follow a design down, deliver up approach to the design of learning programme curricula. Skilful learning programme designers recognise that few (if any) of the desired outcomes will be achieved unless learners are actively involved in the learning process and perceive the learning as valuable to them. This implies moving away from a content-driven approach to a learner-centred approach. The effectiveness of the learning process depends on developing learning outcomes that are meaningful and appropriate to the needs of learners.

ETD practitioners are also required to develop a comprehensive facilitator/trainer guide to demonstrate that the design of their learning programmes complies with the SAQA/ETQA requirements for NQF-aligned outcomes-based learning. The facilitator/ trainer guide also facilitates quality assurance of learning programme delivery, and facilitates evaluation of the value added. Chapter 5 discusses strategies for delivering outcomes-based learning programmes. Chapter 7 explores ways of evaluating the effectiveness of learning programmes.

Tell me and I'll forget; show me and I may remember;
involve me and I'll understand (Chinese proverb).

CHAPTER 5

JEROME KILEY • MELINDE COETZEE

Delivering learning programmes

Effective training delivery does not just depend on the selection of an appropriate delivery method, but also on the expertise, techniques and learning materials used to support the facilitation of learning. Even the best designed training intervention is doomed to fail if ETD practitioners cannot deliver it effectively.

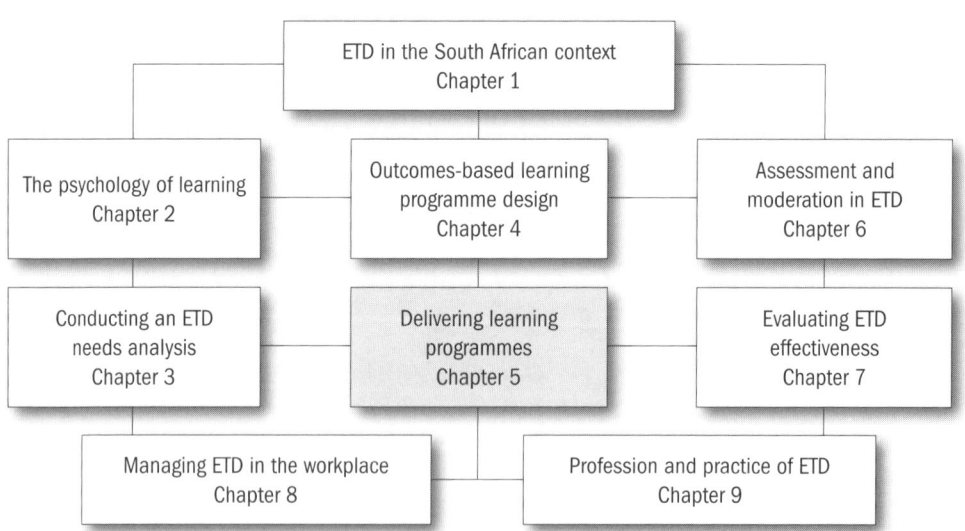

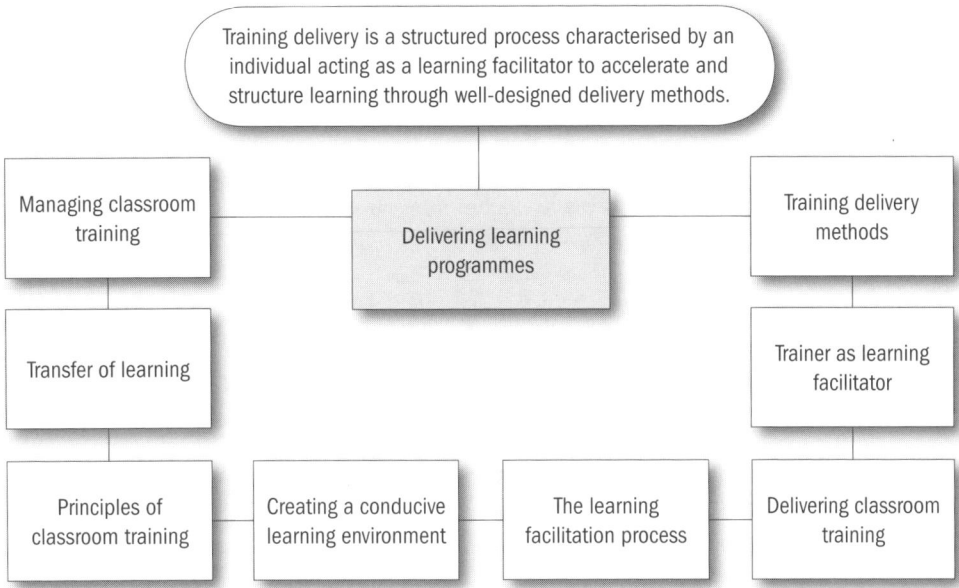

Training delivery is a structured process characterised by an individual acting as a learning facilitator to accelerate and structure learning through well-designed delivery methods.

Managing classroom training

Delivering learning programmes

Training delivery methods

Transfer of learning

Trainer as learning facilitator

Principles of classroom training

Creating a conducive learning environment

The learning facilitation process

Delivering classroom training

Key points of delivering learning programmes
- The effective delivery of training in the workplace depends on a number of factors considered in the design of a learning programme.
- Classroom training and on-the-job training are two of the most common methods for delivering training in the workplace. These two methods are often blended with programmed-instruction and technology-based training approaches to enhance the transfer of learning to the workplace.
- Design and delivery decisions are influenced by the characteristics of the target group and the dynamics of the learning facilitation process.
- Learning facilitation means making the learner more of an active and vital component in the training or learning facilitation process.
- The emotional climate in the classroom has an impact on learners' attitude and willingness to learn.
- Trainers apply principles of learning facilitation to ensure optimal transfer of learning to the workplace.
- Effective trainers are skilful in managing the delivery of learning programmes.

After studying this chapter, you should be able to:
- Describe the various methods of training delivery, including their uses and advantages in the workplace context.
- Explain the elements and characteristics of classroom training.
- Describe how ETD practitioners in their role as learning facilitators can ensure the effective transfer of learning to the workplace.
- Explain how the characteristics of learners and trainers influence the learning facilitation process.
- Evaluate the importance of applying training principles to learning facilitation.
- Explain how trainers can create a classroom environment conducive to learning.
- Describe the options available to trainers when choosing the layout of the classroom.
- Describe the skills and characteristics of a skilled learning facilitator.
- Explain the responsibilities of trainers in managing delivery of learning programmes.

As pointed out in Chapter 2, ETD practitioners use a systematic approach to training that includes assessing training needs, incorporating principles of learning in the design and delivery of learning programmes, assessing learner achievements and evaluating the effectiveness of learning programmes. This scientific approach is also referred to as the Training Cycle (the focus of Chapters 3 to 7). Chapter 5 introduces the delivery of training as a specific way in which learning can take place in an organisation. Learning in the workplace occurs in a variety of situations, some of which are planned and structured and some that are spontaneous and seemingly automatic (Swart, Mann, Brown & Price, 2005).

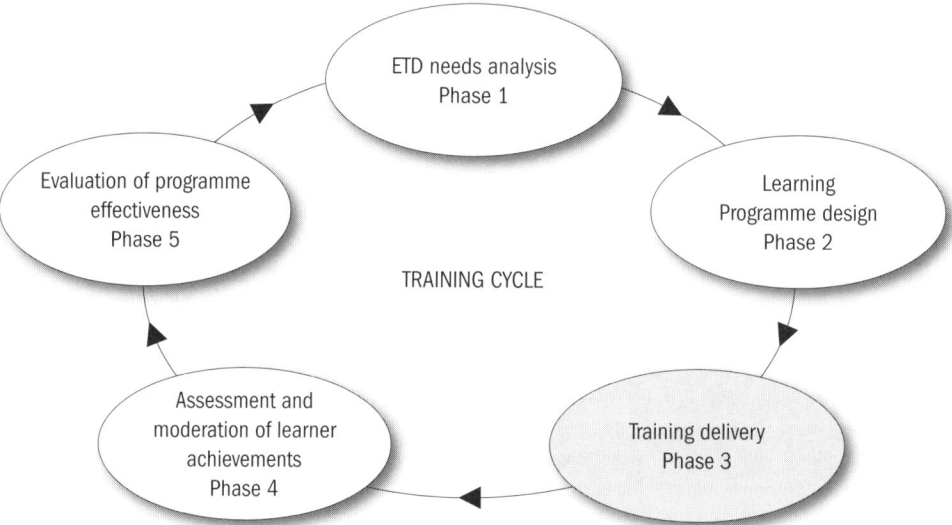

Figure 5.1 The Training Cycle

The focus of this chapter is planned learning or training. It is a structured process characterised by an individual acting as a learning facilitator, who aims to accelerate and structure learning through the delivery of well-designed outcomes-based learning programmes. The effective delivery of training in the workplace depends on a number of factors considered in the design of a learning programme (such as learning outcomes, the characteristics of the learners, the interactions between learners, the skills of the trainer, resources and facilities available, the management of the delivery process and the dynamics within the group of learners). Even the best designed training intervention is doomed to fail if ETD practitioners cannot deliver it effectively.

Training delivery methods

Classroom training and on-the-job training are two of the most common methods for delivering training in the workplace. These two methods are often blended with programmed-instruction and technology-based training approaches to enhance the transfer of learning to the workplace (Cascio & Aguinis, 2005). Even though technology-based training methods (in particular e-learning) have become more popular in recent years, classroom training is still the most popular method to improve employees' job performance (ASTD, 2007).

Classroom training

Classroom training refers to seminars, conferences, lectures and training sessions; all are forms of direct instruction. Direct instruction has strong research support as a method for enabling learners to achieve the learning outcomes of a programme. Direct instruction gives learning facilitators the most control over what, when and how learners learn, and it is also the most appropriate strategy for actively involving learners in developing the required foundational, practical and reflexive competencies (Killen, 2000). Classroom training – when matched with clearly defined learning outcomes – is regarded as a powerful means of enhancing job performance (Aamodt, 2007; Yelon, 1992). However, like all other training or learning facilitation methods, the success of classroom training depends on the ETD practitioner's efforts and expertise.

Table 5.1 *Advantages and limitations of classroom training (based on Killen, 2000)*

Advantages	Limitations
• Trainers are in control of the content and sequencing of information, so they can maintain a clear focus on the outcomes. • It is an effective way of teaching factual information and highly structured knowledge. • It can be effective in all cultures, particularly those in which the trainer is seen as an authority figure. • It can be used equally effectively with large and small groups. • It allows trainers to present a large amount of information in a relatively short time; all learners are given equal access to this information. • It is one of the most effective approaches for teaching explicit concepts and skills to low-achieving learners. • It allows trainers to convey personal interest in the subject (through an enthusiastic presentation). This can stimulate the interest and enthusiasm of learners. • Direct instruction that emphasises listening (for example, lecturing) and observing (for example, demonstrations) help learners who prefer to learn in these ways. • Direct instruction allows trainers to provide a role model for learners in a particular field. They can show how to approach problems, how to analyse information, or how to generate knowledge.	• The success of classroom training depends heavily on the image that the trainer projects. If the trainer does not seem well prepared, knowledgeable, confident and enthusiastic, the learners may become bored or distracted. • Classroom training depends heavily on the communication style of the trainer. If the trainer is a poor communicator, not much learning will occur. • It is difficult to cater for individual differences between learners' abilities, prior knowledge, rates of learning, levels of understanding, learning styles or interest in the subject. • The high level of structure and the trainer's control of learning activities may have a negative impact on learners' problem-solving abilities, independence and curiosity. • If the classroom training does not involve some learner participation (such as asking and answering questions, experimentation and demonstrations), learners will lose interest and remember little of the content. • Some things (such as psychomotor skills) cannot be taught through classroom training alone.

Selecting appropriate classroom training methods

There are a wide variety of training methods available to the trainer. As discussed in Chapter 4, a training method is chosen in the design stage of the Training Cycle. However, design and delivery decisions are influenced by the characteristics of the target group and the dynamics between learners during the learning facilitation process. Figure 5.2 distinguishes between trainer-centred methods and learner-centred methods of classroom training. Trainer-centred methods focus on presenting the learning material, whereas learner-centred methods rely on learning facilitation.

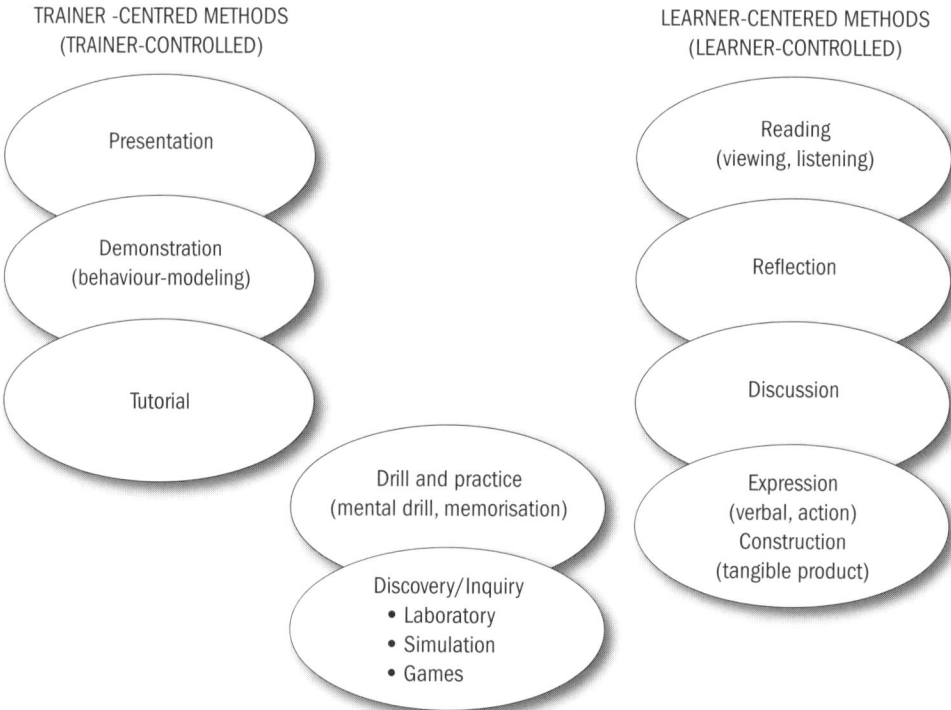

Figure 5.2 Examples of classroom training methods (Molenda & Russell, 2006)

Table 5.2 provides a short summary of the different training methods and their uses in the classroom. It is important to select an appropriate training method based on the nature of the learning outcomes, characteristics of the learners and the dynamics in the classroom situation. Trainer-centred methods might work for some learners, while learner-centred methods will be more appropriate for others. The processes within the group (for example, the levels of energy) will also influence the choice of training method. A training delivery technique is adequate to the extent that it provides the minimum conditions for effective learning to take place. Minimum conditions include:
- Motivate the learner to improve his/her performance.
- Clearly illustrate desired skills.
- Provide for the learners' active participation.
- Provide an opportunity to practise.

- Provide feedback on performance while learners learn.
- Provide some means to reinforce the learner while he/she is learning.
- Structured learning from simple to complex tasks.
- Be adaptable to specific problems.
- Enable the learner to transfer what is learned in training to other situations (Cascio & Aguinis, 2005).

Table 5.2 Classroom training methods and their use (adapted from Molenda & Russell, 2006)

Method	Description	Use
Presentation (by trainer)	One-way flow from trainer to learners Typically verbal with visual aids	Lectures and presentations with: • whiteboard • overheads • Powerpoint slides • videos
Demonstration	One-way flow: 'showing' as opposed to 'telling' Demonstrates device or behaviour	Showing 'how to do it' using trainer, learner or device
Tutorial	Two-way interchange between trainer and learner Learner exerts some control and instructor must respond	• Learnerships • Coaching • Structured tutorials • Technology-assisted training
Reading	Learner reads text at own pace	• Textbooks, modules, handouts • Websites • Self-study modules
Reflection	Learner examines own performance and experience	• Case studies • Experiential learning • Debriefing exercises and games
Presentation (by learner)	Learner creates a verbal product or physical performance	Learner demonstrates knowledge of subject or mastery of technique
Construction	Learner creates a tangible product	• Art, painting or sculpture • Model
Discussion	Two-way interchange between learners Trainer initiates and facilitates	• Seminar • Buzz groups • Small groups • Debates • Panel discussions
Drill and practice	Learner practises skills repeatedly, usually at own pace	• Memorisation drill • Language laboratory • Physical or cognitive skills
Laboratory	Learner acts in 'real' environment with raw materials	• Science experiments • Directly supervised performance
Simulation and games	Learner acts in artificial environment	• Physical simulator • Computer-based simulator • Training games

The effective delivery of training in the classroom does not just depend on the selection of an appropriate delivery method, but also on the selection of learning materials that support the delivery of training.

Learning support materials in classroom training

As discussed in Chapter 4, learning support materials are any materials that support the trainer in the delivery of the learning programme. Materials vary from technologically advanced PowerPoint presentations to pieces of paper used during a training game. The most important requirement for the selection of learning support materials is that materials should enhance and increase the effectiveness of the learning experience. To a large extent, this is achieved by stimulating a wider range of learners' senses. The more senses that are stimulated, the greater the chance that the learning experience will make an impact on the learner. Here are some general points to keep in mind when using learning support materials:

- Make learning support materials visible to all the learners in the class.
- Use a variety of learning support materials.
- Prepare and set up learning support materials before the training begins, and make sure that they work properly.
- Learning support materials are there to enhance content, not to replace it.
- Face the audience rather than the learning support materials.

The most commonly used learning support materials in classroom training are PowerPoint presentations, overhead slides, flip charts, whiteboards or chalkboards, handouts and videos.

PowerPoint presentations

Microsoft PowerPoint is an electronic (and enhanced) version of traditional overhead transparencies. It is fast becoming the standard for learning support material used in a classroom context. It has a number of advantages:

- it is easy to transport and store files;
- presentations can be made colourful and exciting;
- errors can be corrected during the presentation;
- there are numerous resources available online (for example, sound and video can be incorporated into presentations).

The main disadvantages include:

- the cost of computers and data projectors;
- if trainers rely too much on technology in the classroom, the classroom situation will foster passive learners;
- if the equipment fails, the whole learning process is interrupted (or even stopped);
- presentations are more effective when used in a dark room; learners' attention might wander off.

Guidelines for using PowerPoint
- Use keywords. Slides are there to lecture with, not to read.
- Use the default text style to prevent the presentation from becoming too busy.
- Practise using the slide show beforehand to ensure that the animations and layout have the desired effect.
- Use an attractive background (various backgrounds are included with the software).
- Pace the slides. In other words, do not include too many slides in a presentation.
- Check the equipment beforehand to ensure that it is working properly.
- Use a laser pointer to focus learners' attention on particular points.
- The slides must be visible and legible.
- Be careful when using colours such as red, yellow and orange. These colours become unreadable if they are shown with a data projector.
- Keep to the 6x6 rule for slides: 6 words per line x 6 lines per slide.

Overhead transparencies

Overhead transparencies are often used for learning support material. They have a number of advantages:
- They are fairly cheap to produce.
- They do not require expensive equipment.
- You can write directly or print documents on overhead transparencies.
- They can be used repeatedly.

The disadvantages are:
- They are bulky to transport.
- They damage quite easily.
- Errors cannot be corrected easily during the training.

When using overhead transparencies, keep the following points in mind:
- The same usage tips apply as for PowerPoint slides.
- Focus the projector properly, and ensure there is not too much light in the front of the venue.
- Switch off the projector when changing slides.
- Use key points. Do not put too much information on a slide.
- Slides should always be well prepared.

Handouts

Handouts are printed sheets that the trainer can use to supplement training. The following points must be kept in mind regarding the use of handouts:
- Handouts of PowerPoint presentations will ensure that the learners focus on the presentation, rather than on writing down from the slides the whole time. Leave blank spaces for the learners to record information from the lecture.
- When using games or exercises in class, hand out a prepared outline to learners. This saves time, structures the exercises and ensures some form of consistency between the various types of response from the learners.
- Handouts can also provide additional information, such as chapters from books and articles from journals.

Flip charts

Flip charts are powerful learning support materials. They can be used for a number of purposes. The most popular use is to record the inputs of learners. The flip chart pages are then placed on the wall of the training venue so that the learners or facilitator can refer back to inputs later. The facilitator can also use flip charts to illustrate diagrams or record important points. Flip charts have a number of advantages, including the following:

- They allow spontaneity.
- They do not require electricity, so they can be used anywhere.
- They are relatively economical.
- Colour can be used effectively and easily.

Issues to take note of when making use of flip charts are:

- They are better to use with smaller groups of learners (preferably less than 30), otherwise it becomes difficult for all the learners to see.
- Avoid writing in cursive, as this is difficult to read.
- Write in large, legible text. The 7x7 rule should be applied: no more than 7 words in a line and no more than 7 lines on a flip chart.
- Use colours that stand out to make flip charts easy to read. Avoid colours such as yellow, light green and orange. Confirm with learners that the colours are easy to read.
- Use two or three colours on a flip chart, but use colours in a logical way (such as one colour for headings and another for content).
- Use flip chart pens that do not bleed through to the next page or damage the page.
- If the pages need to be put up on the wall, use a tape or adhesive that does not remove paint from the wall.

Whiteboard/chalkboard

Whiteboards and chalkboards are used to record learner inputs, summarise key points or illustrate diagrams. The rules that apply to flip charts also apply here. The main difference is that the information is lost when the board is erased.

Videos

Videos can be used at any point in the delivery of a learning programme. They can serve as ice-breakers, provide an introduction to a topic, illustrate a particular outcome or serve as a powerful conclusion to a learning programme. Issues to consider when using videos include the following:

- When using a video as part of the training, it is critical that the video relates directly to the topic.
- The video must be viewed beforehand. This ensures that the facilitator is familiar with the content and that there are no surprises with regards to quality and content.
- Learners should not be expected to simply understand and remember everything in the video.
- Discuss the video with learners afterwards to gain maximum learning from the video. Learners can be asked to record key points during the video, or a discussion can take place afterwards about the key learning areas in the video. A handout that

summarises the key points can also be helpful.

- It is sometimes helpful to divide a video into smaller segments and deal with these separately.
- The quality of the video should be such that technical aspects do not distract the learners from the content.
- Make sure that the quality of the speakers in the venue is adequate so that all the learners can hear the dialogue.

Blended learning methods

Using a blended learning approach to complement classroom training has been found to be more effective than relying on one particular method only. Blended learning is an integrated approach to the training of adults. It allows ETD practitioners to use a wide range of training methods, including: information presentation techniques, simulation methods, small-group methods, self-instruction and on-the-job training methods (Cascio & Aguinis, 2005; Yelon, 1992). Blended learning allows trainers to involve more of the learners' senses and accommodate a variety of learning preferences (as discussed in Chapter 2).

- Information presentation techniques include lectures, conference methods, videos, CDs, and interactive multimedia in a classroom context.
- Simulation methods include case studies, incident analyses, role playing, experiential exercises, task models (for example, building physical objects), in-basket exercises, business games and behaviour modelling.
- Small-group methods include dyads, simulations and discussions in a classroom context.
- Self-instructional methods include text (for example, books and articles) and technology-based programmed-instruction methods.

Programmed instruction

Programmed instruction is a training method in which learners acquire information at their own pace (Aamodt, 2007). Programmed instruction – whether offered through books, technology-based training or e-learning – is an effective method, because it takes advantage of several important learning principles (Goldstein & Ford, 2002):

- Learning is self-paced, that is, each learner proceeds at his/her own pace.
- Each learner is actively involved in the learning.
- Information is presented in small units or chunks, because learning smaller amounts of material is easier than learning larger amounts.

ACTIVITY

You have to write an examination on the learning outcomes described in each chapter of this book.

- Would you do better in the examination if you read and review one chapter each week, or if you wait until the night before the examination to read and study nine chapters?

Technology-based training

Common forms of technology-based training methods include multimedia learning environments, intranet- and Internet-based instruction, e-learning, full-scale simulations, and virtual reality training. Technology-based training is characterised by its flexibility and adaptability with regards to:

• customising a learning programme to accommodate the characteristics of learners; and

• allowing learners to control or modify the learning environment to suit their learning needs (Cascio & Aguinis, 2005).

As shown in Table 5.3, technology-based learning may be self-paced and asynchronous (it does not involve a 'live' trainer) or synchronous (it does involve a 'live' trainer, subject matter expert or facilitator) (Ward & LaBranche, 2003).

Internet-based programmed instruction or e-learning

E-learning is a popular Internet-based training method. Most e-learning programmes provide learning material in small chunks, and then pose a series of questions to the learner. If the learner does not answer enough questions correctly, the programme informs the learner about the areas in which he/she needs more work, and returns the learner to the appropriate material (Aamodt, 2007). While the design of e-learning programmes vary considerably, the most effective e-learning experiences provide for some way for students to interact with each other or the trainer (for example, online chat, e-mail or discussion forums). Resources such as Internet links, glossary of terms, frequently asked questions and references are also commonly available. Often, online students are asked to complete assignments, complete exercises and take quizzes. Various media are used to convey educational material, including text, dynamic graphics, video and audio (Ward & LaBranche, 2003).

Table 5.3 Learning options in technology-based learning (Ward & LaBranche, 2003)

Synchronous (involvement of a trainer/facilitator)	Asynchronous (no involvement of a trainer /facilitator)
• Classroom training • Internet conferencing • Internet-based training (e-learning) • Simulation methods • Behaviour modelling • Small groups • On-the-job training	• Computer-based training • Self-directed learning • Internet-based training (e-learning) • Message boards/forums • Books • Reading lists • Videos • Audiotapes • DVDs • Internet references • Action learning

Workplace training methods

Workplace training is informal training provided by experienced peers and supervisors. It occurs on the job and during job tasks (DeRouin, Parrish & Salas, 2005). Workplace training methods are popular in basic skills training and management training and development. Broadly, they include:

- orientation training;
- learnerships and apprenticeships;
- on-the-job training;
- near-the-job training;
- job rotation;
- understudy assignments;
- coaching;
- mentoring; and
- performance appraisal feedback (Cascio & Aguinis, 2005).

Table 5.4 On-the-job training methods (Aamodt, 2007; Cascio & Aguinis, 2005)

Method	Description and uses
Orientation training	• Introducing new employees to organisational aspects such as behaviours, attitudes, norms, culture and systems • Also known as induction or socialisation
Learnerships/ apprenticeships	• A structured learning programme that leads to a nationally recognised qualification on the NQF • An integrated, occupation-directed programme that combines learning at a training institution with practical, on-site experience and learning at the workplace
On-the-job training	• Informal training by experienced peers and supervisors that occurs on the job and during job tasks
Near-the-job training	• Training that duplicates the materials and equipment used on the job, but that takes place in an area away from the actual job situation
Job rotation	• Employees are given the opportunity to perform several different jobs in an organisation
Understudy assignments	• An understudy relieves a senior executive of selected responsibilities, thereby allowing him/her to learn certain aspects of the executive's job
Coaching	• A new employee is assigned to an experienced employee, who is told to familiarise the new employee with the workplace and job
Mentoring	• Building of relationships between a mentor and inexperienced employee • Provide the inexperienced employee with an advisor and tutor in the workplace
Performance appraisal feedback	• An effective training method when supervisors meet with an employee to discuss the strengths and weaknesses of job performance • The supervisor and employee determine what training methods would help employees to improve their job knowledge or skills

Team training

A team is a group of individuals who are working together to achieve a common goal. The changing nature of work has led to an increasing emphasis on team performance. Interactions between team members make team training unique. Team training always uses some form of simulation or real-life practice, and always focuses on the interaction of team members, equipment and work procedures. As with individual training, opportunities for guided practice and constructive feedback are particularly important for team training. Forms of team training include the following:

- Team coordination training focuses on teamwork skills that facilitate information exchange, cooperation and coordination of job-related behaviours.
- Cross-training provides exposure to and practice with other teammates' tasks, roles and responsibilities in an effort to increase shared understanding and knowledge among team members.
- Guided team self-correction guides team members in reviewing team events, identifying errors, exchanging feedback, and developing plans for the future (Cascio & Aguinis, 2005).

The trainer as learning facilitator

In conventional training, the emphasis is on the trainer. The trainer is seen as a competent person who has superior knowledge and skills. It is the trainer's task to convey the knowledge and skills to the learner, while the learner has to pick up and master whatever the trainer can offer. The usual method sees the trainer actively disseminating information, while the learner remains mostly passive. In this trainer-centred approach, the trainer is an instructor and presenter. The trainer is responsible for what learners should learn, how and when they should learn, and the effectiveness of their learning. In the context of the outcomes-based approach to education and training, with its emphasis on learner-centred training methods, the trainer has to adopt a facilitative approach to training. A facilitative approach changes the relationship between trainer and learners to one where there is an interdependent sharing of experience and a flow of information. In the outcomes-based context, the trainer is seen as a learning facilitator when delivering a learning programme.

Facilitation involves getting people to work together to achieve a specific outcome. One of the fathers of the facilitative approach to learning, the psychologist Carl Rogers (in Laird, 1993), identifies facilitative trainers (as opposed to instructors or presenters) as:

- less protective of their own beliefs;
- able to listen to learners;
- able to accept ideas that are different or even troublesome;
- able to pay as much attention to the relationship with the learners as to the content of the programme; and
- able to accept both positive and negative feedback and use this to gain insight into and improve their own behaviour.

Learning facilitation is a means to make the learner more of an active and vital component of the learning process. Facilitation is a learning programme delivery strategy that deliberately involves learners and maximises their input and importance in the learning process. Learners take a greater degree of responsibility for their own learning. Facilitation corresponds to the concept of andragogy. Malcolm Knowles (1972) introduced this concept; it comprises the following core principles (discussed in more detail in Chapter 2):

- Adults need to direct their own learning.
- Learners' prior experiences are a rich resource for learning.
- Adults will learn something when they need to; this is normally related to their roles and responsibilities.
- Adults' orientation to learning is problem-centred rather than subject-centred. In other words, they seek to acquire skills that can be applied to real-life problems.

Purposes of learning facilitation (Yelon, 1992)

- Motivate learners to learn and apply the performance in the workplace.
- Help learners to become mentally ready to learn.
- Enable learners to practise.
- Enable learners to improve their performance.
- Help learners to retain learning and transfer what they have learnt to the workplace.
- Facilitate the integration of newly acquired skills with existing skills.
- Certify that learners have accomplished the learning outcomes.

The concept of learning facilitation has several advantages:

- It shifts the focus of training from the trainer to the learners' needs and skills.
- It uses learners' knowledge, experience and frame of reference as a valued and critical input to the learning process. The learners' knowledge and experience serve as a basis for further learning experiences.
- It allows learners to become active partners with a vested interest in their own learning. Learning success is shared with other learners and the learning facilitator.
- It promotes experiential learning that is relevant, significant and meaningful. Facilitated learning relates more directly to everyday, real-life situations.
- It promotes learning that lasts beyond the immediate training sessions. Learning facilitation encourages learning that is readily transferable to the workplace.

Simple rules for facilitating learning in the classroom (based on Cameron, 1998)

- Make the learning in the classroom interesting and stimulating to encourage contributions. Use a variety of facilitation techniques to achieve this.
- The classroom training must have a clear purpose.
- Learners attend because they have something to contribute.
- The classroom training should run according to the agenda.
- The classroom training should be designed to achieve specific, predetermined outcomes.
- Everyone should be included in the discussion and encouraged to participate.
- Learners are encouraged to listen to one another and understand each other's point of view.
- The facilitator should be well informed and unbiased, and should help the learners to distinguish between fact and opinion.
- The classroom training should be part of a larger process; everyone should be kept informed of progress.
- Summarise or conclude learning experiences by asking questions about the experience, comparing and contrasting learners' responses, and helping learners to draw conclusions about the objectives of these experiences.

Learning facilitation skills

The ETD practitioner should know how learning takes place and how the learner can be assisted to make learning easier. Learning facilitators should be able to make the subject matter, learning content and learning process interesting. A facilitator needs the following general skills:

- *Knowledge of and skills in group processes and group dynamics.* Facilitators should understand group behaviour and should have the skills to handle conflict. They have to observe the group carefully and try to determine the mood of the group. It is important to know why the group or individuals in the group behave in specific ways. Facilitators have to be skilful in gauging the attitudes and anticipations of the group, and act accordingly.
- *Listening skills.* By listening to the learners' answers and reactions to discussions, facilitators can determine how they think. Not only the answers are important. The attitude and emotions with which they are given and the ways in which the learners arrive at the answers are equally important.
- *Questioning skills.* Learning facilitators need to be skilful in asking questions that reflect the learners' opinions and feelings, and questions that lead to problem solving and interpretation of information. Open questions that require learners to analyse, synthesise and evaluate and that may have more than one correct answer are important to evoke discussion.
- *Feedback.* The facilitator should be able to summarise, interpret, and communicate the group's performance to the group. At critical and convenient moments during discussions, important information, opinions and conclusions should be summarised and shared with the group. This gives recognition to what was said and achieved and forms the basis for further discussion.
- *Flexibility.* An effective facilitator is not rigid, but flexible and open-minded. Facilitators must be able to adjust, act and react according to the circumstances of the group and the group procedures. Be provocative, supportive, serious or lighthearted as the situation requires, but always be in command of the situation.
- *Time management.* Facilitation must not deteriorate into lengthy, aimless and inefficient discussions. The facilitator should be able to use and manage time in such a way that the group can finish its learning tasks effectively.

The wisdom of learning facilitation (based on Clement, 1992)

- A wise learning facilitator lets others have the floor.
- A good learning facilitator is better than a spectacular learning facilitator. Otherwise, the learning facilitator outshines the learning.
- Facilitate what is happening rather than what you think needs to happen.
- Silence says more than words; pay attention to it.
- Continual classroom drama inhibits inner, or psychological, learning processes.
- Allow time for genuine insight.
- A good reputation arises naturally from doing good work. But do not nourish the reputation: the anxiety will be endless. Instead, nourish the work.
- To know what is happening, relax, and do not try to figure things out. Listen quietly, be calm, and use reflection.
- Let go of selfishness. Let go of your ego, and you will receive what you need. Give away credit, and you

will get more. When you desire nothing, much comes to you. The less you make of yourself, the more you are.

- Instead of trying hard, be easy. Teach by example, and more will happen.
- Trying to be brilliant does not work.
- The gift of a great learning facilitator is to create an awareness of greatness in others.
- Because the learning facilitator can see clearly, light is shed on others.
- Teach as a leader and a healer. Constant force and intervention will backfire, as will constant yielding. One cannot push the river; a leader's touch is light.
- To manage other lives takes strength; to manage your own life takes real power. Be happy, content, and at peace with yourself.

Characteristics of effective learning facilitation

Effective learning facilitation means that learners are active partners in the learning experience and are actively involved in learning new knowledge and skills. Credible and effective learning facilitators inspire learners to learn by demonstrating expertise in the field, using learning facilitation skills effectively and clearly linking the course content to the outcomes. The outcomes are then clearly linked to the learners' work performance. The characteristics of effective learning facilitation are summarised in Table 5.5.

Table 5.5 Characteristics of effective learning facilitation (adapted from Goldstein & Ford, 2002)

Establishing and maintaining credibility
<ul><li>The facilitator negotiates learners' needs and expectations at the beginning of the training programme.</li><li>Together with the learners, the facilitator sets rules so that the learners know what is expected and what they can expect from the facilitator. The ground rules include roles, responsibilities, expectations and group norms. It is important that the facilitator models the agreed-upon behaviours.</li><li>The facilitator briefly refers to his/her own experience and qualifications to build credibility with the group.</li><li>The facilitator arrives early and is ready when the learners arrive.</li><li>The facilitator interacts with the learners individually and uses their names. Name tags are effective.</li><li>The facilitator is well organised and prepared.</li></ul>

Learning facilitation is structured and organised for impact
<ul><li>An outline of the course is presented that links the content to the learning outcomes.</li><li>Materials are sequenced to achieve maximum impact. This may mean that the facilitator adapts the sequence of activities from time to time to match the energy levels of the group.</li><li>The facilitator gives lectures that are well organised and that follow a clear pattern.</li><li>The facilitator clearly links the topics to one another.</li><li>The content in the lectures is linked to other aspects of the course.</li><li>Conceptual learning is emphasised as opposed to simple rote learning.</li></ul>

Learning facilitation is conducted in a responsive and collaborative manner
<ul><li>The facilitator builds responsive and collaborative relationships with the learners.</li><li>Realistic and challenging goals are set.</li><li>Training and communication styles are adapted to meet the needs of the learners.</li><li>The facilitator exhibits energy and enthusiasm.</li><li>The facilitator responds to problems and learners' needs as they arise.</li></ul>

A safe and comfortable learning environment
• The facilitator answers questions thoroughly and clearly and creates a non-threatening environment.

Positive feedback
• The facilitator encourages the learners to participate through positive feedback.
• The facilitator encourages the learners to engage with the material.
• Feedback should be positive and timely when learners have performed well.
• Follow the learners' progress during exercises and activities and provide specific feedback to reinforce correct responses and to correct inaccurate responses.
• Preserve the learners' dignity and self-esteem when giving feedback.
• Actively listen to the feedback of the learners and respond accordingly.

Effective communication and presentation skills
• The facilitator uses examples that are relevant to the learners' frame of reference.
• Class discussions are stimulated and encouraged.
• The facilitator is accessible outside the class situation.
• Manage the physical environment to ensure that it supports the learning process.
• Use audiovisual equipment effectively and have a back-up plan in case of problems.
• Adapt the media used to accommodate the needs of the learners and the realities of the situation.
• Manage the time available to ensure that all learning outcomes are achieved.
• Actively listen to the learners for evidence of learning and engagement.
• Monitor individual and group behaviour.
• Ask for feedback on content and delivery and encourage learners to share new ideas to improve the learning experience.
• Interact with learners during meals and other free time.

Provide opportunities for application of knowledge and skills
• The practical use of the content is emphasised.
• Assessments are used that identify strengths and weaknesses.
• The learners are given opportunities to demonstrate what they have learnt through simulations, role plays, games and case studies.
• Demonstrate skills using anatomical models, role plays and commonly available equipment.
• Show, in a variety of ways, the on-the-job benefits of meeting the learning objectives.
• Develop practical plans to enable the learners to apply their new knowledge and skills on the job.

Delivering classroom training

Classroom training has two distinct attributes. Firstly, classroom training is the training of a group of learners. Secondly, it requires the physical separation of the classroom from the workplace. Separation from the workplace distinguishes classroom training from on-the-job training. Although classroom training differs in certain aspects from other training methods, its purpose is the same: to provide learners with the skills or knowledge they need to perform successfully on the job (Yelon, 1992). ETD practitioners choose classroom training as a solution in the following instances:
• people lack the skills or knowledge to do a job well;
• people must learn and practise the required skills and knowledge; and
• on-the-job training cannot provide the amount or degree of learning necessary to acquire the skills or knowledge (Yelon, 1992).

Classroom training should form part of a comprehensive, coordinated and continuous system for improving performance. Such a system includes training inside and outside the classroom, as well as interventions before and after formal training. In the pre-class intervention, ETD practitioners obtain information from learners and their supervisors before training begins. Next, ETD practitioners combine training in and out of the classroom to teach learners the desired performance. After the training has been completed, ETD practitioners maintain contact with learners and their supervisors to facilitate the transfer of learning to the workplace (Aamodt, 2007; Yelon, 1992).

Pre-class intervention

In the pre-class intervention, ETD practitioners obtain information from potential learners – through an ETD needs analysis (as discussed in Chapter 3) – to make classroom training meaningful, transferable and understandable. The purpose of a target group analysis is to identify the characteristics and specific needs of the group of potential learners. A target group analysis is more specific than the ETD needs analysis, which determines the overall need for training. The following biographical details are important when conducting a target group analysis (Buckley & Caple, 2004):

- *Size of the group.* This will have an impact on the logistical arrangements and the methods that can be used to deliver training.
- *Experience.* What is the learners' level of experience with the topic of the training programme?
- *Age.* What is the average age of learners? Are learners more or less the same age, or are there big differences in age? Age often implies experience.
- *Skills and qualifications.* What is the learners' current level of skills relating to the topic of the learning programme? This will determine the level at which the training is presented.
- *Gender.* What is the distribution of male and female learners?
- *Language proficiency.* What is the learners' level of proficiency in the language that will be used during the training? Is it their first, second or third language?
- *Cultural groupings.* Which cultures do the learners represent? Are there particular cultural practices that need to be considered (for example, diet), or do some topics need to be treated with sensitivity and understanding?
- *Geographical location.* Are the learners all located in one area, or are they spread over a wide geographical area?
- *Specific needs.* Do a particular group of learners have specific needs (for example, a particular focus in the course content, or some specific logistical requirements)?
- *Disabilities.* Are there learners with disabilities? What are their specific needs?
- *Learning styles.* Is there a particular learning style that is dominant in the group?

These and any other relevant characteristics of the learners will have an impact on the delivery of the training and the logistical arrangements of the learning programme. The most effective way to conduct a target group analysis is to send out detailed questionnaires to the potential learners, and then to compile a profile of the learners based on the results of the questionnaires. This approach will help ETD practitioners to determine whether the learners identified for the training programme actually need the training.

Another helpful approach is to conduct a session at the beginning of the learning programme where specific needs are identified. Alternatively, focus groups can be conducted. Another option is to interview learners to identify their specific needs. However, interviews are time consuming. The main advantage of interviews is that it gives the trainer an opportunity to build relationships with individual learners. Once the characteristics and needs of the learners have been identified, the trainer needs to choose the most appropriate training method.

The target group analysis allows ETD practitioners to assess prerequisite skills and knowledge and bring all participants up to the same level of understanding (regarding basic ideas and skills) before the classroom training starts. If ETD practitioners know and understand their learners, they can relate the desired performance to learners' needs and set the emotional climate for the rest of the learning facilitation process. The pre-class intervention also encourages learners to prepare for the training and helps to remove any barriers to the transfer of learning.

How to get the most out of the pre-class intervention (Yelon, 1992)
- To facilitate learning and assess prerequisites, an ETD practitioner gathers information from for example, managers and their supervisors, about managers' performance in meetings.
- To relate the desired performance to the learners' needs, the ETD practitioner might describe what new ideas and skills will be learned and how the resulting performance will be likely to increase productivity.
- To reduce anxiety, the ETD practitioner also explains that meeting procedures will be learned quickly and painlessly.
- To encourage learners to prepare for the formal parts of training, the ETD practitioner might ask managers and their supervisors to choose the next series of meetings as learning programme projects.
- To remove barriers to the transfer of learning, the ETD practitioner discusses with managers and their supervisors ways to eliminate or work around possible blocks to using the new skills on the job.

Learning facilitation

Learning facilitation in the classroom is characterised by three distinctive elements. These elements are an introduction, the actual learning facilitation process and a conclusion to the classroom training.

Introduction

As discussed in Chapter 3, a well-planned introduction captures attention and motivates learners. Good introductions meet the following criteria:
- Establish expectations at the start of the training session by specifically stating what learners must be able to do by the end of the session and how they will be assessed. For example, the ETD practitioner could say, "For your final assessment, you will be required to conduct real meetings according to the meeting performance qualities checklist."
- Orient learners by showing how the content of the learning material and activities are organised. For example, the ETD practitioner provides a content framework by saying, "A good start to a meeting consists of two steps. Firstly, give an introduction to provide context and motivation for the meeting. Next, specify ground rules for the meeting to promote efficient progress."
- Provide a schedule of events (also called an agenda) to help learners follow the progress of the training session. For example, the ETD practitioner says, "You will hear a short lecture about starting a meeting. Then you will see a demonstration. Finally, you will plan, practise and get feedback on the start of your meetings."

Table 5.6 *Example of an agenda*

Day 1 Time	Module	Learning theme	Learning activity
08:30–09:00		Welcoming and orientation	• Introductions • Needs and expectations • Programme learning outcomes • Assessment guidance • Agenda
09:00–10:30	**Module 1** Skills development legislation	Reflection on pre-course learning activity	• Small-group reflections on pre-course learning activity • Completion of Activity 1.1 in the learning manual (competency self-assessment)
10:30–11:00	Break		
11:00–12:30	**Module 1** Skills development legislation	Module activities Lunch	• Small-group reflections on pre-course learning activity • Report back to large group (discussions and learning reflections)
12:30–13:30	Lunch		
13:30–15:00	**Module 1** Skills development legislation		• Learning activity • Small group discussions • Large group reflections and discussion
15:00–15:30	Break		
15:30–16:30	**Module 1** Skills development legislation	• Workplace application briefing • Homework activity briefing • Closure of day	• Reflection on the day's learning • Discussion of workplace application • Homework activity

A useful way to record learners' expectations is to write them down on a flip chart. The trainer should try to ensure that all expectations are addressed during the learning programme. If some of the expectations fall outside the scope of the programme, this needs to be stated before the training begins. Use the list of expectations as a checklist at the end of the learning programme to ensure that all the expectations have been addressed.

Establish ground rules with the group, or learning contracts with individual learners. Ground rules are put in place at the beginning of the programme to serve as guidelines for how the programme is run and how the learners interact. These rules are normally recorded on a sheet of flip chart paper and displayed prominently for the duration of the training programme. Examples of ground rules are: responsibility for learning; administrative arrangements such as starting times, breaks and submission dates for assignments; mutual respect and tolerance. If the nature of the programme allows it (for example, if the programme takes place over a long time), individual learning contracts can be established. In these contracts, the expectations and responsibilities of the learner and facilitator are stated.

Techniques for starting off on a positive note

- Use an ice-breaker exercise to gain the attention of the learners and to help build rapport. There are numerous ice-breakers freely available on the Internet and in books that specialise in training games.
- Relate an anecdote (a short story that is related to the training topic).
- Tell a joke or show a humorous video clip or cartoon. The humour should be related to the topic and it should not be offensive or discriminatory.
- Show a short video that contextualises the topic.
- Ask thought-provoking questions about the topic that challenge the learners and encourage discussion and debate.
- Illustrate the topic graphically (with diagrams or mind maps).
- Quote a startling statistic or make a powerful statement relating to the topic. The aim is to stimulate discussion and debate.
- Get a senior manager to welcome the learners and explain the importance of the learning programme.

Facilitating learning

During learning facilitation, ETD practitioners prepare learners for the most realistic practice possible of new skills and knowledge. In their role as learning facilitators, ETD practitioners do the following:

- explain what the learners need to know to benefit from a demonstration of the desired performance;
- demonstrate the skill;
- allow learners the opportunity to practise the desired performance;
- provide feedback and guidance on improving skills by giving more explanations, demonstrations or practice, as necessary (Yelon, 1992).

Concluding the classroom training

Learning facilitators conclude classroom training in such a way that learners are likely to recall and use what they have learnt:

- They summarise the main ideas.
- They relate the new skill to other job skills and to the job situation in which it will be used. They remind learners of the knowledge and skills they have learnt and why these are important.
- They provide a final supervised practice as a test to assess what learners have learnt, to reinforce the new skills and to instil confidence in learners (Yelon, 1992).

Table 5.7 Elements of learning facilitation in the classroom (based on Yelon, 1992)

Element	Description
Introduction Used for starting training session, learning units and lessons	**Motivation** State or show learners why they should learn to achieve the learning outcomes, where the knowledge, skills, values and behaviour are used, and what its consequences are. **Objective and learning outcomes** State or show learners what performance (knowledge, skills, values and behaviour) they will learn to do and how their performance will be assessed. **Advance organiser** State or show learners the main parts of the performance, how the parts are related to each other, and where this performance fits into their jobs. **Review of past** Remind learners of what they know, and how they can use the existing knowledge to learn this performance (achieve the learning outcomes). **Agenda** State or show learners the order of the learning activities.
Facilitating learning	**Explanation** State or show learners the essential information that they need to perform (that is, the steps to take when performing and the ideas needed to take each step properly). **Demonstration** Show learners how to do the required performance (apply the knowledge, skills, values and behaviour) on the job. **Practice** Ask each learner to try (experiment with) the required performance on the job. **Formative assessment** Assess learners' progress towards mastering the learning outcomes. **Feedback and remediation** Tell learners openly what they did well, what they need to improve on, and what they should do. Include more practice, as needed.
Conclusion Used for ending training session, learning units, lessons	**Summary of main ideas** Remind learners of the main parts of the performance, how the parts relate to each other, and where this performance fits into their jobs. **Integration with other segments** State or show learners how this performance relates to other performances already learnt or to be learned. **Motivation** State or show learners why they have learnt the learning outcomes. **Summative assessment** Assess learners' performance (achievement of learning outcomes) and provide guidance for further learning and development.

Example of a classroom activity for the training of trainers (based on Coetzee & Jansen, 2007a)

Improving my effectiveness as trainer by letting go of old behaviours

Method

1. Before the activity, encourage participants to consider behaviours they wish to change to improve their effectiveness as trainers. Ask them to complete Document 1.1. If people have difficulty defining aspects of behaviour, some discussion might be needed. Examples could be given, as follows:
   - aggressive outbursts;
   - talking too much;
   - being insensitive to learners' problems;
   - being defensive when perceiving criticism; or
   - always saying yes to requests.
2. Encourage participants to discuss the progress they made with their pre-class work. Ensure everyone has done enough preparation to continue with the remainder of the activity.
3. Working in pairs, allow participants time to help each other (through good listening and support) to decide on one behaviour that they wish to change. The following pointers may be helpful in briefing participants:
   - Choose a behaviour that is easy to describe.
   - Choose something that can be practised during the training session.
   - Help each other to identify possible benefits of making the change.
   - Agree on and record a 'contract' that describes what the individual is aiming to achieve, and how the partner is prepared to assist.
4. Bring participants together and ask them to declare their intentions for new behaviours. If possible, each participant should get a commitment from another participant to observe and give feedback about progress. The participants now need to practise their new behaviours. Conduct a short decision-making phase to discuss the different ideas and opportunities available to participants.
5. Ask participants to return to their pairs, and help each other reflect on the decision-making phase.
6. Ask participants to discuss their perceptions of the activity, their aims for further change and any opportunities for mutual support in the future.

Timing

Average total estimated time: 30 minutes

Materials required

1. Enough copies of Document 1
2. Enough space for people to work undisturbed
3. Paper, pens and flip chart

Trainer/facilitator guidance

The activities create opportunities for participants to reflect on their personal characteristics and beliefs, and to give and receive feedback. You need to promote an atmosphere of openness and trust. This may be difficult if the prevailing culture is resistant to these qualities.

Your contribution to this process is as follows:

- Help participants to understand and apply the skills of seeking and receiving feedback. Encourage the group to think about 'feedback contracts'.
- Assist people to define clearly the behaviours they wish to modify.
- Give attention and support when new behaviours are being practised.
- Encourage group members to offer support to each other.

The most important point of the activities is to encourage participants to be honest, take a longer-term view and identify behaviours that will help to unlock their potential ability to improve their effectiveness as trainers. Participants may find it difficult to detach themselves from their immediate situation. You may need to encourage them to think of the activities as an investment in their personal growth. Some may be reluctant to share their personal information and others may feel threatened.

You are well placed to encourage participants to share their concerns within the group. Participants need to know that their right to privacy and confidentiality will be respected and honoured at all times.

A maximum group size of six to eight is recommended owing to the complexity of the tasks.

Document 1

Improving my effectiveness as a trainer by letting go of my old behaviours:

_____
_____

Behaviour(s) being considered:

_____
_____

Example of behaviour(s) to sharpen focus:

_____
_____

Perceived consequences of these behaviours:

_____
_____

New behaviour (what could I change)?

_____
_____

Perceived benefits of new behaviour(s):

_____
_____

Assistance/support available to me?

_____
_____

Post-class intervention

In the post-class intervention, ETD practitioners aim to keep former learners interested in using what they have learnt. They also help learners to continue to improve upon their new skills and remove barriers to the use of the desired performance. For example, the ETD practitioner accompanies learners and observes them on the job. After each observation, the ETD practitioner discusses learners' strengths and further development areas with them and their supervisors. To remove possible barriers, the ETD practitioner asks learners and their supervisors if anything interferes with the use of the newly acquired skills. If barriers are discovered, the ways to remove them are explored (Yelon, 1992).

The learning facilitation process

Learning facilitation emphasises the principles of experiential learning (discussed in Chapter 2). The learning facilitation process should therefore assist learners in their progress through the learning phases described by Kolb's (1985) cycle of experiential learning.

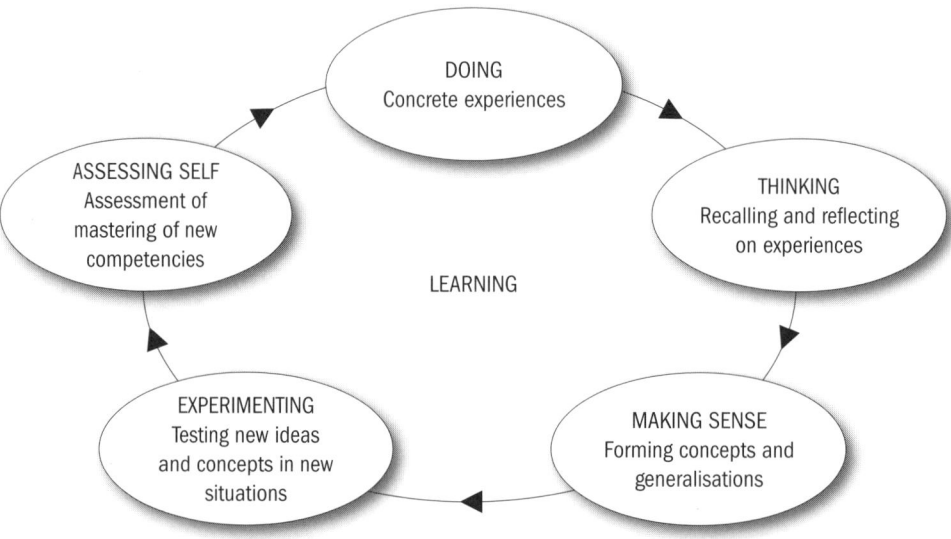

Figure 5.3 *Experiential learning cycle (based on Kolb, 1985)*

Learning facilitators consider the points illustrated in Figure 5.3 before and during the training process. When using activities, facilitators need to think of ways to assist learners in progressing through the learning cycle. Examples of these are given Table 5.8.

Table 5.8 *Examples of behaviours to facilitate throughout the learning cycle (Coetzee & Jansen, 2007a)*

Stage of learning	Behaviours to facilitate the learning cycle
Recall concrete experiences	Guide participants (or pairs helping each other) to recall previous experiences and record these. Use role plays, case studies and video clips as concrete data. Also use group discussions and brainstorm techniques to let thoughts and memories flow.
Share aspects of experiences	Guide pairs/threes to share experiences and the associated thoughts and feelings. Encourage participants to listen, be sensitive towards others' needs and show care. Help participants to give and seek feedback (and see the value of this).
Reflect/process the information	Help participants to reflect in depth. Encourage and seek further feedback in areas that are still not clearly defined.
Arrive at understanding, concepts and generalisations	Help participants to 'see it' and 'believe it' for themselves. Make sense of the feedback and other data.

Stage of learning	Behaviours to facilitate the learning cycle
Test out new ideas and concepts in new situations	Use theoretical information and models to support this process. Encourage others to share the understanding and insights reached.
Move on to further concrete experiences and continue the learning cycle	Express thoughts on areas for improvement and further practice. Use experiential techniques to reinforce and consolidate the learning.
Evaluate mastering of newly acquired competencies and ability to apply in real-life situations by means of self-assessment activities and further development planning	Help participants to draw up action plans for implementing newly acquired competencies. Encourage learners to share plans with others. Help the learners to feel confident about overcoming any perceived obstacles. Agree on a support structure and networks. Assist learners to reflect on their learning. Identify areas for further training and development. Provide guidance on further development resources and networks.

Group dynamics in the learning process

Group dynamics, or the manner in which learners interact with each other, are influenced by the characteristics of the individual learners. In addition, trainers will often have to deal with learners from different generations. Different generations have unique needs and preferences, as shown in Table 5.9. Learners' characteristics have a strong impact on how they interact with one another and how they react to the learning process. Newstrom and Lengnick-Hall (1991) identify ten ways in which learners differ from each other:

1. *Instrumentality* is the degree to which learners are concerned with the immediate applicability of the knowledge and skills being taught.
2. *Scepticism* is the degree to which learners exhibit a questioning attitude that requires logical explanations, evidence and practical examples.
3. *Resistance to change* is the degree to which learners fear the process of moving to the unknown.
4. *Attention span* is the length of time that learners are able to pay attention.
5. *Expectation level* is the level (quality) and quantity (content) that learners expect from the training.
6. *Dominant needs* are the internal and external needs that drive the learners.
7. *Absorption level* is the pace at which learners can absorb new information.
8. *Topical interest* is the degree to which the learners have a personal or job-relevant interest in the topic.
9. *Self-confidence* refers to the degree to which learners view their abilities positively, and the accompanying level of feedback, reinforcement and support required.
10. *Locus of control* is the degree to which learners regard their ability to implement new learning with or without organisational support.

Table 5.9 Learning environment preferences of various generations (Codrington & Grant-Marshall, 2004)

Generation	Learning environment preferences
Silents (born 1920s to 1940s)	• Tend to enjoy conformity, consistency, logic and discipline. • Do not like taking risks and want a clearly understood structure established from the moment they walk in. • Like a classroom style layout for training sessions and prefer conservative trainers who establish the ground rules early on and then stick to them. • It is a good idea to send Silents a list of books and any other reading matter prior to the course. • Like trainers to stick to agendas.
Boomers (born 1940s to 1960s)	• Prefer collaborative learning in large classrooms and enjoy opportunities for interaction, networking and teamwork. • Excel at working in small teams. • Turned off by an authoritarian approach. • Respond to brainstorming, lateral thinking and want to provide their own input.
Generation Xers (born 1960s to 1980s)	• Do not prefer classroom-style interaction. • Prefer training that is related to personal skills development and increased marketability. • Like to absorb learning with CDs, videos and computer-based training with access to a human guide and expert when they get stuck. • Training needs to be fun and multi-styled. • High need for developing life skills.
Millennials (born 1980s to 2000s)	• Care about manners and believe in civic action. • Look for attention and structure. • Prefer personal challenges and team work. • Prefer informal training room structure adaptable to quick seating changes. • Prefer electronic equipment to be part of training.

ACTIVITY

Review chapter 2, in particular Table 2.5 (multiple intelligences) and Table 2.6 (stimulation of intelligences).
• How could trainers make use of the concept of multiple intelligences in increasing learners' participation and learning?

Increasing learners' participation by asking questions

It is important to ask questions in the right way. The amount and type of questions, and the way in which the trainer asks questions influence the level of participation by individual learners and the group dynamics. The aim of asking questions in training is to get input from the learners, get the learners to participate in the learning process and guide the learning process.

Table 5.10 *Guidelines for asking questions (Cameron, 1998)*

Guidelines	Types of question
• Make the meaning clear. If the learners do not understand the question, rephrase it. • Do not ask questions simply to use up time. • Pitch questions at the level of your audience. • Ask questions that will result in insight and reflection, rather than questions that have straightforward answers.	• Open-ended, broad questions that cannot be answered by a simple yes or no • Probing questions, with additional questions to get a more in-depth response • Clarifying questions to check understanding of learners' responses, with additional questions and reflection (repeating in own words) of learners' responses • Example questions that ask learners to provide examples of something • Reflective questions that ask learners to reflect on their feelings or understanding • Closed questions with a simple yes or no answer • Questions to which the facilitator genuinely does not have the answers

Giving and receiving feedback

Feedback plays an important role in learning facilitation. Learning facilitators give feedback on progress, the results of assessment or questions and class discussions. The way in which feedback is given will determine learners' future participation; feedback may either build or obstruct insight and understanding. Most importantly, feedback should treat every input by learners with dignity and respect. It is irrelevant whether the facilitator agrees with learners' inputs or not. Keep the following guidelines in mind when giving feedback:

- Give feedback to learners' answers immediately; encourage learners and tactfully correct when necessary.
- Do not interrupt while a learner is answering a question, even if you do not agree with the answer.
- Rather than simply correcting answers that you do not agree with, probe these answers to understand the reasoning behind the learner's conclusion.
- Always start with a positive remark.
- Be as specific as possible.
- Provide reasons for feedback.
- Address the topic; do not attack the learner personally.
- Be realistic (Erasmus & van Dyk, 2003).

Feedback is an integral part of the learning process. Handled skilfully (both in terms of how it is given and received), feedback shows learners the effect they have on others and provides an opportunity for them to make changes in their behaviour. The learning process will benefit from this.

A feedback contract is an agreement (between all the persons involved in the learning programme, including the trainer) on how to give and receive feedback during the learning process (Coetzee & Jansen, 2007a). Body language is a good indication of how feedback is received.

Table 5.11 *Example of a feedback contract (Coetzee & Jansen, 2007a)*

Receiving feedback	Giving feedback
I agree to: • be prepared to receive feedback as information; • decide for myself what to do with the information; • avoid arguing with the person giving feedback; • seek clarification only if I do not fully understand the feedback; • avoid justifying those aspects of my behaviour that led to the feedback; and • avoid denying the feedback.	I agree to: • check that the other person is receptive for feedback; • address the other person directly; • take responsibility for the feedback; • be specific about which aspect of the other person I am giving feedback; • be clear that these are my reactions to the other person's behaviour; • avoid blaming; • offer feedback as information, free from attached conditions; and • offer as much feedback as I think is useful and avoid giving long lists.

Reading the body language of learners

Body language, also known as non-verbal communication, is the way in which people give information through conscious and unconscious gestures, body movements and facial expressions (Lambert & The Diagram Group, 1996). Our body language expresses our thoughts, attitudes, feelings and intentions. It is an important source of feedback for learning facilitators. Among other things, body language tells facilitators when learners need a break, when they are bored or confused, and whether they agree or disagree with the facilitator. The universal facial expressions such as happiness, sadness, surprise, fear, anger and disgust are examples of body language. Some examples of negative body language include:

• Gestures such as shaking of the head, crossed arms and frowning might indicate negativity and disagreement with learning points.
• Supporting the head with a hand under the chin, looking away, leaning back, stretching out legs and bland facial expressions indicate boredom.
• Drumming the fingers or fidgeting indicate impatience.
• Stroking the throat, putting hands in pockets, pulling at trouser legs or pulling an eyelid may indicate disbelief.
• Fidgeting, a lack of attention and sleepiness indicate tiredness.

Positive body language include positive facial expressions such as smiling, leaning forward, eye contact, nodding and upright heads. These signs all show that learners are interested and involved in the material. Beware: body language is not universal. Different cultures have their own gestures and ignorance can cause offence.

Table 5.12 Reading body language (Coetzee & Jansen, 2007)

Body language	Possible meaning
Eyes looking down or away	Self-consciousness or guilt
Raised eyebrow	Disbelief
Rubbing the nose or pulling the ears	Learners do not understand, even if they say they do
Smiling when greeting someone	Friendly intentions, positive attitude
Hand touching the mouth	Anxious or trying to deceive someone
Folded or crossed arms	Nervous or shut off from someone (or feeling cold)
Hands on hips or active gesturing	Aggression
Tapping on the desk or chair	Nervousness or impatience
Tremor in voice	Nervousness
Shrugging the shoulders	Indifference to what someone says
Facing you squarely, full height, smiling, head forward	Confidence

Apart from reading learners' body language, learning facilitators also need to be sensitive to how they come across to learners. When people communicate, they rely more on the message contained in the body language of the communicator than what is actually said. A trainer's body (including posture, gesture and facial expression) and even their physical appearance (the way they dress) send messages about who they are, how they feel and what they think.

ACTIVITY

How do you come across?

There is a special technique that uses a video camera and monitor to explore the effect you have on your learners, particularly in relation to non-verbal communication. You need another person to help you with this.

- Sit in a chair facing the monitor, while your assistant focuses the video camera on you.
- Your camera operator then invites you to talk about yourself for about four minutes. During the four minutes, the focus of the camera should be changed slowly to include close-ups and angles that concentrate on particular areas of your face and body.
- While you are still looking at yourself on the monitor, your assistant should gently ask the following questions:
  - *Does this person draw your attention?*
  - *Do you dislike what you hear?*
  - *What are your feelings toward him/her?*
- Think about the things that help or hinder your message.
- Does you body language support your message, or does it distract from your message?
- How could you improve your presentation?
- At the end of the exercise, replay the whole video and explore the feelings that the video brought forth in you.

(Source: Coetzee & Jansen, 2007)

Learners often feel accepted or rejected based on what they read in the body language of trainers. Trainers' body language and tone of voice often determine the general classroom atmosphere. Trainers who smile and greet learners in a friendly way make learners feel respected and welcome in the classroom. On the other hand, trainers who are moody and grumpy make learners feel rejected and negatively influence their ability to concentrate on learning tasks. Table 5.13 describes dysfunctional and emotionally intelligent trainer responses to classroom behaviour.

Table 5.13 Dysfunctional and emotionally intelligent trainer responses to classroom behaviour (based on Coetzee & Jansen, 2007)

Dysfunctional behaviours	Emotionally intelligent behaviours
Alienating • Continually stressing conformity • Failing to encourage • Failing to give verbal responses • Listening passively	**Empathic** • Building rapport • Identifying feelings • Being sensitive to emotional needs
Critical • Pointing out inconsistencies • Repeatedly mentioning weaknesses • Belittling	**Supportive** • Acknowledging problems, concerns and feelings • Accepting differences of opinion • Showing understanding • Communicating availability • Committing support • Expressing trust
Directive • Prescribing • Giving orders • Threatening • Failing to provide options • Quoting rules and regulations • Pointing out only one acceptable way	**Exploring** • Asking open questions • Reflecting • Sharing • Probing
Language patterns • "You had better listen to me or I'll kick you out of my class!" • "I'm the boss in this class. If you are not interested in this work, you don't need to attend this class, anyway. I just want to finish this lesson." • "Don't even think of asking questions. Don't waste my time." • "Don't expect from me to remember your names. I have a lot of work to cover." • "Don't try to act smart with me. I don't have time for smart guys."	**Language patterns** • "How are you all feeling today?" • "I really appreciate the effort you've made." • "I'm confident we can achieve these goals." • "What do you think?" • "You really have done a good job, thank you!" • "I am really pleased with what we have accomplished." • "How can we improve the learning process?" • "I really like the idea. It will help us." • "I am really proud of you!" • "Thank you for helping me." • "I appreciate how we all work as a team." • "Now I understand what you have been trying to tell me."

Techniques to encourage positive behaviours (Leatherman, 1990)

- Nod your head affirmatively to encourage learner inputs.
- Voice agreement with learners' constructive inputs.
- Ask the group to comment on points.
- Repeating important points.
- Get learners to repeat or explain statements to the group.
- Ask learners to lead discussions or demonstrate models to the group.
- Smile and make eye contact.
- Listen attentively to questions and inputs from the learners.
- Use positive comments to reinforce learner participation.

Dealing with problem behaviours in the classroom

While learners' inputs, comments and participation are desirable in most instances, some behaviours interfere with the learning process. The facilitator should deal with these behaviours in a timely and efficient manner. Examples of problem behaviours and suggested solutions are set out in Table 5.14.

Table 5.14 Techniques for handling problem behaviours in the classroom (Adapted from Leatherman, 1990)

Learners arriving late or missing sessions
<ul><li>Establish ground rules or individual learning contracts.</li><li>Privately discuss reasons for lateness with the learner.</li><li>Stress the importance of punctuality.</li><li>Offer assistance to the learner.</li><li>Make sure you always start on time.</li></ul>
Challenges to the trainer's credibility
<ul><li>Establish your credibility at the start of training by referring to experience and qualifications.</li><li>Redirect questions to the group or supportive learners.</li><li>Deal with the issues in private.</li><li>Point out that learning is a joint experience that involves all the participants.</li></ul>
Negative comments regarding the course content
<ul><li>Redirect questions to the group.</li><li>Emphasise the positive aspects of the content.</li><li>If the learner already has knowledge and experience in the course, involve them in the presentation.</li><li>If there are mistakes or gaps in the content, make an effort to correct these between sessions.</li></ul>
Undermining the course outside the class
<ul><li>Actively involve the learner in the presentation of the class.</li><li>Confront the learner privately. Express your concern and explain the negative impact.</li><li>Ask the learner what could be done to address his/her concerns.</li></ul>
Learners who dominate the discussions
<ul><li>Tactfully interrupt the learner and redirect to other learners.</li><li>Draw other learners into the discussion by asking them for their inputs.</li><li>Point out to the learner that everyone should have an opportunity to participate.</li></ul>

Individuals who do not participate
• Direct questions at the individual. • Make eye contact. • Give the learner specific tasks to perform. • Positively reinforce any contribution by the learner.
Lack of participation by the group as a whole
• Probe the reasons for non-participation. • Change the nature of the activities (for example, change from a lecture to group activities). • Actively involve the learners in the learning process.
Belligerent attitude or responses
• Let the group handle the learner by asking them for solutions. • Probe the reasons for the learner's behaviour. • Deal with the issue in private. • Appeal to the learner's sense of fairness.
Distracting side discussions
• Set clear ground rules at the beginning of the programme and refer the learner back to these. • Give comments to the group. • Ask the learners who are having discussions on their own to share their ideas. • Stop and wait for the learners to quieten down.
Group becomes sidetracked
• Redirect the learners back to the topic. • Ask questions related to the topic. • Take a break, if it is at an appropriate time.

Creating a conducive learning environment

The classroom environment, or emotional climate, refers to the conditions, circumstances and influences affecting the learning and performance of learners in the classroom. These include the physical conditions of the classroom and the trainer's physical appearance, body language, language patterns, behaviour and attitudes towards learners. The personal values of trainers influence how they treat and interact with their learners. Values are the norms, beliefs, principles, and preferences that determine how people in a particular society, community or family behave and relate to each other (Coetzee & Jansen, 2007).

The values that trainers model through their behaviour create a particular emotional climate. The emotional climate is learners' shared perception of the classroom environment, that is, how they think and feel they are being treated by the facilitator and how they experience the general classroom conditions. The emotional climate can range from warm, welcoming and nurturing to cold and indifferent (Coetzee & Jansen, 2007).

The emotional climate has a significant impact on learners' attitude and willingness to learn. In an emotionally warm emotional climate, learners feel accepted for their uniqueness; their self-esteem is enhanced. Emotionally warm behaviour helps to create an emotional climate that facilitates optimal learning and performance. On the other hand, emotionally cold or distant behaviour slows down facilitation and learning and negatively affects the performance of the trainer and the learners. The distinctive characteristics of emotionally warm and cold behaviour are summarised in Table 5.15.

Trainers with an emotionally warm style are able to create a warm emotional climate. Such an atmosphere is characterised by feelings of mutual goodwill, empathy and cooperation between the trainer and learners. Trainers with a warm style are aware of learners' cognitive and emotional needs and accept and respect learners unconditionally. Furthermore, they show a real interest in learners' well-being through open and honest communication (Coetzee & Jansen, 2007).

Emotionally warm behaviour is linked to emotional intelligence (as discussed in Chapter 2). Research indicates that the ability to manage emotions contributes positively to the quality of social interactions. Individuals who are socially well adapted tend to display emotionally intelligent behaviour. That is, they are aware of their own emotions and how they affect others. Emotionally intelligent people also express their emotions more appropriately and better read and respond to the emotions of others. Emotionally intelligent trainers use their emotional and cognitive presence to monitor the emotional climate and engage in behaviour that facilitates emotional security within themselves and their learners (Coetzee & Jansen, 2007).

Table 5.15 Characteristics of emotionally warm and cold behavioural styles (Coetzee & Jansen, 2007)

Emotionally warm behavioural style	Emotionally cold behavioural style
Shows real interest in the learners, which results in the development of trust and emotional closeness.	Shows emotional indifference, often characterised by an attitude of mistrust and coldness toward learners.
Unconditional acceptance of and respect for learners, which makes them feel safe and sheltered in the classroom context.	Insincerity and disrespect for learners, characterised by superficial, hostile, vindictive, malicious and aggressive behaviour toward learners.
An optimistic and positive attitude with a sense of humour, allowing honest communication between trainer and learners.	Has a negative outlook with closed and secretive behaviour, resulting in an atmosphere of distrust and dishonesty.
Authority exercised in a reasonable, consistent and fair manner, which demonstrates respect for learners.	Authority used to elicit submission inspired by fear and disrespect for the learners. Behaviour typically includes unreasonable and unjust methods to maintain discipline (for example, corporal punishment and abusive language).
Cherishes and embraces the relationship with learners, resulting in feelings of mutual goodwill, empathy and cooperation between the trainer and learners.	Has no concern for the relationship with learners, resulting in disturbed relationships characterised by squabbles and negative criticism.
Has an understanding of and empathy for learners' unique cognitive and emotional development needs.	Lacks understanding of and shows no interest in the unique cognitive and emotional development needs of learners.

Creating an accepting and safe atmosphere

It is important to create a non-critical atmosphere in which learners feels safe and accepted. Optimal learning occurs in an environment where learners feel comfortable to raise opinions, join discussions and experiment. Some strategies to help the learners feel relaxed and comfortable during the learning process include the following:

- Focus on the value of mutual respect between participants. Emphasise that issues should be addressed and that personal attacks are not acceptable.
- Pitch language at a level that is appropriate to the level of the learners. Remember that, although the majority of learning programmes are presented in English, this is often learners' second or even third language.
- Use name boards (on the tables) or name tags. By using names, learners can personalise their interactions with other learners and the facilitator.
- Emphasise that everyone has the right to an opinion. Encourage only constructive criticism that relates to the issues under discussion.

ACTIVITY
Developing a positive learning climate
Think about a training session you would like to present on a favourite topic. How would you ensure that learners will enjoy and learn from the session?

First thoughts
An appropriate starting point for the trainer is to focus on his/her own preferred approach to learning. Where are you in relation to the following statements?
1. "I feel the focus is initially on me and others learn when I show them what to do."
2. "I help others learn. It is okay if I am not in the limelight."

It is no doubt fashionable to be much closer to statement 2 than 1. It is more of a learner-centred approach than the first statement. The occasional inward look can help you to establish what feels right and what is appropriate.

Getting a few basics right
Trainers should ensure that they have prepared everything before the start of the activity. The extent of the trainer's preparation will vary, depending upon the level of experience and willingness to take risks. You will need to think in advance of the activity so that when it starts you feel confident and this is transmitted to the participants. Consider the participants' possible needs and expectations and set out a probable agenda. This may be changed according to the needs of your participants, your own flexibility and your ability and willingness to take risks.

Consider the size of the group. Ideally, the total group size for training sessions is six to 12 participants.

The start
The start can determine the success of your training event. This does not mean that a poor start will automatically lead to disaster. Consider using ice-breakers, and think about the mood you wish to set. Do you want everyone to relax as soon as possible or do you want people to learn under pressure?

Your approach
1. Feelings. Some questions you might ask:

- How am I feeling at the moment?
- How would I feel if I was a participant?
- How do the participants feel?

2. Your behaviour. By being sensitive to the participants' feelings, you can demonstrate empathy. Your behaviour demonstrates that you care for the participants. This is not easy if you feel anxious yourself. Be aware of the effect of your anxiety on others.

3. Your material and how you use it. You will already have considered this at the planning stage. Consider the following:
   - Involve participants at an early stage.
   - Encourage participants to voice their expectations of the training session.
   - Give an indication of the specific outcomes for the training session at an early stage (but not too much, and be prepared to be flexible with the activities).
   - Be prepared to use the 'here and now' method of participants' feelings and experience.
   - Be ready and willing to change direction.
   - Do not work straight through your programme without considering the effect on and needs of the participants.

4. Observe the individuals and their reactions. Use your senses to decide how the individuals or group are developing. Gauge their reactions and feelings. Be sensitive to the participants' needs.

Final thoughts
The learning climate you create is likely to be more significant than all the learning material you have put together. Remember that each group is unique. If you feel frustrated at the rate of progress, do not forget that – even though you might have done 20 similar training sessions – this is the first time for them.

Guidelines for creating an environment conducive to learning (Leatherman, 1990)
- Set out the learning intervention at the start so that the learners know exactly what is expected of them. Deal with the outcomes and how these will be achieved at the beginning of the programme. Revisit outcomes at important points during the learning programme.
- Create a physical environment that is as comfortable as possible for the learners. This includes comfortable chairs, enough working space, comfortable room temperature and sufficient stationery.
- Make sure that all learning support materials are available and working.
- Keep distractions such as noise and visual stimuli to a minimum.
- Make sure there is adequate lighting.
- Make sure that enough learner manuals and other learning support materials are available and that these materials are free from errors.

Arranging the physical learning environment

The venue is an important element of the learning environment. A well-prepared venue gives a professional impression and assists in the transfer of learning. Conversely, a poorly prepared venue has a negative impact on the whole training experience.

ETD practitioners often have to make do with what is available, though, and this is frequently less than desirable. But creating a physical environment that is conducive to training is only part of the job. Trainers can prepare the most comfortable and well equipped training venue possible, but if their learners do not feel safe in an environment that encourages participation and learning, the training programme will fail.

Issues that a trainer will need to consider when deciding on the layout of the venue are:
• the number of learners;
• the training method;
• the physical layout of the venue; and
• the available resources.

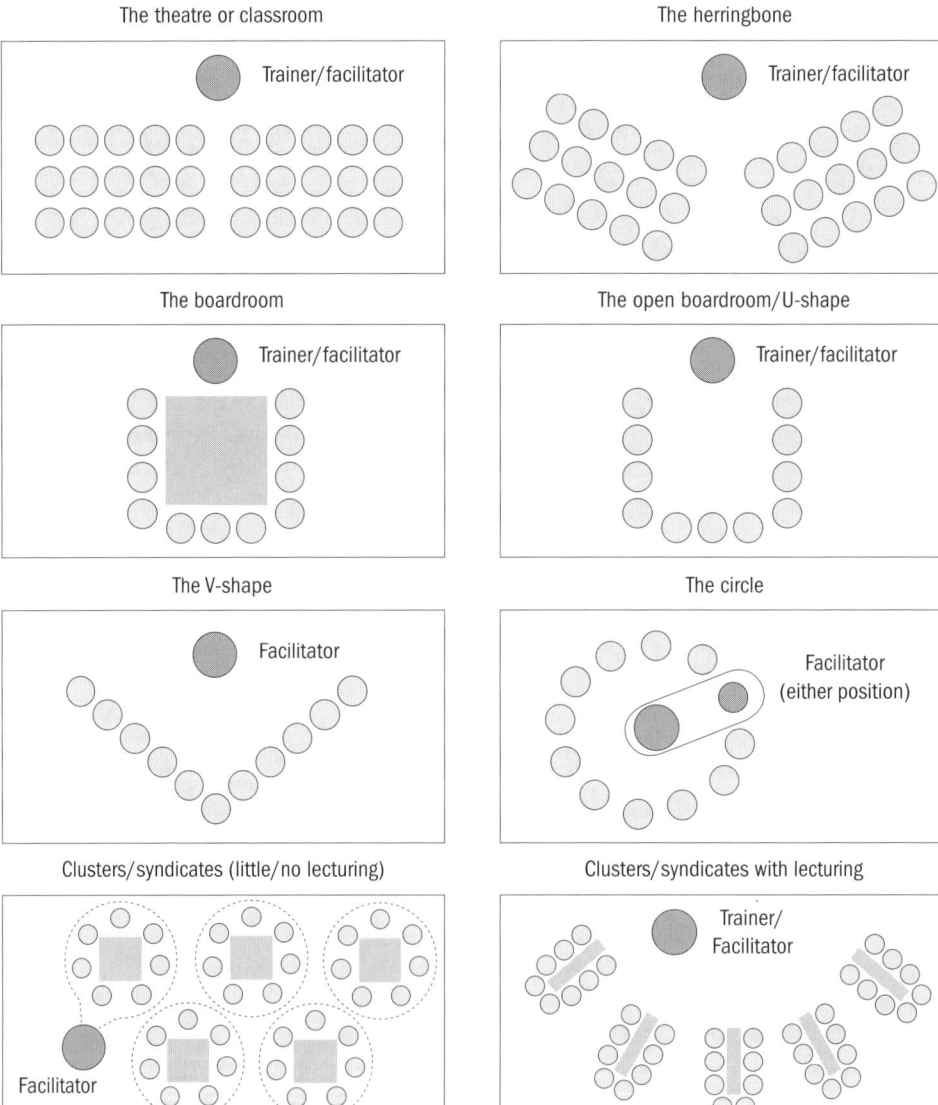

Figure 5.4 The layout of training venues

The training venue can be arranged in a number of ways. The trainer can use different layouts in the course of a training programme. In other words, the layout of the venue can be rearranged to suit the various outcomes of the programme. Different layouts are used for different purposes; the various options are shown in Figure 5.4.

The theatre or classroom

This is the traditional layout for learning. The trainer stands in front and learners are arranged in rows. It is suitable for large groups of learners where the mode of instruction is a lecture or presentation. The interaction between the trainer and learners is limited to questions and answers.

The herringbone

This is similar to the theatre or classroom. The main difference is that the rows are angled diagonally, which allows for greater visibility between learners.

The boardroom

Learners are arranged around a large table or a number of smaller tables put together. This layout is appropriate for small to medium-size groups where interaction is required. It is used in training where learning is facilitated.

The open boardroom or U-shape

Similar to the boardroom, the U-shape leaves a space in the centre where the trainer can move around. This layout works with or without tables and it allows for greater interaction between the trainer and the learners. It is also easy for the trainer to inspect the progress of learners in written exercises.

The V-shape

The V-shape is similar to the U-shape. It can also be used with or without tables. The main advantage is that visibility problems are minimised.

The circle

Seats are arranged in a circle. This format is particularly useful for discussions and debriefings. It also has the advantage of putting the learners on an equal footing with each other.

Clusters/syndicates

Learners are placed together in small groups (normally six to eight members). The groups are separated from one another and placed in various parts of the room. The placing of the groups will depend on the type of training. If there is little or no lecturing, they may be placed randomly. A variation of the U-shape can be used where lecturing occurs. This format is useful if there are a number of group exercises and learning is predominantly facilitated. The trainer can move freely between the groups. Attention must also be paid to the age, race and gender composition of the groups.

Factors to be considered when choosing the physical environment (Michalak & Yager, 1979)
- Arrange seats to ensure maximum visibility of the trainer, while enabling interaction between the learners.
- Provide adequate lighting, preferably natural light.
- The general layout of the training room. Always lay out training materials and the chairs and tables beforehand. Make sure there are no papers or other materials lying around.
- Minimise noise and visual distractions.
- Regulate the temperature in the venue to ensure that it is comfortable for the learners.
- Schedule training and adequate break times. When you break and for how long will generally depend on the type of content and training methods being used. Rather let the training process guide you than rigidly sticking to times for breaks.
- If food is provided, select light meals and snacks that will not sit heavily and induce sleepiness.

Table 5.16 *Quality checklist for the training environment*

The training venue	
Venue booked	
Enough syndicate/breakaway venues available	
Venue laid out properly	
Signs up to indicate to the learners where the training will take place	
Adequate toilet facilities that work properly	
Distractions minimised	
Contact details of person responsible for the venue to assist with problems	
Equipment	
All equipment required available and working properly	
Materials	
Name boards for tables and name plates/stickers for shirts	
Sufficient quantities of learning materials	
Sufficient quantities of consumables such as flip chart paper, notepads and pens	
Physical needs	
Meals and refreshments	
Cold water and glasses on each table	
Comfortable sleeping arrangements for learners (if relevant)	
Facilities for the learners to complete self-study work	

Principles of classroom training

Given the extent and complexity of training delivery, the success of effective classroom training delivery depends on the ETD practitioner's flexible use, revision and adaptation of the following set of general learning facilitation principles (Yelon, 1992).

Meaningfulness

When learners find a topic personally relevant, the topic is considered meaningful to them. When learners can associate a new skill or a new idea with their experience, interests, values or aspirations, it is meaningful to them.

Assumed learning

Learners are said to have the assumed learning (knowledge and skills) for a task when they have mastered all contributing and related basic knowledge and skills. When learners have the assumed learning, they can readily understand instruction for the next level of skills and can learn the new skills without remediation.

ACTIVITY
Study the unit standard in Appendix 1.
• What is the assumed learning that learners need to have before they attempt to master the outcomes specified in the unit standard?

Open communication

Learners must know what they are to learn, how they are to learn, and how they will be assessed before they put their attention and energy into learning. Learning facilitators/trainers must tell learners everything that will help them to focus their attention.

Essential content

Time is a precious resource in learning facilitation. There is always more content than time to learn. One way to be efficient in learning facilitation is to select and give priority to essential content (the 'must know' content elements).

Provision of learning support material

Learners understand messages more quickly and recall them more completely and accurately when learning facilitators use mechanisms that simplify and organise complex content and connect new ideas to old ones. In the design phase, ETD practitioners create learner support material, and in the delivery phase they use the support material. During explanations, demonstrations and practice, learning facilitators provide several types of learning support material:
• mnemonics, to recall a list of ideas and steps;
• flow diagrams,
• decision trees or drawings, to show the path to take in a task;
• highlighted examples on slides or transparencies;
• animated PowerPoint slides or DVDs, using arrows, colours, stars and subtitles to focus attention; and
• checklists, to summarise the qualities of an acceptable performance.

Novelty

People cannot pay constant attention in a classroom situation. ETD practitioners incorporate novelty into the learning facilitation process by varying the format, content and style of learning support materials. In the delivery phase, learning facilitators vary what they do, what they say, and how they say it. They change volume, tone or pace when they want to gain and direct attention to important points. They gesture, move and continue to make moderate changes to maintain learners' attention for the duration of a training session. Learning facilitators use humorous stories and novel experiences to focus learners' attention.

Modelling

Learners can gain the most from practice if, in addition to listening to an explanation, they can observe a good demonstration. Learners are likely to imitate the demonstrated performance if they pay attention to the demonstration, if they perceive all the steps, and if they commit the steps to memory before practice. Therefore, demonstrations should capture attention, focus on the important aspects of each step, and create a mental image of the skill. Behaviour modelling is based on social learning theory, which says that people learn by observing others (discussed in Chapter 2) (Cascio & Aguinis, 2005).

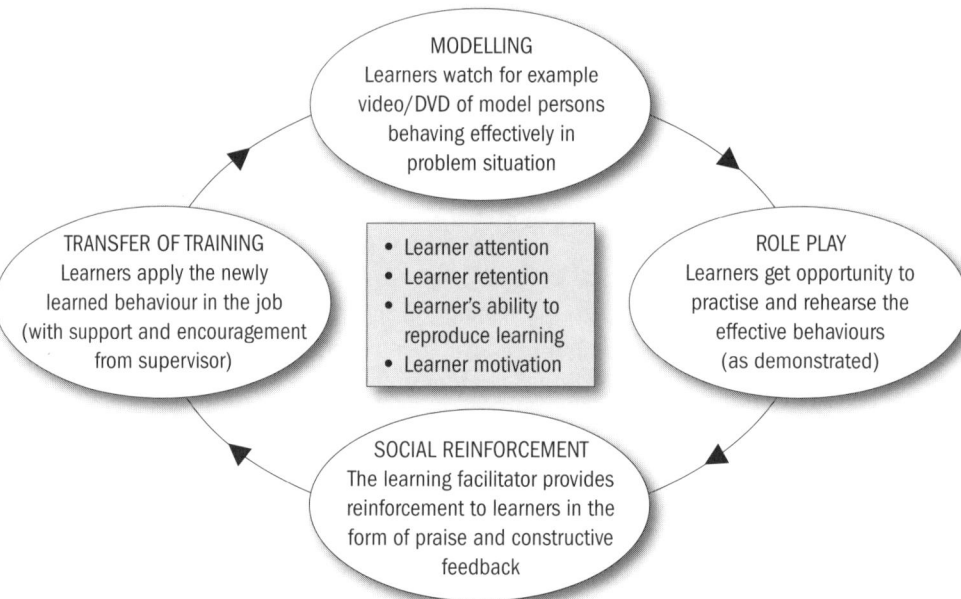

Figure 5.5 *Principles of behaviour modelling (based on Aamodt, 2007; Cascio & Aguinis, 2005)*

Active and appropriate practice

ETD practitioners build in active practice to ensure that learners gain applied competence over learning outcomes. Learning facilitators apply the principle of active and appropriate practice by giving each learner the opportunity to practise the whole skill in a way that matches the performance required on the job. Practice must be challenging. It should allow learners to go beyond previous levels of competency in each practice set. Practice must also be distributed to promote retention and reduce fatigue and error. Learning facilitators therefore schedule skills practice in short sessions over time, and proceed from basic to advanced. Learning facilitators encourage learners to provide their own feedback (as they would on the job). When actual practice is inconvenient or inappropriate, learning facilitators teach learners how to relax and visualise the correct performance.

When learners are given the opportunity to practise far beyond the point where they perform a task correctly several times, the task becomes second nature (this is discussed in more detail in Chapter 2). This is known as overlearning. For some tasks, such as those that must be performed infrequently and under great stress (for example, CPR performed to save a patient's life), overlearning is critical. It is less important in jobs where workers practise their skills on a daily basis (such as mechanics, technicians and language editors). The advantages of overlearning include:

- an increase in the length of time that learned material will be retained;
- learning becomes more reflexive, so tasks become automatic with continued practice; and
- learning is effective for cognitive and physical tasks (Cascio & Aguinis, 2005).

Goal setting

Teaching learners to set goals for their learning helps to improve their motivation and their performance. When learners set explicit, challenging goals, they become highly motivated and committed to the training. They put in greater effort and learn more efficiently (Cascio & Aguinis, 2005). The effects of goal setting on performance can be enhanced even more by explaining to learners how to work on a task, and why the goal and task are important.

Pleasant conditions

People naturally want to learn. When people learn in a comfortable setting, they associate the good feelings they have with the subject and the process. From then on, the subject is associated with pleasant feelings. Learning facilitators provide pleasant conditions during all phases of learning facilitation. Before training, learning facilitators establish a pleasant climate by being friendly and showing interest during interviews. They maintain a pleasant atmosphere during training by attending to the appearance, location and comfort of the classroom. Learning facilitators also create a safe or emotionally warm atmosphere by respecting and supporting learners in their learning process.

Pleasant consequences

To learn from practice, learners need to know how well they have performed. To be willing to perform again, learners must feel confident. Learning facilitators apply the principle of pleasant consequences by providing objective feedback through the use of checklists. They give complete feedback about what was performed correctly, what needs further development, what should have been done, and how to improve. To enhance confidence and self-esteem, learning facilitators add verbal encouragement, emphasise positive qualities of performance, and point out positive consequences of proper performance. Learning facilitators also encourage self-assessment by asking learners to review their own performance before anyone else does. When commenting on an inadequate performance, learning facilitators refer only to the performance and its consequences; they do not comment on a learner's personality.

Knowledge of results (feedback)

If learners know their results or learning achievements, they can use the information to correct mistakes. Learners need to know why they have not achieved the learning outcomes of a programme or task, and how they can correct the behaviour in the future. Learners also need reinforcement. Knowledge of results may be intrinsic (stemming directly from the performance of the task itself) or extrinsic (communicated by an outside individual). It may be qualitative (for example, "that new ad is quite pleasing to the eye"), quantitative (for example, "move the lever two inches down"), informative (for example, "that new machine has just arrived") or evaluative (for example, "you did a good job on that report – it was clear and brief") (Cascio & Aguinis, 2005).

Transfer of learning

Transfer of training refers to learners' ability to apply the behaviours and competencies learned in training to the job itself. Transfer may be positive (for example, improve job performance), negative (that is, hinder job performance) or neutral (Cascio & Aguinis, 2005). To maximise positive transfer, ETD practitioners should consider doing the following before, during and after training (Machin, 2002):

- Ensure that the work climate is positive (for example management support or on-the-job support).
- Maximise the similarity between the training situation and the job situation. Provide a strong link between training content and job content.
- Provide learners with as many opportunities as possible to experience and practise the tasks, concepts or skills being taught.
- Ensure that learners thoroughly understand the principles being taught, particularly in jobs that require the application of principles to solve problems.
- In the context of team-based training, transfer is maximised when:
  - teams have open, unrestricted access to information;
  - membership includes diverse job functions and administrative backgrounds; and
  - a team has sufficient members to draw on to accomplish its activities.
  - Ensure that what is learned in training is used and rewarded on the job.

Table 5.17 Barriers to the transfer of learning (Coetzee, 2006a)

Barriers to the transfer of learning	Description
Training takes place in artificial conditions	Training conditions cannot accurately reflect the reality of the job situation. Irrespective of how much the facilitator tries to recreate the actual situation (through scenarios, role play or simulations), the training venue, the participants, the learning tasks and other variables will be different.
The training setting is a safe and controlled learning environment	Learners are able to disclose and exchange ideas freely, without cynicism or personal attacks. The facilitator manages conflict and poor interpersonal skills. The workplace is different. Training allows for mistakes and failure. In real-life situations, mistakes often have immediate consequences and there is little opportunity to try again.
Learners were not really committed	Learners may not be totally committed to the ideas and strategies developed on the course and may quickly slip back into the old way of doing things.
There is a lack of opportunity to practise acquired skills	If learners do not immediately have the opportunity to practise new competencies in the job situation, they will find it difficult to relate the training to their jobs.

Barriers to the transfer of learning	Description
There is no direct support for the transfer of learning	The opportunity to apply newly acquired knowledge and skills may not arise immediately. Learners' efforts may not be supported by managers, friends or colleagues. Others may persist with old ways of thinking and hinder progress.

Self-management to maintain changes in behaviour

Teaching learners to monitor their own behaviour reduces the likelihood of relapse, or falling back on previous behaviours (Cascio & Aguinis, 2005). The first step is to make learners aware of the relapse process itself. Thereafter, learning facilitators ask learners to identify situations that are likely to sabotage their attempts to maintain the new learning.

For example, in a study designed to control the abuse of sick leave (Frayne & Latham cited in Cascio & Aguinis, 2005), learners listed family problems, incompatibility with supervisors or coworkers and transportation problems as the biggest reasons for using sick leave. Then learners were taught to monitor their own behaviour by recording their own attendance, the reason for missing a day of work, and subsequent steps to get to work. Learners did this using charts and diaries. In addition, learners were also taught coping skills to increase a feeling of mastery and to decrease the probability of relapse. Learners identified their own reinforcers (for example, self-praise, purchasing a gift) and punishers (a disliked activity such as cleaning the garage) to administer if they achieved or failed to achieve their goals. This system of self-management increased the responsibility of learners and their attendance significantly increased.

Adaptive guidance

Adaptive guidance is particularly relevant in technology-based learning. It guides learners about future directions they should take in sequencing study and practice to improve their performance (Bell & Kozlowski, 2002). For example, in Internet-based training, learners can customise the material they work with, determine the sequence of learning and control the amount of time they spend on a particular topic. Adaptive guidance includes evaluative information (formative assessment activities and feedback) to help each learner evaluate his/her progress and individualised suggestions about what the learner should study and practise. Adaptive guidance improves the acquisition of basic knowledge and performance capabilities early in training. It also improves the acquisition of strategic knowledge and performance skills later in training. Adaptive guidance develops the capacity to retain and adapt skills in a more difficult and complex situation (Cascio & Aguinis, 2005).

Managing classroom training

ETD practitioners apply learning facilitation principles to the design and delivery of training. Managing training delivery in the classroom requires that the trainer effectively performs the following functions:
- present lectures;
- facilitate groups (dyads, small groups and large groups);
- administer self-instructed learning;

- follow customised procedures;
- apply principles of learning and learning facilitation;
- deal with easy and difficult learners;
- answer questions;
- create schedules covering all learning facilitation elements;
- account for possible interference;
- allow time to work, practise, think and relax;
- identify, prepare and inform learners;
- fill out the proper forms for training;
- plan and create a comfortable environment;
- choose and control venues, rooms, facilities, furniture and air temperature;
- secure and maintain learning materials, supplies, equipment and staff;
- assess, evaluate and certify learners;
- evaluate the learning programme;
- report outcomes and results;
- implement actions to improve learning facilitation (Yelon, 1992).

ETD practitioners in their role as learning facilitators or trainers have several responsibilities regarding managing classroom training. These include reading and reviewing learning materials before the start of a training session; preparing training session activities; checking the classroom and seating; arranging for equipment; preparing learning materials and learning support materials; announcing the programme/training session; and reflecting on the learning.

Table 5.18 Responsibilities in managing classroom training (Coetzee & Jansen, 2007a)

Responsibility	Description
Preparing training session activities	• Select the activities that will be used and modify them, if necessary, to meet the needs of target audience. • Plan the agenda for the training session, including the learning outcomes, schedule and time for breaks. • Arrange for refreshments.
Check the room and seating	• Reserve a room that is large enough to arrange seats in a way that is conducive to group discussion. • Ensure that there are enough comfortable seats.
Arrange for equipment	• Arrange for a working overhead projector, screen and extra transparencies and markers if needed (or for a laptop computer, data projector and screen). • Provide a flip chart, Prestik, markers and an eraser for a whiteboard. • Arrange for a working video machine and monitor if video material will be used. • When using electronic hardware such as laptop computers and video machines, make sure that you have all the plugs, adapters and leads you need for the machines. Check that the machines work, and check that the electrical outlets in the room are in working order.
Prepare materials	• Print handouts and reading material for all participants. • Comply with copyright laws for reading material. • Prepare overhead transparencies.

Responsibility	Description
Announce the programme	• Give sufficient notice and clearly specify the date, time, and location of the training sessions. Remind participants to bring along course material, pencils, pens and notepads.
Reflect on learning	• Reflect on the questions or issues that are raised during the training session. Record personal thoughts in a journal. Conclude each training session with an entry on any new insights on how to improve the learning facilitation process.

ACTIVITY

You were requested to deliver a learning programme called Managing Conflict in the Work Situation, using classroom training. The following outcomes have been formulated for the learning programme:

After completing the learning programme, learners should be able to:
• Describe the phases of conflict.
• Identify the different processes involved in the management of conflict.
• Apply the conflict management skills in an interpersonal conflict situation.

Questions
• Which characteristics would you need to measure in a target group analysis? Explain why these characteristics are important in this instance.
• How would you arrange the training venue? What are the different factors that you need to consider?
• How would you create a positive learning environment?
• How would you facilitate learning to optimise the learning process and ensure the transfer of learning to the workplace?
• Select one of the outcomes and apply the various stages of the experiential learning cycle. Explain what you would do in each of the steps to optimise the learning facilitation process.
• While conducting the training, you encounter the following problems:
  - learners who feel that the programme is a waste of time;
  - a learner who disrupts the class and dominates the discussions; and
  - a number of learners who do not participate in the discussions and activities.

Explain how you would deal with each of these problems.
• Assume that the learners are middle managers with a great deal of experience. What would be the most effective training delivery methods? Give reasons for your answer.
• Which learning support materials would be particularly useful in the delivery of the programme? Give reasons for your answer.

Key terms

- Blended learning
- Classroom climate
- Classroom layout
- Classroom training
- Learner-centred delivery methods
- Physical learning environment
- Learning facilitation
- Learning facilitation process
- On-the-job training
- Technology-based learning
- Trainer-centred delivery methods
- Training delivery
- Training principles
- Transfer of learning

Review and discussion questions

1. Why is classroom training such a popular training delivery method in the workplace? Which other delivery methods can be used to train people in the workplace?
2. How would you explain the elements and characteristics of classroom training to an inexperienced trainer?
3. How do the characteristics of learners and trainers influence the learning facilitation process?
4. How can trainers ensure the effective transfer of learning in the workplace? What are the barriers to the transfer of learning?
5. Why is it important for ETD practitioners (in their role as learning facilitators) to apply principles of learning? How would you explain these principles to an inexperienced trainer?
6. What can trainers do to create a positive learning environment in the classroom? How do learners' and trainers' behaviours influence the learning facilitation process?
7. Why is the physical layout of a classroom important? What are the various options available to trainers?
8. Why is it important for trainers to be skilful in learning facilitation? Which skills will help trainers to optimise the learning facilitation process?
9. What are the responsibilities of trainers in managing the delivery of their learning programmes?

Suggested reading

Blanchard, P.N. & Thacker, J.W. (2007). *Effective training: Systems, strategies, and practices* (3rd ed.). Upper Saddle River: Pearson Prentice Hall.

Buckley, R. & Caple, J. (2004). *The theory and practice of training* (5th ed.). London: Kogan Page.

Cameron, E. (1998). *Facilitation made easy*. London: Kogan Page.

Cassidy, M.F. & Cassidy, M.M. (2006). Principles and practice of work-group performance. In J.A. Pershing. *Handbook of human performance technology: Principles, practices, and potential*. (3rd ed.). San Francisco: Pfeiffer.

Coetzee, M. & Jansen, C.A. (2007). *Emotional intelligence in the classroom: The secret of happy teachers*. Cape Town: Juta.

Erasmus, B.J. & van Dyk, P.S. (2003). *Training management in South Africa* (3rd ed.). Cape Town: Oxford University Press.

Goldstein, I.L. & Ford, J.K. (2002). *Training in organisations: Needs assessment, development, and evaluation*. Belmont: Wordsworth.

Laird, D. (1985). *Approaches to training and development* (2nd ed.). Reading: Addison-Wesley.

Lambert, D. & The Diagram Group. (1996). *Body language*. London: Harper Collins.

Leatherman, D. (1990). *The training trilogy: Facilitation skills*. Amherst: Human Resource Development Press.

Michalak, D.F. & Yager, E.I.G. (1979). *Making the training process work*. New York: Harper and Roe.

Molenda, M. & Russell, J.D. (2006). Instruction as an intervention. In J.A. Pershing (ed.) *Handbook of human performance technology: Principles, practices and potential*. San Francisco: Pfeiffer.

Nadler, L. (1982). *Designing training programmes: The critical events model*. Reading: Addison Wesley.

Newstrom, J.W. & Lengnick-Hall, M.L. (1991). One size does not fit all. *Training and Development*, 45(6), 43-46, 48.

Rae, L. (1994). *How to design and introduce training and development programmes*. London: McGraw-Hill.

Robinson, D.G. & Robinson, J.C. (1989). *Training for impact: How to link training to business needs and measure the results*. San Francisco: Jossey-Bass.

Swart, J., Mann, C., Brown, S. & Price, A. (2005). *Human resource development: Strategy and tactics*. Oxford: Elsevier Butterworth-Heinemann.

Thiagarajan, S. (1999). Team activities for learning and performance. In H.D. Stolovich & E.J. Keeps. (eds.) *Handbook of human performance technology: Improving individual and organisational performance worldwide* (2nd ed.). San Francisco: Jossey-Bass.

Summary

The effective delivery of training in the workplace depends on a number of factors considered in the design of a learning programme. Design and delivery decisions are mostly influenced by the characteristics of the target group and the group dynamics during the learning process. This chapter explored classroom training and on-the-job training as the most common methods to deliver training in the workplace context. These two methods are often blended with programmed-instruction and technology-based training approaches to enhance the transfer of learning to the workplace.

Learning facilitation was examined as a delivery strategy that deliberately involves the learners and maximises their input and importance in the learning process. Trainers apply principles of learning facilitation to create a learning environment conducive to learning and to ensure optimal transfer of learning in the workplace. Managing the delivery of learning programmes effectively is crucial in helping learners achieve the outcomes of a learning programme. Chapter 6 examines the next phase in the Training Cycle, namely the assessment of learners' achievements.

The mediocre trainer tells. The good trainer explains.
The superior trainer demonstrates. The great trainer inspires.

CHAPTER 6

KIRU TRUMAN

Assessment and moderation in ETD

"Outcomes-based education and training create learning and assessment opportunities that involve applying skills in real-life contexts rather than reproducing facts or ideas. This includes the performance of complex tasks that lead to real and value-adding products or solutions in the workplace."

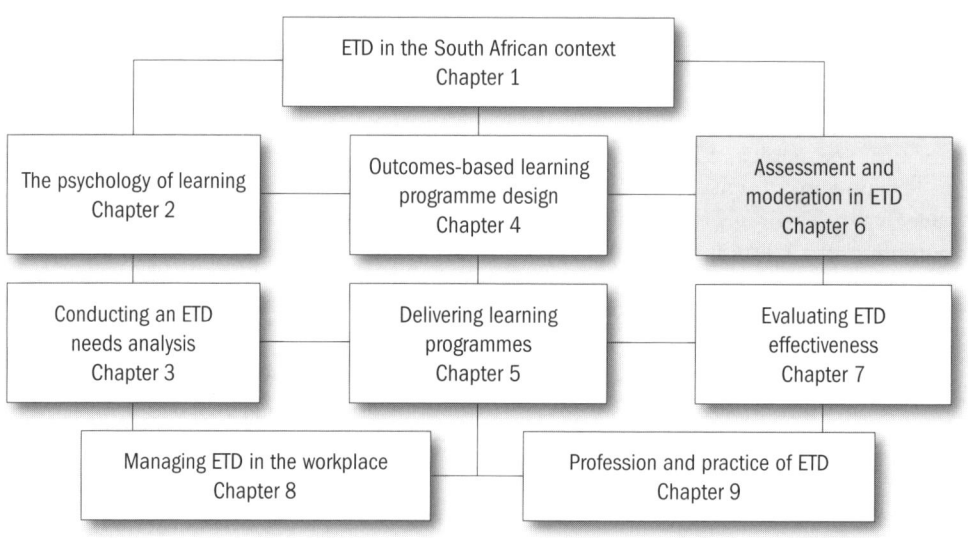

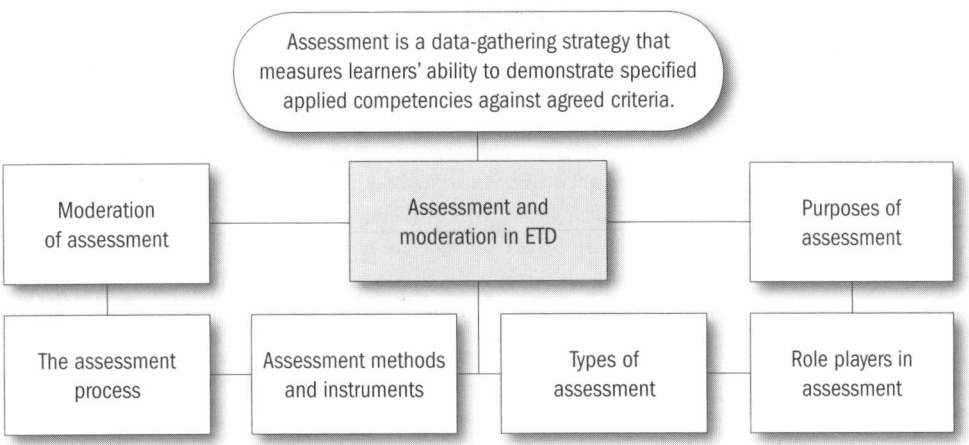

Key points of assessment and moderation in ETD
- Assessment and moderation of learning achievements are significant elements of outcomes-based ETD.
- Valid and reliable assessment procedures, methods and instruments are required to measure whether learners have achieved the learning outcomes of a learning programme.
- Assessors must be qualified subject matter experts who are registered with the relevant ETQA.
- Outcomes-based assessment assesses learners' ability to combine foundational, practical and reflexive competencies with critical cross-field outcomes, and apply these in real-life (practical) contexts or for a defined purpose.
- Moderation is the action of assuring that assessment practices comply with SAQA/ETQA quality requirements.

After studying this chapter, you should be able to:
- Explain the purposes of assessment and moderation in the context of outcomes-based education and training.
- Identify the various role players in the assessment process.
- Discuss the various types of assessment and their uses in the assessment process.
- Evaluate the strengths and weaknesses of various assessment methods and instruments.
- Discuss the various steps in the assessment process.
- Explain the functions and purposes of the assessment plan and assessment guide.
- Explain the requirements for assessors.
- Explain the purpose of moderation in assessment.

Outcomes-based ETD focuses on the achievement of learning outcomes. Assessment and moderation of learning achievements are therefore significant elements of outcomes-based ETD. Accreditation of ETD providers is especially dependent on the quality of their assessment and moderation practices. Valid and reliable assessment procedures are required to measure whether learners achieve the learning outcomes defined for their particular learning programme. As discussed in Chapter 4, assessment is the fourth phase in the Training Cycle. It is an integral part of all ETD planning and design. Assessment procedures should therefore give a clear indication of what learners are intended to learn and achieve. Assessment methods need to be flexible and fair, and should be designed to match the learning outcomes learners are striving to achieve (Van der Horst & McDonald, 1997).

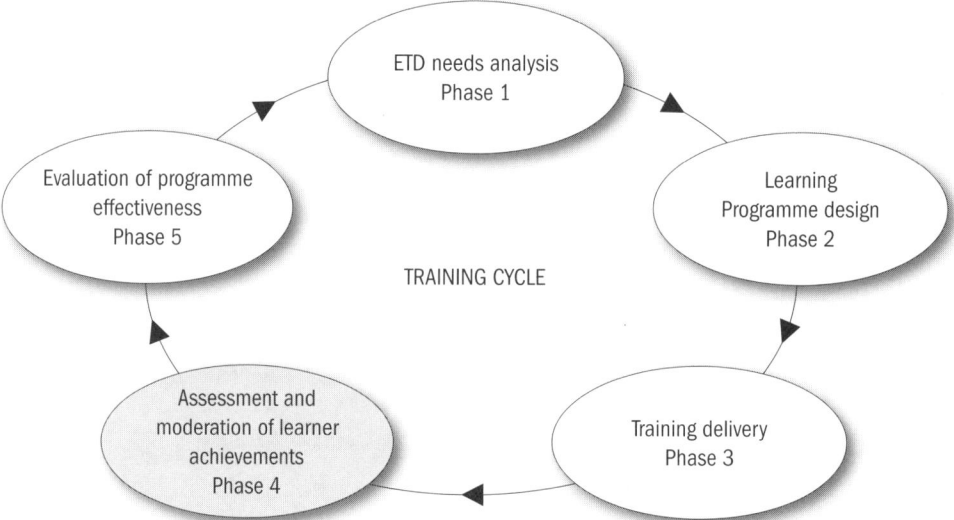

Figure 6.1 *The training cycle*

This chapter sets out the national requirements for outcomes-based assessment and moderation. The functions, principles, types and methodology of assessment are discussed. Sound assessment and moderation practices are tools to ensure that learning programmes lead to measurable outcomes that add value for stakeholders and learners.

Purposes of assessment

SAQA (2001) defines assessment as a structured process in which evidence of performance is gathered and evaluated against agreed criteria. Put simply, assessment is a process that a qualified and registered assessor follows to collect evidence of a learner's learning achievements. Assessment is a data-gathering strategy for measuring knowledge, skills, behaviour or performance, values and attitudes. Assessors use the data gained from the assessment of collected evidence to make informed judgements about learners' competence. In outcomes-based ETD, the evidence is assessed against national standards.

Learning is no longer something that is 'done to' the learner, but something in which the learner is actively involved. As such, the role of the assessor has changed from that of gatekeeper (who uses assessment to prevent learners from developing further) to that of supportive guide (who has the success of the learner at heart). The goal of assessment in outcomes-based ETD is to give learners access to further learning (SAQA, 2000a).

Assessment provides ways to assess the current skills and knowledge of a learner. Assessment also helps to identify further training needs by determining learners' current level of competence. Used appropriately by qualified individuals, assessment can assist in the recruitment and selection of job candidates and can be used to monitor employees' performance.

However, the concept of assessment is relatively new to most organisations. It requires the support of the organisation's management team. Assessment can be costly and time consuming if it is not managed and supported at the appropriate levels.

Outcomes-based assessment is sometimes referred to as authentic assessment. It is the measurement of complex performances and higher-order thinking skills in real-life contexts. Authentic assessment requires learners to demonstrate complex tasks rather than individual skills practised in isolation. This requires a holistic approach to measuring learning achievements (Van der Horst & McDonald, 1997).

The main purpose of assessment is to measure learning outcomes. Additional purposes are to improve learning facilitation, the curriculum, learning programme design and conditions for learning (Van der Horst & McDonald, 1997). Assessment is also used to encourage learners through the feedback they receive. Learners need the feedback that assessment provides: information about their learning and further development, information about their understanding, and information about their accomplishments (Freiberg & Driscoll, 1996).

Assessment will only improve learning if it provides an overall picture of what learners know and are able to do. Assessment should always respect learners' different ways of understanding. Furthermore, sound assessment practice should suggest actions that ETD practitioners can take to enhance the development of their learners and the quality of their learning programmes. ETD practitioners have a broader range of assessment techniques available to them than ever before to accomplish these goals. Using these techniques requires an understanding of assessment goals and procedures for constructing assessments, and criteria for judging and improving the quality of assessments.

Role players in assessment

As shown in Table 6.1, various role players are involved in the assessment process. Not all of these role players are involved at the same time, but it is important to understand their roles and responsibilities within the assessment process.

Table 6.1 Role players in assessment (SAQA, 2001)

Role player	Roles and responsibilities
Assessor	• An assessor must be registered with the relevant ETQA and must be a subject matter expert. • Plan and prepare for the assessment by reviewing the assessment requirements against the standard being assessed. • Prepare the candidate and inform the relevant role players involved in the assessment process. • Conduct the assessment in accordance with the assessment plans and instructions. • Evaluate the evidence and make an assessment decision in accordance with the assessment criteria and guidelines. • Provide developmental feedback and support to the learner. • Record the assessment results in accordance with the organisation's quality management systems (policies, procedures and practices in ETD management, planning and delivery). • Review the assessment to ensure that strengths and weaknesses in the learning programme design and process are captured and implemented in future assessments.
Learner/candidate	• The learner (or candidate) is the person whose knowledge, skills and performance are to be assessed against a particular standard, outcome or criteria. • Provide the assessor with as much evidence as possible of competence of the relevant assessment criteria.
Moderator	• A moderator needs to be registered with the relevant ETQA. • Ensure consistency and quality of assessments. • Ensure that the choice of evidence required and the methods chosen for the assessment meet the assessment criteria of the unit standard. • Sample various assessments by different assessors to ensure that the quality of the assessments is maintained within the organisation. • Conduct regular meetings with assessors to ensure that the principles and process of assessments are maintained.
Designers and developers	• Design and develop assessment guides and tools to be used in an assessment.
Witness or independent assessor	• Ensure objectivity of the assessment process.
Workplace supervisor or manager	• Support the learner throughout the assessment process. • Ensure that the assessment does not disrupt the learner's obligations in the workplace.

Assessor competence

According to SAQA (2001), assessors should have technical and/or occupational expertise related to the field of learning that will be assessed. In general, all assessors should:

- be registered against the national generic assessors' unit standard. (Appendix 1 on page 350 is an example of the generic unit standard for assessors);
- know exactly what the unit standard or learning outcome expects learners to achieve;
- have subject matter and/or occupational expertise;
- have evaluative expertise;
- understand the types of assessment that are appropriate to their field and to the NQF level being assessed;
- understand the language, or jargon, of the field they are assessing;
- keep up to date with developments in the field;
- know the curriculum;
- get to know the trainers through regular contact, and provide them with detailed feedback;
- consider the rights and special needs of learners;
- ensure that learners know what is expected of them;
- treat learners with respect and sensitivity;
- demonstrate a broad understanding of outcomes-based assessment and the NQF.

Assessors also need to demonstrate planning, administrative and management skills. They need to manage assessment documentation and systems in a reliable, efficient and secure manner. Furthermore, assessors need good interpersonal skills and must communicate effectively with learners. The assessor must therefore be an excellent listener and observer. The assessor should also have questioning, feedback and evaluation skills. The learner needs to know that:
- the assessment is fair;
- the assessor acts with integrity;
- the assessor maintains confidentiality;
- the assessment is conducted according to the principles of good assessment;
- the assessor is working on the basis of a relationship built on trust; and
- the assessor has the learner's best interests at heart.

The rights and special needs of learners

All assessment candidates have certain rights. Learners should, as far as possible, be assessed in their first language. Chapter 1, Section 6 of the South African Constitution states:
- *The official languages of the Republic are Sepedi, Sesotho, Setswana, siSwati, Tshivenda, Xitsonga, Afrikaans, English, isiNdebele, isiXhosa and isiZulu.*
- *Recognising the historically diminished use and status of the indigenous languages of our people, the state must take practical and positive measures to elevate the status and advance the use of these languages.*

Chapter 2, Section 29 of the Bill of Rights deals with language of instruction and states the following:
Everyone has the right to receive education in the official language or languages of their choice in public educational institutions where reasonably practicable. In order to ensure the effective access to, and implementation of, this right, the state must consider all reasonable educational alternatives, including single medium institutions, taking into account:

- *equity;*
- *practicability; and*
- *the need to redress the results of past racially discriminatory laws and practices.*

It is worth noting that Section 29 of the Bill of Rights is subject to certain internal limitations: a learner may receive instruction in a language of his/her choice to the extent that it is "reasonably practicable".

These legislative provisions give learners the right to determine the languages of their teaching and assessment. It is important that the organisation's quality management and assessment policies take this into account. The rights of learners should be respected as far as possible. Learners also need information such as the following:
- Learners should know how the assessment process works; they may not be pressured into being assessed when they are not ready.
- Learners may withhold past results.
- Learners have a right to an impartial observer.
- Learners have a right to appeal the assessment decision and should know the procedure to follow if they wish to appeal.
- Learners have a right to an interpreter, where appropriate.
- Learners must know to which qualification the assessment will lead, and should know how to further their learning on completion of the qualification.

Learners' special needs vary from matters related to the work environment to issues that affect the individual learner. These are some of the barriers to assessment:
- special permission is needed for an assessment to take place in a particular area;
- a noisy environment;
- the learner has poor hearing or vision;
- the learner is in a wheelchair;
- the learner is shy, ill or tired;
- the learner is experiencing personal problems that affect concentration; and
- the learner needs special apparatus for the assessment to take place.

The assessor should consider all the rights and special needs of all learners if the assessment is to be fair, reliable and sufficient.

Types of assessment

Van der Horst and McDonald (1997: 172) differentiate between various types of assessment:
- Diagnostic assessment (or pre-testing) is a measure of the learner's prior knowledge, skills, attitudes and values.
- Input-based assessment uses tests and exams and prioritises content recall.
- Norm-referenced assessment compares the learner's performance with the performance of other learners.
- Criterion-referenced assessment occurs when learners' achievements are assessed against a set of external criteria (such as those in a unit standard).
- Formative assessment helps learners to improve their performance, maximise their learning and reflect on and improve their own learning. This type of assessment forms and shapes learning.

- Summative assessment is a summary of the learner's performance. All forms of assessment are added together to sum up acquired competencies at the end of the learning unit, programme, term or year.
- Evaluative assessment compares and summarises information about learner achievements. It is used to assist in curriculum development and evaluate teaching and learning practices.

In outcomes-based education and training, ETD practitioners use an integrated assessment approach that involves mainly four main kinds of assessment. These are diagnostic, formative, summative and evaluative assessment. This means that, as assessors, ETD practitioners have to make assessment decisions before, during and after their learning facilitation (Coetzee, 2007).

Diagnostic assessment

Diagnostic assessment is usually conducted before or at the beginning of a learning session. This form of assessment provides the learning facilitator with valuable planning information. Informal and formal methods are used (in the form of questions) to assess the learners' entry levels. Formal diagnostic assessments are scheduled and structured. A commonly used formal diagnostic assessment is a pre-test, which is a measure of learners' knowledge, skills, attitudes and values with regard to the curriculum. This form of assessment is also known as a baseline assessment; it helps to determine learners' level of competence before starting a learning programme.

A diagnostic assessment can also be used during a learning session. If the facilitator identifies a problem, but cannot quite determine the exact nature of the problem, diagnostic assessment is used to specify the nature of the problem or need. It is essential for ETD practitioners to continually diagnose learners' understanding and interest. This ongoing type of assessment is called formative assessment, because it helps to shape or form the learning.

Formative assessment

Formative assessment is an ongoing assessment that takes place throughout a period of learning. It provides the learner with opportunities to practise what has been learnt with the intention of improving performance in the next assessment. These assessments are conducted to measure learners' rate of progress toward achieving competence in an outcome.

Formative assessments help facilitators to make decisions on learners' readiness to do a summative assessment. Credits may or may not be awarded. Formative assessment credits usually carry a weight towards the summative assessment results. These assessments do not have to be conducted by a registered assessor. The assessments use a range of assessment methods such as observations, oral or written tests, interviews and demonstrations. In some instances, learners can include formative assessments in their portfolios of evidence.

Formative assessment is conducted during instruction. The assessment takes place formally (for example, a test) or informally (for example, the facilitator's questions or observations). Facilitators and learners all receive information, which they can use to adapt learning strategies and methods during the learning session. Formative assessment therefore has a teaching, coaching and development function.

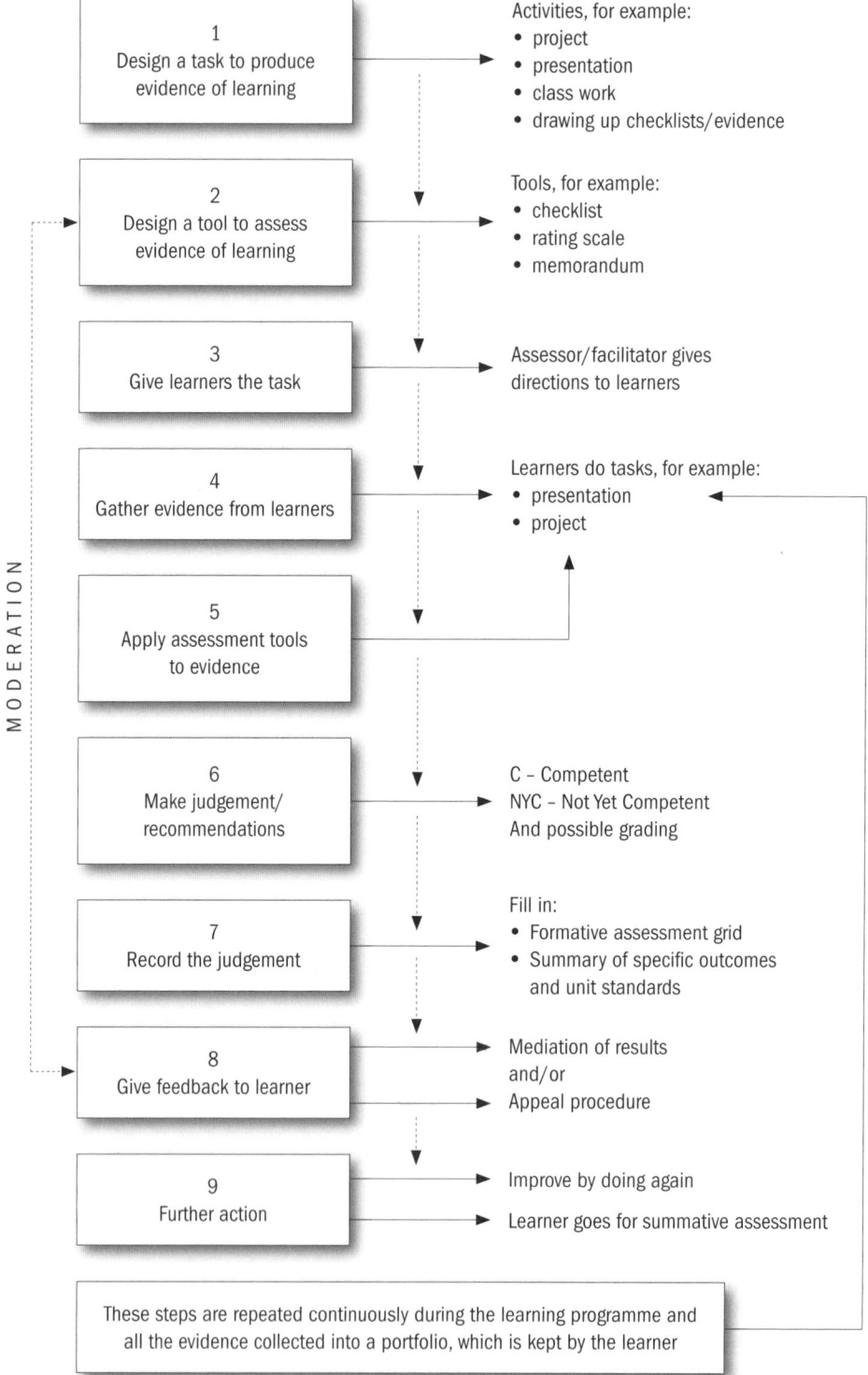

Figure 6.2 Steps and processes involved in the formative assessment of a task (Coetzee, 2007a)

Summative assessment

Summative assessment is usually conducted at the end of a learning programme. It is the final measurement of what was learnt. Summative assessments should include formative assessment evaluations and a final overall assessment of whether learners have achieved the learning outcomes for the programme. Summative assessments often include projects and performance tasks conducted in a real-life context after attending a practical learning programme.

Summative assessment contributes to the final grade for a learning outcome or qualification. A summative assessment is done to determine whether learners have achieved the outcomes of a unit standard or learning programme. Summative assessments are done at the end of a learning programme, a set of outcomes, or a single outcome within the learning programme. This type of assessment summarises the learning process. It results in a formal statement declaring whether a learner has achieved competency, or not.

Summative assessments are not only in the form of written examinations. A range of assessment methods can be used, such as observations, interviews, questioning the learner, listening to the learner and reviewing written material. These assessments provide evidence of the learner's knowledge, application of this knowledge and evidence of the learner's understanding and reflexive abilities. A summative assessment can only be done when:

- the assessor and learners agree that they are ready for the assessment;
- the assessor and learners have decided whether they are doing a summative or formative assessment;
- the learners know when and where the assessment will be held; and
- the learners are informed that the results will be formally recorded and reported.

Table 6.2 *Formative and summative assessment (SAQA, 2001)*

Formative assessment	Summative assessment
<ul><li>Designed to support the teaching and learning process</li><li>Assists with the planning of future learning</li><li>Diagnoses the learner's strengths and weaknesses</li><li>Provides the learner with feedback on progress</li><li>Helps to make decisions on the learner's readiness to do the summative assessment</li><li>Developmental in nature</li><li>Credits or certificates are not awarded</li></ul>	<ul><li>Occurs at the end of a learning programme</li><li>Determines whether the learner is competent or not yet competent</li><li>Learner readiness determines when the summative assessment will take place</li><li>Carried out when the learner and assessor agree that the learner is ready for assessment</li><li>Credits are awarded when the learner is declared competent</li></ul>

Evaluative assessment

Evaluative assessment is a post-assessment activity, which is included in the assessment process to ensure the quality of the overall process. ETD practitioners may use learner feedback to evaluate the effectiveness of the assessment process. Evaluative assessment procedures help the ETD practitioner to explain to learners and moderators how assessment decisions were reached.

Evaluative assessment helps ETD practitioners to identify gaps in unit standards and make recommendations to managers and ETQAs. Information about learner achievements can be used to assist in curriculum development and evaluate the effectiveness of learning programmes.

Integrated assessment

Integrated assessment implies that assessors should focus on assessing learners' ability to combine foundational, practical and reflexive competencies with critical cross-field outcomes (CCFOs) and apply these in a practical context or for a defined purpose. The context of assessment should be as close as possible to real-life application. Integrated assessment refers to the following:

- using one assessment activity for more than one outcome;
- using one assessment activity for more than one unit standard;
- integrating the critical outcomes with the learning outcomes in learning and assessment activities;
- teaching and assessing theory and practice within the same activities;
- using a complex assessment task (for example, a project) to integrate all the outcomes that learners have dealt with throughout the learning period; and
- assessing across learning areas (SAQA, 2005).

Assessing each outcome individually is a long and costly process. Furthermore, the principles of the NQF call for a unifying approach to education and training. If assessments are not integrated, the assessments become fragmented, place undue stress on all the role players and produce a disjointed learning experience. It is important to note that integrated learning comes before integrated assessment. Figure 6.3 is from SAQA's Guidelines for Integrated Assessment.

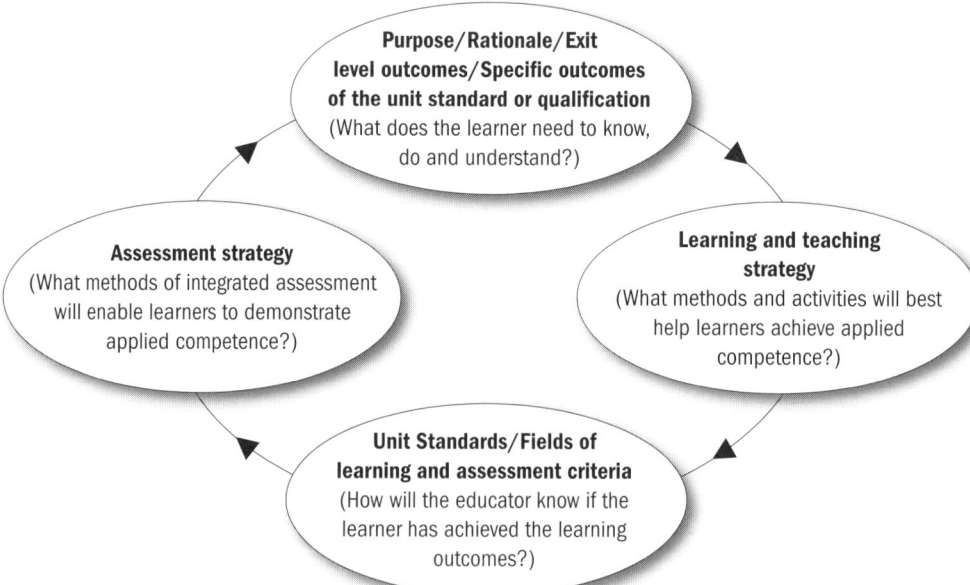

Figure 6.3 *Teaching, learning and assessing in an integrated manner (www.saqa.org.za)*

Integrated assessment demonstrates how teaching, learning and assessment activities could be developed as a coherent process while still upholding the principles of the assessment. The process emphasises the importance of carefully planning integrated teaching, learning and assessment. Other than integrating assessments, there are various ways to ensure that assessments are cost effective:

- Do not involve too many people in the assessment process. This can cause the assessment to become complex and time consuming.
- Ensure that productivity in the workplace is not interrupted by the assessments. A time should be chosen that suits all the role players.
- Keep the resources needed for the assessments to a minimum.
- Encourage learners to do self-assessments. Self-assessments help learners to determine whether they are ready for their final assessment.

Assessment methods and instruments

Assessment methods are tools that an assessor uses to gather evidence of a candidate's performance. Assessment methods relate to what an assessor does to gather and evaluate evidence. Examples of assessment methods include observing learners, questioning learners, interviewing supervisors, colleagues or managers of learners, listening to learners, reviewing written material, and testing products. Assessment activities are the actual activities the learner is supposed to perform when following a particular assessment method. If observation is the assessment method, the actual assessment activity might be, for example, the learner is required to strip the paint off the wall, or the learner cashier is required to pay out money to the customer.

Assessment instruments are designed to make the assessor's use of assessment methods more practical, consistent and effective. For example, a written test (method) needs a test paper and assessment criteria (instrument) to be assessed effectively. Other examples of assessment instruments are scenarios with questions, case studies, descriptions of tasks to be performed and descriptions of role-play scenarios. Table 6.3 shows which methods can be used with which instruments.

Table 6.3 Assessment methods and instruments (SAQA, 2001)

Assessment methods	Possible assessment instrument
Assignments	Assignment sheet and rubric clearly indicating the assessment criteria against which learners are measured
Case studies	Printed case studies and questions based on the case study
Written exams or tests	Examination paper, answer sheet and memorandum
Multiple choice questions	A bank of multiple choice questions and answers
Oral exams	Questions and possible answers, assessment criteria and a rating scale
Personal interviews	Interview format, questions and a clear job description or description of what is required of the candidate
Practical demonstrations	List of expected activities and prescribed levels to indicate required level of competence
Projects	Clear purpose statement, scope of responsibilities, team members and instructions
Role plays	Clear instructions and outcomes to be achieved

The assessment method (or methods) chosen will depend on the type of evidence required, the number of learners and the resources and time available for the assessment. It is important to understand the strengths, weaknesses and uses of the assessment methods. Learners should have a say in the type of method used to assess them. Describe assessment instruments clearly, as this will determine their effectiveness during the assessment process.

Table 6.4 Uses of assessment methods (SAQA, 2001)

Assessment methods	Description	Examples
Observations	Recording evidence of a candidate's competency in carrying out a process or developing a product	• Judging performance against checklists • Logbooks • Diaries
Written tests	Answering questions set by an independent assessor	Aimed at remembering and recalling information, as well as analysing, reporting on and discussing issues and debating viewpoints
Oral presentations	Communicating verbally about a researched and prepared topic	Reporting on a project, briefing other employees and informing a supervisor on work done
Interviews	Discussing issues in a structured way	Aimed at finding out whether an employee understands and can apply knowledge and skills
Documents (reports, portfolios or case studies)	Supplying evidence of competence in written from, clearly demonstrating competence over a period of time	• Job reports • Scientific articles • Certificates • Completed and assessed assignments • Letters of recommendation from employer • Course outlines of previously studied courses • Rough notes and drawings • Photographs • Computer software • Proof of seminars attended • Letters from peers
Simulations	Imitating a real-life situation and a real-life task	• Work-based practical assignments • Rehearsals • Role play • Poster presentations • Models • Simulators
Projects	Tasks undertaken by an individual or group, unique in terms of outcomes, parameters and criteria	• Reports • Dissertations • Models • Computer programmes

Assessment methods	Description	Examples
		• Exhibitions • Portfolios • Posters
Performance tests	Performing in a natural situation (such as a hospital, factory floor or classroom)	Assessing life-saving attempts by a nurse, firefighter or paramedic

Portfolio assessment

A portfolio is a folder that contains samples of the learner's work for a specific learning programme. The portfolio serves as evidence of the learner's ability to demonstrate competency as stipulated in the learning outcomes. Portfolios provide evidence of a learner's knowledge, skills, attitudes and academic development; they can be assessed through formative and summative assessment. Portfolios also allow learners to evaluate their own work. When learners are responsible for deciding what to include in a portfolio, they are forced to examine their work from a new perspective (Van der Horst & McDonald, 1997). Portfolios have the potential to enhance learning facilitation and learning, because they engage the trainer and learners in reflective self-evaluation. Portfolios also accomplish an alignment of curriculum, instruction, and assessment that is seldom achieved with other assessment methods. The main reasons for using portfolios are to:
- assess learners' accomplishments of learning outcomes;
- assess the quality of learners' sustained work;
- allow learners to turn their own special interests and abilities into a showcase;
- encourage the development of qualities such as pride in quality workmanship;
- improve learners' ability to self-evaluate and accomplish meaningful tasks;
- provide a collection of work that learners may use in the future for university applications, employment seeking and continued professional development;
- document improvements in learners' work (Van der Horst & McDonald, 1997).

Portfolios provide important formative assessment data. A portfolio is an accumulated body of work in a real-life context. It provides evidence of the learning and growth that learners have achieved. Portfolios emphasise strengths, the development of skills, improvement and personal reflections. They provide a broad picture of a learner's learning (Coetzee, 2007).

Table 6.5 Uses of assessment instruments (SAQA, 2001)

Instrument	Evidence valid	Evidence authentic	Evidence current	Evidence sufficient	Strengths and weaknesses
Alternative response questions	√	√	√		Assesses the learner's ability to recall information and discriminate.
Knowledge test	√	√	√		This does not test the learner's practical skill. Encourages rote learning and favours learners with good writing skills. Assesses theoretical outcomes and can be cost effective if assessing a number of people.
Assertion/reason questions	√	√	√		Assesses the learner's ability to weigh up options and discriminate.
Simulations	√	√	√		Provides the learner with opportunities to make risk free and non-threatening decisions Depending on the simulation, this can produce evidence of all competencies. Is not a true indication of the actual situation.
Role play	√	√	√		Learners act out a role with other role players. It does not necessarily test the learner's theoretical, practical or reflexive knowledge; hence the evidence is not sufficient. Can be cost effective.
Practical	√	√	√	√	Depending on the practical, this can produce evidence of all competencies – involves the learner performing actual tasks. If conducted in real life situations, it can provide authentic evidence. Might feel self-conscious and nervous when they carry out their practical tasks.
Assignments	√		√		Written evidence is required for an assigned task. Depending on the assignment, this cannot always be verified as the learner's own work. Favour learners with good writing skills.
Portfolio of evidence	√	√	√	√	This method allows the learner to produce a written portfolio of the work he or she has done. Allows the learner to submit evidence of all applied competencies if signed off by role players who have observed the learner's practical abilities.
Oral presentation	√	√	√	√	Allows the learner to prepare a presentation in the form of an oral to an audience. Depending on the oral, this can produce evidence of all competencies. Favours those who speak well. Can make one feel nervous or self conscious.
Examination	√	√	√		Usually given at the end of a programme. Tests the learners foundational and reflexive competencies.
Case study	√		√		This activity can be done orally or in writing, in groups or individually. Allows for creative problem solving. Does not test the learner's ability to actually perform the skill.
Questionnaire	√		√		The competencies of a number of people are assessed. It does not test the theoretical knowledge and practical skill of the learner; hence the evidence is not sufficient.
Demonstration	√	√	√	√	This activity allows the learner to assess all competencies – it can include all aspects of VACS. (Evidence of requirements.)
Oral tests	√	√	√		Depending on the oral, this can produce evidence of all competencies. Favours those with good communication skills.
Personal interviews	√	√	√		This method does not test the learner's ability to actually perform the task.

Instrument	Evidence valid	Evidence authentic	Evidence current	Evidence sufficient	Strengths and weaknesses
Structured questions	√	√	√		Set questions are asked to determine the learners' competence – reflective and foundational skills may be assessed.
Extended response questions	√	√	√		Assesses the learner's problem solving or analysing skills and ability to recall information.
Grid questions	√	√	√		Presented in a grid format. Learners are given two lists – a statement list and a response list. They are to match the responses to the statements given. Each statement may have more than one given response. This method is usually used to simulate open-ended debates and arguments.
Multiple response questions	√	√	√		Comprises of a choice of questions with a possibility of a few answers. Learners are to choose the correct answer.
Oral questions Restricted response questions	√	√	√		The form and the content of the responses are limited by the way in which the questions are asked. They do not have to have specific answers and the assessor can use personal judgement when interpreting a response. This style of questioning allows for self expression and creative thinking.
Log books	√				Use to assess the learners historical evidence. Authenticity cannot always be verified.
Projects	√	√	√		Depending on the project, this can assess most competencies.
Peer assessment	√	√	√		Evaluations done by the learner's peers or co-workers. Does not provide direct evidence of the learner's competencies – can be used as supplementary evidence.
Self-assessment	√	√	√		Cost and time effective methods of assessment. Can be done before an assessment to ensure that the learner is ready for the assessment.

Recognition of prior learning

Recognition of prior learning (RPL) means that people's competencies are recognised and acknowledged (this is discussed more fully in Chapter 1). It does not matter how the competencies were obtained; in other words, competencies acquired through experience are equal to competencies acquired through a formal course. In practice, there is no fundamental difference in the assessment of previously acquired competencies and the assessment of competencies achieved through a full learning programme. RPL involves the following:

- comparing the previous learning and experience of a learner against the learning outcomes required for a qualification;
- accepting that those learning experiences meet the requirements to obtain the qualification;
- allowing for accelerated access to further learning; and
- assessing and giving credit for evidence of learning that has already been acquired in different ways.

As shown in Figure 6.4, the RPL process is about:
- identifying a learner's competencies;
- matching a learner's skills, knowledge and experience to standards and the associated assessment criteria of a qualification;
- assessing learners' achievements against these standards by evaluating the collected evidence; and
- crediting a learner for skills, knowledge and experience built up through formal, informal and non-formal learning that occurred in the past.

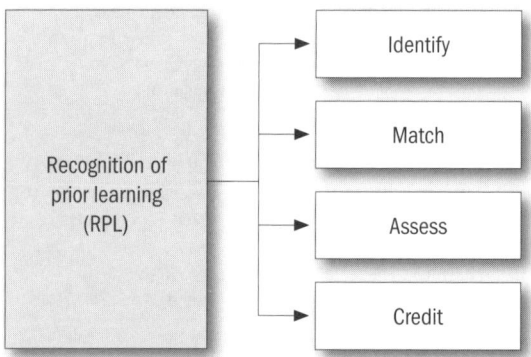

Figure 6.4 The RPL process

According to SAQA, RPL is important for the following reasons:
- to ensure that people's skills and knowledge are current;
- to redress the historical disadvantages, such as exclusion of people from education, training and employment;
- to enhance the development of individuals;
- to facilitate access to jobs and progression in career paths;
- to assist recognition in terms of grading and salary;
- to assist planning through skills audits; and
- to promote employment equity.

The assessment process

All assessments follow the same basic process of planning the assessment, preparing the learner for assessment, conducting the assessment, documenting the evidence, evaluating the evidence and making assessment judgements, providing feedback to the relevant parties and reviewing the assessment.

Planning the assessment

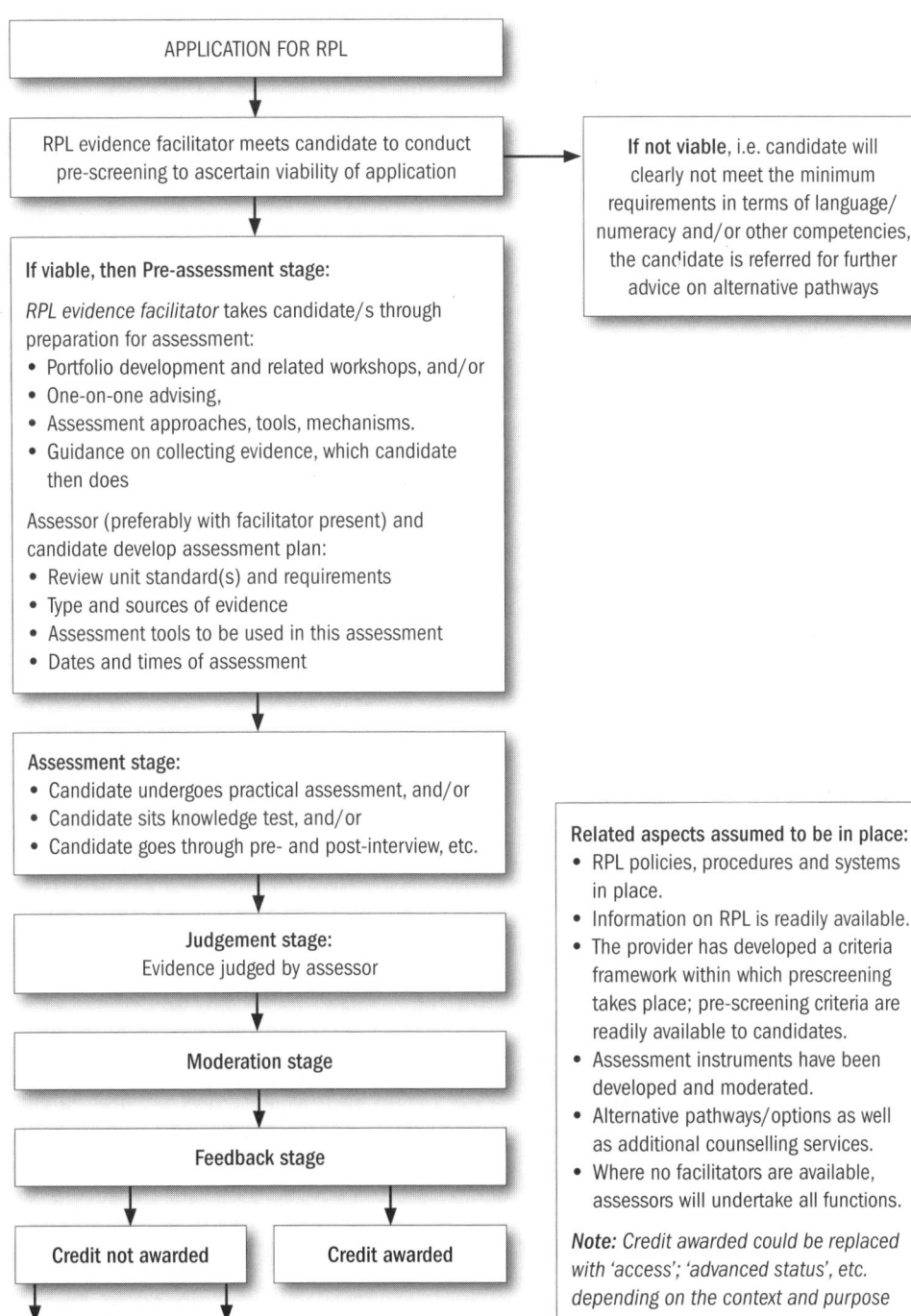

Figure 6.5 *The RPL assessment process*

There are various steps that an assessor should follow when planning the assessment. If the assessor's planning is not adequate, the assessment process will not achieve its goals. Assessors must be familiar with the learning programme and the learning outcomes against which learners will be assessed. To do this, assessors should:

- Familiarise themselves with the overall purpose that has to be achieved. The learning outcomes, critical cross-field outcomes, embedded knowledge, assessment criteria, range statement and other requirements that will influence the design of the assessment should be identified.
- Discuss assessment with other facilitators and assessors to gain as much information as possible about the learning programme, the type of work done with the leaner during the teaching and learning phase and resources used.
- Evaluate and revise previously used assessment processes and materials.
- Develop assessment instruments (if the organisation does not have existing instruments).
- Draw up an assessment plan that addresses all the requirements of the standard being assessed. Its purpose is to provide clarity to all the relevant role players on the assessment and moderation processes.

The assessment plan should cover the following:
- the performance to be assessed;
- the types of evidence that is required to declare the learner competent;
- the assessment methods and instruments that will be used to conduct the assessment;
- the strengths and weaknesses of assessment methods and instruments;
- the sequence of events;
- the period of assessment, indicating the time allocated for each assessment, deadlines and availability of results;
- the physical and human resources that will be required;
- the logistics of the assessment;
- the role players involved in the assessment, and their roles and responsibilities;
- the moderation of the assessment;
- the need for cost-effectiveness in the assessment;
- the special needs of learners and possible barriers to the assessment;
- the plans that are in place in case of unforeseen circumstances;
- the assessment context and strategy;
- the organisation's assessment, moderation, RPL and appeals policies and procedures;
- the accessibility and safety of the environment; and
- the assessment documentation that will be needed.

Table 6.6 provides a detailed example of an assessment plan.

Table 6.6 *Assessment plan*

Assessor's name	
Assessor's contact details Email Cell phone Telephone	
Learner's name	
Learner's contact details ID No Telephone Cell phone Email Address	
Learner's position in organisation	
Manager's name	
Manager's contact details Email Cell phone Telephone	
Assessment context	Give the context of the assessment to be conducted. Describe what is being assessed.
Assessment strategy	State the assessment strategy to be followed. Describe how outcomes will be assessed.
Purpose of assessment	State the purpose of the assessment as given in the learning outcomes or unit standard. Also state whether the assessment is formative or summative. Describe why the outcomes will be assessed.
Performance to be assessed	Mention the specific outcomes to be assessed.
Evidence required	Describe the type of evidence needed to declare the learner competent (for example, direct evidence, indirect evidence and supplementary evidence). Give a thorough explanation of the requirements for evidence.
Methods and instruments to be used (including strengths and weaknesses)	Discuss the methods and instruments needed to determine the learner's level of competence. Also describe the strengths and weaknesses of each method.
Date, time and period of assessment	Mention how long each assessment will take. Give an approximate date for the assessment and confirm it with the learner.
Availability of results	Give an approximate date for the availability of results after the final assessment.
Logistics of assessment, including safety of the environment	Discuss the logistics of the assessment, including where, when and how it will take place. Consider the safety of the environment.

Role players in the assessment	Mention all the role players involved in the assessment. Give their names and contact details, and state how they are involved in the assessment.
Moderation	Describe the role of the moderator in the assessment. Explain exactly how the moderator is involved in pre-assessment and post-assessment moderation.
Policies and procedures	State the organisation's assessment, moderation, RPL and appeals policies and procedures. Note any important matters to be considered in this regard.
Physical and human resources	State what resources you will need for this assessment. Note that this aspect may already be covered in the section on logistics and role players in the assessment.
Cost-effectiveness	Consider ways to keep costs low. Include integrated assessment in the discussion.
Special needs of learners and barriers to the assessment	Note any special needs that have to be considered. Consider any barriers that might impede the assessment.
Contingency plans	Consider contingency plans in the event of circumstances that might hinder the assessment.
Principles of assessment	Indicate how these principles are applied in the assessment.
Documentation	Consider the various documents needed for the assessment, including policy documents and appeals forms. The candidate must have some knowledge of SAQA and the NQF. Ensure that they know the difference between the traditional learning and outcomes-based learning. Prepare this information for the candidate learner. If the candidate does not have this information, he/she will not understand the assessment process.
Sequence of events	Give a step-by-step explanation of the assessment process.
Quality assurance	Explain how feedback will be recorded and stored in keeping with the organisation's quality assurance system.

Assessors are required to compile a comprehensive assessment guide. This should form part of the facilitator/trainer guide (discussed in Chapter 4). The assessment guide is the result of a thorough analysis of the learning outcomes and assessment criteria for the learning programme. Assessors use assessment guides to conduct an assessment. Assessment guides address the following aspects in detail:

* How will the assessment take place?
* What is needed to make the assessment happen?
* How will evidence be gathered, recorded and judged (SAQA, 2007)?

Assessment guides include descriptions of the approach to the assessment, assessment conditions, assessment activities, instructions to assessors and learners, assessment methods, assessment instruments, resource requirements, guidance for contextualising assessments, relevant standard operating procedures, administrative procedures, moderation requirements, assessment outcomes and criteria, observation sheets, quality checklists, possible or required sources of evidence and guidance on expected quality of evidence (SAQA, 2007).

Prepare the learner for assessment

When assessors have planned and prepared the assessment process, the relevant role players must be informed of the assessment. The most important role player is the learner. The learner will probably be unfamiliar with the assessment process and terminology; it is therefore important for the assessor to explain the assessment thoroughly, in a manner and language that sets the learner at ease. Assessors may use the assessment plan as a guide to inform the learner of the process. This plan will inform the learner about the requirements for the assessment and the learner's role and responsibilities during the assessment. It is important for the assessor to reach an agreement with the learner on how the evidence will be collected and presented. Learners should be made aware of the following:

- the process of the assessment and why the assessment will be conducted in a particular way;
- the key elements of outcomes-based assessment within the context of the NQF;
- the kinds of assessment activities that they need to perform;
- the standard and level of performance required;
- the type and amount of evidence to be collected;
- their rights as learners and their responsibilities regarding the collection of evidence; and
- the reassessments and appeals procedure to be followed, if they are not satisfied with the assessment result.

The assessor and learner must reach an agreement on the assessment process. The assessor and learners sign off the assessment plan (or any other document that constitutes an agreement). This gives the assessor documented proof of learners' readiness to proceed with the assessment. This is an important step in the assessment process. If learners later feel that they were forced into the assessment, they may appeal the assessment decision on the grounds that they were not ready for the assessment.

Table 6.7 *Example of an assessment strategy (Coetzee, 2006a)*

Unit Standard 114924: Demonstrate understanding of the outcomes-based education and training approach within the context of a NQF.				
Specific outcomes	Method of facilitation	Reference in manual	Method of assessment	Reference in manual (section where assessment occurs in course)
Specific outcome 1 Explain the outcomes-based approach to education and training.	Pre-course and manual activities Presentation	Pre-course activities Module 1	Questions Learning manual activities Self-assessment Workplace assignments	Relates to all pre-course activities Activity 1.11 Workplace application (Portfolio 1.2)
Specific outcome 2 Describe the NQF.	Group work	Pre-course activities Module 1		Relates to all pre-course activities Workplace application (Portfolio 1.2)
Specific outcome 3 Describe and explain standards.		Module 1 Module 3		Activity 1.11 Activity 3.2
Specific outcome 4 Describe and explain qualifications.		Module 1		Activity 1.11
Specific outcome 5 Develop a broad plan for implementing the NQF within an organisation.		Module 1		Activity 1.11

Essential embedded knowledge	Method of facilitation	Reference in manual	Method of assessment	Reference in manual
The entire unit standard addresses issues of knowledge relative to the outcomes-based approach and the National Qualifications Framework, thus all the outcomes and criteria define the knowledge explicitly.	Pre-course and manual activities Presentation	Pre-course manual Module 1	Questions Learning manual activities Self-assessment Workplace assignments	Relates to all activities and assignments
Critical cross-field outcomes			Method of assessment	Reference in manual
CCFO Communicating CCFO Demonstrating			Questions Learning manual activities Self-assessment Workplace assignments	Relates to all activities and assignments

Conduct assessment

Assessment is a structured process of gathering evidence about learners' achievements in relation to specific learning outcomes. This evidence is used to make assessment decisions about the learners' competence. The collection of evidence is the main focus of the assessment process. Assessors are required to do the following:

- Ensure that the assessment is conducted in an appropriate, non-threatening manner, and in accordance with the assessment plan.
- Collect evidence that is valid, authenticated, current and sufficient to determine the learner's competence. Ideally, collect evidence that is directly observed by the assessor. Other types of evidence are also acceptable, but only if they are verified (Tables 6.8 and 6.9 show ways to verify the authenticity of learners' evidence).
- Collect evidence that covers all the assessment criteria of the programme or unit being assessed.
- Collect evidence from a variety of sources to ensure a consistent and reliable assessment decision. This may include evidence of the learner's previous or current work performance, testimonials and performance appraisals.
- Gather enough evidence – including evidence generated over time – to reach a valid, consistent and fair assessment decision.

Table 6.8 Example of candidate declaration of authenticity (Coetzee, 2006)

Ethics and authenticity declaration	
Please complete the following and sign in the space provided.	
Sign the declaration and ask your manager or a senior colleague to sign the endorsement section. The contents of this portfolio will be verified. The person who signs the endorsement should be willing to stand by their endorsement of authenticity.	
Candidate declaration I declare that I have compiled this portfolio. This is my own work and the contents reflect evidence that I have gathered to demonstrate my competence as an assessor.	Signed: _____ Date: _____
Workplace endorsement Name of person giving the endorsement: _____ Position in the organisation: _____ **Contact details** Telephone (w): _____ Email (w): _____	I confirm that this portfolio of evidence is the work of: _____ Signed: _____ Date: _____

Table 6.9 Example of a witness declaration of authenticity (Coetzee, 2006)

Witness declaration of authenticity

Candidate name: _____

Please ensure that all witnesses who sign the candidate's evidence, observe any activities performed by the candidate or write a report are included on this witness status list.

Name and contact details of witness	Status of witness	Relationship to the learner	Specified activities witnessed	Witness signature	Date

. To ensure that the entire assessment process is credible, certain principles of assessment as outlined in Table 6.10 must be followed. These principles provide guidelines to ensure the integrity of the assessment process.

Table 6.10 Principles of assessment (SAQA, 2001)

Appropriate	The methods of assessment are suited and appropriate to the performance being assessed.
Authentic	The work being assessed and the evidence produced must belong to the learner. In other words, the work submitted must be the work of the person being assessed. The learner or a witness can sign the work to indicate that it is authentic.
Consistent and reliable	The evidence produced must be consistent and reliable. Consistency means the extent to which the same judgement will be made in the same or similar situations. The results of the assessment must be the same if given by another assessor under similar circumstances.
Fair	The assessment process must be fair. There must be no discrimination in terms of race, gender, age, disability, language or ethnicity. The assessment methods must not present any barriers to achieving the learning outcomes. Assessment methods should be suited to the learning outcomes and the evidence required.
Integrative	The evidence collected must be integrated into the job or field of learning, where appropriate. Integrated assessment should assess the ability to combine foundational, practical and reflexive competence with critical cross-field outcomes and apply these in a practical context.
Manageable or practical	The assessment must be manageable and practical. In other words, it must not be expensive and time consuming, or interfere with any learning.

Relevant	The evidence must be relevant to the outcome. For example, if the aim of an assessment is to assess a learner's ability to drive a truck, it is not necessary to assess a learner's ability to drive a car. The assessor must ensure that only the required outcomes are assessed.
Sufficient	The assessor must collect enough evidence to make an accurate judgement. The amount of evidence needed will depend on the type of assessment. The assessor will only know sufficient evidence has been collected if the evidence assesses the learner's foundational knowledge, practical skill and reflective thinking.
Systematic	The assessment process must be planned and recorded in a systematic way.
Transparent or open	The assessment process should be transparent and open to all. Learners must be able to contribute to the assessment process and give their input regarding the collection of evidence.
Valid	An assessment is valid if it tests what the unit standard states it is supposed to test. The evidence provided must be relevant to the required outcomes.

Gather and document evidence

Gathering evidence is a crucial part of the assessment process. Assessment evidence can be defined as evidence collected from workplace performance, supplemented by other performance. This evidence is weighed up against the assessment criteria in the unit standard. The evidence that assessors are looking for may differ from one type of assessment to the next. Evidence will be different for assessing technical competence, occupational competence, critical outcomes, team performance or a learner's ability to transfer knowledge. There are many different ways to collect evidence:

- *Direct evidence* is obtained when you directly observe learners' performance in a normal or non-routine workplace situation, and in the execution of specific tasks.
- *Indirect evidence* is the opposite of direct evidence. It is collected through simulations, projects, and the assessment of products or services.
- *Supplementary evidence* may be required to see whether a learner can perform in a variety of situations. Learners will have to give proof of their competence, and evidence can be gathered in a variety of ways (such as through written or oral exams). Third party reports (from supervisors, fellow learners and clients) may also contribute to the evidence.

Table 6. 11 Types of evidence

Direct evidence	Indirect evidence	Supplementary evidence
This is the preferred type of evidence. It is valid, authentic, current and sufficient. Direct observations give the assessor direct evidence of learners' competence.	Indirect evidence can be used to supplement or support the direct evidence. It is evidence about the learner, usually from another source.	Supplementary evidence may include additional evidence that supports direct or indirect evidence and historical evidence. Historical evidence informs the assessor how learners performed in the past. It does not necessarily prove learners' current competence.

Assessment documents should be developed to collect and record evidence. This will ensure the consistency of assessment results, especially if more than one assessor is involved in the assessment process. Assessors are required to record all the evidence collected in the learner's portfolio of evidence. It is best to keep an assessment record for each learner, stating the outcomes assessed, the date and time of the assessment and the assessor's details. These documents should be dated and signed by the learner, assessor and moderator.

Table 6.12 Example of a summative assessment form (Coetzee, 2006a)

Learning programme: Developing people Unit standard title: Analyse the skills development legislation and apply it in the workplace (US 14551) NQF Level: 4　　　　　Credits: 4 Candidate name:			
Learning Unit 1	Assessor initials	Candidate initials	Date
Outcome title Demonstrate an understanding of the social contexts and values underpinning skills development.			
Assessment criteria • The principles and values underpinning the institution are identified and explained in terms of their operations. • Current skills development legislation is identified and a summary of the underpinning principles and values is given in writing. • Batho Pele principles are explained with examples. • Skills development priorities are linked to labour market opportunities.			
Application • Interpret the objectives of the NSDS, HRDS and Batho Pele principles as they apply to the public service. • Explore the challenges regarding people development within the public service and the specific department. • Explore the roles of the various stakeholders in implementing the NSDS, HRDS and Batho Pele principles in the public service.			

Competent ☐   Not yet competent ☐

General comments: _____

_____

Assessor: _____   Candidate: _____

Signature: _____   Signature: _____

Date: _____   Date: _____

Evidence is the tangible proof that learners produce to show that they meet the criteria of the applicable learning outcomes or unit standard. The evidence must include the following:

- *Evidence of knowledge.* Learners should provide evidence of theoretical knowledge of the work (foundational knowledge). For example: The chef has theoretical knowledge about planning menus.
- *Evidence of application of knowledge.* Learners should show that they can actually apply the knowledge to practical situations (practical knowledge). Example: The chef plans the menu for a dinner.
- *Evidence of understanding and reflection.* In addition to foundational and practical knowledge, learners must show that they understand the work (reflective knowledge). Example: The chef designs and creates menus for various different events.

Evidence should meet certain criteria before it can be used in the assessment process. These are shown in Table 6.13.

Table 6.13 The VACS analysis of evidence

Valid	The evidence must be relevant to the standard or outcomes assessed.
Authentic	The evidence must belong to the learner.
Current	The evidence must indicate the current competence of the learner.
Sufficient	The learner must provide enough evidence (as defined by performance criteria and the range statement) to enable the assessor to declare the learner competent.

Evaluate evidence and make assessment judgements

Plan Prepare Conduct Document Evaluate Feedback Review

When the evidence has been gathered and documented, assessors need to judge learners' competence. This judgement is based on an evaluation of the evidence. Assessors are expected to evaluate the evidence against each assessment criterium. The assessment decision must take into account any unexpected circumstances that may compromise the fairness and correctness of the assessment. In other words, learners must not be penalised for something that was not their fault.

The assessment decision must be consistent. Consistency is the extent to which the same result will be reached if the assessor uses different methods to assess the learner or if someone else assesses the learner. If the results are not consistent, the assessor must reconsider the assessment methods and activities and reassess the learner. If the assessment takes place in an organisation, assessors are also required to store assessment records safely within the quality assurance system. This is done in case the assessment results are questioned, and for moderation and quality assurance purposes.

Provide feedback to the relevant parties

Assessment is considered a learning tool, because it provides learners with continuous feedback on their performance. Assessors are required to provide written and oral feedback to the learner and other role players. However, assessors should handle assessment results with confidentiality.

During the feedback phase of assessment, assessors provide detailed, clear and accurate feedback on the learner's achievements. Feedback gives learners information about their performance on each assessment criterium and learning outcome.

Assessors should provide positive and constructive criticism, because feedback has a significant impact on learners' further learning. The assessor should also advise learners on further learning opportunities or, if the learner has been declared not yet competent, discuss ways to improve performance and opportunities for reassessment.

CASE STUDY

Read carefully through the case study and answer the questions that follow.

Sibongile and Pamela must each assess three supervisors in the organisation. The unit standard that the supervisors worked towards is US 10981, Supervise Work Unit.

Sibongile calls her three supervisors in for a meeting on Friday afternoon. She asks them to prepare themselves for their assessments on Monday. She asks all three to be available for a group interview at 10:00 Monday morning.

When they ask her if they should prepare any documents or observations with their floor staff, she tells them no. The assessment will be in the form of a 20-minute group interview. She tells the group that, as they have been with the company for more than two months, they do not have to worry about having to do additional assessments. Their work records can be drawn from the HR department; this can be their evidence. One of the employees states that she is not comfortable with this process; everything seems too quick and rushed. Another employee, Crystal, got a written warning a year ago. She does not want this to influence the assessor's decision. Sibongile tells the whole group that time is money – they have no reason to worry. She abruptly ends the meeting.

The second assessor, Pamela, contacts the HR department for more information about the three employees that she has to assess. She reads through their files and the unit standard and draws up a detailed assessment plan. She then approaches the manager of the division and reviews the timetable with him. Finally, she contacts the three supervisors and invites them to a meeting to discuss their assessments.

At the meeting, she informs them that their prior learning will be recognised (RPL) in the assessment. She explains the process and arranges a time on the following Friday with each supervisor. Pamela asks the group for their suggestions on the assessment. There are none. She then gives them a detailed breakdown of her plan for the RPL. She asks the group to read the documents and contact her if they have any questions. All the employees leave her office excited about the prospect of being assessed.

Questions
1. Compare Sibongile and Pamela's assessment planning and preparation.
2. Discuss the assessment method Sibongile used.
3. Sibongile says the supervisors can be assessed because they have been with the organisation for more than two months and their work records can be drawn from the HR department. Explain why her reasoning is flawed.
4. Discuss Sibongile's approach to the assessment.
5. How should she have conducted this assessment?
6. Why do you think Pamela decided that her group could be recognised for their prior learning?
7. What methods and activities do you think Pamela suggested to the group that made them excited about the assessment?
8. Explain how you would conduct this RPL assessment.

Review the assessment process

Assessors are required to review the assessment process. They do this by identifying the strengths and weaknesses in the process to improve future assessments. An evaluation of the assessment process will include the following:

- Consult the learner and other relevant role players for feedback about and suggestions to improve the assessment.
- Evaluate the impact the assessment process may have had on the results of assessments.
- Review the entire process with other assessors and moderators.
- Make appropriate changes, including recommendations about the learning outcomes or qualification.
- Use the assessment results to evaluate the learning programme and strategies.

The aim of such a review is not to be critical and destructive, but rather to influence future assessments and ensure that errors are not repeated. The positive aspects of the assessment process must also be noted. These positive aspects add to the quality of future assessments and support the overall quality assurance of the organisation's practices.

Table 6.14 Example of candidate evaluation of the assessment process (Coetzee, 2006)

Candidate evaluation *Please answer the questions below.*	
Was your assessor's manner encouraging and designed to put you at ease?	
Was the assessment procedure explained and agreed with you? Was it clear and understandable?	
Were you encouraged to participate and be involved?	
Did your assessor ensure that all specific outcomes and the appropriate range were covered?	
Were you given clear, evaluative feedback against each specific outcome?	
Were all pieces of evidence considered?	
In what manner were assessment decisions communicated to you?	
Did you agree with the decisions?	
Was all the appropriate documentation completed and signed? Did you receive copies for your records?	
Candidate's name: _____	
Candidate's signature: _____ Date: _____	

Moderation of assessment

Effective quality assurance gives everyone involved in the particular learning programme confidence in assessment decisions. Internal moderation is one aspect of quality assurance. It is the process of monitoring and verifying assessment practices to ensure that assessment decisions are consistently accurate. Moderation and verification involve:

- monitoring the conduct of assessment;
- evaluating assessment design, instruments and methods;
- sampling candidate evidence to verify assessment decisions;
- assuring quality of the assessment and moderation system and procedures;
- supporting and advising assessors;
- keeping verification and assessment records up to date; and
- providing information for analysis by the assessment centre and ETQA (Coetzee, 2007).

According to SAQA, the following points need to be considered when establishing a moderation system: management structure; functions of the moderation system; components of the moderation system and moderation methods to be used.

Management structure

The management team in the organisation is responsible for ensuring the implementation of a moderation policy and procedure that complies with SAQA's requirements and the national unit standard for moderation and verification. Moderation is an integral part of the ETD provider's quality assurance.

Functions of the moderation system

The organisation may use internal ETD practitioners (who are not involved in presenting the learning programme) as internal moderators. The ETQA of the relevant SETA acts as external moderator of the assessment procedures, methods and learner achievements. Internal moderators are responsible for:

- checking the credibility of assessment methods and instruments;
- checking the assessment system for effectiveness (including the use of resources);
- monitoring and observing assessment processes and candidates' evidence (through sampling);
- checking assessors' decisions;
- providing advice and guidance to assessors on system improvements;
- checking that all the staff involved in assessment are appropriately qualified and experienced; and
- assuring that learners with special needs have been accommodated in the assessment process.

Components of the moderation system

The components of the moderation system include appropriate timing, extent, materials and personnel.

Timing

Assessment guides should be moderated before assessment takes place and after the final assessment decisions have been made. Moderation must be conducted on an annual basis.

Extent

The moderation activities should be evaluated in terms of the extent to which they protect the integrity of unit standards. Unit standards, assessment materials, assessor competence and learner evidence are assessed in the moderation process.

Materials

Moderation materials should include the following:

- assessment activities;
- assessment guides;
- case studies; and
- learners' worked samples (for example, portfolios of evidence, knowledge questionnaire answer sheets, assignment answers, case study solutions, observation checklists and self-assessments).

Personnel

The personnel chosen as moderators need to have unquestionable expertise in the curriculum and assessment practices. Moderators should understand the expectations of all users. Moderators also need to be registered with the relevant ETQA.

Methods

Moderation methods that must be employed are:

- revising moderation materials and benchmark materials;
- recognising expert assessors;

- doing statistical moderation;
- reviewing common assessment activities and assessment guides;
- getting external moderators to do site visits;
- getting external moderators to conduct panel meetings;
- establishing site consultative committees; and
- reviewing the moderation system for effectiveness.

Moderation tools

Table 6.15 *Example of a moderator report (Coetzee, 2006a)*

Scope of moderation	Evidence	Compliance Yes/No	Recommendations
Assessment instruments covered the curriculum and unit standard	Assessment guide		
Assessment design and methodology relevant to the unit standard and curriculum design and consistently applied by all assessors	Assessment guide		
Assessment decisions recorded	Assessment records		
Report and feedback mechanisms in place	Assessment records and reports		
Assessment decisions: • Fairness • Reliability • Appropriateness • Validity • Sufficiency • Practicality	Assessment records and reports Worked samples Learner evidence (portfolios, case studies, assignment answers, knowledge questionnaire answer sheets)		
Candidates with special needs and RPL cases considered	Assessment records and reports Candidate feedback		
Assessment practice reviewed for quality assurance purposes Improvement areas identified	Quality review report		
Learner support and guidance practices regarding assessment in place	Assessment guide		
Assessor registered and competent	Assessor registration and qualifications		
Assessment decision outcomes confirmed/rejected	Moderator report		

General comments: _____

Moderator name and signature: _____   Date: _____

Assessor name and signature: _____   Date: _____

The moderation tools that must be employed are:
- a moderation plan;
- a moderation report; and
- the national unit standard for moderation.

Key terms

- Assessment
- Assessment activities
- Assessment guide
- Assessment instruments
- Assessment methods
- Assessment plan
- Diagnostic assessment
- Evidence
- Formative assessment
- Integrated assessment
- Moderation
- Portfolio assessment
- RPL assessment
- Summative assessment

Review and discussion questions

1. Why does outcomes-based ETD emphasise quality assessment and moderation practices?
2. Why should ETD practitioners take into account the various role players in the assessment and moderation process? What are the functions of these role players?
3. How can assessors and ETD practitioners apply the various types of assessment to enhance the quality of learning?
4. How do the various assessment methods and instruments help to assure valid and reliable assessment practices?
5. What is the function and purpose of drawing up a comprehensive assessment plan and assessment guide? What aspects of assessment should be included in these documents?
6. What are the various steps involved in the assessment process?
7. What are SAQA's requirements for assessors?
8. How does moderation support the assessment process?

Suggested reading

Coetzee, M. (2007). *Getting and keeping your accreditation: The quality assurance and assessment guide for ETD practitioners* (2nd edition). Pretoria: Van Schaik.

Van der Horst, H. & McDonald, R. (1997). *Outcomes-based education: A teacher's manual.* Pretoria: Kagiso.

SAQA website (www.saqa.org.za)
- RPL in the context of the NQF
- Department of Education Language Policy
- Education Rights Project – The Law and Transformation programme, The Education Policy Unit
- The National Qualifications Framework and Standards Setting
- The National Qualifications Framework – An Overview
- Quality Management Systems for ETQAs
- Criteria and Guidelines for Providers
- Guidelines for Integrated Assessment

- Assessment of NQF Registered Qualifications and Unit Standards.
- Department of Labour Criteria for SETAs: Implementation of Monitoring and Evaluation processes for Learnerships – prepared by the Monitoring of Quality Learning Provisioning Working Group appointed by the Department of Labour: Quality Learning Forum.
- The National Qualifications Framework and Curriculum Development
- Criteria and Guidelines for ETQAs
- Draft Policy in General Education and Training

Summary

Assessment and moderation of learning achievements are significant elements of outcomes-based ETD. Outcomes-based assessment assesses learners' ability to combine foundational, practical and reflexive competencies with critical cross-field outcomes and apply these in real-life (practical) contexts or for a defined purpose. This chapter discussed the importance of identifying and applying valid and reliable assessment procedures, methods and instruments in measuring learners' achievement of learning outcomes. Assessors must be qualified subject matter experts who are registered with the relevant ETQA.

Moderation (as an aspect of quality assurance) was explored. Assessment and moderation of learners' achievements are important to ensure that a learning programme adds value and contributes to the overall HRD strategy of a company. Chapter 7 explores methods of evaluating the effectiveness of learning programmes.

> *"I never teach my (learners); I only attempt to provide the conditions in which they can learn" (Albert Einstein).*

CHAPTER 7

JEROME KILEY

Evaluating ETD effectiveness

The purpose of ETD interventions is to improve performance in the organisation on an individual, group or organisational level. ETD evaluation is the process of determining to what extent this has been achieved. The ETD evaluation process allows ETD practitioners and managers to collect descriptive and judgemental information that is used to improve the quality of learning programme design and delivery.

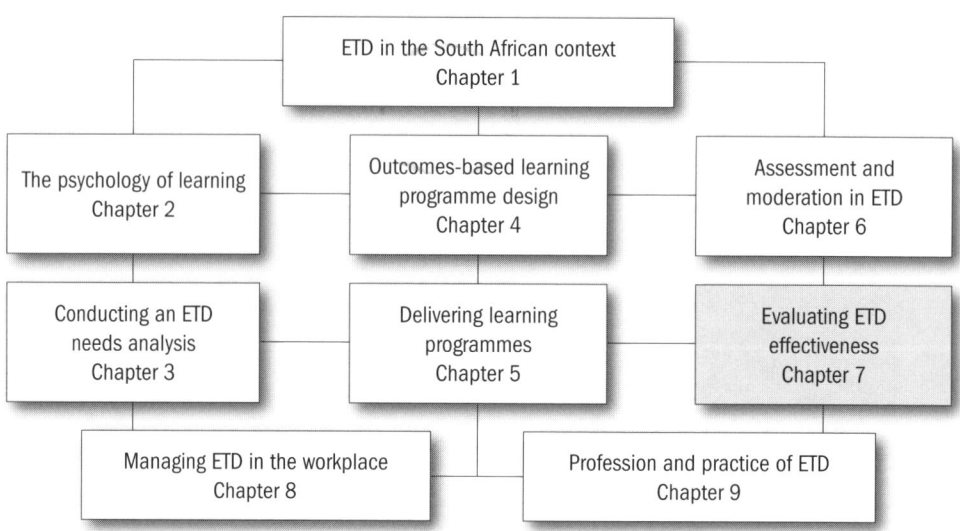

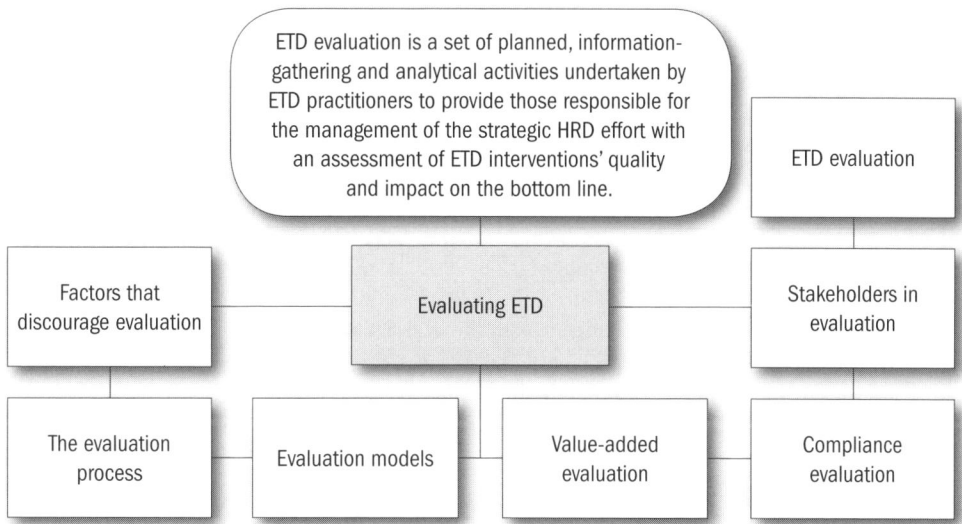

ETD evaluation is a set of planned, information-gathering and analytical activities undertaken by ETD practitioners to provide those responsible for the management of the strategic HRD effort with an assessment of ETD interventions' quality and impact on the bottom line.

ETD evaluation

Factors that discourage evaluation

Evaluating ETD

Stakeholders in evaluation

The evaluation process

Evaluation models

Value-added evaluation

Compliance evaluation

Key points of evaluating ETD

- Evaluation is a significant component of ETD provision. Compliance evaluation and value-added evaluation of ETD interventions and practices allow ETD practitioners and managers to collect descriptive and judgemental information. This information is used to make effective ETD decisions regarding the selection, adoption, modification and financial evaluation of various ETD activities.
- ETD evaluation can take place before, during, at the conclusion of, or some time after a learning programme.
- Evaluation models are useful frameworks to determine the ETD evaluation dimensions and criteria to be measured.
- The ETD evaluation process should be planned properly and executed in a systematic manner to ensure the validity and reliability of compliance and value-added measurements.

After studying this chapter, you should be able to:

- Explain how properly planned and executed ETD evaluations help ETD practitioners and managers to prove the quality of and value added by their learning programmes and other ETD interventions.
- Explain the purpose of compliance evaluation and value-added evaluation in the South African workplace.
- Evaluate the factors that discourage ETD evaluation in the workplace.
- Describe the steps that ETD practitioners follow to ensure that their evaluations produce valid and reliable data.
- Describe how ETD practitioners demonstrate to management the cost-effectiveness, resulting change and impact of learning programmes.
- Describe how the various evaluation models guide ETD practitioners in determining evaluation dimensions and criteria.
- Explain the timing of conducting an ETD evaluation.

As the fifth phase in the Training Cycle, the evaluation of learning programmes is a significant component of ETD provision. The aim of any ETD intervention (in particular learning programmes) is to sustain employee and organisational performance capability (including present and future performance) or to solve problems that occur in the organisation. Organisations invest in ETD initiatives such as learning programmes because they want to improve performance, reduce costs or improve working conditions. In this regard, ETD evaluation is the process of determining whether the ETD intervention has achieved its goals in the most effective and efficient manner possible (Swart, Mann, Brown & Price, 2005).

The long-term success of ETD initiatives and the ETD function is dependent on the following three principles:
1. ETD practitioners need to excel at their job.
2. They need to plan, design, manage and evaluate ETD programmes that not only positively influence the mission and purpose of the organisation, but also add value for stakeholders.
3. They need to use information about their performance to prove to the organisation and its stakeholders that they are doing an excellent job and that they should be provided with the necessary resources to sustain their performance.

ETD evaluation allows ETD practitioners and managers to collect descriptive and judgemental information. This information is used to make effective ETD decisions. Such decisions include the selection, adoption, modification and financial evaluation of various ETD activities (Goldstein & Ford, 2002).

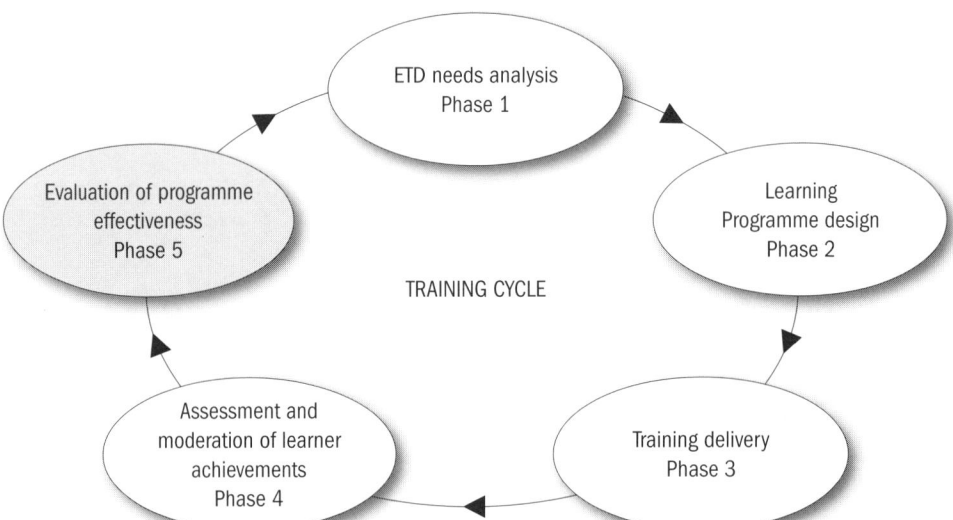

Figure 7.1 The Training Cycle

This chapter clarifies what evaluation means in ETD and describes the various stakeholders involved in ETD evaluation. In addition, the various types, criteria and models of ETD evaluation relevant to the workplace are discussed. We explore the evaluation process, examine data collection tools and discuss factors that discourage ETD evaluation in general.

ETD evaluation

ETD evaluation is a set of planned, information-gathering and analytical activities. ETD practitioners undertake these activities to provide those responsible for the management of the strategic HRD effort with a satisfactory assessment of the effects, progress, quality and added value of ETD interventions. ETD evaluation also means placing a value on the ETD initiatives (in particular, the learning programmes that employees attend). Evaluations of the effectiveness of learning programmes are usually done to provide information and influence a decision that must be made about the HRD strategy, practices and procedures. Evaluation provides diagnostic information that shows where remedial actions should be undertaken and whether the ETD intervention should be continued. More broadly, the purpose of ETD evaluation is to identify performance solutions for improving the organisation as a whole.

ETD evaluation is a continuous process. It requires proper planning and a clear statement, in the form of objectives, of what is to be evaluated. It is a systematic process of making judgements about the quality of a programme in terms of effectiveness (how well it works and whether it adds value to the organisation's bottom line) and efficiency (how well it is designed, delivered and managed). ETD evaluation also makes use of valid and reliable measuring instruments, or data collection tools, to achieve its objectives. Validity is the extent to which the measuring instrument reflects the concept it is intended to measure. Reliability is the extent to which scores obtained on a measure are reproducible in repeated administrations under similar measurement conditions (Rossi, Freeman & Lipsey, 1999).

Advantages of ETD evaluation (Phillips *et al*, 2004)

- Measure the difference between what was required and what has been achieved. The purpose of training is to improve performance in the organisation on an individual, group or organisational level. Evaluation shows to what extent this has been achieved.
- Justify the HRD department's budget. Evaluation gives the department the opportunity to justify its existence to management.
- Improve the design and delivery of learning programmes. Evaluation serves as a feedback system to judge the design and delivery of learning programmes.
- Improve the transfer of learning. Evaluation measures the extent to which learning is transferred to the workplace and helps to identify barriers to transfer.
- Identify unnecessary or ineffective programmes. Evaluation helps the organisation to identify learning programmes that do not contribute to the goals of the organisation or do not achieve their purpose.
- Improve the credibility of the HRD department. Evaluation data build respect and credibility for the HRD department and its staff.
- Meet the needs of management and gain their support. Evaluation data illustrate to management that their needs have been met by the HRD department. This creates loyalty and support.
- Show the financial return on training. Depending on the type of evaluation conducted, evaluation data provide information on the return on investment in training.

Similar to assessment, evaluation can take place at different times: before a training intervention (known as diagnostic evaluation), during a training intervention (known as formative evaluation), at the conclusion of a learning programme (known as summative evaluation), or some time after a learning programme (known as longitudinal evaluation) (Rothwell *et al*, 1995). Assessment focuses on evaluating collected evidence of learners' achievements against a set standard. Evaluation, on the other hand, makes judgements about the quality and added value of learning programmes and whether changes and/or improvements in learners' performance in the workplace occurred as a result of the learning programme. The moderation of assessment practices, methods and instruments and learners' achievements is an example of an evaluation activity.

Diagnostic evaluation

Diagnostic evaluation is relevant in the design phase of a learning programme (design is discussed in Chapter 4). Some of the questions that can be asked in the evaluation are:
- Are the selected training and learning facilitation methods appropriate to achieve the outcomes? In other words, will the training methods be effective in providing the learners with the necessary knowledge, skills or attitudes?
- Do the training methods coincide with the learners' preferences and learning styles?
- Has the learning programme been designed in the most efficient manner? In other words, is the programme curriculum designed to achieve the programme objective and learning outcomes in the shortest time and most cost-effective manner possible, without sacrificing quality?

The most effective method to review these issues is to run a pilot learning programme.

Formative evaluation

Formative evaluation is relevant to the delivery phase of a learning programme (delivery is discussed in Chapter 5). During this phase, ETD practitioners need to pay attention to the following issues:
- Are the learners enjoying the delivery of the programme?
- Are the methods being used in the delivery of the programme effective in achieving the programme objective and learning outcomes?
- What is the quality of the delivery of the learning programme? In other words, are the trainers doing their jobs properly?
- Are all the administrative arrangements running smoothly?

The most important time to discover errors or problems with a learning programme is while it is being implemented. The piloting, or testing, of a learning programme is therefore recommended to ensure that the most obvious problems are identified and corrected before the learning programme is implemented.

Summative and longitudinal evaluation

A number of important issues need to be evaluated during the summative and longitudinal evaluation processes. These evaluations occur when the learning programme has been completed. Summative evaluation occurs immediately after the learning programme. Longitudinal evaluation occurs some time after the learning programme (from a few weeks to a year). Issues that are relevant during these evaluations are:
- Have the learners achieved the learning outcomes? What are learners' assessment results?
- Was the learning programme effectively delivered?
- Did the learning programme achieve its overall objective?

It is important for ETD practitioners and learners to reflect on the learning programme after it has been completed. Questions such as the following can be asked:

- What could we have done differently?
- What needs to be changed?
- How can we improve the learning programme?

However, it is a lot more effective to identify problems before (diagnostic evaluation) or during the process (formative evaluation). Diagnostic and formative evaluation provide an opportunity to address and rectify the identified shortcomings during the ETD delivery process. The timing and purpose of evaluation are crucial to the relevance of and value added by an evaluation effort.

Table 7.1 Timing of evaluation and its related purpose

Evaluation timing	Focus of evaluation
Diagnostic evaluation Before the delivery of the ETD intervention	• The design of the programme • Existing skills levels of learners as part of the ETD needs analysis
Formative evaluation During the ETD intervention	• The quality of the delivery process • The adequacy of the learning material • The appropriateness of the delivery methods
Summative evaluation Directly after the ETD intervention	• Satisfaction of the learners with the learning programme • The achievement of the outcomes by the learners • The overall effectiveness of the learning programme
Longitudinal evaluation On the job Three to 12 months after completion of the ETD intervention	• Transfer and application of learning in the workplace • Support for new knowledge, skills and attitudes in the workplace • Impact on individual performance in the organisation • Impact on the performance of the organisation

As shown in Table 7.1, learner assessment data and other measures are used to determine the effectiveness of learning programmes. The ETD evaluation process not only determines whether a learning programme has achieved its objective, but also determines whether the assessment instruments were effective or appropriate in assessing learners. As pointed out in Chapter 4, the learning programme objective and learning outcomes are used to judge the effectiveness of the learning programme. ETD evaluation needs to be planned in advance, based on the overall learning programme objective and learning outcomes (Landy & Conte, 2004). The analysis of ETD needs (discussed in Chapter 3) and the design of learning programmes (discussed in Chapter 4) therefore form the foundation of any ETD evaluation activity.

Table 7.2 Example of a formative evaluation (Coetzee, 2006)

Module 6 Management and evaluation of ETD practices

Name: _____

Assess your own skills by rating yourself with a √ on each aspect mentioned.

I can	Poor	Fair	Excellent
Conduct an analysis of learning needs within the current and potential scope of provision			
Evaluate the provider's current management of learning			
Plan the development of learning programmes and learning provision			
Contribute to and promote ETD policies and quality assurance procedures within the organisation			
Support the ETD team			
Monitor and review learning provision and related systems			

What did you like about the module and learning process?

What about the module and learning process did you not like?

What additional learning support do you require from the facilitator to achieve the learning outcomes set for the programme?

Stakeholders in ETD evaluation

Stakeholders in ETD evaluation refer to those individuals, groups, or organisations that have a significant interest in a learning programme or ETD intervention (Rossi, Freeman & Lipsey, 1999). Any of the following persons may be considered as stakeholders in the context of an ETD evaluation:

- Present and past learners are the direct customers of any learning programme. They are directly affected by the quality of the programme.
- Learners' supervisors and managers. Learners are sent on a learning programme to change or improve their performance. Learners' managers or supervisors depend on the performance of learners in the workplace; they are thus directly affected by the effectiveness of learning programmes.
- Top management. The performance of learners affects the overall performance of the organisation. As this is the responsibility of top management, they will have an interest in the overall effectiveness of learning programmes.
- ETD practitioners in the organisation. The ETD practitioners are affected by the quality and effectiveness of learning programmes. This is their job, so evaluations may influence their future within the organisation.
- Representatives of labour unions represent the interests of their members (the learners). They are concerned with the quality and effectiveness of interventions that have an impact on the skills levels of their members.

Table 7.3 *Example of summative evaluation (Coetzee, 2007)*

Name of learning programme: Name of facilitator(s): Date learning programme was attended: Evaluate your learning experience				
Questions	Absolutely yes	Fairly so	In a small measure	Absolutely not
The purpose of the programme is clear to me.				
I understand the learning outcomes I have to achieve to successfully complete this programme.				
The learning objectives of the programme helped me to achieve the learning outcomes.				
The time we spent on the various activities was appropriate.				
The learning material helped me to improve my understanding of what I needed to learn.				
Instructions for learning activities were clear.				
The learning experience satisfied my personal learning needs.				
I could relate the learning activities, case studies and examples to my work situation.				
I was encouraged to participate in the learning activities.				
I was treated with respect.				
The facilitator was professional and approachable at all times.				
I was given a lot of help and support to complete the programme activities.				
The venue, time, refreshments and breaks were well organised.				
The facilitator helped me to identify ideas/actions that could assist me to learn more effectively.				
The assessment of my competencies was well planned and clear to me.				
I knew what evidence to provide to prove my competence in terms of the learning outcomes.				
The assessment of my competence was fair and objective.				
I was given the opportunity to ask questions about the assessment results.				
The feedback provided by the facilitator helped me to know how to build on my strengths and how to develop my weaknesses.				
I feel confident in applying the knowledge and skills I have learnt in my job.				
My learning points from the learning programme are: The most useful part of the learning programme was: The least useful part of the learning programme was: The actions I am going to take as a result of the learning programme are:				

- The training committee. As discussed in Chapter 1, the Skills Development Act, Act 97 of 1998, states that each organisation is required to have a training committee that is responsible for ETD matters within the workplace.
- SETAs are concerned with the development of skills within their particular sector. To this effect, organisations develop workplace skills plans (read more about this in Chapter 1). The SETA's success is influenced by the effectiveness of learning programmes in the organisation.
- SAQA is concerned with the standards of qualifications and learning programme design, delivery and management. ETD providers are therefore required to comply with the national standards for NQF-aligned outcomes-based ETD practices. They have to apply for recognition and accreditation of their learning programmes, qualifications and ETD management systems with the relevant ETQA.
- Customers of the organisation are affected by the performance of the learners in the workplace.
- ETD practitioners in other organisations may have conducted similar learning programmes or may be planning to do so in the future.
- Academic experts and consultants are valuable sources of expertise. They may be consulted for advice and support in conducting ETD evaluations.
- Professional associations such as the South African Board for Personnel Practice (SABPP) and the Institute for People Management (IPM) are valuable sources of information and expertise.
- Communities and the broader society. The communities within which organisations operate and the broader society are affected by these organisations. By implication, they are affected by the performance of the learners (Rothwell & Sredl, 1992: 94-98).

The list of stakeholders is exhaustive. All of these will not necessarily be involved in every evaluation. The criteria for involving stakeholders in an evaluation should relate to whether they have a significant interest in the success of a particular learning programme.

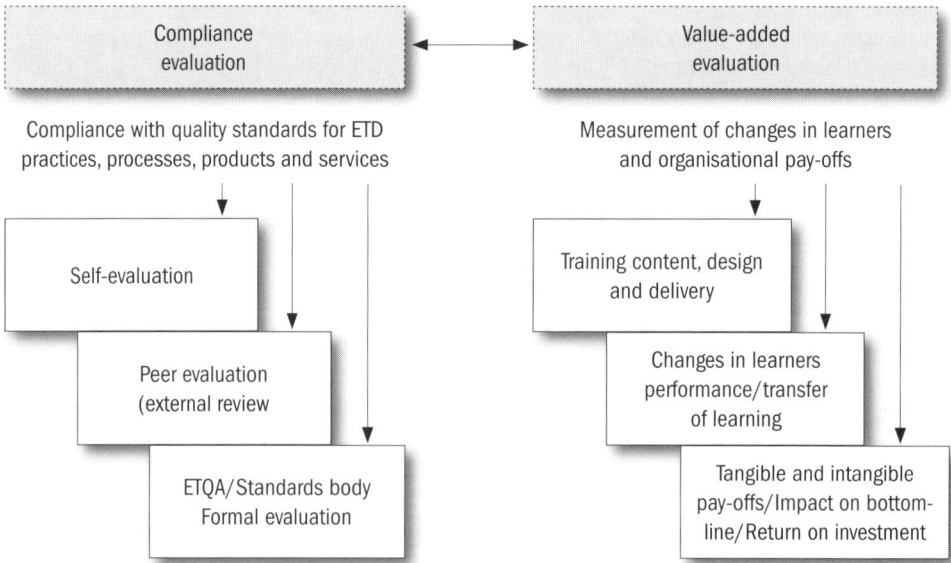

Figure 7.2 Integrated ETD evaluation (Coetzee, 2007a)

As shown in Figure 7.2, there are two types of evaluation in the workplace, namely compliance evaluation and value-added evaluation:

- Compliance evaluation emphasises the organisation's compliance with international and national quality standards for outcomes-based ETD practices.
- Value-added evaluation addresses the organisation's bottom line. It measures the cost-effectiveness of ETD interventions (Coetzee, 2007a).

Compliance evaluation

In terms of the national requirements for quality outcomes-based learning programme design, delivery and ETD management, compliance evaluation (also called quality audit or quality evaluation) is a compulsory activity for all ETD providers. Compliance evaluation is a three-step process:

1. ETD providers first conduct a self-evaluation of their ETD practices, procedures and processes against the SAQA/ETQA requirements for ETD provision. Self-evaluation will typically comprise evaluating the effectiveness of learning programme design, delivery, assessment, moderation, evaluation and management practices. Based on the findings of such a self-evaluation, ETD providers compile and implement an action plan aimed at improving the identified aspects.
2. The second step is to arrange a peer evaluation by external quality reviewers, based on the self-evaluation. This is done in preparation for the external compliance evaluation by the relevant ETQA or standards body.
3. The third step is to prepare for and undergo a formal quality audit by the ETQA or relevant standards body (such as the South African Bureau for Standards) for accreditation and recognition.

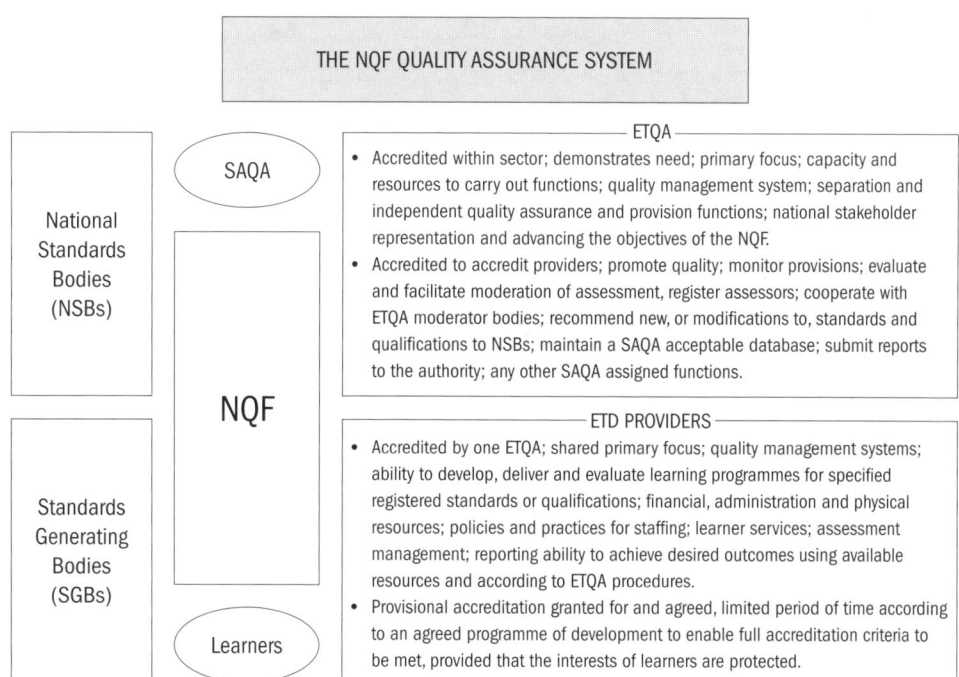

Figure 7.3 NQF quality assurance system for quality outcomes-based ETD in the workplace (SAQA, 2001)

ETD quality assurance refers to all the activities that assure the quality of the design, delivery, management and evaluation of learning programmes and their outcomes. These activities include the following:

- Clarify and describe customer expectations and needs.
- Ensure ETD providers, practitioners, assessors and moderators have a clear, comprehensive and accurate understanding of the quality standards.
- Ensure that the required resources are available for the design, delivery and management of qualifications and learning programmes, and that they meet the required standards.
- Ensure that ETD providers, practitioners, assessors and moderators have the necessary skills, knowledge and motivation to make the products or deliver the service.
- Ensure that quality assurance evaluation systems are in place to monitor the design, delivery, management and evaluation of qualifications and learning programmes.
- Ensure the independent auditing and monitoring of quality and feedback systems by providers of learning programmes and other stakeholders who are in a position to contribute to enhancing quality (SAQA, 2001a).

Table 7.4 *SAQA quality requirements for ETD providers (adapted from SAQA, 2001a)*

1. Policy statement
• What are the values and principles of your ETD department?
• Are these values and principles aligned with those of the NQF?
• What structures, systems and activities are in place in your department to apply these values and principles?
2. Quality management systems
• How does your ETD department/organisation create and sustain a quality culture?
• How, when and by whom is information collected about the workings of your ETD department?
• What processes are in place to ensure that you meet the needs of your learners?
• How often are programmes delivered by your ETD department reviewed?
• What processes are in place to ensure that the facilitators are competent to facilitate and assess the learning standards, according to the requirements of the NQF?
• What processes are in place to monitor and review assessment activities?
• What processes are in place to ensure that the information gathered from reviews, audits and monitoring lead to improvements in your ETD department?
• What mechanisms exist for your ETD department to report back to people within your organisation?
• How does your ETD department ensure that its resources are utilised effectively and efficiently?
• How does your ETD department report to and generally relate to the ETQA?
• How does your ETD department relate to other providers in the subject area in which they work?
3. Review mechanisms
• What review, monitoring, research and/or auditing mechanisms are in place in your ETD department?
• What process do these mechanisms follow?
• How often are reviews, research and audits carried out?
• Who is responsible for carrying out the reviews, research and audits?
• What process is used to report back findings within the organisation?
• How do the findings of the reviews lead to improvements in your ETD department?

4. Programme delivery

- What types of learning programme does your ETD department deliver?
- On which level/s of the NQF do these programmes fall?
- What are the different components of these programmes?
- How frequently are the programmes delivered?
- What processes are used to deliver the programmes (for example, classroom-based instruction, distance learning, computer-based instruction)?
- To what extent is the delivery of the programmes flexible?
- How do you ensure learner-centredness in the delivery of the programmes?
- How do you ensure that the delivery methods are relevant to learners?
- What assessment processes are used (when, where, how often and by whom)?
- What are the processes used to give the learners feedback on their performance?

5. Staff policies

- Who is responsible for the selection of your staff in your ETD department?
- What are the criteria used for selecting ETD department staff?
- What selection procedures are used for the selection of staff?
- How is the Employment Equity Act applied in the selection process?

6. Learner policies

- What processes are followed to select learners for training programmes?
- How is recognition of prior learning applied in the selection procedures?
- What processes are in place to ensure programmes are relevant to the needs and aspirations of learners?
- How is learner participation encouraged through the delivery of the programmes?
- What processes are in place to identify the nature of the support that learners require?
- What is the nature of the support given to learners?
- What guidance is offered to learners? What is the motivation for this?
- What opportunities for further learning are provided for by your ETD department?
- What process is used to give the learners feedback on their performance?

7. Assessment policies

- What is your ETD department's approach to assessment?
- How are assessments conducted, by whom and how often?
- How is your department's assessment policy aligned with the NQF's principles?
- How does your ETD department/organisation's assessment policy incorporate principles of lifelong learning, recognition of prior learning and integration of theory and practice?
- What mechanisms are in place to ensure the quality of assessments?
- How are learners given feedback on their assessments? Who does this and how often?
- How are assessments used to identify and provide the support and guidance that learners require?
- How are assessment results used in programme development?

8. Management systems and policies

- What is the management and administrative structure of your ETD department?
- What decision-making processes are used in your organisation?
- What process is used to allocate financial resources to your ETD department?
- Does your ETD department have adequate resources (physical, human and financial resources) to carry out its intended functions?
- What systems does your ETD department use to manage and account for its finances?

Table 7.5 *Steps to establish an ETD quality assurance system (Coetzee, 2006)*

Action	Evidence
1. Review current training practices, policies and procedures.	Review report
2. Evaluate these practices, policies and procedures in terms of alignment with the NQF OBET quality system requirements.	Review report
3. Identify areas for improvement.	Improvement plan
4. Draft a quality plan containing: • quality statement; • goals, objectives and performance targets; • resource plan (people, finance, administrative and physical resources); • quality areas to be managed; • list of policies that need to be written; • customer relations plan; • communication plan; and • quality audit plan.	Quality plan Quality manual containing plan and policies
5. Draft an organogram (structure of people required). The structure should address the following functions: • manager/coordinator of quality assurance; • assessors; • internal and external assessors; • ETD practitioners; • mentors; • RPL advisors; • administrative support; and • quality auditors.	Organogram in quality manual
6. Draft occupational (job) profiles for the identified positions.	Job profiles
7. Draft a selection, screening and appointment plan.	Recruitment plan
8. Appoint identified people. Follow formal authorisation and accreditation procedures.	Advertisements Interview report Competency certificates Authorisation letters
9. Draft performance contracts with people.	Performance contracts
10. Conduct a competence assessment and draft a development plan with appointed people.	Development plans
11. Identify ETD interventions for people and integrate these in the workplace skills plan.	Workplace skills plan
12. Draft organisation quality policies and procedures and obtain formal approval.	Approval
13. Orientate organisation management, stakeholders and employees in quality assurance system, policies and procedures.	Minutes of sessions Attendance reports Unit standards

Action	Evidence
14. Train management and HRD people in the quality auditing process.	Evaluation reports Unit standards
15. Obtain management and other customer requirements in terms of reporting on progress and standards.	Record and documentation system
16. Draft unit standards for in-house training programmes.	Management information system policy
17. Set up a documentation and record system for learner achievements, assessment reports, skills development needs and audits, ETQA and provider evaluation reports.	Documentation system
18. Set up a management review system, including: • monthly progress review; and • audit reviews and corrective action planning.	Management review system Minutes of meetings Audit review reports Corrective action plan
19. Conduct quality culture and climate surveys.	Survey results
20. Establish effective computerised information systems to support decision making.	HR information system

Organisations who have to follow international standards and regulations are exposed to compliance evaluations by bodies such as the South African Bureau for Standards (SABS). The results or outcomes of a compliance evaluation point out the remedial actions that must be taken to ensure national recognition and accreditation as an ETD provider. ETD providers are also required to draw up and execute development plans that address the shortcomings highlighted by the compliance evaluations.

Table 7.6 Steps in conducting a compliance evaluation (based on Coetzee, 2006)

In place		Key performance areas	Responsible person	Evidence
Yes	No			
		Prepare and orientate the stakeholders (management, ETD staff, providers and learners).		
		Plan a time and compliance evaluation schedule with them.		
		Give a written notice of the compliance evaluation (date, time, venue, area to be audited, evidence required and process).		
		Prepare the compliance evaluation (checklist, measurement scales, evidence to be collected, assessment criteria and performance areas).		
		Orientate all evaluators to ensure reliability, validity and fairness of the evaluation process. Use assessment criteria as guideline.		
		Conduct the evaluation. Use worksheets to record findings.		
		Analyse the findings.		
		Meet with the stakeholders to discuss the report on findings and recommendations.		

In place		Key performance areas	Responsible person	Evidence
Yes	No			
		Do joint action planning with them on corrective actions to be taken.		
		Determine follow-up evaluations on corrective actions implemented.		
		Draw up a formal plan of action and let all involved sign the plan.		
		Keep minutes of these meetings as evidence and distribute to all involved.		
		Conduct a formal follow-up evaluation, following the same process as described above.		
		Coach and mentor people involved. Evaluation is a development process; the aim is continuous improvement.		

Value-added evaluation

Value-added evaluation is concerned with the organisation's bottom line. It is conducted to measure the cost-effectiveness of ETD interventions. The decision resulting from a value-added evaluation may involve continuing, expanding, or eliminating the learning programme. Evaluation may be carried out to determine if the cost of a learning programme is justified by its effects, or the value it adds to the organisation. Evaluation of a learning programme's effectiveness also provides useful information to market the programme or get the support of stakeholders (Smith & Geis, 1992).

Evaluation criteria

Organisations often neglect to evaluate the value added by their ETD interventions because they are uncertain about what should be evaluated. There is a wide range of evaluation models, each with a different emphasis and focus. ETD practitioners find it difficult to decide which model to use (Ostroff cited in Goldstein & Ford, 2002). One approach to overcome this problem is to classify the purpose of evaluation into broad categories or dimensions. Each of these dimensions has a number of criteria. These are the standards or rules by which the dimensions are judged. Typical dimensions of evaluation are discussed below and on the following pages.

Learning programme design

The design of the learning programme is evaluated in terms of the selection of appropriate content, training methods and the physical design of the curriculum and learning materials. These are examined in the context of good ETD design practices (discussed in Chapter 4) and their appropriateness for achieving the objectives and learning outcomes of the learning programme. For example, if an ETD needs analysis indicates that knowledge of electronic circuitry is required to perform a job, then a seminar about electronic circuitry would have content validity. Although content analysis may ensure that a learning programme is job related, it still does not indicate whether a particular training method is effective (Aamodt, 2007). But if the content of a learning programme is valid, and if the learning programme is conducted by a professional ETD practitioner, the learning programme will most probably be successful.

Examples of criteria for evaluating the content validity and overall design of a learning programme include the following:

- Are the methods selected appropriate to the learners?
- Is the programme pitched at the level of the learners?
- Does the content adequately relate to the outcomes?
- Is this the most efficient way to deliver the learning?
- What is the quality of the learning materials?

Training delivery

The evaluation of the quality of the training delivery is based on learner satisfaction and sound learning facilitation practices. The evaluation also includes the administrative and support processes related to the programme. Examples of criteria for the delivery of a learning programme include:

- Were the learners satisfied with the quality of the delivery of the learning programme?
- What was the quality of the logistical arrangements?
- Were the most appropriate delivery methods used for delivering the programme?
- Were the characteristics of the learners identified by means of a target group analysis?
- Were the characteristics and ETD needs of the learners taken into account in the delivery of the programme?
- Were the assessments appropriate in light of the learning outcomes?

Competence

Competence relates to the quality of the assessment process, methods and instruments. The question that the evaluator asks is, "To what extent did the learners achieve the outcomes of the learning programme?" The main criterion for competence is whether learners demonstrated mastery of the learning outcomes.

Transfer of learning

In this dimension, the extent to which acquired competencies are transferred to the workplace, is evaluated. The evaluation question here is, "Does the workplace support the transfer of the competencies acquired during the learning process?" Examples of criteria for the transfer of learning to the workplace include:

- Does the workplace allow the implementation of new knowledge, skills, attitudes and behaviour?
- Are learners provided with opportunities to practise their new skills?
- Do supervisors and managers encourage the implementation of knowledge, skills, attitudes and behaviour?
- Are the knowledge, skills, attitudes and behaviour acquired in the learning programme appropriate to the workplace?

Impact on the performance of the organisation

The main aim of learning programmes is to address present problems, improve current performance or to address future requirements (Swanson, 1994). The last dimension that is evaluated is the extent to which the delivery of the learning programme and the accompanying transfer of knowledge, skills, attitudes and behaviour affect the performance of the organisation. Examples of criteria to measure the impact of a learning programme on the performance of the organisation include:

- Have the tangible outputs of the organisation increased (see Table 7.7)?
- Have the intangible outputs of the organisation increased (see Table 7.8)?

Table 7.7 *Tangible organisational results (based on Rothwell & Kazanas, 1994)*

Organisational outputs (usually expressed in terms of productivity)	
• Number of units produced • Tons of goods manufactured • Sales volume • Forms processed • Shipments sent • Number of rejects	• Patients visited • Applications processed • Students graduated • Tasks completed • Targets achieved
Time	
• Equipment downtime • Overtime paid • Orders and shipments on time • Lead times • Time to process orders	• Training and retraining time • Time taken by meetings • Work stoppages • Lost time • Repair time
Monetary outputs	
• Difference between budget and actual expenses • Overhead expenses • Cost reductions	• Operating expenses • Cost savings on projects
Quality outputs	
• Number of rejects and product defects • Levels of waste • Error rates • Product repairs • Deviations from set standards	• Product failure • Percentage of tasks correctly completed • Number of accidents • Sick leave and days off • Number of products that have to be reworked

Table 7.8 *Intangible organisational results (based on Rothwell & Kazanas, 1994)*

Work habits	
• Levels of absenteeism • Lateness • Accidents at work	• Violations of health and safety rules • Communication breakdowns • Excessive and prolonged breaks
Application of new skills	
• Quality of decisions made • Problems solved • Conflicts avoided • Grievances resolved	• Listening skills • Reading skills • Use and application of new skills • Frequency of use of new skills
Work climate	
• Number of grievances • Levels of job satisfaction	• Relations with the unions in the workplace • Employee turnover

• Instances of discrimination • Requests for transfer	• Sick leave

Development and advancement of employees	
• Number of promotions • Number of pay increases • Training programmes attended	• Product failure • Ratings in performance appraisals • Increases in job performance levels

Attitudes and opinions	
• Favourable attitudes towards the organisation and management • Perceptions of duties and responsibilities	• Perceived changes in performance • General attitude towards colleagues and clients

Initiative	
• Implementation of new ideas • Successful completion of projects • Employees taking responsibility and initiative	• Number and type of suggestions submitted • Suggestions implemented

Measuring value added in ETD

Measuring the value added by ETD interventions plays an important role in managing the quality and cost-effectiveness of learning programme design and delivery. A measurement system provides a frame of reference that helps managers and ETD practitioners to carry out several important responsibilities:

- Measurement focuses staff on important issues. A measurement system is a management decision-making tool that helps to prioritise tasks. Measurement also shows ETD practitioners the return on investment in a learning programme. ETD staff learn that cost, time, quality, quantity and learners' and stakeholders' reactions are all factors that influence ETD decisions and actions.
- Measurement clarifies expectations. Once the objectives for ETD interventions are set in terms of cost, time, quality, quantity and stakeholder satisfaction, ETD staff understand what is expected of them. Standards of performance and acceptable levels of deviation from those standards are known.
- Measurement involves, encourages and fosters creativity. Once a measurement system is in place, staff tend to compete to meet or exceed the objectives. When the system is fully functioning, people bring forth new and important issues to measure and clever ways to measure them.
- Measurement brings the ETD function closer to departments. The ETD measurement system should include factors that relate to quality, productivity, services and profitability within the organisation. For example, it is important to track and report learners' success rate, but connecting a new ETD delivery strategy to an improvement in operational quality, productivity and service is much more valuable to managers.
- Measurement improves ETD management and control. If ETD practitioners and managers measure the value added by ETD initiatives, they can manage it. If they can manage it, they can improve it (Fitz-ens, 1995).

Value-added measurement of ETD emphasises the following components of the value chain (Fitz-ens, 1995):

PROCESS ──▶ OUTCOME ──▶ IMPACT ──▶ VALUE ADDED

Figure 7.4 The value chain (Fitz-ens, 1995)

All ETD processes (for example, ETD needs analysis, planning, design and delivery of learning programmes) must be cost effective and fit for purpose. The objective of value-added measurement is to develop ways to measure and evaluate changes in the ETD processes, results and the resulting value. For every improvement in a process, there should be a resulting improvement in results or outcomes. The difference between the improved outcome and the outcome before the improvement in the process is the impact. The cost improvement as a result of the impact is the value added.

Example of cost improvement as a result of impact

Here is an example of cost improvement as a result of impact. An ETD practitioner decides to shorten the hours of training provided (outcome) without affecting the quality of delivery, by improving the learning programme design and delivery process. More employees can be trained in a shorter period of time; the resultant cost savings can be calculated. If learning programmes are delivered in a more cost-effective and efficient manner, the organisation will save on operating expenses. Furthermore, the cost of the product or service is lowered and the ETD initiative reaches the market faster. Lower product cost and shorter delivery time creates a competitive advantage in the marketplace, thereby increasing the organisation's market share.

The three general measures of training are cost, change and impact:
- Cost refers to the expense per unit of training delivered.
- Change refers to the gain in competence or positive change in attitude and behaviour among learners.
- Impact refers to the results or outcomes of the learners' use of new competencies. Impact is measurable in monetary terms (Fitz-ens, 1995).

Cost

Measuring the cost of training is relatively simple. The simplest calculation is a matter of adding up all the expenses and dividing the total by the number of people trained. Expenses will differ, depending on the number of direct and indirect costs included. Examples of direct costs are: consultant fees, training room rental, supplies, refreshments, travel and accommodation, and ETD provider costs. Examples of indirect costs (mostly overhead costs) include learning facilitators' salaries and benefits, learners' salaries and benefits and use of departmental equipment.

Example of cost calculation per learner (Fitz-ens, 1995: 228)

$$C/L = \frac{CC + TR + S + RC + T\&A + TS + PS + OH}{PT}$$

C/L	Cost per learner	
CC	Consultant costs	15 000
TR	Training facility rental	950
S	Supplies, workbook, paper and pencils	5 000
RC	Refreshments	1 500
T&A	Travel and accommodation for learners and trainers	30 000
TS	Trainer's salary and benefits	15 000
PS	Participants' salaries and benefits	60 000
OH	ETD department overheads	3 000
PT	Number of people trained	30

$$C/L = \frac{15\ 000 + 950 + 5\ 000 + 1\ 500 + 30\ 000 + 15\ 000 + 60\ 000 + 3\ 000}{30}$$

$$= \frac{130\ 450}{30}$$

$$= R\ 4\ 348.33$$

Table 7.9 *Example of a training cost spreadsheet (based on Fitz-ens, 1995)*

Phase	Costs					
	People	Material	Facilities	Equipment	Miscellaneous	Total
ETD needs analysis						
Design and development						
Delivery						
Evaluation						
Total						

Input analysis

An input analysis approach is a systemic method of identifying and comparing the many costs involved in two or more learning programmes (Fitz-ens, 1995). The ETD practitioner forms a matrix of the main phases of the ETD process and the basic cost inputs. Each cell of the matrix is filled in with the appropriate cost, and the totals for all phases and inputs are calculated. One matrix is completed for each learning programme. The final set of matrices is compared for differences in cost. This approach only shows which programme costs the least (cost-efficiency). It does not compare the cost-effectiveness of different programmes. Cost-effectiveness is measured in terms of the impact of the change or improvement; in other words, the outcome or result of the learning programme.

Change or outcome

Change or outcome usually describes the immediate consequences of a learning programme or ETD intervention (Smith & Geis, 1992). Change can be measured at individual level in terms of improvements in knowledge, skill, attitude or behaviour. Comparisons can be made across groups. The text box below gives an example of a calculation for measuring skill changes. Data for the skill change ratio can be gathered through questionnaires, interviews, demonstrations or observations with ETD practitioners, employees, peers or supervisors. The key to obtaining something of value from any measurement is to be specific in describing the skills or behaviours to be evaluated (Fitz-ens, 1995).

Example of skill or behaviour change calculation (Fitz-ens, 1995)

$$SC = \frac{Sa}{Sb}$$

SC   Observable change in skills as a result of training

Sa   Skill level after training, demonstrated by work output, critical incidents, or other observable phenomena

Sb   Skill level before training, using the same criteria as for Sa

---

Impact

Impact describes the long-term effect of the change brought about by the learning programme (Smith & Geis, 1992). The relationship between change and impact measurement is one of value. Whereas change and cost are two distinctly different variables, change and impact are sequential measures along the value chain continuum. The text box below is an example to illustrate the distinction between the measurement of change and impact (Fitz-ens, 1995:234).

Example of impact measurement (based on Fitz-ens, 1995)

A machine operator, Johannes, is taught to run a cutting machine. At the end of the learning programme, Johannes's skill and knowledge is tested with a performance test. Before attending the learning programme, he could cut 80 units per hour. After the learning programme, the test shows that he can now cut 100 units per hour. Clearly, the level of skill and knowledge changed in a positive way: Johannes is more efficient as a result of the training. If he goes to work and consistently averages 100 cuts per hour, the training has an impact on the cost of goods manufactured. Assuming the reject and scrap rate is the same as before, Johannes is now 25% more productive. This is the amount of change. The cost of labour (as an input to the cutting cost) is thus reduced by 25%. That is the impact. If Johannes's on-the-job performance was not measured, the ETD practitioner and supervisor would not have known that the training added value to the organisation.

Levels of value-added evaluation

There are several levels of sophistication in evaluating the value added by training. As the degree of sophistication increases, the value of the evaluation tends to increase as well (Fitz-ens, 1995). These levels include: learner reaction surveys, which are administered during or at the end of the learning programme; knowledge tests; performance measurements after the learning programme; and performance measurements before and after the learning programme.

- The learner reaction survey is the lowest-value method, as the survey generally measures only learners' subjective experience of the learning programme.
- Knowledge tests are a slightly more useful method. They are given after the programme to measure how much the learner knows. However, as there is no pre-test against which to compare scores, there is also no proof that the learners' knowledge level increased as a result of the programme.
- Measuring learners' performance after the programme helps to evaluate learners' ability to apply the newly acquired competencies in the workplace.
- Measuring performance before and after the learning programme is even more sophisticated. It includes a follow-up check some months after the learning programme.

Evaluation models

There are many different models that focus on different dimensions and levels of ETD evaluation. This section will examine four different models that have a wide range of focuses.

Kirkpatrick's taxonomy of training evaluation criteria

Donald Kirkpatrick is recognised as the father of ETD evaluation. He published one of the first papers on the subject in 1954. Kirkpatrick (1994) defines ETD evaluation as "the determination of the effectiveness of a training program." His model still has a major impact on evaluation practices today. His model is known as a hierarchy or taxonomy, because the different levels build upon one another.

Level 1: Reaction
This level measures the extent to which learners liked the learning programme. Reaction evaluation normally takes place immediately after the learning programme. Questionnaires (often referred to as smile sheets) are used. Learners indicate their satisfaction with the various elements of the learning programme. Questions make use of Likert-scales (five or seven-point scales that range from, for example, like to dislike, or poor to excellent). An example of some reaction questions are provided below.

Example of a reaction evaluation

1 = Poor; 2 = Okay; 3 = Good; 4 = Very good; 5 = Excellent

1. How would you rate the presentation of the course?	1 2 3 4 5
2. What was the quality of the support materials?	1 2 3 4 5
3. How supportive was the trainer?	1 2 3 4 5

Kirkpatrick (1994: 37) provides the following guidelines for evaluating learners' reactions:
- Determine what you want to find out.
- Use a written comment sheet that covers these items.
- Design the sheet in such a way that reactions can be tabulated and quantified.

- Keep the forms anonymous to encourage honesty.
- Encourage the learners to include comments not covered by the questionnaire (see Tables 7.2 and 7.3 for examples).

Alliger, Tannenbaum, Bennet, Traver and Shotland (1997) suggest that Kirkpatrick's taxonomy should be enhanced to include multiple criteria at Level 1 (reaction). Their framework divides Level 1 criteria into affective reactions (for example, "I found this learning programme to be enjoyable") and utility reactions (for example, This learning programme had practical value" or "This learning programme was job relevant"). They conclude that affective reactions can be important, particularly when unfavourable reactions to training have negative effects on perceptions of the ETD department and future training efforts. However, utility reactions are more closely linked with learning and behavioural criteria than affective reactions. Accordingly, if the purpose of collecting reaction criteria is to predict the transfer of learning, ETD practitioners should ask questions that require utility reactions.

Level 2: Learning
Kirkpatrick (1994) emphasises that a favourable reaction to a learning programme does not ensure learning. To understand this, one simply has to think about all the pleasant experiences in life that do not lead to learning. The learning level evaluates whether there has been a change in the level of knowledge, skills, attitudes and behaviour. The main question is whether the learning outcomes set for the learning programme have been achieved. At this level, assessment and evaluation overlap. Evaluation occurs through the use of assessment instruments such as tests, examinations, assignments, presentations and portfolios of evidence. Again, Alliger and colleagues (1997) suggest multiple criteria for Level 2. According to their framework, learning outcomes should be divided into immediate knowledge, knowledge retention, and demonstration of behaviours or skills.

Level 3: Behaviour
The question here is whether the knowledge, skills, attitudes or behaviour that have been acquired as a result of the learning programme are transferred to the workplace. In other words, do learners use what they have learnt on the job? Kirkpatrick (1994) notes that five requirements must be met before change in behaviour can occur:
- desire to change;
- know-how of what to do and how to do it;
- the right climate in the workplace;
- support in applying the learning in the workplace; and
- rewards for applying learning.

Various methods can be used to collect the data, from questionnaires and interviews to observations and work samples. The people involved in the evaluation include all those that are affected by the learners' performance in the workplace, including learners, their supervisors and managers and their subordinates or colleagues.

Level 4: Results
This is one of the most important but also one of the most difficult areas to evaluate. It is often difficult to determine the exact impact of a learning programme on the

performance of an organisation. For example, it is difficult to measure the impact of a learning programme that addresses interpersonal relations in the sales department. With poor interpersonal relations, sales will suffer. But what percentage of sales can be attributed to good interpersonal relations, and not to other factors?

If we refer back to the dimensions of evaluation, we see that Kirkpatrick's model is concerned with the dimensions of competence, transfer of learning and impact on the performance of the organisation. To a lesser extent, the design and delivery of the programme is measured through learners' reactions to the learning programme.

Phillips' return on investment model

Phillips' (1994) model incorporates the four steps of Kirkpatrick's model, but adds a fifth step, namely return on investment (ROI). ROI attempts to determine the return on invested capital. The expected benefits are divided by the costs of the intervention.

ROI is expressed as a formula:

$$ROI = \frac{\text{Operational savings + Increase in revenue}}{\text{Full cost of the intervention}}$$

A distinction is made between the direct and indirect costs of an intervention. Direct costs include expenses such as the salary of the trainer, cost of the venue, printing of training materials, meals and refreshments, travelling, accommodation and allowances. Indirect costs are more difficult to determine and include expenses such as loss in production, and salaries of learners. All expenses related to the learning programme need to be determined; this is the sum of the direct and indirect costs.

Nadler's model of evaluation

Nadler's model focuses on the evaluation of the design and delivery process of the learning programme. There are eight steps in his model. Every step from analysis to delivery of the learning programme is evaluated for effectiveness and efficiency. As Nadler (1982) notes, "… that which is happening is directly related to the needs of those in the organisation who are involved as learners or decision-makers. It is not the performance of the designer that is being evaluated, but the outcomes of the activities for which the designer has responsibility." As shown in Figure 7.5, Nadler's model states that:

- Evaluation is a continuous process as opposed to a once-off activity.
- Evaluation should be integrated into every part of the training and delivery process.
- Each step in the process should be evaluated before moving to the next step.
- The emphasis is on formative evaluation, where the results of the evaluation of one stage serve as a point of departure for the next stage.

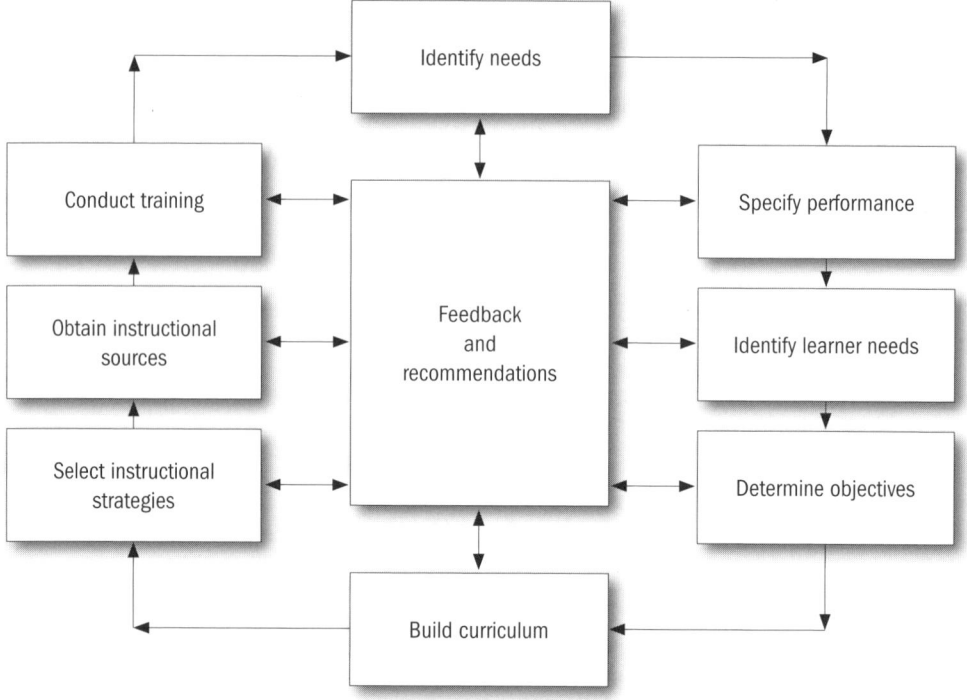

Figure 7.5 *Nadler's model of evaluation (based on Nadler, 1982)*

Guba and Lincoln's fourth generation evaluation

Fourth generation evaluation is a form of evaluation in which the claims, concerns and issues of the stakeholders serve as focus points. These focus points determine what information is needed (Guba & Lincoln, 1989). The model falls within the constructivist inquiry paradigm. This is the view that social reality is a creation of the observer, which means that reality is different for each person. Guba and Lincoln (1989) propose a 12-step model of evaluation:

1. Initiate contact with the client or sponsor. The client is the person/s who is requesting the evaluation.
2. Organise the evaluation. Select a team of evaluators who will carry out the evaluation.
3. Identify the stakeholders. Identify all the persons who are affected in any way by the learning programme and the evaluation thereof.
4. Develop the evaluation constructs between the various groups of stakeholders. Here the stakeholders (through interviews and focus groups) indicate what they view as the main concerns, claims and issues relating to the intended programme.
5. Test and validate the constructs with stakeholder groups. The different claims, concerns and issues are discussed with the other groups, which leads to the acceptance of some and the rejection or revisiting of others.
6. Sort out resolved concerns, claims and issues between the stakeholders. The concerns, claims and issues that the various stakeholders agree upon are listed and described.

7. Prioritise unresolved concerns, claims and issues. The unresolved concerns, claims and issues are prioritised according to criteria developed by the stakeholders. Examples of how these may be prioritised include: possibility of resolution; possibility of achieving a compromise; or importance to the value system of the stakeholder.
8. Collect information about unresolved concerns, claims and issues. Detailed information is collected about the unresolved concerns, claims and issues. This gives both the evaluator and stakeholders an in-depth understanding of exactly what is involved with each concern, claim and issue.
9. Prepare agenda for negotiation. An agenda is set up with as much information as possible about each concern, claim and issue. Stakeholders prepare for the negotiations.
10. Carry out the negotiation process between the stakeholders. Negotiations are carried out between the various stakeholders in an attempt to attain consensus regarding the unresolved concerns, claims and issues. The aim is to create joint constructions about the learning programme with the input of all different stakeholders.
11. Report the joint construction as a case study. The results of the evaluation process are reported in such a way that the reader can see the facts pertaining to the evaluation as well as the process that the constructors used to create these facts.
12. Recycle. Many issues will remain unresolved and many questions unanswered. Repeat the process. As Guba and Lincoln (1999) put it, "Fourth generation evaluations never stop; they merely pause."

The main difference between the fourth generation model and earlier models is that the stakeholders decide what should be evaluated. Where earlier models assume an objective reality, fourth generation evaluation assumes that reality is a construction of those involved.

The ETD evaluation process

Formal, professional evaluation of learning programmes is systematic. It relies on a whole range of special skills and knowledge, including the following:
- Planning skills are used to determine evaluation options and decide what information would be useful.
- Conducting the evaluation is the process of collecting information.
- Communicating outcomes includes putting the information in some convenient form and feeding it into the decision-making process (Smith & Geis, 1992).

As shown in Figure 7.6, the steps in the evaluation process are similar to the steps that one would follow in any research process.

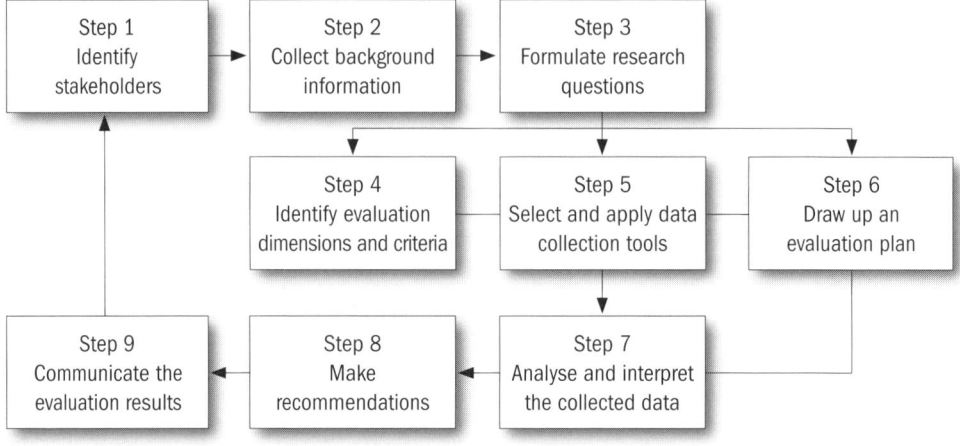

Figure 7.6 The evaluation process

Step 1: Identify stakeholders

The first step in evaluating a learning programme is to identify the decision makers or stakeholders and their expectations or requirements. Stakeholders include programme designers, ETD practitioners involved in the learning programme, learners who will attend the programme and managers or supervisors. The main reasons for identifying the decision makers or stakeholders are:

- to gain their commitment and support;
- to identify their needs and expectations;
- to communicate to them about the progress of the evaluation; and
- to ensure that the findings and recommendations of the evaluation are implemented.

Step 2: Collect background information

The ETD practitioner needs to collect background information about the learning programme and the organisational context. The information that will be collected about the ETD intervention include:

- the objective(s);
- the learning outcomes;
- the size and scope; and
- the expected results.

In addition, the ETD practitioner needs to collect background information about the organisation including:

- the strategic direction of the organisation (vision, mission, goals and objectives) to determine the extent to which the objectives and outcomes of the programme are aligned;
- the culture of the organisation and how this supports learning;
- the political climate, including who supports and who opposes the changes brought about by the learning programme;
- the business policies and procedures, especially those that are related to training and development;

- the history of the performance problem that led to the initial implementation of the learning programme;
- the communication channels; and
- the human and financial resources available.

Step 3: Formulate research questions

The next step is to translate decisions about requirements into research questions. Research questions describe the type of data to be collected, the people who will be measured and the standard or benchmark for evaluating a learning programme's success. For example, an ETD practitioner might be asked to demonstrate the value of a new management development process. The evaluation might deal with the following research question: "Do managers change their approaches to self-development as a result of the learning programme?" This question implies that the data will be a measure of self-initiated development activities; that the people are managers who participate in the learning programme; and that the standard will be the level of activity before the learning programme. Research questions should indicate what data the decision maker will consider as valid and credible. This implies that the research question should be tested with the decision maker before proceeding (Smith & Geis, 1992).

Step 4: Identify the evaluation dimensions and criteria

Once the research questions have been formulated, evaluators and stakeholders need to define the dimensions of the evaluation. These are the aspects of the learning programme that will be evaluated and include issues such as the design and delivery of the learning programme, competence, transfer of learning to the workplace and impact on organisational performance. ETD practitioners need to choose criteria to evaluate the different dimensions. In choosing the evaluation dimensions and criteria, evaluators can make use of various evaluation models. The choice of an evaluation model will depend on the purpose and focus of the evaluation. Using a particular model will help the evaluator to focus and structure the evaluation process.

Step 5: Select and apply data collection tools

Data collection tools or measuring instruments include questionnaires, observations, interviews, and organisational records. The evaluator needs to select the most appropriate data collection tool based on the information that needs to be collected.

Questionnaires

Questionnaires measure learners' reactions and opinions. They provide data that can be easily summarised. Petersen (in Lee, 2006) argues that there are seven distinct tasks in constructing an effective questionnaire:
- Identify the specific information required.
- Develop and prioritise a list of questions that will access the required information.
- Carefully assess each potential question.
- Determine what types of question need to be asked.
- Decide on the specific wording of each question.
- Determine the structure of the questionnaire.
- Evaluate the questionnaire.

Guidelines for writing effective questions (Lee, 2006)

- Write simple, clear and short questions.
- Questions should be specific and precise.
- Language usage should be appropriate to the audience.
- Make sure the respondents are able to answer the questions.
- Include one topic per question.
- Emphasise important words in the questions.
- Take care with sensitive questions.
- Avoid negatives and double negatives.
- Avoid biased or loaded questions.
- Do not base questions on false premises.

Interviews

Interviews collect information directly from people. They provide in-depth information; during interviews, responses can be probed and checked. Interviews can be conducted on a one-to-one basis, in groups or by telephone. Interviews, as an evaluation technique, require a high level of skill (Swanson, 1994). Focus groups are group interviews during which the opinions and attitudes of group members are tested. Focus groups involve a targeted group of stakeholders who provide information about a specific topic (Swanson, 1994).

Table 7.10 Advantages and disadvantages of interviews as an evaluation technique (Adapted from Pershing, 2006: 783)

Advantages	Disadvantages
• The interviewer can seek clarification on issues. • They provide opportunity to build rapport. • A wider range of subjects can be addressed, including unexpected issues that have arisen.	• Interviewers may influence or lead respondents. • Note taking can distract respondents. • Interviews are expensive and time consuming. • Results are often difficult to analyse if semi-structured or unstructured questions are used.

Table 7.11 Steps to follow in an interview process (Adapted from Pershing, 2006: 786-793)

Step 1: Determine the objective of the interview
• The evaluator needs to ask questions relating to the dimensions of the training intervention that is being evaluated.

Step 2: Preparing for the interview
• Select the respondents. Who will be interviewed? • Develop an interview protocol (the list of questions to be asked). • Prepare a timetable for conducting the interviews. • Conduct a pilot interview to test the protocol. • Train interviewers. • Schedule the interviews.

Step 3: Carrying out the interview
• Open the interview by setting the respondent at ease. • Conduct the interview. Go through the questions in the interview protocol. • Close the interview and thank the respondent. • Record the interview. If the interview has been taped, the interview needs to be transcribed.
Step 4: Concluding the interview
• The interviewing process is concluded when the information from several respondents become repetitive.
Step 5: Compiling and analysing results
• The data is analysed either statistically (if the interview comprised closed questions) or qualitatively (if the interview comprised open-ended questions).

Observations

Learners can be observed before, during and after a learning event. Observation is particularly useful to evaluate the mastery of skills (Gibb, 2002; Swart *et al*, 2005). The evaluator observes employees performing their jobs in their natural environment. When practised in a systematic way, observing people at work will yield a great deal of qualitative and quantitative information about the work, the worker and the environment (Swanson,1994).

Observations are divided into two broad categories, namely overt observations (employees are aware that they are being observed) and covert observations (employees are unaware that they are being observed). A distinction is also made between structured and unstructured observations. Unstructured observations are characterised by an absence of premeditated tasks; the observer simply takes in as much as possible. Structured observations have specific goals, and structured instruments (such as checklists) guide the observation. The observer's degree of involvement also varies from an independent observer, to an observer who participates to some degree, to a participant that also observes. The purposes of observation as an evaluation technique are also regarded as the advantages of observation (Pershing, Scott & Rowe, 2006):

- First-hand information is obtained about task performance problems in the work situation.
- Task, individual and group processes can be observed.
- Findings from interviews and questionnaires can be confirmed.
- Predicted performance can be compared to actual performance.

Organisational records

Organisational evidence and learners' work samples can serve as evidence of the transfer of learning to the workplace. Organisational records are any documents (paper or electronic) kept by the organisation. Examples include employee turnover, sick leave, grievances, production statistics, policy and procedure manuals, memoranda and minutes of meetings. The method used to analyse organisational documents is known as content analysis. This is the process of searching through documents to answer specific questions (Thomas, cited in Gilmore, 2006). The following questions need to be answered before analysing business records (Pershing, cited in Gilmore, 2006):

- Who has access to the required records?
- Where will these be analysed? Can they be moved?
- Do the documents contain sensitive or proprietary data?
- Are confidentiality agreements required?
- Who should be consulted if additional documents are required?
- Is training needed to analyse the documents?
- Are there built-in biases in the documents?

Assessment instruments

Assessment instruments are the tests, assignments, projects, portfolios of evidence or other tools used to measure the competence of learners (read more about assessment in Chapter 6). These instruments provide information on learners' competence after completing a learning programme. This information can also be used to determine whether the programme is achieving its intended goals. In this regard, pre- and post-course tests are valuable as evaluation tools.

Once the appropriate data collection tool(s) have been selected, the evaluator starts to collect the data. The process of selecting and applying an appropriate data collection tool comprises a number of steps:
- Determine the type of information that is required.
- Select a data collection tool that is appropriate to the type of information required.
- If an appropriate tool is not available, design a valid tool that will enable the evaluator to collect the required data.
- Test the data collection tool on a pilot group.
- Collect the information from the target group.
- Analyse and summarise the collected data.
- Report the findings.

Step 6: Draw up an evaluation plan

Research questions are expanded into an outline of the evaluation plan. From the example used in step 3 (formulate research questions), the way to measure self-initiated development activities might be selected from such options as training requests, self-reports by means of questionnaires or interviews, superior ratings, subordinate ratings, or a combination of techniques. In addition, the standard that will be used to evaluate performance is determined (the term 'standard' refers to a benchmark for judging the performance of the learning programme). Standards may be relative (norm-referenced) or absolute (criterion-referenced).

Relative standards compare two sets of data: one set to represent the effects of the learning programme (its impact); and the other to represent performance unaffected by the learning programme. For example, a learning programme may be evaluated by comparing pre-test performance to post-test performance; comparing learners' performance to the performance of untrained employees, or a combination of these (Smith & Geis, 1992). Absolute standards are fixed indicators expressed in numbers; they are set independently of any group's performance in the evaluation study. These standards may be derived from corporate policy or objectives, historical records of productivity, work quality, turnover rates, opinions of job experts, legal or government requirements (for example, SAQA quality requirements) or assessment requirements. For example, the evaluator may choose to compare the managers' development activities to their activities before the process, or to the activities of a similar group of managers who do not attend the learning programme (called a control group), or to both.

When formulating research questions, participants are also described. The target groups are identified and the characteristics that define each group are listed. In an evaluation of a learning programme for managers, the group of managers will be defined by such characteristics as: managers participated in the learning programme; and they have been back at work for at least two months to demonstrate the expected behaviour. Managers from different departments and levels will be included in the target group.

In the planning of an evaluation, the ETD practitioner identifies any constraints that may hinder the evaluation effort and the resources required for the evaluation (such as people, time, finances and instruments). The administrative requirements for the evaluation effort are also specified in the plan. The actual evaluation plan should be written and documented (Smith & Geis, 1992). Table 7.12 is an example of an evaluation plan.

Table 7.12 *Example of an evaluation plan (based on Smith & Geis, 1992)*

Evaluation of management development programme	
Purpose	
Client	JB – Human Resources
Programme	Learning programme to help executives with self-development. Participation is voluntary.
Objective	Develop skills for executive succession.
Decision	Continue or modify programme design?
Concerns	Learning facilitators (trainers) say it is too early to look for tangible outcomes.
Design question	Do executives do more self-development because of participation in the learning programme?
Constraints	JB wants a report in two months.
Measurements	Interviews to determine types and frequency of developmental activities
Sampling	Random selection of 20 participants and 20 non-participants
Standards	Participants' change is greater than non-participants' change over the same period.
Analyses	• Frequency counts of different types of development activity reported by each group for each time period • Statistical test to see if groups differed significantly in frequency of development activities • Summary of suggested improvements
Administration	
Staffing	One evaluator, half-time position for two months
Budget	Salary and expenses estimated at R45 000
Schedule	Measurement materials designed 4 April 2008 Samples selected 10 May 2008 Interviews completed 20 June 2008 Report available 15 July 2008

Step 7: Analyse and interpret the data

Analysis of the data is about making sense of the data. The evaluator has now collected data from various respondents. Once the data has been analysed, the evaluator needs to explain what the findings drawn from the data mean. This is known as the interpretation of data. The data are structured in such a way that the evaluator can make sense of the data. There are two broad categories of data analysis, namely:

- Statistical analysis uses various statistical techniques to analyse quantitative data (data that can be expressed in numbers, such as data from questionnaires).
- Content analysis is the analysis of qualitative data (such as organisational records and interviews) to identify trends.

Step 8: Make recommendations

This step in the evaluation process is where the evaluator makes recommendations to the stakeholders about how the learning programme needs to be changed or improved based on the findings of the evaluation. This is the most important step in the evaluation process as this is the reason why the evaluation was conducted in the first place.

Step 9: Communicate the evaluation results

Once the evaluation process has been conducted, the results should be communicated to the stakeholders. The evaluation process and the results are put together in a report and presented to the stakeholders. Based on this report, the stakeholders will make decisions about their course of action. The quality of this report is therefore extremely important. The evaluation results are communicated in the form of an evaluation report. The following elements are generally included in an evaluation report:

- an executive summary, which provides an overview of the main points covered in the report;
- the methodology used to collect and analyse the data and reach conclusions;
- the programme costs per item, in as much detail as possible;
- the design of the learning programme, identifying what was done well and what needs to be improved;
- the reaction of the learners, expressed in terms of their level of satisfaction with the delivery of the learning programme;
- the learning results, where the results of the assessment of learner achievement are satisfactory;
- transfer of learning to the workplace, identifying barriers and enablers of transfer of learning to the workplace;
- the impact on the results of the business, showing the extent to which the results of the organisation were improved;
- the return on investment, weighing up the costs of the programme against the financial benefits for the organisation; and
- conclusion and recommendations.

There are also a number of important principles that need to be followed when communicating evaluation results. They include the following (Block, 2000; Phillips *et al*, 2004):

- Communicate at the right time. There is normally a 'window of opportunity' related to evaluation data; in other words; evaluation results need to be communicated when it will have the most impact.

- Communicate quickly. It is important to get evaluation results and communicate them to the relevant stakeholders as quickly as possible.
- Aim the communication at the right audience. Make sure that the appropriate stakeholders (the ones affected by the learning programmes and those who have influence over the HRD department) are kept in mind.
- Keep the data simple and concise. Present the data in as simple and concise a manner as possible so that it is easy to read and understand.
- Present negatives positively. Discuss negative results as development opportunities rather than as criticisms.
- Use simple descriptive data. Describe the data in language that all the stakeholders can understand.
- Select the appropriate media. Select the media that will have the most impact and get the message across effectively.
- Provide unbiased and modest data. Provide honest, unexaggerated data.
- Communicate consistently. Communicating evaluation results is not a once-off process. It should take place on a regular basis.
- Get the reactions of the stakeholders. Ask stakeholders for their reactions to the data and the recommendations.
- Communication should be planned. Communicating evaluation results is not a random process. When planning the communication, decide why the communication is taking place, who will receive the communication, what will be communicated, and when, where and how the communication will take place.
- Act on the findings. It is pointless to evaluate if you do not do anything with the findings. Use findings to bring about improvements to the organisation's learning interventions.

Table 7.13 Quality checklist for an evaluation report

Does the report contain the following sections?	Yes	No	Comments
1. The purpose of the report • Why was this report drawn up and for whom? • What is the aim of the report?			
2. Executive summary • What programme was evaluated? • What was the aim of the programme? • How, when and where was the programme conducted? • Who requested the evaluation? • When was the evaluation conducted and over what period of time? • The process followed in the evaluation? • Who was responsible for conducting the evaluation? • What were the major findings of the evaluation?			
3. Background • The aims of the training programme? • What outcomes is the programme intended to achieve? • The process followed to deliver the programme? • Where was the programme delivered?			

Does the report contain the following sections?	Yes	No	Comments
• Unique challenges that the programme faced? • Who was responsible for the delivery of the programme?			
4. Evaluation • What dimensions were evaluated? • What criteria were used to evaluate the different dimensions? • The evaluation design or process used? • Any limitations on the results as a consequence of the design? • A description of the data collection methods used? • Motivation for the appropriateness of the data collection methods? • A description of the data collection process? • A description of how the data was organised? • A description of the process used to analyse the data?			
5. Findings • Presents the findings of the evaluation? • Summarises the main findings in a user-friendly format? • Explains the meaning of the findings?			
6. Recommendations • How the findings should impact on future training programmes? • How the findings should be used to adjust the curriculum? • How the findings will impact on any and all relevant stages of the training and development process? • Other (specify):			

Factors that discourage evaluation

There are a number of reasons why organisations avoid evaluating their ETD interventions. These include barriers to evaluation and problems experienced with the evaluation process. Barriers to evaluation generally include:

- Top management tend not to emphasise the importance of evaluation and tend to simply accept that training is valuable and effective.
- Managers of HRD departments do not have the necessary skills to conduct evaluations; they avoid this aspect of the HRD process.
- There is uncertainty about what exactly should be evaluated. Owing to the wide range of models, each with a different emphasis, it is often difficult to decide what to evaluate.
- Evaluation is viewed as risky and expensive. It is often felt that the costs outweigh the benefits. There is also a fear that an evaluation may bring negative attention to the HRD department (Grove & Ostroff, cited in Goldstein & Ford, 2002).

A number of problems results in organisations doing superficial evaluations in most instances, or no evaluations at all. Some of these problems include:

- Too many models and theories. There are many theories and models for evaluation. This is confusing, as the different models and theories focus on a wide variety of issues.
- The complexity of models. Models and theories tend to be complex and contain

many variables. This makes it difficult for the average ETD practitioner to use them.

- A general lack of understanding about evaluation.
- The lack of research skills. Effective evaluation comprises a research process. This implies that ETD practitioners should have research skills; this is not always the case.
- Difficulty in identifying the impact of training on specific variables. It is often difficult to identify specific variables, or the specific impact that a training intervention has on an organisation.
- Evaluation is considered a post-programme activity. Most evaluation focuses on the end results of training programmes, rather than on the process.
- Managers do not see the long-term advantages. Evaluation is often aimed at individual programmes and interventions, rather than the overall training and development function.
- Little support from main stakeholders. Managers and other stakeholders often see evaluation as a 'nice-to-have' rather than a 'must-have'.
- Evaluation is not focused on management needs. Evaluation data often focus on the learners' needs rather than on those of management.
- Evaluation data not used appropriately. Evaluation results are not used at all, do not reach the appropriate stakeholders, are not used to bring about improvements, or are used for political or disciplinary purposes.
- Inconsistent use. Evaluation will not be taken seriously if it is used in an inconsistent way across different learning programmes.
- No clear standards. No consistent standards exist for evaluation in terms of the process, methods and techniques.
- Lack of sustainability. Evaluations tend to be short-term processes aimed at specific goals, rather than strategic long-term processes (Phillips *et al*, 2004).

ACTIVITY

Case study

Read carefully through the following case study and answer the questions that follow.

The WiFi Corporation is a large retail chain that specialises in the sale of electronic goods to the public. They have 20 branches located across South Africa, with an average of 25 staff members in each branch. These include a store manager, department managers, sales people and administrative staff. They also have a head office located in Johannesburg that is responsible for the overall management of the organisation. The CEO and the regional managers are located here. A call centre is also located in the head office. It deals with customer complaints and provides support to customers for the various products that they buy from WiFi Corporation.

Previously, training and development took place on an ad hoc basis, as it was needed. Training was conducted by external providers at the request of the store managers and regional managers. Examples of learning programmes that members of the staff of WiFi Corporation have undergone include courses on Sales Management, Effective Sales and Improving Your Interpersonal Relations.

Management has now decided that, with the growth of WiFi Corporation, they need an in-house ETD department. An ETD manager, two ETD practitioners and an administrative assistant have been employed. The ETD manager, John Mabasa, has been given the instructions to review all learning programmes currently used by the organisation, and to develop a WiFi Corporation Customer Service programme.

Questions
1. What problems can John expect to encounter when evaluating the learning programmes of WiFi Corporation?
2. Describe the process that John would need to follow when evaluating the existing learning programmes?
3. Who are the stakeholders that need to be involved in the process? Explain why each stakeholder should be included.
4. What dimensions should be the focus when evaluating the Improving Your Interpersonal Relations learning programme? List at least three criteria to measure these dimensions.
5. What data collection instrument would be the most appropriate to collect data about the identified dimensions when evaluating the Improving Your Interpersonal Relations learning programme? Give reasons for your answer.
6. What dimensions should be the focus when evaluating the Effective Sales programme? List at least three criteria to measure these dimensions.
7. What data collection instrument would be the most appropriate to collect data about the identified dimensions when evaluating the Effective Sales learning programme? Give reasons for your answer.
8. Which evaluation model would be the most effective to evaluate the new WiFi Corporation Customer Service programme? Give reasons for your answer.
9. What issues will you focus on when communicating the results of your evaluations?
10. What dimensions or issues will the ETD department of WiFi Corporation need to address if they wish to become a SAQA accredited ETD provider?

Key terms
- Compliance evaluation
- Data
- Data collection tools
- Diagnostic evaluation
- ETD evaluation
- Evaluation criteria
- Evaluation dimensions
- Evaluation process
- Formative evaluation
- Reliability
- Return on investment
- Stakeholders
- Summative evaluation
- Validity
- Value-added evaluation

Review and discussion questions

1. How does a properly planned and executed ETD evaluation help ETD practitioners and managers to prove the quality of and value added by their learning programmes and other ETD interventions?
2. What is the purpose of compliance evaluation in the South African workplace? How does it differ from and complement value-added evaluation?
3. Why do organisations sometimes neglect ETD evaluation?
4. How can ETD practitioners ensure that their evaluations produce valid and reliable data? What steps would you recommend in executing an evaluation?
5. How would you demonstrate to management the cost-effectiveness, the change that occurred because of a learning programme, and impact of a learning programme?
6. How do the various evaluation models guide ETD practitioners in determining evaluation dimensions and criteria?
7. When should ETD practitioners conduct evaluation? Give reasons for your answer.

Suggested reading

Alliger, G.M., Tannenbaum, S.I., Bennet, W., Traver, H. & Shotland, A. (1997). A meta-analysis of the relations among training criteria. *Personnel Psychology*, 50, 341-358.

Block, P. (2000). *Flawless consulting* (2nd ed). San Francisco: Jossey-Bass/Pfeiffer.

Erasmus, B.J. & van Dyk, P.S. (2003). *Training management in South Africa* (3rd ed.). Cape Town: Oxford University Press.

Fitz-ens, J. (1995). *How to measure human resources management*. New York: McGraw-Hill.

Gibb, S.E. (2002). *Learning and development: Processes, practices and perspectives at work*. Houndmills: Palgrave Macmillan.

Gilmore, E. (2006). Using content analysis in human performance technology. In J.A. Pershing (ed.) *Handbook of human performance technology: Principles, practices and potential*. San Francisco: Pfeiffer.

Guba, E.G. & Lincoln, Y.S. (1989). *Fourth generation evaluation*. Newbury Park: Sage.

Goldstein, I.L. & Ford, J.K. (2002). *Training in organisations: Needs assessment, development, and evaluation*. Belmont: Wordsworth.

Kirkpatrick, D.L. (1994). *Evaluating training programs – The four levels* (2nd ed.). San Francisco: Berrett-Koehler.

Lee, S.H. (2006). Constructing effective questionnaires. In J.A. Pershing (ed.) *Handbook of human performance technology: Principles, practices and potential*. San Francisco: Pfeiffer.

Nadler, L. (1982). *Designing training programmes: The critical events model*. Reading: Addison Wesley.

Pershing, J.L. (2006). Interviewing to analyse and evaluate human performance technology. In J.A. Pershing (ed.) *Handbook of human performance technology: Principles, practices and potential*. San Francisco: Pfeiffer.

Pershing, J.A., Scott, S.J. & Rowe, D.T. (2006). Observation methods for human performance technology. In J.A. Pershing (ed.) *Handbook of human performance technology: Principles, practices and potential*. San Francisco: Pfeiffer.

Philips, J.J., (1994). *Measuring ROI: Progress, trends and strategies*. ASTD Press.

Phillips, J.J.; Phillips, P.P. & Hodges, T.K. (2004). *Make training evaluation work*. Alexandria: ASTD Press.

Rossi, P.H., Freeman, H.E. & Lipsey, M.W. (1999). *Evaluation: A systematic approach*. Thousand Oaks: Sage.

Rothwell, W.J. & Kazanas, H.C. (1994). *Human resource development: A strategic approach*. Massachusetts: HRD Press.

Rothwell, W.J. & Sredl, H.J. (1992). *The ASTD guide to professional roles and competencies: Volume 1*. Amherst: ASTD Press.

SAQA (2000). *Quality management systems for ETQAs*. Pretoria: SAQA.

SAQA (2001). *Quality management systems for education and training providers*. Pretoria: SAQA.

Smith, M.E. & Geis, G.L. (1992). Planning and evaluation study. In: H. Stolovitch & E.J. Keeps (Eds.). *Handbook of human performance and technology* (pp. 151-166). San Francisco: Jossey-Bass.

Swanson, R.A. (1994). *Analysis for improving performance: Tools for diagnosing organisations & documenting workplace expertise.* Thousand Oaks: Sage.

Swart, J., Mann, C., Brown, S. & Price, A. (2005). *Human resource development: Strategy and tactics.* Oxford: Elsevier Butterworth-Heinemann.

Terre Blanche, K. & Durrheim, K. (eds.). (1999). *Research in practice: Applied methods for the social sciences.* Cape Town: University of Cape Town Press.

Summary

This chapter concluded the discussion of the Training Cycle by exploring evaluation as a significant aspect of quality and value-adding ETD provision. The South African workplace emphasises compliance evaluation and value-added evaluation of ETD interventions and practices to measure the quality and impact of ETD interventions. Well-planned ETD evaluation allows ETD practitioners and managers to collect descriptive and judgemental information. This information is used to make effective ETD decisions regarding the selection, adoption, modification and financial evaluation of ETD interventions. Various evaluation models were presented to indicate how they can be used to determine the ETD evaluation dimensions and criteria to be measured. The ETD evaluation process should be executed in a systematic manner to ensure the validity and reliability of compliance and value-added measurements.

Chapter 8 discusses the function of ETD management to ensure that the quality of and value added by ETD interventions, practices, services and products are sustained in the workplace.

Wise ETD practitioners create an environment that encourages learners to teach themselves.

CHAPTER 8

Melinde Coetzee

Managing ETD in
the workplace

"Effective ETD management allows ETD experts to help sustain organisational capability. ETD is managed effectively when the ETD function operates as a strategic business partner and delivers results that add value for stakeholders."

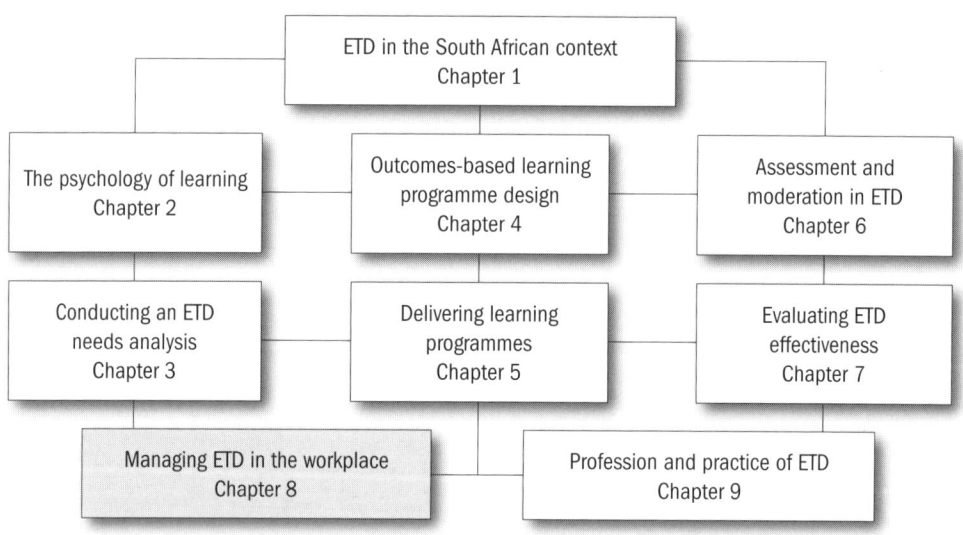

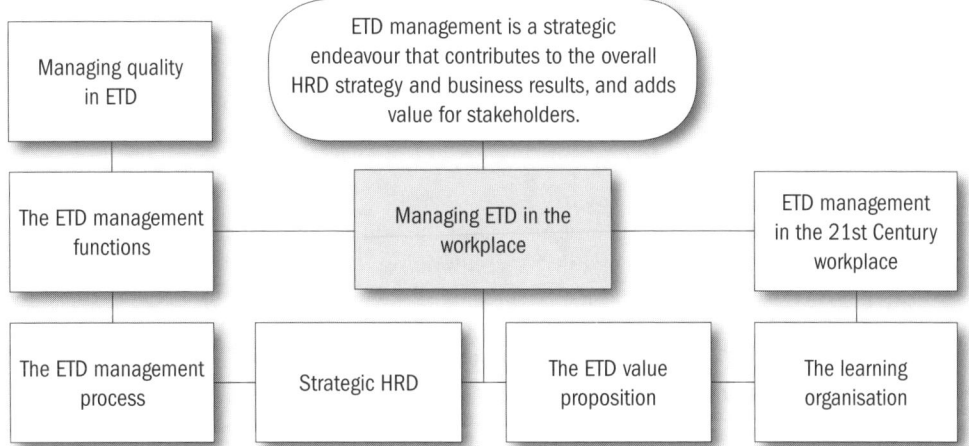

After studying this chapter, you should be able to:

- Explain why the 21st century workplace requires a dynamic and flexible approach to ETD management.
- Explain how the concept of knowledge management relates to individual and organisational learning.
- Evaluate and discuss the concept of strategic ETD management.
- Describe the role of ETD management in addressing the seven core workplace issues in the 21st century workplace.
- Discuss the importance of defining the ETD value proposition.
- Explain the link between the HRD strategy and ETD management.
- Discuss the ETD management process and the functions that support the effective and efficient implementation of the strategic ETD plan.
- Discuss the importance of establishing and managing an ETD quality management system.

Managing ETD requires a dynamic and flexible approach that not only contributes to organisational flexibility and capability, but also adds value for stakeholders. ETD management is therefore a strategic activity that contributes to measurable, value-adding business results. An important role of the ETD function is to help build and enhance the organisation's learning capability by supporting the implementation of the organisation's overall HRD strategy. Learning capabilities are the set of core competencies that differentiate an organisation from its competitors and processes that enable an organisation to adapt to its environment and sustain its competitive advantage. The ETD function is therefore responsible for challenging the organisation and its members with new ideas, information and performance enhancement solutions. This is done by constantly scanning the external environment, ensuring the expertise and professionalism of ETD practitioners, identifying talent pools and groups within the organisation for specific ETD interventions, and devoting resources to educate, train and develop these groups.

Learning organisations are results oriented. The ETD function needs to foster an environment in which employees are encouraged to expand their knowledge and skills, and use the newly acquired behaviours and operational processes to achieve corporate goals (Kinicki & Kreitner, 2006).

This chapter explores the context of and approach to managing ETD in the 21st century workplace. The ETD value proposition, management process and functions are discussed to demonstrate how these contribute to the overall HRD strategy of an organisation. Quality assurance is also discussed as a critical aspect of managing outcomes-based ETD.

ETD management in the 21st century workplace

Managing ETD activities in the 21st century workplace makes heavy demands on managers and ETD practitioners. They have to handle interactions with stakeholders and operate flexibly in response to changing information and conditions. Effective ETD management requires a balance between doing the right things (effectiveness) and doing them in the right ways (efficiency). As discussed in Chapter 7, measuring the return on investment (ROI) of training efforts is a typical indicator of effectiveness. Such measures show that ETD costs are offset by improved skills and knowledge (for example, sales knowledge related to increased sales). Effectiveness also requires compliance with stakeholder requirements and legal regulations, reducing the risk of costly legal actions. Efficiency in ETD processes refers to the efficient use of resources such as time and money.

ETD priorities change all the time as new challenges confront organisations. But many observers believe that seven issues are receiving the highest priority in the 21st century workplace (Cascio, 2003; Grobler *et al*, 2006; Ulrich & Brockbank, 2005):
1. Quality improvement programmes are instituted in response to increasingly higher demands for quality from the customer and the need to be more competitive in a global economy.
2. Technological change-related programmes will continue to challenge organisations. The rate of advancement of technology continues to accelerate. Employers must continue to offer ETD opportunities to employees to keep them from obsolescence.
3. Customer service employee development programmes are now a priority for organ-

isations that consider themselves service orientated. Financial, banking, insurance and government organisations are placing an increased emphasis on service to the customer as a possible competitive advantage. Total quality management or customer service excellence programmes focus on the responsibility that each employee has to the customer or client.

4. Promoting employability and sustainable livelihoods. Employability is people's ability to gain access to, adjust to, and be productive in the workplace. It is the set of competencies that enables a person to meet the demands of the 21st century workplace. According to Herr *et al* (2004), employability relates to the ability to hold a job even if no jobs exist. The South African government's societal transformation agenda, in particular, requires concerted efforts to address the career development and upskilling needs of the country (Coetzee & Roythorne-Jacobs, 2007). People need adaptive skills; the goals of ETD in the workplace therefore go beyond increasing motivation, productivity and job satisfaction to focus on lifelong adaptability, employability and performance capability.

South Africa has a high rate of unemployment, which is a cause of social issues such as poverty and a high crime rate. As discussed in Chapter 1, the government provides financial support to companies, non-governmental organisations and community-based organisations to stimulate skills development initiatives. All skills development initiatives include strategies for the placement of individuals in employment, self-employment or social development programmes, or further educational studies.

5. Enhancing employability of designated groups. The National Skills Development Strategy emphasises the assistance of unemployed people from designated groups, including new entrants, to participate in accredited work, integrated learning and work-based programmes. In these programmes, unemployed people acquire critical skills to enter the labour market and self-employment. Programmes include learnerships, apprenticeships, internships, bursaries and new venture creation initiatives.

6. Promoting and accelerating employment equity. To address the inequalities in terms of the educational and equity profile of the workforce, the skills development legislation makes provision for levy grants initiatives for employers who promote and accelerate the development of blacks, women and the disabled.

7. Developing human capital. Capital comes from the Latin word caput, meaning head. In business, capital refers to the most important assets of a organisation (Ulrich & Brockbank, 2005). The competencies of people in an organisation are regarded as valuable assets that enhance the organisation's ability to sustain its competitive advantage (Robinson, 2006). People are therefore increasingly recognised as critical assets, and ETD professionals are often regarded as human capital developers. As human capital developers, ETD practitioners focus on the future, often one employee at a time. They assess skills gaps, develop competency profiles and development plans that offer each employee opportunities to develop, and match development needs with opportunities. In this role, ETD practitioners also help employees to unlearn old skills and master new ones to enhance their employability and performance capability (Ulrich & Brockbank, 2005). ETD efforts focus on those areas where human capital makes the biggest difference to strategic success.

Case example of human capital development (Ulrich & Brockbank, 2005)

Eli Lilly demonstrates commitment to human capital through many initiatives. The company generally recruits people right out of school, then invests in their development and reviews their skills annually. Lately, in an effort to accelerate growth, Eli Lilly has also been recruiting experienced scientists whose worldwide reputations make them talent magnets.

Pedro Granadillo, senior vice president of human resources, meets regularly with the CEO and leaders of every major Eli Lilly component. The group invests a day per year reviewing worldwide talent for sales and marketing, manufacturing and research. They discuss business strategy, organisation capabilities and development plans for high-potentials – including the second and third generation of talent, people in their late twenties and early thirties, whom the business leaders are expected to know by name. The CEO meets with the board annually to review organisation changes and the talent pipeline, using an early identification tool based on learning agility.

Eli Lilly measures success of talent by how outsiders comment on the talent in the organisation. Informed observers note that Eli Lilly has smart, global, and business-orientated people who get targeted by competitors (which is regarded as a compliment).

The learning organisation

A learning organisation is one in which all employees have access to learning, and that transforms constantly in response to employees' new knowledge and abilities. This description suggests that organisations can also adapt to new circumstances; they can undertake a learning process similar to people (Martin, 2005). The text box below shows the main characteristics of a learning organisation.

Characteristics of a learning organisation (Mumford, cited in Martin, 2005: 186)
- Encouragement for managers to accept responsibility for the identification of their own ETD needs
- Encouragement for managers to set challenging learning and development goals for themselves
- The provision for all employees of regular performance reviews and feedback on learning achieved
- Encouragement for managers to identify learning opportunities in jobs and to provide new experiences from which employees and managers can learn
- Encouragement of a questioning attitude to the accepted ways of doing things within the organisation
- The acceptance that, when learning, some mistakes are inevitable, but that individuals should learn from them
- Encouragement of on-the-job training and other learning activities

---

The notion of a learning organisation is of fundamental importance in creating a modern, flexible and adaptable organisation. It allows the organisation to meet the needs of all the stakeholder groups associated with it more effectively (Martin, 2005).

Knowledge management

Learning at an individual level has strong implications for learning in (and by) the whole organisation. Knowledge management allows organisations to translate the advantages of being a learning organisation into a competitive advantage.

Knowledge management is a process of creating, acquiring, capturing, sharing and using knowledge to enhance learning and performance in organisations (Rollinson, 2005). It is also the management of all knowledge available to the organisation, for the benefit of the organisation and the individuals within it (Martin, 2005: 190). Furthermore, there is a growing realisation that management objectives can be more easily achieved if managers seek to ensure that employees are trained to absorb management's values and norms in addition to technical and job skills (Martin, 2005). This often finds expression through ETD being driven by business objectives rather than just technical needs, and delivered through management-controlled provision.

There are different forms of knowledge within a organisation. Nonaka (cited in Rollinson, 2005) draws a distinction between two types of knowledge: explicit and tacit.

- Explicit knowledge is knowledge that is easily communicated, codified and expressed. It is available to anyone within a particular context. This is the type of knowledge and understanding that most people in organisations have about what to do or how to function in certain circumstances (Rollinson, 2005).
- Tacit knowledge is much more personal and individualised. It is difficult to articulate and communicate to others because it is part of a person's experience and skill.

According to Nonaka and Takeuchi (1995), explicit and tacit knowledge complement each other. They are both needed in an organisation if it is to be creative and innovative. Taken together they are the accumulated wisdom of the organisation or, to put it differently, part of its intellectual assets. An organisation that knows how to use both is likely to have a significant competitive edge (Martin, 2005; Rollinson, 2005).

Harrison (2000:153) suggests that knowledge management can be used in three broad ways: to provide banks of information that enable employees to record and access explicit knowledge across the organisation; to provide access to data across boundaries; and to allow groups of people to interact and create new knowledge through virtual communities where they can share expertise and tacit knowledge.

CASE STUDY

Knowledge management in practice

The Post Office, with 210 000 employees, is one of the largest and most complex organisations in Great Britain. In recognition of the vital importance of information of this type it has recently set up a knowledge management team to try to capture this tacit or implicit learning that accumulates in people's minds. To do so the team has developed two novel methods. First, what it calls 'after action reviews' are used when someone has completed a novel task or special project. These seek to identify the aims of the project, what actually occurred, why things happened as they did and whether matters could be improved if something similar arose in the future.

The second and perhaps most important tool is the 'knowledge interview'. In an attempt to become aware of important insights that the person has gained and what might otherwise be lost, this is used when a senior member of staff moves on. It is also used with people who are recognised as having particularly important knowledge that should be more widely disseminated, and sometimes for new employees who could have gained relevant and useful information in other employment. Interestingly, the Post Office explored the use of computerised knowledge-capturing packages for this task, but these turned out to be nowhere near as effective as face-to-face, in-depth interviewing techniques.

By learning about itself in this way and spreading best practice more widely throughout the organisation, the Post Office is reported to have become more efficient and saved a considerable amount of expenditure. Source: Whitehead, M. (1999). Collection Time. People Management, 28 October: 68-71.

Questions

Think about the role and function of the ETD department and ETD practitioners.
- What are the types of knowledge that ETD managers and practitioners need to manage?
- How can ETD managers and practitioners apply mechanisms such as knowledge management teams, after action reviews and knowledge interviews in improving the effectiveness of the design, delivery and evaluation of learning programmes?

Improving organisational flexibility and capability

Organisations see flexibility as a strategic goal to increase competitiveness (Birkinshaw, 2000). Sanchez (1995) distinguishes between resource flexibility (the extent to which a resource can be applied to a wide range of alternative uses) and coordination flexibility (the extent to which the organisation can rethink and redeploy resources). Flexibility requires specific competencies (Baruch, 2004). It needs to be developed through a variety of human resource management practices, of which ETD is a critical component.

A main focus of ETD practices in the workplace is to help employees understand how their personal competencies help to build organisational capability. ETD investments produce deliverables and add value when it develops both capability and ability (Brockbank, 2005). Capability represents the identity and reputation of the organisation and includes factors such as talent management, collaboration, learning, speed of change, leadership, shared mindset, accountability, customer connection, innovation and efficiency. Ability represents the capacity of an organisation to use resources, get things done, and behave in ways that accomplish goals. Abilities characterise how people think and behave in the context of the organisation and form the organisation's personality (Ulrich & Brockbank, 2005).

Case example: The learning organisation (www.jcpenny.net/)
JC Penny's virtual university

In order to keep key employees and stay competitive and profitable, organisations are sometimes turning from classroom training to highly customised learning. Competition and increasing consumer demand mean that organisations must respond quickly to change. At the same time, corporate mergers and related job cuts mean that the remaining employees have more responsibilities without the education, training and development to fulfil them. How can companies meet all these demands?

JC Penny's corporate university, The Learning Place, is run by Jane Masten from the company's headquarters in Plano, Texas. There, a production studio holds video conferences via satellite for employees around the world. Participants use touch-pad technology to ask questions or make comments – and all the other participants can hear them, in real time. Masten, the director of human resources development, says, "There is no bricks-and-mortar facility for our university, outside of the production studio. We have created a completely virtual university. When people need knowledge, they need it immediately. They can't wait until it can be scheduled, then hop on a plane and spend a week in a seminar." In addition to its video conferencing capabilities, The Learning Place provides all of its training material online, available at any time to JC Penny's 200 000 employees (Garger, 1999).

Table 8.1 Organisation capabilities (Ulrich & Brockbank, 2005:51)

Capability	Definition
Talent	Attracting, motivating, and retaining competent and committed people
Speed	Making important changes happen fast
Shared mindset	Ensuring that customers and employees have positive images of and experiences with the organisation
Accountability	The disciplines that result in high performance
Collaboration	Working across boundaries to ensure both efficiency and leverage
Learning	Generating and generalising ideas with impact
Leadership	Embedding leaders throughout the organisation who deliver the right results in the right way, who carry the organisation's leadership brand
Customer connection	Building enduring relationships of trust with targeted customers
Innovation	Doing something new in both content and process
Strategic unity	Articulating and sharing a strategic point of view
Efficiency	Managing operational costs

ETD practices make a significant contribution to the organisation when ETD practitioners shift from a focus on just people to a focus on organisations where people work. By helping to create and build organisational capabilities, ETD practices, processes, products, services and technology are integral to the success of the organisation. These capabilities enhance (or reduce) investor confidence in future earnings and increase (or decrease) market capitalisation. ETD practitioners who link their practices to capabilities and who then find ways to communicate those capabilities to investors and stakeholders deliver long-term sustainable value (Ulrich & Brockbank, 2005).

The concept of organisation capability is closely related to the emerging focus on organisational sustainability. Human resource professionals and business leaders increasingly include sustainability as a factor when assessing organisational effectiveness or success. Sustainability is the ability to meet the needs of the present and achieve success today without compromising the ability of future generations to meet their own needs (Losey, Meisinger & Ulrich, 2005). Sustainability includes values, governance, transparency and ethics, and goals such as diversity, social responsibility, supporting human and employee rights, protecting the environment and contributing to the community. Sustainability also considers the bottom line because financial viability is necessary for organisational survival, but it defines success as something more than financial results (Losey *et al*, 2005).

The emphasis on flexibility, capability and sustainability has various implications for managing ETD. ETD efforts should focus on those areas where human capital makes the biggest difference to strategic success. Human resource and ETD practices should also be aligned to ensure compliance with legal regulations or to provide incentives that reflect community, environmental or social goals. This requires an evaluation of the effects of human resource policies (including ETD policies and practices) on human capacity (people's capabilities, opportunities and motivation). Capability includes people's knowledge about the organisation's social responsibility and ethics codes;

opportunity includes time off from work to do volunteer tasks in the local community; and motivation includes employee perceptions that activities related to sustainability are noticed and rewarded (Losey *et al*, 2005).

These workplace issues have a profound impact on the role and function of ETD. ETD professionals are increasingly expected to function as business partners and to align their ETD activities with business strategies. ETD programmes need to add value for stakeholders and help to deliver business results. This requires a non-traditional approach to ETD management.

The ETD value proposition

The ETD value proposition means that ETD practices (along with other supportive human resource practices), departments and practitioners produce positive outcomes for main stakeholders: employees, line managers, customers, investors and government. As discussed in Chapter 7, when stakeholders see the value of ETD interventions, the ETD department will be credible, respected, and influential. Value, in this sense, is defined by the receiver. In a world of increasingly scarce resources, activities that fail to add value are not worth pursuing (Ulrich & Brockbank, 2005). Effective ETD management is therefore crucial to ensure that all ETD activities deliver results that add value for main stakeholders. The text box below provides an example of a typical ETD value proposition.

Example of an ETD value proposition

To enhance its service delivery role and strategic human capital development role, the ETD department developed a consolidated ETD strategy, products and service offerings guided by the following value proposition:

We will provide ETD products and services that will assist our clients to become capable and competent and provide leadership and stature to the company in their respective fields, areas of expertise and endeavours. We as an ETD function will provide or obtain the necessary expertise in ETD services, product development and technology so that we can provide a full capability that supports the effective implementation of the company HRD strategy. We will form partnerships with our clients in the company and the various departments we assist, by being responsive and adaptive, and developing and providing solutions, products and services that add value for key company stakeholders. We will do all this by acting as a seamless function, devoid of functional and geographic separations. We will become a service provider that is responsive, highly valued, recognised for its professionalism, expertise and effectiveness.

Implications of a value proposition

Managing ETD within the context of a value proposition has five important implications for ETD practitioners. These are described in the following section.

Value is defined by the receivers

Since value is defined by the receivers, not the provider, the ETD value proposition begins with a focus on the needs, goals and beliefs of the main stakeholders. The ultimate receivers of the value added by ETD interventions are customers. Therefore, ETD practitioners must balance the multiple and frequently conflicting demands of stakeholders, who range from internal clients (such as managers and employees) to external stakeholders (such as customers and investors) (Ulrich & Brockbank, 2005).

Create competitive advantage

The value proposition needs to position the ETD department, practitioners, products, services and technology as a source of competitive advantage. Ulrich and Brockbank (2005:6) describe the creation of competitive advantage as the 'wallet test'. An internal operation passes the wallet test if it inspires customers or shareholders to take money out of their wallets and put it into the organisation's wallet, instead of into the wallets of competitors. If the ETD department is to create competitive advantage, it must create substantial value with measurable and concrete results. For example, ETD products and services must measurably contribute to the creation of human abilities and organisational capabilities that are substantially better than those of competitors. An organisation's capabilities give investors confidence in future earnings and increase market capitalisation. ETD practitioners who link their activities, products and services to capabilities and who then find ways to communicate those capabilities to investors deliver shareholder value.

Alignment with customer requirements

ETD practitioners must align their ETD practices, products and services with the requirements of internal and external customers. To employees worried about retrenchment, the ETD practitioner should demonstrate that participating in a training event will enhance their employability and help them to stay employed. To a line manager worried about reaching strategic goals, ETD practitioners need to show how investment in training and development will help to deliver business results. ETD practitioners need to remember that their interest in customers must create value in the products or services customers receive. For shareholders who are worried about returns and growth, ETD practitioners must implement and manage training strategies that deliver results, enhance employee employability and productivity, and deliver intangibles that give owners confidence that results will be sustained in the future. Intangibles represent the hidden value of the training and development function; this is shareholder value not shown by financial results (Lev, 2001).

Continued professional development

The ETD value proposition directs ETD practitioners to acquire the personal competencies necessary to link training activities to stakeholder value.

Value the link between investors and internal operations

The ETD value proposition leads ETD practitioners to understand the powerful connection between managers' and employees' jobs inside the organisation and what happens with customers and investors on the outside. Focusing on the implications of the ETD value proposition (listed in Table 8.2) helps the ETD function to:

- emerge as full strategic contributors;
- add greater value for main stakeholders (customers, investors, line managers, employees and government);
- enhance business productivity;
- achieve measurable and valuable results;
- create sustainable competitive advantage; and
- have more job and career satisfaction (Ulrich & Brockbank, 2005).

Table 8.2 Implications of the ETD value proposition (based on Ulrich & Brockbank, 2005)

Implication	Description
Know external business realities Serve external and internal stakeholders	• What capabilities does the organisation need to create products and services that result in customers investing their capital in the organisation? • What abilities and competencies do our people need to understand and respond to short-term and long-term market demands? • How do we invest in ETD practices, products and services that deliver business results and add value for main stakeholders?
Align ETD practices, products and services with internal and external stakeholders' requirements	• Who are the main stakeholders of the ETD activities? • What are the goals and values of the receiving stakeholders? • What is important to them? • What do they want? • What are their requirements?
Build ETD resources	• How do we organise ETD activities to deliver maximum value? • How do we create an ETD strategy that will help our organisation to achieve its business goals?
Ensure ETD professionalism	• How do we ensure that ETD practitioners will know what to do and have the skills to do it?

Table 8.3 provides an overview of the criteria for an effective ETD function and shows how these link with the five implications of the ETD value proposition.

Table 8.3 Criteria of an effective ETD function (based on Ulrich & Brockbank, 2005: 16)

Criteria for an effective ETD function	Elements of the ETD value proposition
• Recognises external business realities, adapts its practices and allocates resources accordingly	Knowing external business realities
• Creates market value for investors by increasing intangibles • Increases customer share by connecting with target customers • Helps line managers to deliver strategy by building organisation capabilities • Clarifies and establishes an employee value proposition and ensures that employees have the competencies to do their work and sustain their employability	Serving external and internal stakeholders
• Adds value by managing training and development practices and processes	Creating training and development practices, products and services
• Has a clear strategic planning process for aligning training and development investments with business goals • Aligns the training function to the strategy of the business	Building training and development resources
• Has staff who play clear and appropriate roles • Builds staff ability to demonstrate training function and ETD practitioner competencies and professionalism • Invests in ETD practitioners through training and development experiences	Ensuring ETD professionalism

Strategic human resource development

ETD is an integral part of the larger field of human resources (HR). ETD consists of education, training and development. It is defined as organised learning experiences provided by employers within a specified period of time to bring about the possibility of performance improvement, personal growth and enhancement of employees' employability orientation. The goal is to satisfy the current and future ETD needs of the organisation (Rothwell, Sullivan & McLean, 1995; Van Dam, 2004). Employability orientation refers to the attitudes of employees toward interventions aimed at increasing the organisation's flexibility and performance capability. Employability interventions often imply a change in the employees' current work situation. To be or to become employable, an employee may have to change work content, jobs, or departments, or engage in ETD programmes (Van Dam, 2004).

Training is one way in which learning can take place within the organisation. Training is regarded as a planned, short-term change effort intended to modify competencies by helping employees to achieve effective performance in an activity or range of activities (Rothwell *et al*, 1995; Robinson, 2006). Education is an intermediate-term change effort intended to prepare individuals for promotions (vertical career progression) or for enhanced technical abilities in their current jobs (horizontal career progression). Education is broader in scope than training and aims to develop employees' knowledge, social understanding and skill and intellectual capacity. Development is a long-term change effort intended to broaden individuals through experience and to give them new insights about themselves and their organisation. Development focuses on the longer-term growth and development of the individual in a way that fulfils their potential (Rothwell *et al*, 1995).

Education, training and development are equally weighted components of a holistic capability-building process. This process forms the foundation for all programmes and activities that cater for the strategic HRD needs of the organisation. ETD efforts are therefore linked to the organisation's business goals, objectives and strategies (Grobler *et al*, 2006). This process is known as strategic human resource development. Below is an overview of the principles that drive the human resource development strategy for the public service. The text box on pages 301-302 sets out the main components of the public service's HRD strategy.

Principles underlying the White Paper on Public Service Training and Education

The White Paper on Public Service Training and Education (1997)

According to the White Paper on Public Service Education and Training (July 1997), the formulation, implementation and evaluation of programmes of public service training and education will be carried out in accordance with the following broad principles:

- **Access and entitlement.** All public servants will be entitled to ongoing and meaningful opportunities for training and education, on recruitment and throughout their working lives. This broad principle will also be extended to cover potential recruits to the public service through the development and improvement of the current bursary scheme).

- **Needs analysis.** Programmes of training and education will be based on the detailed assessment of the needs of individual organisations and employees, and will be designed in particular to secure an optimal fit between these two sets of needs.

- **A competency-based approach to learning outcomes.** The new approach to public service training and education will focus on outcomes rather than inputs, with particular reference to the competencies required at different levels to build individual and organisational capacity.

- **Integration between policy-formulation, strategic planning and transformation.** Far from being marginalised, as in the past, it will be expected of government departments and provincial administration to systematically link training and education to the broader process of policy formulation, strategic planning and transformation, at national, departmental and provincial levels, particularly in relation to service delivery, institution building and management, human resource development, and representivity and affirmative action.
- **Adequate resourcing.** This will be vital for the success of the training and education system, and will be ensured in particular by integrating plans and priorities for training and education as a central element in the budget planning process, at national, departmental and provincial levels.
- **Flexibility and decentralisation.** To ensure that programmes of training and education are designed flexibly to meet the individual and changing needs of particular departments and provinces, responsibility will be decentralised as much as possible, within agreed national norms and standards.
- **Career pathing.** Programmes of training and education will be targeted in particular at facilitating career paths for all staff that promote progression (vertical and lateral) and productivity, and for this reason such programmes will need to be positively related to policies on recruitment, promotion, grading, remuneration and performance appraisal.
- **Lifelong learning.** Public service training and education (PSTE) will be linked to the National Qualifications Framework (NQF) in ways which promote lifelong learning and the development of portable skills and competencies. PSTE will also be linked to the Department of Labour's Skills Development Strategy, particularly through the development of appropriate learnerships for the service.
- **Learning organisations.** Training, education and development will be promoted in ways which enable public service institutions to become learning organisations, capable of continuous development and adaptation through the creative integration of learning with work at all levels.
- **Quality and cost-effectiveness.** This will be promoted through the effective utilisation of available resources; the avoidance of duplication; the establishment of effective structures and mechanisms for the coordination of training and education at national and provincial levels; the introduction of improved forms of standard setting and accreditation; and the targeting of training and education at activities that add value by developing skills; knowledge and attitudes that can be readily transferred to the job.
- **Equity and empowerment.** Training and education will be linked to broader plans and programmes for promoting employment and occupational equity and will be targeted in particular at the empowerment of historically disadvantaged groups.
- **Consultation and participation.** To ensure broad commitment and support at all levels within the public service, plans and programmes for training and education will be formulated, implemented and evaluated with the full participation and involvement of the public service unions and all other relevant stakeholders.
- **Information and communication.** Information about training and education opportunities will be collected and collated, and effectively disseminated at all levels throughout the public service.
- **Effective design and delivery.** To enhance the relevance, quality and cost-effectiveness of training and education, programmes will be designed and delivered in accordance with the twelve training principles set out in Chapter C of the Public Service Staff Code.
- **Monitoring and evaluation.** In order to ensure that plans and programmes of training and education are carried out throughout the public service in accordance with the above principles, effective mechanisms for ongoing monitoring and evaluation will be put into place.
- **Elevating the status of training and trainers.** To ensure that training, education and human resources development more generally play an increasingly strategic and integral part in building a new public service in South Africa, the position, role and status of trainers as human resource specialists will need to be significantly redefined and enhanced.

Human resource development refers to a set of methods and processes for solving problems or realising opportunities related to people's performance capability and employability. Managing ETD involves seeing that those methods and processes are applied with economy and care to ensure stakeholder value. The ultimate goal of any ETD effort is always a change in human behaviour to facilitate organisational capability and employee employability (Ulrich & Brockbank, 2005).

HRD is linked to most other human resource management functions. Workforce planners identify the quality and quantity of employees that the organisation requires. Projected workforce needs enable the human resource function to plan the ETD of both current and new employees. The recruitment and selection functions locate candidates with the required skills in the market. The need for formal ETD depends on the level of the job in the organisation. For example, high entry requirements will diminish the need for intensive formal training, while a good in-house training course may reduce the need to recruit highly skilled candidates. Performance assessments and career planning are also directly related to HRD. Performance assessments allow for the identification of possible training requirements and possible career opportunities in an organisation. Similarly, remuneration and reward should also be linked to employees' competencies (Swanepoel, Erasmus, Van Wyk & Schenk, 2003).

One of the main reasons why people development efforts fail is the lack of a systematically developed ETD model. The aim of people development is to contribute to an organisation's overall business objectives and add value for important stakeholders. However, in many instances such objectives are not clearly formulated, stakeholder goals and requirements are not identified, ETD programmes are never evaluated, and it seems that behaviour changes do not form part of the HRD effort. A systematic approach to HRD would typically involve the following activities:

- Do a proper job analysis as an input to the workforce planning process.
- Do a proper job and competency profiling.
- Identify and define the skills requirements of the organisation as derived from the workforce planning process and the business strategic goals.
- Conduct a skills audit to determine the gap between the actual skills of the current workforce and the skills required to sustain organisational capability.
- Identify pivotal talent pools and their ETD needs.
- Compile a skills inventory of critical skills and competencies of pivotal talent pools.
- Identify skills programmes to address the skills gaps.
- Draft and implement the workplace skills plan by means of a strategic ETD plan and management efforts.
- Monitor, evaluate and report on the ETD and workplace skills plans.
- Establish a quality assurance system to ensure effective and value-added ETD interventions.

Key elements of the Human Resource Development Strategy for the Public Service

The Human Resource Development Strategy for the Public Service

The Human Resource Development Strategy (HRDS) concept was adopted to support a holistic approach to human resource training and development in the Public Service. The HRDS requires that the development and training of people should take place primarily on the basis of relevant training policies. If training is further linked to departmental strategies, the impact of training could be enhanced in terms of job performance, service delivery and attitudes.

The following are the key challenges facing human resource development in the Public Service:
1. Ensuring effective service delivery
2. Keeping effective managers and people with scarce skills
3. Coping with limited resources
4. Effective financial practices
5. Integration of career and life goals
6. Meaningful advancement of women and the disabled in the Public Service
7. Coordinating missions and goals
8. Establishing effective management information systems
9. Establishing effective interfaces between systems
10.Impact of HIV/Aids
11.Performance management in the Public Service

The HRDS for the Public Service aims at addressing the major human resource capacity constraints currently hampering the effective and equitable delivery of public services, including dealing with the consequences of the HIV/Aids epidemic and the threat that it poses to the development of the public sector.

The Public Service at national, provincial and local government levels needs the relevant skills to implement the policies and programmes that have been introduced to improve living standards and reduce levels of poverty.

Strategy for human resource development within the Public Service
Vision
A dedicated, responsive and productive Public Service.
Mission
To maximise people development, management and empowerment through quality skills development to accelerate transformation and service delivery that will benefit the people of South Africa.
Strategic objective
By the end of 2006 the Public Service competently delivers effective and equitable services to the people of South Africa.

The strategic objective will be achieved by attainment of the following key results:
1. Full commitment to promote and implement the HRDS in all Public Service institutions and organisations
2. An effective strategic and operational HRD planning framework established within the Public Service
3. Relevant competencies established within the Public Service
4. Effective management and coordination of the implementation of the HRDS for the Public Service ensured

The implementation framework is underpinned by the vision of an integrated human resource management system. In order to ensure that required competencies are effectively utilised, developed and nurtured, it is critical that the development of human resources in the Public Service is integrated with other human resource processes and systems.

The ETD management process

To ensure the effective implementation of the human resource development strategy, ETD managers typically follow a systematic process. An effective ETD management process needs to comply with the following ten criteria (see Figure 8.1 on page 305):

Develop a holistic HRD strategy

All ETD interventions should form part of the overall HRD strategy of the business. These interventions should add value for stakeholders and contribute to the organisation's performance capability and long-term sustainability. The strategic HRD plan has a long-term focus (usually three to five years), while the annual ETD plan has a short-term focus (one year). As discussed in Chapters 1 and 3, the ETD plan describes the strategies for implementing the workplace skills plan and the relevant HRD objectives for a particular year.

Consider external and internal forces

External and internal forces create the need for specific HRD strategies. An awareness of these forces can help ETD managers and practitioners to prioritise ETD interventions and methods. External forces for change originate outside the organisation and have global effects. These may cause an organisation to question the essence of its business and the ways that products and services are produced. External forces typically include technological advancements, market changes and social and political pressures. Internal forces for change come from inside the organisation. These forces can be subtle (such as low job satisfaction) or can manifest in outward signs (such as low productivity or high staff turnover and conflict) (Kinicki & Kreitner, 2006).

Define the ETD value proposition

The ETD function needs to define the ETD value proposition by determining the requirements of main stakeholders and documenting these requirements in the strategic HRD and annual ETD plans.

Conduct a strategic skills gap analysis

A proper diagnosis must be conducted of the biggest performance problems and industry-related skills gaps that impact on the effectiveness of the business. ETD solutions to these problems need to be identified. As discussed in Chapter 3, assessing the industry-related skills gaps helps managers to forecast the supply and demand of critical skills that could affect the business' current and future performance capability. A proper ETD needs analysis helps managers to compile a skills inventory of critical and scarce skills, and identify the skills development needs of talent pools in the organisation. An ETD needs analysis also assists managers to develop and implement an effective HRD strategy.

Conduct an organisational ETD needs analysis

Once the biggest problem areas and skills gaps have been identified, a thorough skills audit must be conducted to determine the ETD needs of the groups targeted for ETD interventions. These groups usually include scarce and critical skills groups, employment equity groups and talent pools. An ETD analysis is based on job and competence profiles; it describes the competencies required to perform a job. On the other hand, a skills audit determines the skills development needs of the current employees.

Compile the workplace skills plan and ETD plan

The next step is to compile a workplace skills plan, which reflects the skills development needs of targeted groups and the planned ETD interventions for a particular financial year. To implement the workplace skills plan effectively, an ETD plan needs to be developed. This means setting specific, realistic and measurable targets, determining implementation strategies, setting progress review dates, allocating resources and appointing people who will be responsible for executing and managing the ETD plan. The ETD plan should also consider constraints that might hinder the achievement of the identified goals.

Specify the execution strategy

The ETD plan should also indicate the delivery methods of the planned ETD interventions. Delivery methods include on-the-job training, formal university education programmes, in-house workshops or external learning programmes. Another important aspect is to determine whether the ETD intervention will be outsourced to an external ETD provider.

Implement the ETD plan

Once the ETD plan has been finalised and approved, it needs to be implemented. Depending on the methods used, this can be a lengthy process. It is important to actively monitor the success of the implementation stage. Frequent evaluation of the effectiveness of the ETD interventions and measurement of results are essential. Actions at this stage include evaluating learners' assessment results, attendance records, feedback on the ETD provider's effectiveness and ETD targets achieved.

Evaluate the effectiveness of the ETD plan

The ETD plan and the ETD interventions are never perfect. An evaluation of outcomes achieved and the feedback received on the effectiveness of interventions is crucial to identify problem areas. A number of follow-up ETD interventions may be conducted to ensure that the workplace skills plan targets and ETD goals are achieved.

Evaluate value added by ETD interventions

A challenging aspect of managing the implementation of the ETD plan is to evaluate whether employees' on-the-job behaviour and performance have changed for the better, as a result of the ETD intervention. The ETD practitioner needs to assist line managers to measure behavioural changes in employees. As discussed in Chapter 7, the outcomes-based assessment process and the performance management system of the organisation are useful mechanisms in determining behavioural changes related to employees' on-the-job performance.

ENVIRONMENTAL ANALYSIS

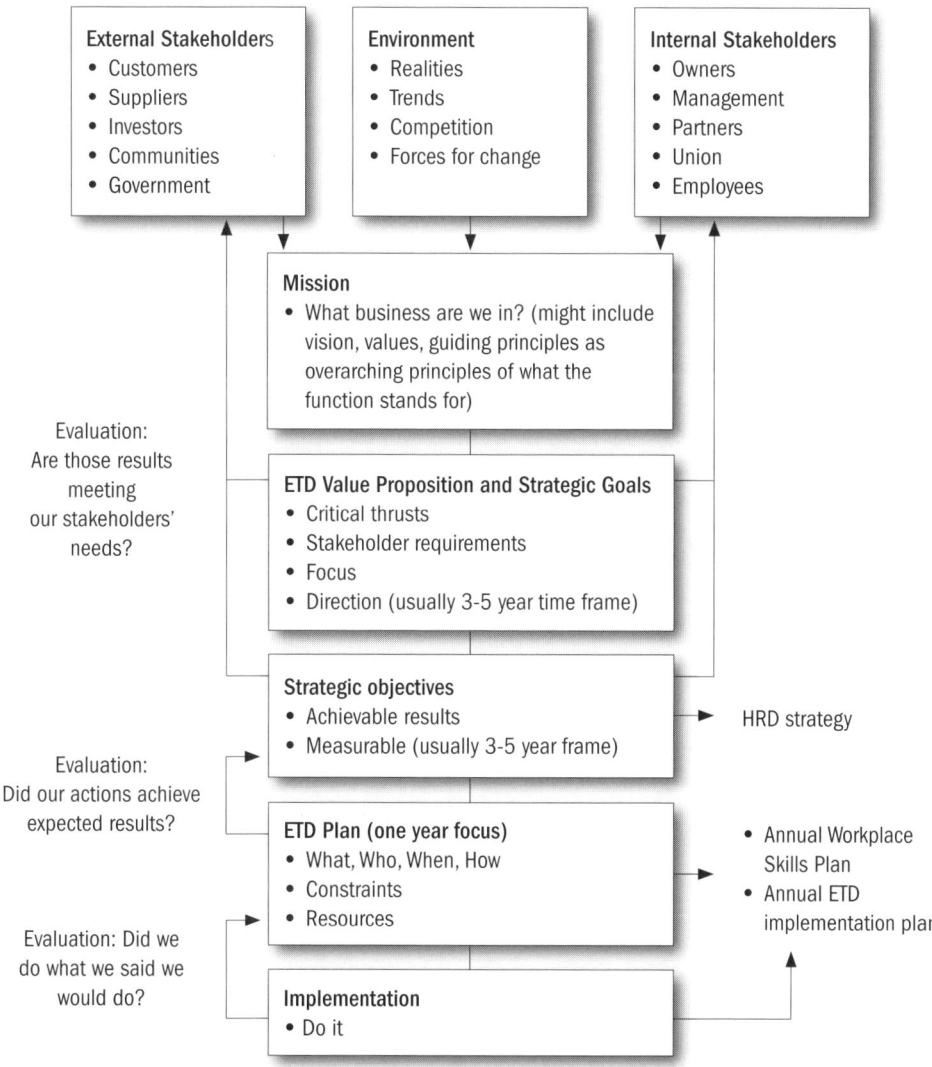

Figure 8.1 The strategic ETD management process (based on Rothwell et al, 1995)

CASE STUDY

The Social Security Administration Office of Systems (OS) in the United States of America employs more than 3 200 Information Technology (IT) professionals skilled in a wide variety of specialties. As Social Security has automated processes and improved efficiencies during the last four years, the OS hired approximately 1 100 new IT professionals and managers to serve the changing systems needs of the growing agency. Complicating the staffing challenge was a large wave of looming retirements of managers and IT workers with specialised programming knowledge. OS leaders knew that it was critical to attract and retain skilled talent to stay ahead of technological advances and the agency's IT needs.

Assessing the skills gap

Since 2001, the OS workforce increased from 2 800 to almost 3 200 employees today, most of whom are IT specialists. By 2015, 51% of the OS workforce will be eligible to retire, and another 12% could exercise early retirement. With half of the OS workforce under age 50 and the other half over age 50, retiring IT workers with significant programmatic knowledge and technical expertise could leave. OS leaders knew that it was essential to upskill the current workforce and recruit new workers with the necessary technical expertise that is critical to maintaining the agency's systems now and in the future.

The strategy

During the initial assessment phase, OS leaders conducted research and benchmarking with other government agencies and held discussions with subject matter experts to understand best practices in undertaking a skills audit. With more than 250 managers, OS leaders conducted a skills audit to evaluate skills and competencies for the OS workforce and determine what skills were needed in the next three years. Serving a baseline benchmark, the skills audit measured more than 200 skills and 90 competencies for each IT professional in the OS. The skills inventory that resulted from the skills audit quantified what OS leaders knew from anecdotal evidence: technical skills, management expertise, and programmatic knowledge were in short supply.

By comparing baseline data from the inventory with the skills and competencies identified as critical in the next three years, OS leaders identified the 10 largest gaps. While they initially focused on the largest gaps, OS leaders were careful to look at all gaps from top to bottom as the need for certain skills and competencies may change over time. OS leaders set into motion an organisation-wide plan involving ETD, recruitment and retention. Working closely with managers, the ETD staff conducted needs assessments and created ETD solutions and strategies to address the largest gaps. And, as managers hired new employees or replaced those who had left, they evaluated what type of skills and competencies were lacking and actively recruited new hires with those skills.

In addition to the skills inventory, the OS created a long-term process to strategically manage human capital. This process, including the steps of targeting, assessing, planning, executing and monitoring, provides an opportunity for the OS to proactively address skills shortages and demographic changes in the workforce before significant gaps in skills and competence occur. Between 2003 and 2005, OS data revealed a 46% decrease in the gap of critical skills and competencies. The overall retention rate for the OS has increased from 77% in 2003 to 91% in 2006.

(based on ASTD, 2006:22)

Questions

Reflect on the current ETD practices of an organisation that you are quite familiar with, then answer the following questions:

- What are the ETD priorities, as described in the HRD strategy and the workplace skills plan?
- Does the organisation conduct skills audits to determine the skills development needs of its employees?

- Does a skills inventory exist of critical and scarce skills?
- If not, what could be the implications for the organisation in terms of sustaining its competitive advantage and performance capability as a business?
- What advice would you offer to the ETD manager regarding the importance of following a strategic ETD management approach in planning and managing ETD efforts?

The ETD management functions

The ETD management process requires managers to be competent in performing the six functions described in the following section.

Define the ETD value proposition

The ETD value proposition shows the ETD department's intent to achieve excellence. As discussed earlier, the ETD value proposition means that ETD practices, departments and practitioners produce positive outcomes for main stakeholders. The ETD value proposition ensures that all ETD activities, products and services are aligned with the strategic business goals of the organisation to support the effective and efficient implementation of the HRD strategy.

Strategise

ETD managers need to decide what needs to be done and how and when things need to be done. ETD managers identify the scope, resources and constraints of the ETD activities as required by the HRD strategy, strategic ETD plan and the workplace skills plan.

Scope deals both with quantity (how many people, departments, situations, groups, and ETD programmes) and consequences (who and what may be affected; the importance of the identified ETD interventions). The scope of the ETD plan will determine what resources are required to implement the plan. Questions to ask about available resources are shown in Table 8.4. The scope of the ETD plan is weighed against available resources to make decisions about how to manage the implementation of the plan. ETD managers and practitioners also need to consider constraints that may affect the implementation of the ETD plan, including:

- limitations or requirements regarding when and how resources can be used (for example, times when people will be unavailable or under heavy pressure, or deadlines that must be met to coordinate with other activities);
- actions required or prohibited to conform to laws, contracts or government regulations (for example, union agreements that restrict access to people, requirements for appropriate representation of historically disadvantaged or designated groups, or safety or environmental regulations that limit certain activities);
- organisational policies or cultural expectations that direct or influence the conduct of some activities (for example, protocols and policies to be observed in contacting people, conducting training or requesting information); and
- decision-making limits and sensitivities that might influence how people respond to the ETD interventions (for example, requirements for decision-making processes; concerns about loss of jobs or status; or sensitivities about similar ETD interventions in the past).

Table 8.4 ETD resource questions (based on Jackson & Addison, 1992)

Resources	Important questions
People	• How many people are involved in the ETD activities? • What skills, backgrounds and experience do they have? • What limitations are placed on the amount or nature of their participation? • Do we make use of outsourced ETD providers? • What kind of performance problems do the ETD activities address? • How many ETD practitioners do we need? • Do we need assessors and moderators? • Are ETD practitioners competent in delivering the ETD programmes?
Time	• How much time is required? • What are the deadlines? • What are the consequences of changing deadlines?
Money	• How much money is available? • How are funds allocated?
Information	• Do we know the ETD needs and expectations of the targeted groups? • What information do we need to implement the ETD plan? • What are the requirements of main stakeholders? • What are the workplace skills plan targets? • What ETD programmes are available? • Who are the target group and sponsor?
Locations	• How many different locations or settings are involved? • How varied are they? • How far apart are they?
Materials, equipment and systems	• What materials, equipment and systems are available for use? • How much materials, equipment and systems can be used? • How can they be accessed?

Organise

ETD managers decide how to arrange, deploy and use the organisation's resources, processes and core activities. For example, an ETD practitioner has to arrange the training facilities for an upcoming training course. Organising makes it possible to achieve the goals set out in the strategising process. From an ETD management perspective, organising includes the following:

• Management has to allocate human, physical and financial resources to the planned ETD interventions.
• Duties and roles need to be defined.
• Performance agreements, competence profiles and personal development plans need to be compiled and negotiated.
• Policies and procedures need to be in place to enable the ETD function to attain its goals and objectives. These need to be attained at specific deadlines and according to set standard requirements.

Lead

Leading, or directing, has to do with mobilising the resources of the organisation to achieve goals. For example, leading the ETD staff to conduct the training courses entails the following:

* Give directions and guidelines.
* Motivate the staff to direct their actions in accordance with the goals of the ETD plan and quality requirements.
* Influence and motivate ETD staff, line managers and employees through effective communication.
* Conduct performance appraisals and development planning discussions at regular intervals.
* Make available feedback on performance and mentoring for development purposes to motivate and encourage staff.
* Involve ETD staff in decision making and problem solving.

Assure quality

Quality assurance (QA) is the implementation of the ETD function's (or the ETD provider's) quality management system. It includes the following:

* quality management policies that define what the ETD function wishes to achieve;
* quality management procedures that enable the ETD function to practise its quality management policies;
* review mechanisms, which ensure that the quality management policies and procedures are applied and that they remain effective.

As shown in Table 8.5, the quality management system governs all ETD practices (Coetzee, 2007).

Table 8.5 Setting up the ETD quality assurance system (Coetzee, 2006)

In place		Key performance areas	Responsible person	Evidence
Yes	No			

		1. Establish the QA structure:
		  • manager responsible for ETD provision QA;
		  • assessors;
		  • ETD practitioners;
		  • coaches;
		  • moderators;
		  • RPL advisors;
		  • mentors;
		  • quality auditors;
		  • administrative support; and
		  • job profiles for all these positions.		

		2. Recruit, appoint and train QA staff.		
		3. Negotiate performance contracts and development plans with QA staff.		

In place		Key performance areas	Responsible person	Evidence
Yes	No			
		4. Obtain physical, administrative and financial resources to operate the learning provision QA function.		
		5. Draft strategies and an operational business plan for the learning provision QA function (including mission, vision, values, goals and objectives).		
		6. Identify the quality assurance areas to be managed.		
		7. Draft policies and procedures for each of these areas. These will form the basis of the quality management system, which must be formally managed using ISO guidelines.		
		8. Set up a management information system to review, on at least a monthly basis, the established goals.		
		9. Train stakeholders, management and staff in learning provision QA (orientation sessions). Ensure that they understand policy and procedure requirements.		
		10. Set up a documentation and administrative system that complies with SAQA standards.		
		11. Design an internal quality audit (self-assessment) and customer review system (identify main quality areas; draw up checklists, measurement scales and other tools; and draw up quality audit procedures).		
		12. Orientate stakeholders and involve staff in the quality audit process.		

Evaluate

As discussed in Chapter 7, evaluation refers to the ETD manager's task of continuously monitoring and checking whether the ETD staff are achieving goals and standards. Examples include checking the required standard of training on a particular learning programme, and measuring the extent to which the workplace skills plan targets have been achieved. ETD managers evaluate the ETD department's progress in terms of achieving the goals of the ETD plan and the workplace skills plan, and the extent to which ETD interventions added value to the organisation's bottom line. Through evaluation, ETD managers also detect any deviations from these plans and make corrections. For example, they have to monitor, check and control the expenditure on planned ETD interventions. Furthermore, they need to do quality audits to ensure that all ETD activities comply with the ETQA or SETA quality requirements. An evaluation of the cost-effectiveness and impact of ETD interventions should cover the following aspects:

- the impact that ETD interventions had on improving workplace performance and the employability of learners (as discussed in Chapter 7);
- the appropriateness of the design and delivery of the ETD interventions (as discussed in Chapters 4 and 5);
- the curriculum, learning programme delivery and assessment strategy described in

the facilitator/trainer guide (as discussed in chapter 4);
- the learning facilitation (delivery) and assessment process (as discussed in Chapters 5 and 6);
- the ETD strategic and operational plans, the workplace skills plan and the management and administration of these plans;
- the difficulties that managers, ETD providers, ETD practitioners and learners experienced (for this purpose, ETD managers and practitioners need to analyse the data and reports generated during implementation to identify trends, problem areas and successes).

Learners' progress needs to be monitored during the course of any ETD intervention. This makes it possible to address problems as they arise. The overall success of the ETD plan must be evaluated. The implementation of an ETD plan is successful if:
- targets set out in the plans are achieved;
- ETD practices comply with the standards for quality and best practices;
- learners achieve competence within the stipulated time frames;
- the ETD interventions lead to an increase in productivity levels; and
- learners' employability and educational levels increase and they are able to progress in their careers.

Table 8.6 Key functions of strategic ETD management

Function	Description
Define the ETD value proposition Management determines the requirements of the key stakeholders.	• Identify the main stakeholders of the ETD activities. • Determine the goals and values of the receiving stakeholders. • Clarify what is important to them. • Specify their requirements.
Strategise Management decides what needs to be done.	• Determine the ETD needs of the enterprise. • Analyse the tasks and the learning outcomes of a programme. • Draw up a strategic plan for ETD. • Draw up an annual ETD plan and schedule of courses. • Plan every learning intervention. • Plan the ETD budget for the following year.
Organise Management decides how it should be done.	• Organise the ETD department (for example, allocate responsibilities to various staff members in the ETD department). • Organise a course for supervisory training or in communication skills. • Identify and coordinate the resources, including ETD staff required to implement the plan (for example, identify the training facilities and catering requirements). • Select suitable training methods, training aids and facilities, and the trainers themselves. • Arrange accommodation and make administrative arrangements for the training programme and learners.
Lead Management says how and when it should be done.	• Motivate ETD and support staff. • Provide direction and guidelines to ETD staff. • Provide support for the achievement of the objectives.

Function	Description
	• Conduct performance appraisals and provide coaching and mentoring support.
Assure quality Management ensures that all ETD practices comply with the national quality outcomes-based ETD requirements.	• Establish a quality management system that governs all ETD practices, including learning provision, design and development, assessment and moderation practice, record keeping and competence of ETD staff. • Draft policies and procedures to ensure compliance with ETQA requirements. • Train and educate ETD staff in quality requirements. • Ensure that ETD staff are trained and competent in ETD, assessment and moderation.
Evaluate Management determines whether ETD practices comply with standards and whether ETD interventions added value for stakeholders.	• Determine the extent to which the required results have been achieved. • Determine whether the ETD programmes were implemented as planned. • Determine whether the objectives and targets were achieved. • Assess whether learners have achieved outcomes and are able to transfer learning to the workplace. • Decide what changes need to be made for future programmes. • Measure the value added to the organisation's bottom line. • Measure compliance to quality and best practice standards.

Reasons why ETD efforts fail
• Only the ETD manager is interested in the end result.
• No one is in charge.
• There is no effective or efficient IT infrastructure.
• The ETD plan lacks structure.
• The ETD plan lacks detail.
• The ETD plan is under-budgeted.
• Insufficient resources are allocated.
• The actual ETD interventions are not tracked against the workplace skills plan targets.
• The manager, ETD practitioners and learners are not communicating.
• The ETD plan strays from its original goals.
• There is no HR support for managers.
• A quality management system has not been established.
• The human resource information system is poorly managed or does not exist.
• ETD interventions are not followed up.
• There is no improvement planning.
• A communication framework to communicate and review progress has not been established.

ACTIVITY

Approach the ETD manager of your organisation (or any organisation you are familiar with). Ask him/her the following questions and make notes about his/her responses:

- What is the value proposition of the ETD department?
- What strategising activities are conducted in respect of ETD in the organisation?
- What organising activities are conducted in respect of ETD in the organisation?
- What leading activities are conducted in respect of ETD in the organisation?
- What quality assurance activities are conducted in respect of ETD in the organisation?
- What evaluation activities are conducted in respect of ETD in the organisation?

After your discussion with the ETD manager, draw up a list of all the activities and classify them under the headings: value proposition, strategising, organising, leading, assuring quality and evaluating. Do you think the list is complete? What would you add to the list?

Managing quality in ETD

In the South African workplace, HRD operates within the national requirements for quality outcomes-based ETD. The Concise Oxford Dictionary defines 'quality' as 'degree of excellence' and 'assurance' as 'formal guarantee' or 'positive declaration'. From these definitions, 'quality assurance' is a formal guarantee of excellence. The SAQA Act defines quality assurance as the process of ensuring that the specified degree of excellence is achieved. The unit standards and regulation requirements specify these degrees of excellence. Quality management is defined as all activities of the overall management function that determine the quality policy, objectives, strategies, responsibilities and implementation of these by means of a combination of managerial processes (Coetzee, 2007).

In ETD, the move towards a quality management system approach is being driven by:

- stakeholders (particularly the state) that demand a higher level of quality in education and training, particularly where learners and employers have to invest in learning opportunities;
- international expectations that each country will ensure the quality of its graduates and learners;
- ETD providers that demand flexibility, requiring self-approval and review of new learning programmes;
- a move away from expensive, unresponsive centralised systems; and
- standards and qualifications.

South African organisations that want to use the NQF to best advantage will need to establish their own ETD quality management systems. This approach is consistent with the international trend towards self-management and devolved responsibility for quality; this means that everyone is responsible for quality. Quality management is also fundamental to every other qualifications framework in the world. A robust and coherent ETD quality management system provides learners and other stakeholders with an assurance that the ETD department and its staff have the capacity to meet the needs of its clients. Quality can only be measured when these requirements are known and defined.

Table 8.7 Elements of the ETD quality management system (Coetzee, 2007)

Quality assurance element	Description
Management system	Management is responsible for overseeing the design of the quality management system. The following are management functions regarding the quality management system: • Compile the departmental business plan, workforce plan, workplace skills plan, strategic ETD plan and budget. • Establish policies and procedures, which specify the standards of performance and service delivery. • Review performance and service delivery against the set standards. • Develop a strategy to achieve business goals and strategies. • Develop a quality and service delivery culture.
Personnel and material resources	Management should provide sufficient and appropriate resources to implement the quality system and achieve the quality objectives. The motivation, competence and thus ETD, communication capacity and performance of personnel involved in quality management are crucial. Effective performance management processes must be in place for all staff involved in facilitating the quality management system. Employees must also be educated in the principles of the quality management system. Regular communication on quality performance is essential for improvement purposes.
Administrative, physical and financial resources	These include service provisioning equipment and stores; accommodation, transport and information systems; quality assessment facilities; operational and technical documentation; the funding of learning provision; administrating, recording and storing of learner achievement, education, training and development. An employee's biographical information, qualifications, educational level and performance appraisal data should be maintained and updated on the personnel administration system.
ETD records	ETD records are normally kept to: • Make strategic skills development decisions. • Keep track of the status of skills in the department/organisation. • Enable HRD management staff to respond to enquiries from top management and outside institutions. • Guide employees to reach their full potential in the organisation by devising individual development plans that suit their particular needs. The types of record could be any of the following: • strategic ETD plan, Workplace skills plan and Annual Training Report • ETD budget and expenditure; • workforce planning data; • records of learning programmes attended; • employees' personal ETD records; • performance and development appraisal records; • in-service training records; • assessment and moderation records of learner achievements; • course evaluation records; and • quality audit and self-evaluation records.

Quality assurance element	Description
Communication system	An effective communication system allows for an effective flow of information between all the parties involved in the development of people. The communication system must eliminate the blockages and obstacles interrupting the flow of information and ensure that all information is available to all levels of staff within the agreed time frames.

Quality assurance in ETD is one of the most important principles of the NQF. Every unit standard and qualification registered on the NQF (and all the learning and assessment that take place) are subject to a quality assurance process. This ensures that ETD providers, assessors, moderators and organisations adhere to best practice ETD standards and continually improve their ETD practices.

As discussed in Chapter 1, the quality assurance process of ETD begins with designing and registering unit standards and qualifications on the NQF. Standard Generating Bodies develop and design the unit standards and qualifications and the National Standard Bodies recommend these to SAQA. If SAQA approves them, the standards and qualifications are registered on the NQF. As part of the quality assurance process, ETD providers and their learning and skills programmes must be accredited. Accreditation refers to the certification (usually for a specified period of time) of an ETD provider that has the capacity to provide the training on a specific area. The aim of the NQF quality assurance system is continuous improvement of learning provision practices and alignment with the NQF's quality outcomes-based training and assessment practices. SAQA established Education and Training Quality Assurance Bodies (ETQAs) to assure the quality of learning achievements according to registered unit standards and qualifications. The ETQA accredits ETD providers who comply with the accreditation criteria determined by SAQA (SAQA, 2001a).

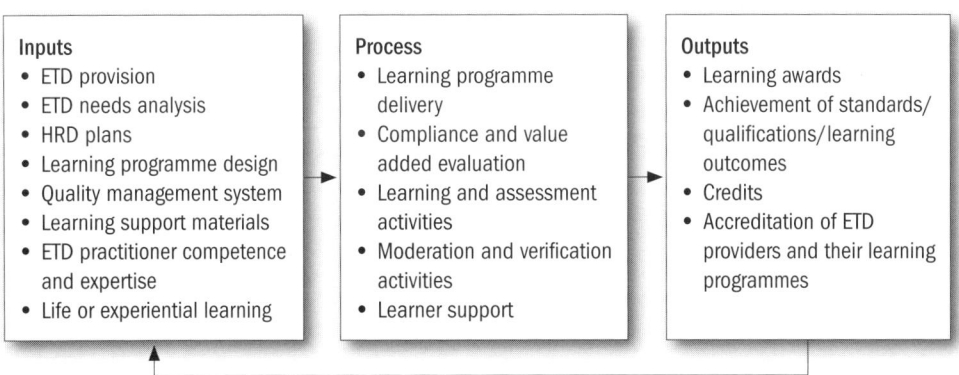

Figure 8.2 Critical points in the ETD quality management process

According to SAQA (2000), the three critical points in the ETD quality process are:
1. The product, or outcome, which comprises learning awards; achievement of standards or qualifications; credits and accreditation of learning programmes and providers;
2. The inputs, which are learning provision; outcomes-based learning and skills programmes; learning and learner resources; and experiential learning; and

3. The process, which includes the quality of the learning and assessment interactions; moderation and verification activities; the quality of the monitoring and auditing interactions.

Table 8.8 Provisional accreditation criteria (based on SAQA, 2001a)

Criteria	Principle	Quality assurance requirement
The primary focus of the provider coincides with that of the ETQA.	*External provider:* Core ETD provision is targeted at SETA ETD focus. *Internal provider:* Registered with the SETA as a levy payer and core ETD provision is targeted at SETA ETD focus.	Internal providers are registered for payment for Skills Development levy with the SETA. Providers will be offering learning towards SETA-related unit standards and qualifications. Providers have entered into partnerships with employers to offer workplace learning.
The provider seeking accreditation is registered in terms of the applicable legislation at the time of seeking accreditation.	The provider must be a legal entity and registered as such.	A provider must be registered as a: • CC; • Pty; • Trust; • NGO; or • statutory body.
Organisational practices reflect the provider's quality management system, which includes but is not limited to: • quality management policies that define what the provider wishes to achieve; • quality management procedures that enable the provider to practice its defined quality management policies; • review mechanisms, which ensure that the quality management policies and procedures defined are applied and remain effective; and • ETD-specific policies and procedures.	The provider must have a quality management system in place that governs all ETD practices, including learning provision, design and development, assessment practice, record keeping and ETD staff.	Policy 1: Managing quality management Policy 2: Managing learning provision Policy 3: Managing assessment Policy 4: Managing administration Policy 5: Developing ETD staff Policy 6: Assessment practice and assessor staff Policy 7: Learner record keeping system Site visit: Electronic database for learner information
The provider has the necessary resources, such as financial, administrative and physical resources.	• Appropriate, skilled staff are utilised for the delivery and assessment of learning.	ETD practitioners, facilitators, mentors and coaches are identified and appropriately qualified per unit standard in planned provision.

Criteria	Principle	Quality assurance requirement
	• Appropriate and required learning facilities and equipment are available and operational.	Physical premises of learning delivery is identified and operational.
The provider is able to develop, deliver and evaluate learning programmes that culminate in specified, registered unit standards and qualifications.	Learning programmes are designed and aligned to: • enable the learners to achieve the outcomes stated in the unit standard and/or qualification/ learning programme; and • facilitate the achievement of competence in the workplace. The provider has the staff to design and develop outcomes-based learning programmes or contracts the required capacity to meet requirements. Where the provider outsourced learning programme design and development, the provider has the ability to evaluate whether those products meet the OBET requirements.	• All equipment required per unit standard for which provision is applied for, is available and operational. • Learning programmes are aligned to OBET. • Opportunity for workplace learning is designed into the programme. • Outsourced programmes meet requirements of SETA, ETQA and OBET principles.
The provider has the appropriate policies and practices for: • learner entry, guidance and support; and • the management of off-site practical or work-site components, where applicable.	• Learners are supported during the learning process. • Arrangements are made with workplaces to provide learners with workplace learning opportunities. • Workplace assessments are accommodated within the workplace and programme design.	QMS policy regarding learner support throughout learning process in operation.
Appropriate policies and practices for the management of assessments are in place.	• Policies and practices are implemented to ensure the quality of assessments during learning on-the-job and off-the-job. • Sufficient and appropriate assessments are designed to assess learner progress and competence. • Individuals earmarked to assess learners are identified and selected for assessor training.	Resources required for quality assessment is in place and operational.

Criteria	Principle	Quality assurance requirement
	• The provider's development plan makes provision for assessors to be trained and declared competent to assess learners before learners complete the learnership.	
The provider has the capacity and ability to produce the appropriate reports.	The provider has a system in place to ensure that: • learner information is captured and stored correctly; • learner registration and achievement information are captured; and • the confidentiality of learners' information is maintained. The provider has the ability to store, retrieve and forward learners' reports and information to the SETA and ETQA.	Provider reporting system. Provider record keeping system.
The provider strives for continuous improvement.	The purpose of the development plan is to assist the provider in identifying areas in the organisation where: • alignment still needs to take place; or • no system exists to ensure quality.	Provider's continuous development plans per development area in place.

Table 8.9 Example of an ETD improvement plan

Development area	Provider activity	Responsible person	By when	ETQA review
Assessment management	• Identify assessors required per region/unit standard. • Identify assessors. • Select and orientate assessors. • Train master assessors. • Assess assessors in technical and assessment competence. • Train assessors in required areas. • Register assessors with ETQA.			

ACTIVITY
Reflect on the five ETD management functions and the ETD provider accreditation criteria in Table 8.8. Also, study the quality checklist provided on the following four pages.
- How do these functions apply to the activities ETD practitioners perform in designing, delivering and evaluating a learning programme?
- Which elements would you like to add?

Study the following suggestions.

Defining the value proposition
The learning programme design, delivery and outcomes must add value for stakeholders and measurably contribute to business results.

Strategising
The learning programme must be planned, including the schedule for training, the training location and resources, facilities to be allocated and support required.

Organising
All the aspects of the learning programme have to be organised, for example the coordination of ETD practitioners, the lecture room, the learning support material and equipment required.

Directing/leading
The relevant ETD practitioners have to be appointed, briefed and motivated and given guidance in the presentation of the learning programme.

Assuring quality
ETD practitioners have to ensure that policies and procedures (external and internal) are adhered to in the management and support of the learning programme. For example, there may be certain organisational policies and procedures for the design, delivery and evaluation of learning programmes, and the assessment and moderation of learner achievements. There may also be external policies and procedures, for example those imposed on ETD providers by SAQA and the ETQAs. There may be other requirements and procedures laid down by the relevant SETA (see Tables 8.7 and 8.9).

Evaluating
ETD practitioners will have to carry out certain checks that everything is running according to schedule, that the required learning outcomes are being achieved and that the required standards are maintained (as discussed in Chapter 7).

Table 8.9 *Quality checklist: Learning facilitation, administration and quality assurance management*

	Yes √	No X	Comments
Planning of learning/training event			
1.1 I know and understand the learning outcomes to be achieved.			
1.2 I have thoroughly studied the facilitator guidelines:			
• sequencing of training methods and learning activities;			
• time allocation;			
• opportunities for application and practice;			
• use of projector, video, textbook, learner workbook; and			
• formative and summative assessment activities.			
Organisation resources for a learning event/programme			
2.1 I have identified the equipment and resources I need:			
• writing boards;			
• flip chart;			
• projector;			
• pens;			
• transparencies;			
• monitor and visual equipment; and			
• tape recorder.			
2.2 Requisitions for equipment and materials are submitted in time to the appropriate person.			
2.3 Quantity of learning support materials/equipment ordered matches anticipated number of learners.			
2.4 Materials/equipment to be used are available and organised in an orderly manner.			
2.5 Venue is arranged in a way that promotes learner participation and suits learning activities.			
Facilitation of learning programme			
3.1 I make a conscious effort to be seen and heard by all learners when speaking.			
3.2 The pace, and level of language are suitable for the learning group.			
3.3 I repeat, rephrase and sum up new information at adequate intervals.			
3.4 Demonstrations of practical tasks are done at a pace slow enough for learners to assimilate essential information.			
3.5 Learning is contextualised into real-life situations whenever possible.			
3.6 Previous learning is referred to and built on.			
Use of materials to facilitate learning			
4.1 Learning support materials are used in an appropriate manner at appropriate stages of the learning cycle.			
4.2 Clear instructions are given to learners regarding the use of materials.			
4.3 Checks are carried out to ensure that learners understand and follow instructions regarding the use of materials.			

	Yes √	No X	Comments
4.4 Gaps in existing materials are identified and simple strategies are used to address these (for example, extra explanation is offered to learners; supplementary materials are introduced).			
4.5 Audiovisual material can be seen and heard by learners.			
Effectiveness of learning programme			
5.1 Purpose and intended outcomes of the learning event are explained to learners.			
5.2 Training methods and learning activities are appropriate for the subject matter.			
5.3 Opportunities for application and practice are provided within the learning event.			
5.4 Activities are varied within a single learning event.			
5.5 Learners are actively involved in each stage of the learning event.			
5.6 Learning needs of individual learners are dealt with adequately.			
5.7 Each learning event is summarised and an indication of what is planned for the following event is given to learners.			
Assessment of learners within a learning situation			
6.1 Learners are informed of impending assessment events.			
6.2 Purpose of the impending assessment event is explained to learners (placement; formative; summative).			
6.3 Outcomes that learners will be expected to demonstrate in the assessment are explained to learners in accessible terms.			
6.4 Prescribed assessment instruments are used as specified.			
6.5 Learners are given clear instructions regarding the assessment event.			
6.6 Judgements on learners' performance are made in accordance with prescribed guidelines.			
6.7 Moderation/verification procedures for internal assessment are followed where necessary, according to policy.			
6.8 Results of internal assessment are made available to learners within a specified period.			
6.9 Administrative requirements of the external assessment agency is fulfilled.			
6.10 Specified measures are taken to ensure the security of the assessment documentation.			
6.11 Assessment is ethically administered.			
6.12 Learners are given an opportunity to ask questions about their assessment results.			
6.13 Feedback is given to all learners on their individual strengths and weaknesses with regard to their performance in the assessment event.			
6.14 Implications of assessment results are clarified with learners in a sensitive manner (for example, the need to repeat a level, the need to improve on identified weaknesses).			

	Yes √	No X	Comments
6.15 Records are kept of learners' performance in assessment events, in accordance with the requirements of the organisation.			
6.16 Information from assessment results is used in lesson planning in order to build on learners' strengths and help them to improve their weaknesses.			
6.17 Appropriate forms of formative and summative assessment for illiterate/semi-literate learners are used, where applicable.			
Fulfilling administrative requirements of a learning group			
7.1 I have an attendance register, which records learners' names, surnames, dates and times of classes and absenteeism.			
7.2 I have records of learners' addresses, contact telephone numbers and contact persons.			
7.3 Reasons for collecting personal information are explained to learners.			
7.4 Records are accurate, complete and up to date.			
7.5 Records are available to learners and relevant authorities			
7.6 Records are systematically organised.			
7.7 Venue is secured (through relevant authority) for the duration of the event.			
7.8 Venue and equipment are organised timeously.			
7.9 Damage to equipment or venue is promptly reported to appropriate person.			
7.10 Situations that may affect the health and safety of learners are promptly reported to the appropriate person.			
7.11 Dates; times of learning events; venues; registration procedures; fees; absentee procedures are communicated to learners.			
Evaluation of own facilitation performance			
8.1 Feedback on learning event is sought from learners in the form of open-ended questions.			
8.2 Learner feedback is synthesised into a few valid points.			
8.3 Relatively successful and unsuccessful aspects of a learning event are identified.			
8.4 Actual outcomes of the event are compared to planned outcomes.			
8.5 Plausible reasons are given for relative success/failure of the event.			
8.6 Feedback from learners and own reflection are formulated into resolutions about future learning events.			
8.7 Own learning and development needs and areas for self-improvement are identified.			
8.8 Resolutions are formulated to build on own strengths or address own development needs.			
8.9 Assistance and advice are sought from a senior practitioner or supervisor when necessary.			

	Yes √	No X	Comments
8.10 Reports on progress of learning groups are produced according to requirements.			
8.11 Reports accurately indicate progress made and difficulties encountered.			
8.12 Exceptionally high incidents of absenteeism and dropout are recorded and plausible explanations offered.			
Helping learners with language and literacy across the curriculum			
9.1 Learners are consulted on language(s) to be used for all activities (for example, in whole group, small groups, materials, written and oral work).			
9.2 Strategies for dealing with language difficulties, which may affect learning, are suggested.			
9.3 Relevant terminology of the subject (including acronyms and abbreviations) is explained.			
9.4 Level and style of language used for instructions is suitable for learners.			
9.5 Relevant symbols and their uses are explained to learners.			
9.6 Layout and style of visuals used in support materials are explained to learners.			
9.7 Learners are helped to use the different parts of a text (for example, contents page; glossary; index; page numbers; charts; graphs; diagrams; uses of colour; worksheets).			
9.8 Learners are questioned on the purpose of a text to ascertain how much is understood; fuller and alternative explanations are given when required.			
9.9 Learners are shown how to use textbook and learner workbooks.			
9.10 Learners are helped to fill in forms and worksheets relevant to the learning situation.			
Identifying and responding to learners who have special needs			
10.1 Learners who may have special learning, counselling or health needs are referred to relevant services and appropriate actions are taken within the learning situation.			
10.2 Learners who have special needs (for example, physical disability such as sight or hearing impairment; impairment of movement or motor skills; learning disability as a cause of impaired performance in writing, reading, spelling, numeracy ability) are recognised.			
10.3 Learners with special needs are referred for further intervention by someone other than the trainer.			
10.4 Adequate information regarding the referral is provided to learner in order to reduce anxiety (for example, address, time, nature of referral, people involved).			
10.5 Strategies are implemented to assist learner.			
10.6 Learning environment is organised to alleviate difficulties (for example, seating closer to the front, negotiating help from other learners).			

Key terms

- Critical skills
- Employability
- ETD management
- ETD plan
- ETD value proposition
- Evaluating
- HRD strategy
- Leading
- Learning organisation
- Organisational capability
- Organisational sustainability
- Organising
- Quality assurance
- Quality management
- Stakeholders
- Strategising
- Talent pool
- Workplace skills plan

Review and discussion questions

1. Why does the 21st century workplace require a dynamic and flexible approach to ETD management?
2. ETD management is a strategic activity that not only contributes to the overall HRD strategy and business results, but also adds value for stakeholders. Do you agree with this statement? Give reasons for your answer.
3. How would you describe the role of ETD management in addressing the seven core workplace issues in the 21st century workplace?
4. What is the link between individual learning and organisational learning?
5. Why is the management of knowledge critical to organisational learning? How does the concept of knowledge management relate to training?
6. Why is it important for ETD managers and practitioners to define the ETD value proposition?
7. What is the link between the HRD strategy and ETD management?
8. How do the ETD management process and the functions support the effective and efficient implementation of the strategic ETD plan and workplace skills plan?
9. Why is it important to establish and manage an ETD quality management system? What are the national requirements for ETD provision?
10. How would you describe the roles of the ETD manager and the ETD practitioner in managing ETD in the workplace? Study Chapter 9 before you formulate your answer.
11. Why do ETD efforts fail in organisations? What can ETD managers do to ensure the success of ETD efforts?

Suggested reading

Coetzee, M. (2004). *Empowering the skills development facilitator.* Johannesburg: Knowres.

Coetzee, M. (2007). *Getting and keeping your accreditation: The quality assurance and assessment guide for ETD providers* (2nd edition). Pretoria: Van Schaik.

Erasmus, B.J., Loedolff, P.v.S., Mda, T. & Nel, P.S. (2006). Managing training and development. Cape Town: Oxford University Press.

Hattingh, S. & Smit, S. (2004). *Building learning organisations to enhance competitiveness.* Johannesburg: Knowres.

Kinicki, A. & Kreitner, R. (2006). *Organisational behaviour: key concepts, skills and best practices* (3rd edition). New York: McGraw-Hill.

Losey, M., Meisinger, S. & Ulrich, D. (Eds.). (2005). *The future of human resource management.* Hoboken, New Jersey: John Wiley & Sons.

Marchington, M. & Wilkinson, A. (2005). *Human Resource Management at Work.* London: CIPD.

Robinson, I. (2006). *Human Resource Management in Organisations.* London: CIPD.

SAQA. (2000). *Criteria and guidelines for Providers.* Pretoria: SAQA.

Swanepoel, B., Erasmus, B., Van Wyk, H. & Schenk, H. (2003). *Human Resource Management.* Cape Town: Juta.

Ulrich, D. & Brockbank, W. (2005). *The HR value proposition.* Boston, Massachusetts: Harvard Business School.

Summary

This chapter explored the changing focus of managing ETD in the 21st century work-place. ETD management is an integral part of the overall HRD strategy of an organisa-tion. The focus of the strategic ETD management process and functions are defined by the ETD value proposition and the quality requirements specified by national legisla-tion. Chapter 9 explores the profession and practice of ETD with specific reference to the roles and functions of the ETD practitioner.

In a world class organisation both the ETD practitioner and the learners should feel encouraged to excel in their ability to create a very special learning experience. Aspiring to be world class should identify real development opportunities, provide experiences which are dynamic, positive and challenging. ETD practitioners should be curious, have a thirst for knowledge, and seek to be inspiring, innovative and wanting to lead in the field of ETD. The organisation should be supportive, and want to be the one that others benchmark against (Thorne & MacHray, 2000).

CHAPTER 9

MELINDE COETZEE

Profession and practice of ETD

When ETD professionals develop the knowledge and skills necessary to link ETD practices, processes, products and services to stakeholder value, they become partners in the business. They are respected not only for their professionalism and expertise, but also for the results they deliver.

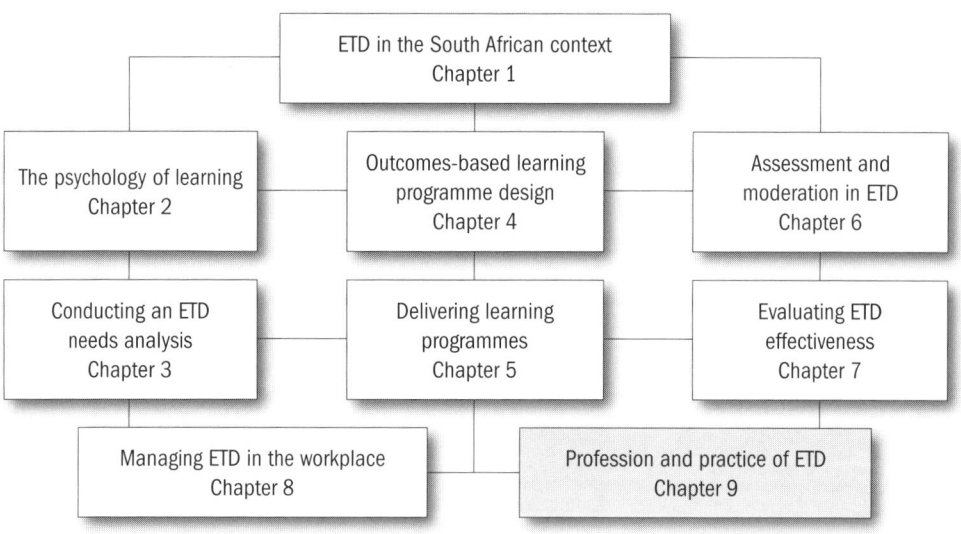

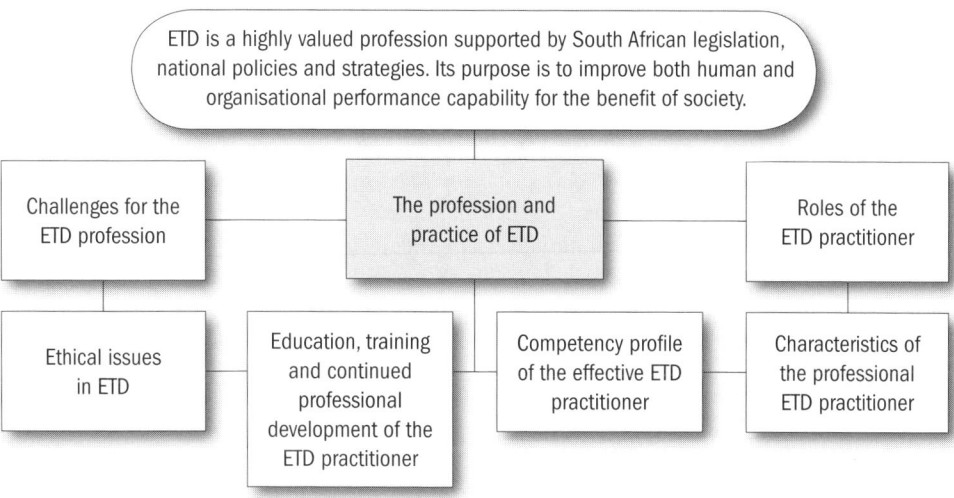

ETD is a highly valued profession supported by South African legislation, national policies and strategies. Its purpose is to improve both human and organisational performance capability for the benefit of society.

Challenges for the ETD profession	The profession and practice of ETD	Roles of the ETD practitioner
Ethical issues in ETD	Education, training and continued professional development of the ETD practitioner	Competency profile of the effective ETD practitioner	Characteristics of the professional ETD practitioner

Key points of the profession and practice of ETD

- ETD is a highly valued profession supported by South African legislation, national policies and strategies. Its purpose is to improve both human and organisational performance capability for the benefit of society.
- Professional ETD practitioners add value to the organisation by fulfilling their key roles ethically, competently and with expertise.
- The rapid transformation of societies within a turbulent and uncertain world of work will continue to challenge the professional ETD practitioner to be creative in improving human and organisational performance capability and proving the value added for stakeholders.

After studying this chapter, you should be able to:

- Evaluate the value that the key roles of the professional ETD practitioner add to the performance capability of employees and the organisation.
- Explain the importance for ETD practitioners to be professionally educated and trained.
- Describe the core competencies that ETD practitioners need to demonstrate in the South African workplace.
- Explain how ETD practitioners benefit from continued professional development and how they can ensure that they stay abreast of new technology and developments in the ETD field.
- Explain why ethical behaviour is an important characteristic of effective ETD practitioners.
- Describe the challenges for the ETD profession in the next decade.

In this chapter, the role, personal characteristics and competency profile of the professional ETD practitioner are discussed. Training and credentialing issues, professional ethics and continuing development are reviewed as they apply to ETD practitioners in the South African workplace.

Within the context of the NQF, ETD is a highly valued profession rooted in human values, quality outcomes-based ETD principles and relevant theory. Its purpose is to improve human and organisational performance capability for the benefit of society. Furthermore, the unique and challenging socio-economic circumstances in South Africa increasingly demand professionally qualified and experienced ETD practitioners (ETDP SETA, 2006). The national scarce skills guide (Department of Labour, 2005) also lists ETD practice as a scarce skill. ETD needs to make creative and proactive contributions to organisational effectiveness and capability, as well as to the employability and performance capability of employees. ETD practitioners therefore need to extend their professional skills beyond ETD tools and methods to address the concerns and requirements of internal and external stakeholders.

ETD practitioners are becoming more accountable for gaining the skills they need to perform their jobs. It is important that they share responsibility for their own learning and development with their employers. The National Skills Development Strategy, and skills development and employment equity legislation create an environment in which continuous learning is valued by organisations and employees.

Roles of the ETD practitioner

The professional ETD practitioner has a very important role in an organisation. Organisations draw on many sources to develop their talent and enhance the employability and performance capability of their employees. These sources include school systems, national and local workforce development programmes, professional associations, and private and higher education organisations. With rapidly changing skills needs, the efficiency of technology-enabled learning and an increasing shortage of qualified and skilled workers across many industries, business leaders understand that they too must educate, train and develop their employees. They rely on the expertise of their human resource and ETD professionals to manage ETD, measure its impact on performance and demonstrate business results based on the change in performance (ASTD, 2006).

Traditionally, ETD practitioners are responsible for designing learning programmes and delivering training to employees in classroom settings. But in the 21st century workplace, they are responsible for much more. ETD practitioners are managing and leading integrated systems of talent management that provide learning and skills development. They use a variety of learning technologies at every step of employees' careers (ASTD, 2006). ETD practitioners work with human resource professionals to:

- assess skills needs;
- develop job and competence profiles;
- map performance goals and development plans to the business strategies of the organisation;
- manage opportunities for coaching, mentoring and leadership development;
- assess and moderate employees' learning achievements;
- collect evidence of employees' performance capability in the workplace; and
- manage and implement other activities that may be part of the organisation's talent development and succession plans.

Table 9.1 provides an overview of the roles that ETD practitioners fulfil in the workplace.

Table 9.1 Roles of the ETD practitioner (based on Erasmus et al, 2006; Killen, 2000)

Role	Description
Mediator of learning	• Mediating learning in a manner that is sensitive to the diverse needs of learners • Constructing learning environments that are appropriately contextualised and inspirational • Demonstrating sound knowledge of subject content and various principles, strategies and resources appropriate to ETD in a South African context
Mediator and designer of learning programmes and materials	• Understanding and interpreting provided learning programmes • Designing original learning programmes • Identifying the requirements for a specific context of learning • Selecting and preparing suitable textual and visual resources for learning • Selecting, sequencing and pacing the learning in a manner sensitive to the differing needs of the learning area and learners
Developer of skills	• Developing skills and ETD plans that address individual learning needs and are aligned with organisational strategic objectives and the organisation's HRD strategy • Providing information and advice regarding skills development and related issues • Conducting skills audits and ETD needs analyses to determine outcomes of learning for skills development and other purposes • Developing plans for implementing learnerships and skills programmes within a learning organisation
Leader, administrator and manager	• Making decisions appropriate to the level • Managing learning • Carrying out administrative duties efficiently • Participating in workplace learning and development decision-making structures • Supporting learners and colleagues • Demonstrating responsiveness to changing circumstances and needs
Strategist	• Formulating the ETD value proposition and plans, organisation policies and practices to contribute to the effective implementation of the organisation HRD strategy and workplace skills plan, including talent management and succession plans
Scholar, researcher and lifelong learner	• Achieving ongoing personal, academic, occupational and professional growth through pursuing reflective study and research in learning area, in broader ETD matters, and in other related fields
Collector of evidence, assessor and quality assurer	• Understanding that the collection of evidence of learners' achievements and learning application in the workplace, assessment and quality assurance are essential features of the ETD process • Understanding the purposes, methods and effects of assessment

Role	Description
	• Designing and managing both formative and summative assessment in ways that are appropriate to the level and purpose of the learning, and meeting the requirements of accrediting bodies • Keeping detailed and diagnostic records of assessment and quality assurance • Understanding how to interpret and use assessment results to improve learning programmes
Learning area/ subject/discipline specialist	• Being well grounded in the knowledge, skills, values, principles, methods and procedures relevant to the learning area • Knowing different approaches to learning facilitation, research and management and how these may be used in ways that are appropriate to the learner and the context • Understanding the content knowledge of the learning area
Evaluator	• Measuring results, evaluating and communicating the impact of ETD on the performance capability and employability of employees and the organisation's business results • Developing improvement plans to address performance or outcome gaps
Needs analyst	• Identifying stakeholder requirements • Assessing gaps between required competencies and the organisation's HRD strategies • Identifying learning and/or development needs of employees, groups and the organisation • Identifying goals, ETD solutions, priorities and strategies to fill skills gaps
Community, citizenship, coach and mentor role	• Practising and promoting a critical, committed and ethical attitude towards developing a sense of respect and responsibility towards others, one that upholds the ethical standards of the ETD profession • Promoting democratic values and practices in the workplace and society • Demonstrating the ability to develop a supportive and empowering environment for the learner • Responding to the ETD and other needs of learners and fellow workers • Developing supportive relationships with line managers, employees, customers and other stakeholders, based on a critical understanding of strategic HRD issues

ETD practitioners can grow throughout their professional lives. Their work is purposeful. When ETD professionals effectively contribute to the interests of the organisation and the people within it, they can make an enormous impact. The reward is personal satisfaction. According to Losey *et al* (2005), ETD practitioners (along with their partners in human resources) will fulfil these emerging roles:
• chief integrative officer – responsible for connecting different parts of an organisation;
• deliverer of business success – participant in the success of the business;
• diversity manager – responsible for helping to manage all types of employee diversity;

- employee champion – responsible for human capital development;
- productivity csar – responsible for doing more with less; and
- chief effectiveness officer – responsible for making the organisation, not just people, effective.

As they start to play these roles, ETD practitioners will have more visibility and responsibility. To fulfil these emerging roles successfully, they will require more complex competencies, such as understanding and managing people; rethinking organisations as capabilities, not structures; creating collaboration throughout the organisation; responding to social expectations and policy; and learning to play new roles (Losey *et al*, 2005).

Characteristics of the professional ETD practitioner

Some general characteristics apply to all professions in the human resource development field. However, the following eight characteristics are especially important for ETD practitioners. In the organisational context, professional ETD practitioners are:

- driven by results;
- investigative;
- able to set and comply with quality standards;
- cooperative and collaborative;
- willing and able to add value for stakeholders;
- flexible, while maintaining important principles;
- responsible for their own continuous professional development; and
- ethical and responsible in their service to the profession and clients (Coetzee, 2004; Rothwell, Sullivan & McLean, 1995; Sink, 1992).

Results driven

Outstanding ETD practitioners are results orientated. They document stakeholder requirements and implement well-planned (and cost-effective) strategies to achieve their ETD goals. They manage these strategies and evaluate the outcomes of each ETD intervention in terms of the value they add for stakeholders.

Investigative

Successful ETD practitioners are investigators. They make sure that they fully understand stakeholder requirements and the particular performance problem or opportunity. Only then do they identify the most appropriate and cost-effective ETD solution. They document all the important requirements of stakeholders and characteristics of the target groups. They make few assumptions and remain open to expert opinions.

Able to set and comply with quality standards

One of the main ingredients of successful ETD practice is setting and complying with outcomes-based ETD quality standards. ETD practitioners set and model standards, but they also plan how to sustain these standards. They do quality checks at key points in an ETD intervention. ETD practitioners always review and evaluate products, services, practices and processes to make sure that all expectations and requirements are met.

Cooperative and collaborative

Successful professional ETD practitioners are flexible and cooperative. They analyse performance problems in collaboration with human resource practitioners, line managers and employees. Collaboration ensures that the best possible decisions are made, which in turn creates ETD solutions that achieve the desired results.

Willing and able to add value for stakeholders

ETD practitioners' abilities to focus on identified priorities and work cooperatively with clients and stakeholders enable them to achieve value-adding results. Clients are not asking for what they can do themselves. They expect the ETD practitioner to add value to the performance of the business. Their anticipation is that ETD solutions will be better because of their interaction with the ETD professional.

Flexible while maintaining important principles

Professional ETD practitioners are flexible, but they adhere to key principles. For example, they pay more attention to the substance than the form of a training solution. Their concern is with providing the learner with appropriate practice and feedback and using the correct language level, rather than with the physical characteristics of particular delivery systems or media. They know that, if a learning programme does not suit the needs of the learners, the delivery method will not solve the performance problem or meet the development need. In the South African ETD context, ETD practitioners are also required to comply with the principles and regulations for quality ETD provision.

Responsible for continuous professional development

Successful ETD practitioners acknowledge their personal needs and desires. They deal with them in a responsible way as they fulfil their professional roles. ETD practitioners strive for self-knowledge and personal growth, but they also want to achieve and maintain a high level of competence. They achieve this by developing the full range of their competence and by establishing networks with other ETD professionals. They practise within the limits of their competence, culture and experience.

Ethical and responsible

Professional ETD practitioners serve the long-term well-being, interests, and development of their clients and their clients' stakeholders, even if the ETD intervention has a short-term focus. They define and protect the confidentiality of their relationships with clients. Public statements (including promotions and advertisements) are accurate, and services are provided as advertised. ETD practitioners are aware of how their cultures affect their view of the world. They respect cultures that are different from their own, and they are sensitive to cross-cultural and multicultural differences.

ETD practitioners want to contribute to the continuous professional development of themselves, other practitioners and the profession. They share ETD knowledge and skills. They advocate ethical ETD practices and they use appropriate channels for dealing with unethical practices. ETD professionals bring credit to the ETD profession and respect colleagues in other professions.

A competency profile of effective ETD practitioners

Competent ETD practitioners have the same basic skills as other professionals in the human resource development field. Being competent as an ETD practitioner means that the practitioner has the ability and capability to perform the tasks and roles required to the expected standards. ETD practitioners understand ETD theory and keep up to date with the latest theoretical information. The competent ETD practitioner must be prepared to meet the challenges of multicultural workplace settings and the unique skills development needs of clients.

Based on recent studies of ETD skills, all ETD practitioners should have the following basic skills and knowledge:

1. *Intrapersonal skills.* ETD is a human craft. The intrapersonal skills listed in Table 9.2 can help ETD practitioners to be effective. ETD practitioners must often process complex, ambiguous information and make informed judgements about its relevance to clients' skills development needs and stakeholders' requirements. This requires considerable conceptual and analytical ability. ETD practitioners must also know their own values, feelings and purposes; they should have the integrity to behave responsibly in a supporting relationship with others. The practice of ETD requires constant adjustment and creativity; therefore, ETD practitioners need active learning skills and a reasonable balance between their rational and emotional sides. Finally, the practice of ETD can be highly stressful; ETD practitioners need to know how to deal with stress in an emotionally intelligent way.

2. *Interpersonal skills.* ETD practitioners must create and maintain effective relationships with their clients. The interpersonal skills listed in Table 9.2 promote effective supporting and collaborative relationships with clients. Such working relationships start with an understanding of the organisational skills development culture. ETD practitioners need to listen to clients' perceptions and feelings to understand how they see their own performance and growth needs within their organisation and industry. This understanding provides a starting point for diagnosing problems and creating ETD solutions.

3. *General ETD counselling skills.* All ETD practitioners should have diagnosis, assessment and ETD intervention development planning skills. An ETD intervention starts with a diagnosis of the client's performance problems and skills development needs. The ETD practitioner tries to understand the causes of problems and the client's uniqueness. Thereafter, ETD practitioners develop ETD solutions to equip clients with competencies that will contribute to their job satisfaction and work performance.

4. *ETD theory.* ETD practitioners should understand ETD theories and how they apply to diverse clients from multicultural backgrounds. They should be creative in designing and applying a range of outcomes-based ETD tools and techniques to enhance clients' employability and performance capability. Most importantly, ETD practitioners should understand their role in the field of ETD in the 21st century workplace (particularly with regard to the National Skills Development Strategy).

Table 9.2 *Core and advanced skills for ETD practitioners*

General ETD skills
- Individual and group training and counselling
- Facilitation of learning and development
- Personal development planning
- Multicultural ETD contexts
- Learner-centred training
- Outcomes-based ETD assessment and moderation technology
- Group dynamics
- Outcomes-based ETD design and development
- ETD interventions
- Outcomes-based ETD tools and techniques
- ETD diagnostics and interpretation
- Skills audits/Skills profiling/Job and competence profiling
- Computer-based ETD practices and technology
- ETD practice evaluation and value-adding measurement
- Collecting evidence for assessment purposes
- ETD quality assurance skills

Intrapersonal skills
- Conceptual and analytical ability
- Integrity (educated moral judgement)
- Personal focus (staying in touch with one's own purpose and values)
- Active learning skills
- Innovative thinking
- Adaptability
- Leadership skills
- Business skills
- Rational–emotional balance
- Emotional intelligence
- Personal stress management skills
- Personal responsibility for learning

Interpersonal skills
- Listening
- Establishing trust and rapport
- Giving and receiving feedback
- Interviewing skills
- Aptitude in speaking client's language
- Ability to model credible behaviours
- Development counselling and coaching
- Cross-cultural skills
- Telephone intervention skills
- Suggestion skills (metaphors)

Workplace learning, development and training knowledge
- Outcomes-based ETD theory
- Individual and cultural differences
- Personality theories
- Organisational behaviour/Industrial and organisational psychology/Organisational capability theory
- Learning organisation
- Human resource management and development
- Performance management and improvement
- Motivation and leadership
- Theories of adult learning
- Human capital development/Employability/Talent development
- Outcomes-based assessment and moderation
- Job design and competence profiling
- Cross-cultural theory
- Generational theory
- Ethical and legal practices
- National Skills Development Strategy
- Skills development governing structures and principles
- Employment equity
- Skills development legislation
- ETD management
- Workplace skills plan compilation and management
- Skills development facilitation
- ETD provider accreditation requirements

Research and evaluation knowledge and skills
- Action research
- Diagnostic research
- Evaluation research
- Theory-building research
- Case method research and writing methods
- Use and design of outcomes-based assessment and programme evaluation tools and techniques

Data analysis
- Behavioural science statistics
- Computer literacy/IT skills
- Writing reports/Communication skills
- Graphic and audiovisual skills

Management knowledge and skills
- ETD management

• Negotiation skills	• Defining value proposition for ETD
• Conflict resolution skills	• ETD management policy and strategy
• Training skills	• Information systems
• Presentation skills	• Legal and socio-political environment
• Networking	• Finance/Economics/Accounting
	• Marketing/International business

Education and training of ETD practitioners

ETD practitioners receive unique education and training. This distinguishes ETD from other human resource disciplines such as industrial and organisational psychology and human resource management.

A rich history of ETD theories informs ETD practitioner education and training. ETD practitioners work to bridge the theory–practice gap by supplementing theoretical descriptions with practical techniques. ETD practitioners are involved in the day-to-day activities of ETD in the workplace. They continually acquire knowledge and experience about ETD methods, techniques and processes. They aim to produce consistent, measurable and high-quality results that add value for stakeholders. To achieve this goal, ETD practitioners implement what they learn through education and experience.

ETD practitioners should have a solid theoretical foundation. Professional ETD practitioners use theories (such as those discussed in this book) to understand what they see in practice. The theories also provide guidelines in solving each new and unique performance problem and opportunity. ETD practitioners should also remain aware of current research that can give them new perspectives on ETD theory, principles, practices, technology and methodology.

Professional associations, such as the American Society for Training and Development (ASTD), have a history of playing a leading role in advancing ETD practice. ASTD is the world's largest association dedicated to workplace learning and performance professionals (including ETD and HR practitioners). South African ETD practitioners can also apply for membership. ASTD has members in more than 100 countries and connect locally through 24 global networks. ASTD has widened the profession's focus by linking learning and performance to individual and organisational results. ASTD is also a renowned source of insightful and practical information on workplace learning and performance topics, including training basics, evaluation and return on investment (ROI), instructional systems development, e-learning, leadership and career development (ASTD, 2006).

In South Africa, ETD practitioners working in organisations can also apply for professional status to the South African Board for Personnel Practice (SABPP). The SABPP's mission is to establish, direct and sustain a high level of professionalism and ethical conduct in personnel practice (which includes ETD practice). The SABPP strives to establish a career path in HR with no glass ceilings, acknowledges and honours every step up the career ladder and challenges the professional to new heights in knowledge acquisition, bottom-line contribution, professional conduct and responsible work ethic (www.sabpp.co.sa). Table 9.3 provides an overview of the SABPP's professional levels of registration.

Table 9.3 SABPP professional levels of registration

Category of registration	Requirement
Master HR practitioner	NQF level 8: postgraduate 3 and 4 / Master's or Doctorate degree
Chartered HR practitioner	NQF level 8: postgraduate 1 and 2 / Honours, BTech or Master's diploma
HR practitioner	NQF level 7: three years post-matriculation study / National diploma
HR associate	NQF level 6: two years post-matriculation study / SGB diploma
HR technician	NQF level 5: one year post-matriculation study / Certificate

ETD practitioners can apply to the SABPP for registration as a Generalist or ETD specialist in one of the categories described in Table 9.3. To apply for registration as an ETD specialist, the practitioner must provide evidence of relevant qualifications, experience and competence in outcomes-based ETD assessment, moderation and verification practice, coaching and mentoring, education and lecturing, induction, career planning, job training, management development, skills facilitation and ETD quality management (www.sabpp.co.sa).

The National Skills Development Strategy also emphasises the professional education, training and development of ETD practitioners. The education and training of ETD practitioners in South Africa must therefore be aligned with the unit standards for ETD. Only those qualifications that have been accredited by the ETDP SETA are recognised. As discussed in Chapters 1, 4 and 6, competencies based on standards are now driving ETD practice worldwide. Table 9.4 gives an overview of typical accredited, occupation-directed ETD practitioner qualifications and a developmental pathway for ETD practitioners in South Africa.

Table 9.4 Example of accredited, occupation-directed qualifications and developmental pathway for ETD practitioners (info@maccauvlei.co.sa)

Qualification	Developmental pathway	NQF level and credits
Coach the learner (short learning programme)	Year 1	NQF level 3 10 SAQA credits
Certificate in Occupation-directed ETD Practice		NQF level 4 120 SAQA credits
Higher Certificate in Occupation-directed ETD Practice	Year 2	NQF level 5 120 SAQA credits
Diploma in Occupation-directed ETD Practice	Year 3	NQF level 6 240 SAQA credits
Career-focused Bachelor's Degree in Occupation-directed ETD Practice: B.Tech (HRD) in partnership with the Vaal University of Technology	Year 4	NQF level 7 360 SAQA credits

ACTIVITY
Self-assessment

This self-assessment questionnaire contains the specific outcomes and assessment criteria for the Bachelor's Degree: Occupation-directed Education, Training and Development Practices (SAQA ID: 50330; NQF level 6; 360 credits).

For each of the following items, indicate the strength of your knowledge/skill in the area. If a particular competence is not listed here, or if your knowledge/skill is weak, mark that specific item as a development priority.

Competence	Knowledge/skill Weak/Strong	Development priority Low/High
Learning design and development • Conduct an organisational skills audit. • Define training needs in terms of outcomes and link these to performance requirements on the job. • Develop and design outcomes-based learning programmes. • Align learning outcomes with given standards, including unit standards, assessment standards, qualifications or job requirements. • Ensure that the design meets target audience needs, and is appropriate to the subject matter. • Ensure that the design caters for learners with special needs. • Identify and use approaches that comply with adult learning principles and are suitable for achieving the defined outcomes. • Identify and employ designs that include evaluation strategies capable of revealing the value of programmes or interventions. • Ensure that learning and assessment design are compatible and promote integration.		

Learning facilitation
• Demonstrate understanding of the outcomes-based education and training approach within the context of the NQF.
• Facilitate learning and development that:
  – is professional and ensures the physical and psychological safety of the learners;
  – is self-monitored and allows behaviour to be modified to address weaknesses or difficulties; and
  – has an approach that creates opportunities for assessment.
• Give direct, relevant, honest and valuable feedback on performance in a constructive manner.
• Provide recommendations to facilitate the personal and professional growth of learners.
• Facilitate transfer and application of learning in the workplace.		

Competence	Knowledge/skill Weak/Strong	Development priority Low/High
Learning support • Proactively and sensitively identify learners requiring support . • Give support in a manner that enables learners to define objectives, clarify issues, help manage expectations and identify learning paths and opportunities. • Give support that assists learners to identify and understand assessment opportunities, processes and benefits, including the nature and benefit of RPL. • Give support that ensures that learners experience the maximum benefit from learning and assessment, and helps them to prepare for and cope with learning and assessment. • Diagnose barriers to learning and solve problems cooperatively within given frameworks. • Make referrals, as required, to appropriate professionals. • Give support that helps to create a safe learning environment and promotes objectives of learning and the principle of life-long learning. • Give advice that is helpful, realistic, relevant, valid, impartial and based on learner needs.		
Assessment • Support assessors adequately. • Prepare and assist assessors in assessment and/or RPL processes, without compromising the assessment process or results. • Design and use assessment instruments that are fit for the purpose and facilitate the integration of assessment in learning and work environments. • Engage in assessment practices that are in line with the principles of outcomes-based assessment. • Make assessment decisions that are reliable and relevant to predetermined outcomes. • Give constructive, relevant feedback. • Conduct moderation of outcomes-based assessments.		
Strategic management • Demonstrate an understanding of the transformative elements of the HRD legislation. • Develop an organisational (strategic) ETD plan. • Allocate resources and use these effectively and within budgets. • Provide leadership that gives focus and direction in line with individual needs and organisational strategy. • Manage learning and assessment to meet learners' and the organisation's needs, according to relevant ETD plans. • Cost projects and activities according to sound budgeting principles.		

Competence	Knowledge/skill Weak/Strong	Development priority Low/High
• Ensure that management activities make the best use of diversity within the workplace, while promoting productivity. • Facilitate team-building activities to ensure the achievement of set goals and objectives. • Empower team members by building on strengths and provide scope for development. • Deal with conflicts in a manner that supports established conflict management principles and that is in line with organisational policies and procedures. • Ensure that records are accurate and up to date. • Design and develop instruments to evaluate ETD. • Evaluate and promote ETD providers, services and products for organisational use. • Define the ETD value proposition for an organisation.		
Quality assurance • Develop ETD policies and procedures for an organisation. • Ensure that contributions to policies and procedures provide a quality framework for the organisation and practitioners to deliver quality ETD practices. • Promote a learning culture in the organisation. • Use evaluation instruments that provide reliable feedback on the ETD cycle. • Administer evaluation instruments as designed. • Measure and assess the factors that influence labour productivity and establish the relative impact of each factor. • Report findings from the evaluation fairly and accurately and make recommendations that facilitate improvements and changes that add value to the learning environment and process. • Promote a productivity improvement strategy. • Advise management on the establishment and implementation of a quality management system for ETD practices in an organisation. • Manage learner information using an information management system. • Manage the capture, storage and retrieval of HR information using an information system. • Manage the design, development and review of an HR information system.		
Standards setting and qualifications design • Use consultative processes that meet stakeholder needs in determining required standards. • Ensure that standards are based on a thorough analysis of needs.		

Competence	Knowledge/skill Weak/Strong	Development priority Low/High
• Define stakeholder requirements in clear, measurable terms. • Present standards in a format as required by the registering body. • Evaluate standards in a manner that identifies the extent to which they are fit for purpose, with resulting recommendations meeting stakeholder needs.		
Skills development facilitation • Develop ETD and workplace skills plans that address individual learning needs and that are aligned with organisational objectives. • Promote learning in line with individual and organisational needs, using appropriate and effective communication techniques. • Keep records that are clear, accessible, accurate and up to date. • Coordinate ETD interventions in line with the ETD and workplace skills plans.		
Self-management and responsible citizenship • Identify and solve problems using critical and creative thinking. • Work effectively with others as a member of a team, group, organisation or community. • Organise and manage myself and my activities responsibly and effectively. • Collect, analyse, organise and critically evaluate information. • Communicate effectively using visual, mathematical and/or language skills in the modes of oral and written communication. • Use science and technology effectively and critically, showing responsibility towards the environment and the health of others. • Demonstrate an understanding of the world as a set of related systems by recognising that problems do not exist in isolation. • Reflect on and explore a variety of strategies to learn more effectively and continue professional development. • Participate as a responsible citizen in local, national and global communities. • Be culturally and aesthetically sensitive across a range of social contexts. • Explore education and career opportunities and develop entrepreneurial opportunities.		

Now complete the following:

Action plan

I would still like to improve:

_____

_____

_____

My ultimate goal is to:

_____

_____

_____

These are my long-term learning and development outcomes:

_____

_____

_____

These are my short-term learning and development outcomes:

_____

_____

_____

I will start by:

_____

Thereafter:

_____

Time limits for achieving the outcomes are the following:

In the short term:

_____

_____

_____

In the long term:

_____

_____

_____

ETD is an important area in the South African context; it is supported by legislation, national policies and strategies. To meet the ETD requirements of the workplace, it is important to identify competent ETD practitioners at various levels and in particular, to have access to the services of ETD practitioners with high-level specialist skills (SAQA, 2007).

Occupationally directed qualifications give recognition to experienced ETD practitioners. With this recognition, practitioners can increase their employment prospects, and organisations can appoint experienced practitioners with proven competencies.

Continuous professional development

As the ETD profession evolves, so ETD professionals must adapt. It is crucial to invest in your own continuous professional development to stay employable as an ETD professional. Continuous professional development aims to improve ETD practitioners' employability and performance capability, as well as the effectiveness and performance capability of the organisation as a whole (Elmore, 2001 cited in ETDP Seta, 2006). Continuous professional development is an integral part of being professional, as it supports the principle of lifelong learning. For example, the SABPP requires that registered professionals provide proof of continuous professional development to retain their registration.

Continuous professional development does not normally lead to a higher qualification. Rather, it ensures that the professional returns to or retains the level of expertise required in the profession (or required by a professional body). Continuous professional development also helps professionals to stay up to date with developments in the profession. Continuous professional development usually involves the following (Steyn & Van Niekerk, 2002):

- Personal development advances ETD practitioners' competencies and achievements for personal and professional use.
- Career development supports the professional advancement of ETD practitioners to higher-level or broadened positions by providing them with the necessary qualifications and developing their skills to prepare for anticipated vacancies.
- Organisation development improves employability and performance capability to benefit the organisation as a whole.

ETD as a profession will remain viable only as long as practitioners continue to develop and enhance their competencies. ETD practitioners who engage in continuous professional development activities benefit in the following ways (Coleman, 1992):

- Professional development increases practitioners' breadth and depth of understanding and their ability to apply the principles of quality outcomes-based ETD.
- Professional development provides a way to keep up to date with developments in the field. When ETD practitioners use the most current technology and techniques, they are able to produce the most value-adding solutions.
- Professional development also expands professional networks. Such networks are useful when looking for employment opportunities or seeking help with a problem.
- Professional development makes ETD practitioners more valuable to employees and employers. Better skills, up-to-date knowledge, and broad professional networks increase practitioners' ability to handle each new assignment.

Apart from formal further education at a university, there are many ways to acquire or enhance the knowledge and skills that an ETD practitioner needs (these are listed in Table 9.2 on page 334 and in the self-assessment activity on page 337). A regular, systematic and integrated personal development plan helps the ETD practitioner to get the most out of their continuous professional development. There is always more to do than time available to do it, so ETD practitioners have to invest their time, money and effort in the most effective way. ETD practitioners need to examine the range of continuous professional development activities available, especially in the following five areas (Coleman, 1992):

1. *Joining* refers to becoming a member of professional societies in the ETD field. Membership in one or more professional society provides opportunities to explore,

participate in and influence the profession. Practitioners from a variety of settings become members, attend meetings, make presentations, write for society publications, network and serve as volunteers.

2. *Reading* involves interpreting written materials produced to explain, report on and expand ETD information. The information ranges from personal opinion to factual accounts, from promotional expositions to scholarly inquirys. Typical reading materials include books, periodicals, journals, newsletters, trade publications, vendor literature, professional society publications, training materials, research reports, monographs, conference proceedings and reports of ETD interventions. Reading materials are often the cheapest source of information, the easiest to share, and the most convenient to use. The information can be read and reread, as necessary.

3. *Attending* refers to participating in a wide variety of events designed to bring practitioners together to share information and ideas. Interactions include face-to-face interactions, closed-circuit broadcasts, online discussions, and videos or DVDs of presentations. Events include workshops, conferences, lectures, courses, seminars, video screenings, vendor promotions and exhibitions. While attending is often the most expensive and time-consuming activity of professional development, it is also often the source of the most current information.

4. *Networking* refers to making contact with other professionals to seek their help or to offer support. Many experienced practitioners believe that networking is the single most valuable source of continuous professional development. Networking activities include face-to-face discussions, telephone discussions and electronic bulletin boards.

5. *Sharing* refers to contributing time or expertise to individuals or groups to explore ideas, give help, provide services or act as an advisor. Specific activities include serving as a member of a committee; serving as an appointed officer; publishing; teaching; making presentations at conferences or workshops; and mentoring. Professional growth comes from imparting knowledge, interacting, serving, counselling, mentoring, and helping others to grow. By engaging in these activities, ETD practitioners learn while they teach.

These five types of activity – joining, reading, attending, networking and sharing – are the ways in which continuous professional development takes place. Every effective skills development programme involves a combination of these five types of activity. However, professional ETD practitioners must always remember that, as members of a knowledge society, they need to ensure that furthering their higher educational qualifications form the basis for any continuous professional development activities.

ACTIVITY
Action plan for continued professional development
Reflect on the development areas (and the action plan) you identified in the previous self-assessment activity. Study the five activities for continuous professional development. Also, keep your current formal higher education qualification level in mind. Now complete the action plan below. Indicate activities that you could engage in to ensure your continued professional growth as an ETD practitioner.

Review the plan every three months and at the beginning of any new ETD project or assignment. Modify the plan as necessary to adapt to changes in interests, job demands, available financial resources and other relevant factors. Creating, using and revising this action plan is a systematic approach to developing and enhancing your employability and performance capability as a professional ETD practitioner.

Activity for continued professional growth	This is what I plan to do	This is how I will do it
Joining	I belong to (or will join) the following organisations and/or societies:	
Reading	I plan to read _____ hours per week from the sources listed below:	
Attending	I plan to attend the following events in the next _____ months:	
Networking	I currently estimate my professional network to contain _____ sources. Within the next _____ months, I plan to have _____ sources in my network.	
Sharing	I now engage in the following activities: During the next _____ months, I plan to do the following:	
Furthering my higher education qualifications	My current higher education qualifications are the following: During the next _____ years, I plan to obtain the following higher education qualifications:	

Ethical issues in ETD

Ethics are the application of standards of conduct to specific situations or decisions. A code of ethics defines good standards of conduct for the profession. Codes of ethics do not result in ethical behaviour, but rather give ETD practitioners a basis for exercising judgement about ethical matters in ETD practice.

General ethical issues that ETD practitioners need to consider are the following (Coetzee, 2004; Rothwell *et al*, 1995; Westgaard, 1992):

- maintaining appropriate confidentiality and integrity;
- saying no to inappropriate requests;
- showing respect for copyrights, sources, and intellectual property and complying with laws and regulations governing the ETD position;
- ensuring truth in claims, data and recommendations;
- balancing organisational, stakeholder and individual needs and interests;
- ensuring client and user involvement, participation and ownership;
- avoiding conflicts of interest;
- managing personal biases;
- showing respect for, interest in, and representation of individual and population differences;
- making the ETD intervention appropriate to the client's needs;
- ensuring transparency, fairness, integrity, reliability, consistency and validity in the application of ETD processes, tools and techniques;
- being sensitive to the direct and indirect effects of ETD interventions and acting to address negative consequences;
- pricing or costing products or services fairly;
- using power appropriately;
- recognising the rights and dignities of each individual;
- developing human potential;
- providing the employer, clients and learners with the highest quality education, training and development;
- striving to keep informed of pertinent knowledge and competence in the human resource field;
- supporting peers and avoiding conduct that hinders them in practising their profession;
- conducting oneself in an ethical and honest manner;
- improving the public understanding of human resource development and management;
- fairly and accurately representing one's ETD credentials, qualifications, experience and ability; and
- contributing to the continuing growth of the ETD profession.

Example of ethical principles stated by SABPP (www.sabpp.co.sa)

We value what we can offer as a profession and recognise the stewardship role of the profession and its members. The role is embodied in the norms and principles we stand for. The purpose of our code of conduct is to entrench the obligation we have as professional HR practitioners to uphold the profession's norms and principles and to conduct our activities in a professional and ethical manner. To ensure the trust of all our stakeholders, we strive to build the reputation of the profession and its members through the values of responsibility, integrity, respect and competence.

Our ethical identity

As members of the profession of human resource management in South Africa, we actively pursue the ideals of professionalism and are therefore ethically obliged to:

- Bring meaning and quality of worklife to the people we serve in our professional capacities.
- Ensure the sustainability of the organisations that we serve.
- Make a difference to the communities we touch.

ETD practitioners can occupy an important position in any organisation by being committed to ethical standards and making valuable contributions to the organisation's capability goals. Below is a checklist for being a proactive and ethical ETD professional.

Checklist for being a proactive and ethical ETD professional (Kaufman & Watters, 1992)

- Can I justify, both financially and ethically, my intended actions and interventions on the basis of benefits to society, benefits to the organisation and its stakeholders, and contributions to internal clients?
- For each intended action and intervention, did I ask, "Why?" and "What will happen if I accomplish this?" Did the answers meet ethical and financial standards?
- Did I relate means and ends for each action and intervention?
- Did I define quality in terms of results and added value, not just compliance with accepted procedures?
- On the basis of research and development, can I substantiate what I intend to do and deliver?
- Am I willing to forego the job if ethical standards will not be met?
- Do I define quality in terms of delivering the right results to the right place at the right time, the first time?
- Would I be comfortable reading in tomorrow's newspaper about what I am planning to do and deliver?

ACTIVITY
Case study

Diversity training – fad or here to stay? (Based on Cascio, 2003:308)
Diversity training is a flourishing business in South Africa. Most South African companies are engaged in one form or another of diversity training. All are built on the assumption that 'understanding builds better relationships'. Fair enough. However, some diversity consultants promise corporations they will increase their profits by 'empowering their whole workforce'. How could one support that claim? To some, the preferred solution to the problems of measurement and description is to declare them irrelevant and proceed on faith alone.

Question
Is diversity training ethically justifiable in light of the principles of sound ETD practice (value-added learning programme design and delivery, needs assessment, careful specification of programme objectives and learning outcomes, and the evaluation of training in terms of the original objectives and stated outcomes)? Give reasons for your answer.

Challenges for the ETD profession

Future trends in ETD closely follow trends in business and society. Most organisations are already trying to find ways to automate ETD practices. The use of information technology, computers and other sophisticated technologies to help practitioners perform their work will continue to grow. Clients will become more sophisticated.

The most successful practitioners will depend not only on their ETD expertise, but also on highly developed training expertise and consulting skills. Multicultural and multigenerational skills development issues will require innovation and creativity. Furthermore, as more sophisticated delivery systems and technologies are implemented, sharing expertise will become more critical to the success of ETD interventions.

The future is bright for ETD practitioners. As more and more organisations recognise the value-adding benefits of ETD, the demand for ETD practitioners' services and products will grow. In South Africa, more professionally educated, trained and competent ETD professionals are currently needed to address the skills development needs of the country. However, the future is not without challenges. As the ETD profession matures, the practice of quality outcomes-based ETD broadens. Organisations will also have a greater choice of ETD professionals. Quality, reliability, and value-adding services and products will become determining factors in gaining and retaining clients as an ETD provider.

As discussed in Chapters 7 and 8, quality is achieved by competently applying ETD skills, focusing on relevant performance capability issues, and generating cost-effective and proactive ETD solutions that add value for stakeholders. Reliability and service are dependent on the commitment and philosophy of the ETD practitioner. Clients and stakeholders are increasingly concerned with reliability and value-adding services and products. ETD practitioners should do their jobs with uncompromising integrity and timeliness, aim to satisfy the needs of stakeholders, and be accountable to their client. The quality of ETD products and services must always meet or surpass the client's expectations.

The ETD profession will have many opportunities during the next decade. Opportunities include expanding the tools to teach interesting and engaging ETD courses in outcomes-based ETD; conducting research in aspects of the ETD process, technology and methodology; and expanding the skills for the practice and measurement of quality outcomes-based and value-adding ETD. Within the context of the National Skills Development Strategy, the pressure to produce value-adding services and products is very high. ETD practitioners require more advanced tools and techniques to deal with the demands. These demands include issues such as rapid change in organisations, the use of advanced delivery systems for ETD, multicultural needs in the workplace, stakeholder requirements for value and quality compliance and measurement of their own productivity and contribution to business goals.

Key terms

- ETD practitioner roles
- ETD competency profile
- ETD practitioner characteristics
- Ethical behaviour
- Continued professional development

Review and discussion questions

1. What value do the key roles of the professional ETD practitioner add to the performance capability of employees and the organisation?
2. Why is it important for ETD practitioners to be professionally educated and trained?
3. What are the core competencies that ETD practitioners need to demonstrate in the South African workplace?
4. How do ETD practitioners benefit from continued professional development? How can they ensure that they stay abreast of new technology and developments in the ETD field?
5. Why is ethical behaviour an important characteristic of effective ETD practitioners?
6. What are the challenges for the ETD profession in the next decade?

Suggested reading

ASTD. (2006). *Bridging the skills gap.* Alexandria: ASTD Press.
Coetzee, M. (2004). *Empowering the skills development facilitator.* Johannesburg: Knowres.
Erasmus, B.J., Loedolff, P.v.S., Mda, T. & Nel, P.S. (2006). *Managing training and development.* Cape Town: Oxford University Press.

Useful learning and development resources

Centre for Community Training and Development (ctdregistration@unisa.ac.za)
Programme in Training Practices for Educators and Trainers
Short Course in the Design of Integrated Assessment of Learning Programmes
Short Course for Assessors
Short Course in Mentoring, Guidance and Support for Teachers and Trainers

Centre for Industrial and Organisational Psychology (iop@unisa.ac.za)
Programme in Skills Development Facilitation
Short Course in Skills Development Facilitation

Websites:
ASTD: www.astd.co.sa
Department of Labour: http://www.gcis.gov.sa/gov.labour
ETDP SETA: http://www.etdpseta.org.sa
info@skillsportal.co.sa
SABPP: www.sabpp.co.sa
SAQA: http://regqs.saqa.org.sa

Summary

In this chapter, we reviewed ETD as a profession and practice. ETD practitioners need to engage in continued professional development to ensure that they capitalise on the exciting opportunities for networking and the design of innovative ETD techniques. The rapid transformation of societies within a turbulent and uncertain world of work will continue to challenge the professional ETD practitioner to be creative. ETD practitioners who engage in ethical behaviour and continued professional development activities will get the benefits of being highly valued for the results they deliver through their continued expertise and professionalism.

CONCLUSION

ETD is an important part of an organisation's strategy to sustain its learning and performance capability. ETD has an impact on all aspects of the employment of people, from the induction of new employees to the development of future generations of directors. Unless individuals are exposed to learning and development opportunities, they cannot be expected to fulfil their roles, even if they know what their roles are. The challenge facing managers, ETD practitioners and organisations is how to make cost-effective use of ETD interventions within the organisation. ETD practitioners who apply the principles, theories and practices in this book will be recognised for their contributions to the organisation's and its employees' performance capability and productivity.

Learning and development, along with knowledge management, gain increasing significance from the inclusion of a strategic perspective to the education, training and development of the human resource within the organisation. The stakeholder approach to strategic ETD management ensures that ETD efforts add value for stakeholders. ETD practitioners who take pride in their professionalism and realise that learning continues throughout the lives of individuals will assist organisations and individuals to sustain their competitive edge in a changing business environment.

> *If people have talent and cannot use it, they have failed.*
> *If they have a talent and use only half of it, they have partly failed.*
> *If they have a talent and learn somehow to use the whole of it,*
> *they have gloriously succeeded and won a satisfaction and a*
> *triumph few people ever know*
> *(Thomas Wolfe cited in Palmer, 2002)*

Appendix 1: Example of a SAQA Unit Standard

SOUTH AFRICAN QUALIFICATIONS AUTHORITY
REGISTERED UNIT STANDARD:

Conduct outcomes-based assessment

SAQA US ID	UNIT STANDARD TITLE		
115753	Conduct outcomes-based assessment		
SGB NAME		REGISTERING PROVIDER	
SGB Assessor Standards			
FIELD		SUBFIELD	
Field 05 – Education, Training and Development		Higher Education and Training	
ABET BAND	UNIT STANDARD TYPE	NQF LEVEL	CREDITS
Undefined	Regular	Level 5	15
REGISTRATION STATUS	REGISTRATION START DATE	REGISTRATION END DATE	SAQA DECISION NUMBER
Registered	2004-08-11	2007-08-11	SAQA 0555/04

PURPOSE OF THE UNIT STANDARD

This generic assessor unit standard is for those who assess people for their achievement of learning outcomes in terms of specified criteria using pre-designed assessment instruments. The outcomes and criteria may be defined in a range of documents including but not limited to unit standards, exit level outcomes, assessment standards, curriculum statements and qualifications.

Those who achieve this unit standard will be able to conduct assessments within their fields of expertise. This unit standard will contribute towards the achievement of a variety of qualifications, particularly within the fields of Education, Training and Development Practices and Human Resource Development.

People credited with this unit standard are able to carry out assessments in a fair, valid, reliable and practicable manner that is free of all bias and discrimination, paying particular attention to the three groups targeted for redress: race, gender and disability.

In particular, people credited with this unit standard will be able to:
• Demonstrate understanding of outcomes-based assessment;
• Prepare for assessments;
• Conduct assessments;
• Provide feedback on assessments; and
• Review assessments.

LEARNING ASSUMED TO BE IN PLACE AND RECOGNITION OF PRIOR LEARNING

The credit calculation is based on the assumption that those starting to learn towards this unit standard have no previous assessment experience. It is assumed, though, that the learner-assessors have evaluative expertise within the area of learning in which they intend to assess (see Definition of Terms for a definition of "evaluative expertise").

UNIT STANDARD RANGE

1. This generic assessment unit standard applies to assessment in all fields of learning. However, it is expected that assessments will be contextualised to meet the requirements of different contexts.
2. Assessment of learner-assessors will only be valid for award of this unit standard if the following requirements are met:

- Assessments carried out by the learner-assessor are in relation to significant, meaningful and coherent outcome statements that include criteria for assessment purposes, and allow for judgements of competence in line with SAQA's definition of competence i.e. embrace foundational, practical and reflexive dimensions of competence. Outcomes that are highly task-orientated and do not demand much, if any, in the way of reflexive competence, will not be sufficient for measuring competence as an assessor in terms of this unit standard. It is important that learner-assessors select outcomes that enable them to meet the requirement laid out here.
- The learner-assessor demonstrates repeatability by carrying out at least two assessments:
  - One of which may be a simulated assessment (in order to cover a range of typical assessment situations); and
  - At least one of which must involve a real learner in a real assessment situation, preferably under the guidance of a mentor.

The assessments may involve two or more learners in relation to the same outcome.

- Learner-assessors produce evidence that they can conduct assessments in RPL situations and for learners who may have fairly recently acquired the necessary knowledge and skills through courses or learning programmes. However, learner assessors do not need to carry out both kinds of assessments in practice for the award of this unit standard. Should learner-assessors carry out an RPL-related assessment for the purposes of this unit standard, then it is sufficient for them to show how they might have conducted the assessment differently had it been an assessment linked to recent learning, and vice versa.

3. For the purposes of assessment against this unit standard, learner-assessors should have access to Assessment Guides and will not be expected to design assessments. (See Definition of Terms for a definition of Assessment Guides). Learner assessors will be expected to interpret the standards at hand in order to ensure their assessment judgements are in accordance with the requirements of the standard. In cases where Assessment Guides are not available, providers should seek ways to make such guides available for the purposes of this assessment. Where learner-assessor also intend to design assessments, then providers are encouraged to integrate the learning and assessment of the unit standards:
   - Conduct outcomes-based assessments
   - Design and develop outcomes-based assessments

4. Learner-assessors should have access to organisational assessment policies, procedures and systems (including moderation). It is assumed the organisational policies and procedures are of a quality sufficient for accreditation purposes. Where such policies and procedures are not yet available, the provider may make general policies and procedures available for the purposes of this assessment.

Further range statements are provided in the body of the unit standard where they apply to particular specific outcomes or assessment criteria.

UNIT STANDARD OUTCOME HEADER
N/A

SPECIFIC OUTCOMES AND ASSESSMENT CRITERIA:
SPECIFIC OUTCOME 1
Demonstrate understanding of outcomes-based assessment.

ASSESSMENT CRITERIA:
ASSESSMENT CRITERION 1
Comparisons between outcomes-based and another form of assessment of learning highlight key differences in terms of the underlying philosophies and approaches to assessment, including an outline of advantages and disadvantages.

ASSESSMENT CRITERION 2

RPL is explained in terms of its purpose, processes and related benefits and challenges. Explanations highlight the potential impact of RPL on individuals, learning organisations and the workplace.

ASSESSMENT CRITERION 3

A variety of assessment methods are described and compared in terms of how they could be used when conducting assessments in different situations.

ASSESSMENT CRITERION RANGE

The description of methods should cover situations for gathering evidence of:
- Problem solving ability;
- Knowledge and understanding;
- Practical and technical skills; and
- Attitudinal skills and values.

ASSESSMENT CRITERION 4

Key principles of assessment are described and illustrated in practical situations. The descriptions highlight the importance of applying the principles in terms of the possible effect on the assessment process and results.

ASSESSMENT CRITERION 5

The approach to giving feedback on assessment results is described in terms of the possible impact on learners and further learning and assessment.

SPECIFIC OUTCOME 2

Prepare for assessments.

OUTCOME RANGE

Preparation for assessments relates to organising and preparing resources, people, schedules, venues, assessment instruments and documentation for a particular assessment and/or related assessments for an individual or a number of assessment learners/learners. Preparation is to be carried out in situations where the learner assessor has access to:
- Relevant organisational assessment and moderation policies and procedures; and
- Assessment guides and instruments for the assessment at hand, including the relevant outcomes and criteria.

ASSESSMENT CRITERIA:
ASSESSMENT CRITERION 1

Preparation of assessment resources, logistics, documentation and environment meets the requirements of the assessment at hand and ensures fairness and safety of assessment.

ASSESSMENT CRITERION 2

Parties involved in the assessment are notified in good time. Checks are carried out to ensure parties involved in the assessment are ready and available to meet required schedules.

ASSESSMENT CRITERION RANGE

Parties include assessment learners and moderators, and may include assessment facilitators and/or assistants, teachers, trainers, invigilators and safety personnel.

ASSESSMENT CRITERION 3

All pre-assessment moderation requirements are carried out in accordance with relevant assessment policies, moderation plans and ETQA requirements.

ASSESSMENT CRITERION 4

Assessment details are explained to learners clearly and constructively. Opportunities for clarification are provided and responses promote understanding of the requirements.

ASSESSMENT CRITERION RANGE

Assessment details cover the specific purpose, process, expectations, roles, responsibilities and appeals procedures related to the assessment at hand, as well as the general context of assessment in terms of the principles and mechanisms of the NQF, as applicable to the situation and assessment context.

ASSESSMENT CRITERION 5

Inputs are sought from learners regarding special needs and possible sources of evidence that could contribute to valid assessment, including RPL opportunities. Modifications made to the assessment approach on the basis of the inputs do not affect the validity of the assessment.

ASSESSMENT CRITERION 6

Learner readiness for assessment is confirmed. In cases where learners are not yet ready, actions taken are in line with assessment policies.

SPECIFIC OUTCOME 3

Conduct assessments.

OUTCOME RANGE

The ability to make assessment judgements using diverse sources of evidence must be demonstrated. Assessments to include cases where learners have special needs and where evidence arises through RPL situations. Should it not be feasible to gather evidence for assessments of special need learners or in RPL situations, evidence may be produced through scenarios.

Learner-assessors must show they can make judgements in situations where:
- Learners meet all criteria for a particular outcome;
- Learners clearly do not meet the criteria for a particular outcome;
- Learners meet some, but not all criteria; and
- More evidence is required in order to make a judgement of competence.

ASSESSMENT CRITERIA:
ASSESSMENT CRITERION 1

Assessment practices promote effective, manageable, fair and safe assessment. Assessment practices are in line with quality assurance requirements, recognised codes of practice and learning-site or work-site standard operating procedures where applicable.

ASSESSMENT CRITERION RANGE

Professional, industry or legislated codes of practice.

ASSESSMENT CRITERION 2

The assessment is carried out according to the assessment design and in line with the assessment plan. Adjustments are justified by the situation, and unforeseen events and special needs of learners are addressed without compromising the validity or fairness of the assessment.

ASSESSMENT CRITERION 3

Questioning techniques are appropriate and have the potential to successfully elicit appropriate responses. Communication with learners is non-leading, and is appropriate to the assessment at hand and the language ability of the learner.

ASSESSMENT CRITERION RANGE

"Leading" refers to the practice of inadvertently or deliberately influencing the evidence learners produce through the style of questioning, instructions or responses to learners.

ASSESSMENT CRITERION 4

Sufficient evidence is gathered, including evidence generated over time, to enable valid, consistent, reliable and fair assessment judgements to be made.

ASSESSMENT CRITERION 5

Assessment judgements are consistent with judgements made on similar evidence and are justified by the authenticity, validity, sufficiency and currency of the evidence.

ASSESSMENT CRITERION 6

Records of the assessment are in line with the requirements of the organisation's quality assurance system. Records meet requirements for making assessment judgements, giving meaningful feedback, supporting internal and external moderation, and addressing possible appeals.

SPECIFIC OUTCOME 4

Provide feedback on assessments.

OUTCOME RANGE

- Parties include learners, educators, trainers, managers and moderators as applicable to the situation.
- Evidence must be provided of the ability to give written and oral feedback.
- The ability to give feedback must be demonstrated in situations where:
    - Learners meet all criteria in relation to an outcome;
    - Learners clearly do not meet the criteria in relation to an outcome;
    - Learners meet some, but not all criteria; and
    - More evidence is required before a judgement is possible.

ASSESSMENT CRITERIA:
ASSESSMENT CRITERION 1

Feedback is given to relevant parties in accordance with confidentiality requirements, in an appropriate sequence and within agreed timeframes.

ASSESSMENT CRITERION 2

Feedback is clear and confined to strengths and weaknesses in performance and/or requirements for further evidence in relation to the outcome/s at hand.

ASSESSMENT CRITERION 3

The type and manner of feedback is constructive, culturally sensitive and related to the relevant party's needs. Sufficient information is provided to enable the purpose of the assessment to be met, and to enable parties to make further decisions.

ASSESSMENT CRITERION RANGE

Further decisions include awarding of credit, redirecting learners to further learning or guiding learners to further application or re-assessment.

ASSESSMENT CRITERION 4

Feedback on the assessment process is obtained from the learner and opportunities are provided for clarification and explanations concerning the entire assessment.

ASSESSMENT CRITERION 5
Disputes and/or appeals that arise are dealt with according to the assessment policy.

ASSESSMENT CRITERION 6
Agreements reached and key elements of the feedback are recorded in line with the requirements of the organisation's quality assurance system.

SPECIFIC OUTCOME 5
Review assessments.

OUTCOME RANGE
The review should address at least the following aspects:
- The quality of the assessment instruments, including the outcomes against which assessment takes place and Assessment Guides used.
- The assessment process.
- Learner readiness for assessment.

ASSESSMENT CRITERIA:
ASSESSMENT CRITERION 1
The review identifies strengths and weaknesses in the instruments and process, and records these for incorporation in assessment redesign.

ASSESSMENT CRITERION 2
Feedback from relevant parties is analysed and used to influence future assessments positively.

ASSESSMENT CRITERION 3
Weaknesses in the assessment design and process that could have compromised the fairness of assessment are identified and dealt with according to the organisation's assessment policy.

ASSESSMENT CRITERION 4
Weaknesses in the assessment arising from poorly defined outcomes and criteria are identified, and effective steps are taken to inform relevant bodies.

UNIT STANDARD ACCREDITATION AND MODERATION OPTIONS
- A learner-assessor wishing to be assessed against this unit standard may apply to an assessment agency, assessor or provider institution accredited by the relevant ETQA.
- Anyone assessing a learner-assessor against this unit standard must meet the assessor requirements of the relevant ETQA. In particular, such assessors of learner-assessors must demonstrate that they assess in terms of the scope and context defined in all the range statements.
- Any institution offering learning towards this unit standard must be accredited as a provider with the relevant ETQA.
- External moderation of assessment will be conducted by the relevant ETQA at its discretion.

UNIT STANDARD ESSENTIAL EMBEDDED KNOWLEDGE
The following knowledge is embedded within the unit standard, and will be assessed directly or indirectly through assessment of the specific outcomes in terms of the assessment criteria:
- Outcomes-based education, training and development
- Principles of assessment – directly assessed through assessment criterion 'Key principles of assessment are described and illustrated in practical situations. The descriptions highlight the importance of applying the principles in terms of the possible effect on the assessment process and results', and indirectly assessed via a requirement to apply the principles throughout the standard.

- Principles and practices of RPL – directly assessed through assessment criteria 'RPL is explained in terms of its purpose, processes and related benefits and challenges. Explanations highlight the potential impact of RPL on individuals, learning organisations and the workplace.', 'Inputs are sought from learners regarding special needs and possible sources of evidence that could contribute to valid assessment, including RPL opportunities. Modifications made to the assessment approach on the basis of the inputs do not affect the validity of the assessment' and specific outcome 'Conduct assessments', as well as through application in the rest of the standard.
- Methods of assessment – directly assessed through assessment criterion 'A variety of assessment methods are described and compared in terms of how they could be used when conducting assessments in different situations', and indirectly assessed through application of the methods.
- Potential barriers to assessment – assessed when dealing with special needs.
- The principles and mechanisms of the NQF – this knowledge underpins the standard.
- Assessment policies and ETQA requirements
- Moderation requirements

UNIT STANDARD DEVELOPMENTAL OUTCOME
N/A

UNIT STANDARD LINKAGES
N/A

CRITICAL CROSS-FIELD OUTCOMES (CCFO)

UNIT STANDARD CCFO IDENTIFYING
Identify and solve problems using critical and creative thinking: preparing for contingencies, learners with special needs, problems that arise during assessment, suggesting changes to assessment.

UNIT STANDARD CCFO WORKING
Work effectively in a team using critical and creative thinking: working with learners and other relevant parties during assessment, as well as post-assessment.

UNIT STANDARD CCFO ORGANISING
Organise and manage oneself and ones activities: preparing, conducting and recording the assessment.

UNIT STANDARD CCFO COLLECTING
Collect, analyse, organise and critically evaluate information: gather, evaluate and judge evidence and the assessment process.

UNIT STANDARD CCFO COMMUNICATING
Communicate effectively: prepare learners for assessment, communicate during assessment, and provide feedback.

UNIT STANDARD CCFO DEMONSTRATING
Demonstrate the world as a set of related systems: understanding the impact of assessment on individuals and organisations.

UNIT STANDARD CCFO CONTRIBUTING
Be culturally and aesthetically sensitive across a range of social contexts: give feedback on assessments in a culturally sensitive manner.

UNIT STANDARD ASSESSOR CRITERIA
N/A

UNIT STANDARD NOTES

This unit standard replaces unit standard 9927, "Conduct an assessment", Level 4, 12 credits.

This unit standard replaces unit standard 7978, "Plan and conduct assessment of learning outcomes", Level 5, 15 credits.

Supplementary information :

NOTE FROM AUTHORS: The Definition of Terms (available on original SAQA document), were omitted here for abbreviation purposes. The Glossary of terms in the book captures most of the SAQA definitions.

Principles of assessment

Methods of Assessment:

- Appropriate: The method of assessment is suited to the outcome being assessed i.e. is capable of gathering evidence in relation to the intended outcome, and not something else.
- Fair: The method of assessment does not present any barriers to achievements, which are not related to the achievement of the outcome at hand.
- Manageable: The methods used make for easily arranged, cost-effective assessments that do not unduly interfere with learning.
- Integrated into work or learning: Evidence collection is integrated into the work or learning process where this is appropriate and feasible. (Often referred to as naturally occurring evidence.)

Evidence

- Valid: The evidence focuses on the requirements laid down in the relevant standard and matches the evidence requirements of the outcome/s at hand under conditions that mirror the conditions of actual performance as closely as possible.
- Current: The evidence is sufficient proof that the learner is able to perform the assessment outcomes at the time the assessor declares the learner competent.
- Authentic: The assessor is satisfied that the evidence is attributable to the person being assessed.
- Sufficient: The evidence collected establishes that all criteria have been met and that performance to the required standard can be repeated consistently in the future i.e. the performance to standard is not a "once-off".

Overall Assessment Process

- Systematic: The overall process ensures assessment is fair, effective, repeatable and manageable.
- Open: The process is transparent i.e. assessment learners understand the assessment process and the criteria that apply and can contribute to the planning and accumulation of evidence.
- Reliable/Consistent: The same assessor would make the same judgement again in similar circumstances and judgements match judgements made on similar evidence.

Appendix 2

ANNUAL TRAINING REPORT (ATR)

1 April 2006 – 31 March 2007

&

WORKPLACE SKILLS PLANNING GRANT (WSP)

1 April 2007 – 31 March 2008

50 Employees and more

Name of Organisation: _____

Trading as: _____

Skills Development Levy (SDL) Number: _____

Skills Development Levy (SDL) Numbers to be linked to main number (if applicable):

    1. _____

    2. _____

This Grant application form is to be used in conjunction with the guidelines on the Web-site

www.wrseta.org.za

WSP / ATR Due Date 30 June 2007. No extensions will be granted.

Kindly send completed applications to your Regional Office (details on pg. 19)

W&RSETA Date Stamp	SETA Office Use
	Captured by:...............................
	Date:...
	Approved by:...............................
	Date:...

TABLE OF CONTENTS

Section 1:		
1.1	SDF Details	3
1.2	Company Details	4
1.3	Company Contact Person (Other than SDF)	4
1.4	Confirmation of Banking Details	5
Section 2		
2.1	Annual Training Report	6-8
2.2	Scarce Skills ATR	9-11
2.3	ABET ATR	12
Section 3		
3.1	Provincial Profile	13
3.2	Training Committee	13
3.3	Current Employment Profile	14
3.4	Training Plan (WSP)	15-17
3.5	(A) Scarce Skills List	18
3.5	(B) Scarce Skills Plan	19-21
3.6	ABET Plan	22
Section 4:		
4.1	Development and Consultative Process	23
4.2	Declaration by Employer	23
4.3	Confirmation Form	24
Appendix A: Contact Details for W&RSETA		25
Appendix B: Checklist for SDF and SETA		26

SECTION 1

1.1 SDF DETAILS

Please confirm your details to ensure that our database can be updated

Title _____   Surname _____

First Name _____   Initials _____

Gender   Male [ ]
(for statistical purposes only)   Female [ ]

Population Group   African [ ]
(for statistical purposes only)   Coloured [ ]
   Indian/Asian [ ]
   White [ ]

Disability Status [ ]
(for statistical purposes only, please tick if applicable)

Current Occupation _____

Cell Phone Number   Postal Address

_____   _____

Telephone Number (work)   _____

_____   _____

Fax Number (work)   City & Province   Postal Code _____

_____   _____

E-mail Address _____

ID Number _____

(Compulsory – needed for verification purposes)

Acting in capacity of:

Company SDF   [ ]

Independent SDF   [ ]

1.2   COMPANY DETAILS

Please confirm your details to ensure that our database can be updated

Company Name _____

Skills Development Levy (SDL) number _____

SIC Code: _____

Annual Payroll: Above R500K [ ]   Below R500K [ ]

Physical Address

_____

_____

_____

City _____   Postal Code _____

Province _____

Telephone Number (work)   Fax Number (work)

_____   _____

Postal Address

_____

_____

City _____   Postal Code _____

1.3   COMPANY CONTACT PERSON (OTHER THAN SDF)

Please confirm your details to ensure that our database can be updated

Title _____   Surname _____

First Name _____   Initials _____

Telephone Number (work) _____

Cell Number _____

Fax Number (work) _____

E-mail Address _____

1.4 CONFIRMATION OF BANKING DETAILS

To be completed by first time participants and companies whose banking details have changed.

Company Name _____

Address _____

_____

_____ Postal Code _____

Skills Development Levy (SDL) number _____

Details of Company/Entity bank account are as follows:

Name of Bank _____ Branch _____

Type of account *(please tick the applicable box)* ☐ Current   ☐ Savings

Branch Code _____   Account Number _____

Attach at least one of the following to confirm banking details:

- Copy of cancelled cheque (preferable).
- A copy of an entity bank statement.
- See website for banking details criteria.

Please Note:

The Organisation's name, Bank account number, Branch code, etc. on the attached

cancelled cheque, must be the same as the detail reflected in section above

Payment instructions

To Whom It May Concern:

The Organisation hereby requests and authorises W&RSETA to pay any amounts, which may accrue to the credit of the Organisation's account with the mentioned bank. The Organisation understands that the credit transfers hereby authorised will be processed by computer through a system known as the "ACB ELECTRONIC TRANSFER SERVICES", and the Organisation also understands that an additional advice of payment will be printed on the Organisation's bank statement. The Organisation understands that a payment advice will be supplied via the Seta Management System (SMS) and which will indicate that funds are deposited into the Organisation's bank account.

Compiled by	Signature	Job Title	Date

Authorised by	Signature	Job Title	Date

Company/Entity Registration Number	Company/Entity VAT Registration Number

SECTION 2

2.1 ANNUAL TRAINING REPORT (ATR) 1 APRIL 2006 – 31 MARCH 2007

Please refer to the Workplace Skills Plan for the previous financial year 1 April 2006 – 31 March 2007 when completing this form.

Occupational Categories	People trained during the current financial year		African			Coloured			Indian			White			Total		
			M	F	D	M	F	D	M	F	D	M	F	D	M	F	D
Senior Officials, Managers / Owner	Current employees (at this level)	Planned															
		Completed															
	Current employees (earmarked for accelerated development)	Planned															
		Completed															
	External recruits (incl 18.2 learners at this level)	Planned															
		Completed															
Professionals	Current employees (at this level)	Planned															
		Completed															
	Current employees (earmarked for accelerated development)	Planned															
		Completed															
	External recruits (incl 18.2 learners at this level)	Planned															
		Completed															
Technicians and Associate Professionals	Current employees (at this level)	Planned															
		Completed															
	Current employees (earmarked for accelerated development)	Planned															
		Completed															
	External recruits (incl 18.2 learners at this level)	Planned															
		Completed															

Occupational Categories	People trained during the current financial year		African			Coloured			Indian			White			Total		
			M	F	D	M	F	D	M	F	D	M	F	D	M	F	D
Clerical and/or Administrative Workers	Current employees (at this level)	Planned															
		Completed															
	Current employees (earmarked for accelerated development)	Planned															
		Completed															
	External recruits (incl 18.2 learners at this level)	Planned															
		Completed															
Service Workers and Sales Workers	Current employees (at this level)	Planned															
		Completed															
	Current employees (earmarked for accelerated development)	Planned															
		Completed															
	External recruits (incl 18.2 learners at this level)	Planned															
		Completed															
Agricultural and Fishery Workers	Current employees (at this level)	Planned															
		Completed															
	Current employees (earmarked for accelerated development)	Planned															
		Completed															
	External recruits (incl 18.2 learners at this level)	Planned															
		Completed															
Skilled Workers	Current employees (at this level)	Planned															
		Completed															
	Current employees (earmarked for accelerated development)	Planned															
		Completed															
	External recruits (incl 18.2 learners at this level)	Planned															
		Completed															

Occupational Categories	People trained during the current financial year		African			Coloured			Indian			White			Total		
			M	F	D	M	F	D	M	F	D	M	F	D	M	F	D
Plant and Machine Operators and Assemblers	Current employees (at this level)	Planned															
		Completed															
	Current employees (earmarked for accelerated development)	Planned															
		Completed															
	External recruits (incl 18.2 learners at this level)	Planned															
		Completed															
Labourers and Elementary Occupations	Current employees (at this level)	Planned															
		Completed															
	Current employees (earmarked for accelerated development)	Planned															
		Completed															
	External recruits (incl 18.2 learners at this level)	Planned															
		Completed															
Apprentices and Learnerships	Current employees (at this level)	Planned															
		Completed															
	Current employees (earmarked for accelerated development)	Planned															
		Completed															
	External recruits (incl 18.2 learners at this level)	Planned															
		Completed															
Casual / Temporary Workers	Current employees (at this level)	Planned															
		Completed															
	Current employees (earmarked for accelerated development)	Planned															
		Completed															
	External recruits (incl 18.2 learners at this level)	Planned															
		Completed															
TOTAL	Current employees (at this level)	Planned															
		Completed															
	Current employees (earmarked for accelerated development)	Planned															
		Completed															
	External recruits (incl 18.2 learners at this level)	Planned															
		Completed															

2.2 SCARCE SKILLS (ATR) 1 APRIL 2006 to 31 MARCH 2007

Kindly enter the corresponding number (1, 2, 3 etc.) of the relevant scarce skill from the list in section 3.5(A) where training has taken place. Also, indicate the type and level of training linked to this scarce skill as well as the race, gender and disability status of the beneficiaries trained. See example below.

Occupational Categories	Scarce Skill	Type of Training			Level			African			Coloured			Indian			White			Total		
		Skills Programme	Learnership	Short Course*	Entry	Intermediate	Advanced	M	F	D	M	F	D	M	F	D	M	F	D	M	F	D
Senior Officials, Managers	5			√	√			2												2		
	2	√				√						1						1			1	
	4		√			√			3												3	

Occupational Categories	Scarce Skill	Type of Training			Level			African			Coloured			Indian			White			Total		
		Skills Programme	Learner-ship	Short Course*	Entry	Inter-mediate	Advanced	M	F	D	M	F	D	M	F	D	M	F	D	M	F	D
Senior Officials, Managers																						
Professionals																						
Technicians and Associated Professionals																						

Please note:

- A short course can be any training programme which is not Unit Standard-aligned.
- Only formal training (and not on-the-job training) should be entered

Occupational Categories	Scarce Skill	Type of Training			Entry	Level		African			Coloured			Indian			White			Total		
		Skills Programme	Learner-ship	Short Course*		Inter-mediate	Advanced	M	F	D	M	F	D	M	F	D	M	F	D	M	F	D
Clerical and/or Administrative Workers																						
Service and Sales Workers																						
Agricultural & Fishery Workers																						
Skilled Workers																						

Occupational Categories	Scarce Skill	Type of Training			Level			African			Coloured			Indian			White			Total		
		Skills Programme	Learner-ship	Short Course*	Entry	Inter-mediate	Advanced	M	F	D	M	F	D	M	F	D	M	F	D	M	F	D
Plant & Machine Operators and Assemblers																						
Labourers & Elementary Occupations																						
Apprentices and Learnerships																						
Casual / Temporary Workers																						
Total																						

2.3 ABET – ATR (1 APRIL 2006 – 31 MARCH 2007)

This table records those beneficiaries who have completed ABET. It also indicates the Population Group, Gender, Disability Status and level of ABET completed.

| Name | ID Number | Population Group | | | | Gender | | Disability Status | ABET Level | | | |
		A	C	I	W	M	F	D	1	2	3	4

A – African
C – Coloured
I – Indian
M – Male
F – Female
D – Person with disability (for the disability description please consult the guidelines which may be found on our website)

SECTION 3

3.1 PROVINCIAL PROFILE AS AT 1 APRIL 2007

National Province	Number of Employees	Number of Stores
Eastern Cape		
Free State		
Gauteng		
KwaZulu-Natal		
Mpumalanga		
Northern Cape		
Limpopo		
North West Province		
Western Cape		
TOTAL NUMBER OF EMPLOYEES		

3.2 TRAINING COMMITTEE (Skills Development Committee)

Title	Surname	First Name	Initials	Constituency

3.3 CURRENT EMPLOYMENT PROFILE (as at 1 APRIL 2007)

Occupational Group	African			Coloured			Indian/Asian			White			Total		
	M	F	D	M	F	D	M	F	D	M	F	D	M	F	D
Senior Officials, Managers / Owner Managers															
Professionals															
Technicians & Associated Professionals															
Clerical and/or Administrative Workers															
Service Workers															
Agricultural & Fishery Workers															
Skilled Workers															
Plant / Machine Operators & Assemblers															
Labourers															
Apprentices and Learnerships															
Casual / Temporary Workers															
Total															

M – Male
F – Female
D – Person with disability

Disability definition: The Employment Equity Act of 1998 defines people with disabilities as 'people who have a long term or recurring physical or mental impairment that substantially limits their prospects of entry into or advancement in employment'. Physical impairments include hearing and visual impairments, paralysis, amputations and problems with internal organs. Mental impairment includes clinically defined mental and emotional illnesses and learning disabilities.

3.4 TRAINING PLAN (WSP) (1 APRIL 2007 – 31 MARCH 2008)

This table identifies those beneficiaries that will participate in learning interventions. Please indicate the number of beneficiaries who will receive training and NOT the number of programmes to be run during the course of the year. Please note that a beneficiary can receive training on their current level as well as training for a potential promotion to a higher level. Therefore a beneficiary can be indicated on more than one occupational level.

Occupational Categories	People to be trained during the current financial year		African			Coloured			Indian			White			Total		
			M	F	D	M	F	D	M	F	D	M	F	D	M	F	D
Senior Officials, Managers / Owner	Current employees (at this level)	Planned															
	Current employees (earmarked for accelerated development)	Planned															
	External recruits (incl 18.2 learners at this level)	Planned															
Professionals	Current employees (at this level)	Planned															
	Current employees (earmarked for accelerated development)	Planned															
	External recruits (incl 18.2 learners at this level)	Planned															
Technicians and Associate Professionals	Current employees (at this level)	Planned															
	Current employees (earmarked for accelerated development)	Planned															
	External recruits (incl 18.2 learners at this level)	Planned															

Occupational Categories	People to be trained during the current financial year		African			Coloured			Indian			White			Total		
			M	F	D	M	F	D	M	F	D	M	F	D	M	F	D
Clerical and/or Administrative Workers	Current employees (at this level)	Planned															
	Current employees (earmarked for accelerated development)	Planned															
	External recruits (incl 18.2 learners at this level)	Planned															
Service Workers and Sales Workers	Current employees (at this level)	Planned															
	Current employees (earmarked for accelerated development)	Planned															
	External recruits (incl 18.2 learners at this level)	Planned															
Agricultural and Fishery Workers	Current employees (at this level)	Planned															
	Current employees (earmarked for accelerated development)	Planned															
	External recruits (incl 18.2 learners at this level)	Planned															
Skilled Workers	Current employees (at this level)	Planned															
	Current employees (earmarked for accelerated development)	Planned															
	External recruits (incl 18.2 learners at this level)	Planned															

Occupational Categories	People to be trained during the current financial year		African			Coloured			Indian			White			Total		
			M	F	D	M	F	D	M	F	D	M	F	D	M	F	D
Plant and Machine Operators and Assemblers	Current employees (at this level)	Planned															
	Current employees (earmarked for accelerated development)	Planned															
	External recruits (incl 18.2 learners at this level)	Planned															
Labourers and Elementary Occupations	Current employees (at this level)	Planned															
	Current employees (earmarked for accelerated development)	Planned															
	External recruits (incl 18.2 learners at this level)	Planned															
Apprentices and Learnerships	Current employees (at this level)	Planned															
	Current employees (earmarked for accelerated development)	Planned															
	External recruits (incl 18.2 learners at this level)	Planned															
Casual / Temporary Workers	Current employees (at this level)	Planned															
	Current employees (earmarked for accelerated development)	Planned															
	External recruits (incl 18.2 learners at this level)	Planned															
TOTAL	Current employees (at this level)	Planned															
	Current employees (earmarked for accelerated development)	Planned															
	External recruits (incl 18.2 learners at this level)	Planned															

SECTION 3

3.5 (A)   SCARCE SKILLS LIST

No.	Scarce Skill	No.	Scarce Skill
1	Blockman	20	Food technologists
2	Buyers	21	Shelf Packers
3	Logistics Planners (Stock movement)	22	Plumbers
4	Supply Chain Management	23	Polishers (furniture)
5	Product developers	24	Polishers (jewellery)
6	Sellers	25	Chefs
7	Merchandisers (incl. visual merchandisers)	26	Cashiers/Till Operators
8	Bakers	27	General administration and finance
9	Butchers	28	Accountants and book-keepers
10	Fresh Food Operators (e.g. deli supervisor)	29	Creditors and debtors
11	Fresh Food Operators (e.g. fruit and vegetable supervisor)	30	Retail managers
12	Fresh Food Operators (e.g. fish supervisor)	31	Human Resource Practitioners
13	Electricians	32	Inventory management
14	Mechanics	33	Labour Law Specialists
15	Marketers	34	Assessors
16	Sewers	35	Moderators
17	Pattern Cutters	36	Shop stewards
18	Industrial over locker operator (carpets)	37	Call Centre/Help desk staff
19	Planners	38	Sales People

Please note:

The above numbering is merely for the purpose of listing the Scarce Skills and has no relevance to pri-oritisation. It is simply numbered for the purpose of aligning the relevant Scarce Skills to the type and level of training as required in section 3.5 (B).

3.5 (B)   SCARCE SKILLS PLAN (WSP) 1 APRIL 2007 to 31 MARCH 2008

Kindly enter the corresponding number (1, 2, 3 etc.) of the relevant scarce skill from the list in section 3.5(A) where training has taken place. Also, indicate the type and level of training linked to this scarce skill as well as the race, gender and disability status of the beneficiaries trained. See example below.

Occupational Categories	Scarce Skill	Type of Training			Level			African			Coloured			Indian			White			Total		
		Skills Programme	Learnership	Short Course*	Entry	Intermediate	Advanced	M	F	D	M	F	D	M	F	D	M	F	D	M	F	D
Senior Officials, Managers	5			√	√			2												2		
	2	√				√						1						1		1	1	
	4		√			√			3												3	

Occupational Categories	Scarce Skill	Type of Training			Level			African			Coloured			Indian			White			Total		
		Skills Programme	Learner-ship	Short Course*	Entry	Inter-mediate	Advanced	M	F	D	M	F	D	M	F	D	M	F	D	M	F	D
Senior Officials, Managers																						
Professionals																						
Technicians and Associated Professionals																						

Please note:

- A short course can be any training programme which is not Unit Standard-aligned.
- Only formal training (and not on-the-job training) should be entered

Occupational Categories	Scarce Skill	Type of Training			Level			African			Coloured			Indian			White			Total		
		Skills Programme	Learner-ship	Short Course*	Entry	Inter-mediate	Advanced	M	F	D	M	F	D	M	F	D	M	F	D	M	F	D
Clerical and/or Administrative Workers																						
Service and Sales Workers																						
Agricultural & Fishery Workers																						
Skilled Workers																						

Occupational Categories	Scarce Skill	Type of Training			Level			African			Coloured			Indian			White			Total		
		Skills Programme	Learner-ship	Short Course*	Entry	Inter-mediate	Advanced	M	F	D	M	F	D	M	F	D	M	F	D	M	F	D
Plant & Machine Operators and Assemblers																						
Labourers & Elementary Occupations																						
Apprentices and Learnerships																						
Casual / Temporary Workers																						
Total																						

3.6 ABET – PLAN (1 APRIL 2007 – 31 MARCH 2008)

This table identifies those beneficiaries who require ABET. It also indicates the Population Group, Gender, Disability Status and level of ABET required.

Name	ID Number	Population Group				Gender		Disability Status	ABET Level			
		A	C	I	W	M	F	D	1	2	3	4

A – African
C – Coloured
I – Indian
M – Male
F – Female
D – Person with disability (for the disability description please consult the guidelines which may be found on our website)

SECTION 4

4.1 DEVELOPMENT AND CONSULTATIVE PROCESS

1. What process was used to develop the WSP (Please tick)?

1.	Training/Skills Development Committee	
2.	Employees were consulted	
3.	Other e.g. Performance appraisal system	

Should you wish to expand on your choice above, please do so in the space below:

_____

_____

2. Will the WSP assist the organisation in achieving its Employment Equity Plan goals?

Yes	
No	

Should you wish to expand on your choice above, please do so in the space below:

_____

_____

4.2 DECLARATION BY EMPLOYER

This is to confirm that this organisation is up-to-date with levy payments to the Commissioner of the South African Revenue Services.

SARS
SDL Number

Name _____

Signature _____

Position in organisation _____ Date _____

(Must be signed by senior manager/director)

Please Note:

It is a legal requirement that Grants may only be paid to organisations who are up-to-date with their Skills Development Levy Payments to SARS
(See Regulation No. 8627 Volume 500, 2 February 2007, 9(b) c)

4.3 CONFIRMATION FORM (ATR 2006-2007 AND TRAINING PLAN 2007-2008)

SARS
SDL Number

Skills Development Facilitator

Name _____

Signature _____

Position in organisation _____

Date _____

Representative of Workforce (Duly elected by the Workforce)

Name _____

Signature _____

Position in organisation _____

Date _____

CEO/MD/HR Director

Name _____

Signature _____

Position in organisation _____

Date _____

Please Note:

- The above three signatures are a declaration by the organisation confirming the validity of the information in this document and the W&RSETA will not approve any grant payments to organisations without the original three signatures above.
- Please take note of the draft regulation (Regulation No. 8627, Volume 500, 2 February 2007, 9(b) e) whereby the SETA may require companies to complete a certain percentage of training in order to qualify for their Mandatory Grant. Pending the final Regulations as well as W&RSETA Board-approval, organisations will be informed and this requirement would then be effective on submission of the 2007/2008 ATR.

APPENDIX A - CONTACT DETAILS FOR W&RSETA

It is important to note that the SETA will not be able to approve any Grant payments to organisations without the original signed hard copies of sections 1.4, 4.2 & 4.3

Please return the completed Workplace Skills Planning Grant to:

W&RSETA Head Office	Gauteng Office	KwaZulu-Natal Office	Western Cape Office	Limpopo/Mpumalanga Office	Eastern Cape Office	Free State Office
PO Box 9809, Centurion 0046	PO Box 14780 Hatfield 0028	PO Box 18473 Dalbridge Durban, 4014	PO Box 13913 Mowbray 7705	PO Box 17717 Emalahleni 1035	Not yet available.	PO Box 1419 Bloemfontein 9300
W&RSETA House 224 Witch-Hazel Street Highveld Techno Park Centurion	1267 Pretorius Street Hadefield Office Park Block B, Ground Floor Hatfield, Pretoria	Ground Floor Smart Xchange Building 5 Walnut Road Durban	Ground Floor, Old Warehouse Building Black River Park Fir Road Observatory	64 Mandela Street Parkmed Building Office 202 Emalahleni 1035	Office No. 8 Malcomess Park Southernwood East London	Justitia Building Corner Aliwal and St Andrew Streets Bloemfontein 9300
Tel: (012) 676 9000 Fax: (012) 665 2559	Tel: (012) 430 4930 Fax: (012) 430 4935	Tel: (031) 333 8800 Fax: (031) 333 8815	Tel: (021) 442 6700 Fax: (021) 442 6777	Tel: (013) 690 1214 Fax: (013) 690 1190	Not yet available. Please contact H/O	Not yet available. Please contact H/O
skillsadmin@wrseta.org.za	wmkhombo@wrseta.org.za	bdlamini@wrseta.org.za	jedwards@wrseta.org.za	dmametsa@wrseta.org.za	joycem@wrseta.org.za	lmotshabi@wrseta.org.za

APPENDIX B - CHECKLIST FOR SDF AND SETA

Please note that the WSP / ATR should comply with the requirements below to qualify for approval and the subsequent payment of the Mandatory Grant to the company.

Section	Description	SDF Check √	SETA Check √
SDF Details	Name, ID No. and Contact details must be completed.		
Company Details	All details to be completed.		
Company Contact Person	All details to be completed.		
Banking Details	If a cancelled cheque has been submitted previously and no changes have occurred it is not necessary to resubmit a cancelled cheque or to complete this section.		
Annual Training Report	Beneficiaries of training completed are recorded.		
Scarce Skills ATR	Beneficiaries who received Scarce Skills training are recorded.		
ABET ATR	Beneficiaries who completed ABET are recorded.		
Provincial Profile	If a consolidated WSP is submitted on behalf of a number of branches, the number of branches per province must be indicated.		
Training Committee	For companies with more than 50 employees. Refer to the Skills Development Act of 1998.		
Current Employment Profile	Total Permanent Staff complement of the organisation. (Employees who fall under annual payroll)		
Training Plan	Beneficiaries of planned training are identified and recorded according to occupational category and level		
Scarce Skills	List of Scarce skills identified through Sector Skills Audit.		
Scarce Skills Plan	Scarce skills are selected from the list on page 18 and aligned to the relevant occupational category, type and level of training, race, gender and disability status.		
ABET Plan	Identifies beneficiaries who require ABET.		
Development and Consultative Process	Consultation steps followed to complete Grant application.		
Declaration by Employer	Confirm that levy payments are up to date.		
Authorisation	All three signatures must be present.		

Appendix 3

Skills Development for Economic Growth

SMME ANNUAL TRAINING REPORT (ATR)

1 April 2006 – 31 March 2007

&

SMME GRANT APPLICATION FORM

1 April 2007 – 31 March 2008

Levy-Paying Companies with Less Than 50 Employees

Name of Organisation: _____

Trading as: _____

Skills Development Levy (SDL) Number: _____

Skills Development Levy (SDL) Numbers to be linked to main number (if applicable):

_____

_____

This Grant application form is to be used in conjunction with the guidelines on the Web-site

www.wrseta.org.za

WSP / ATR Due Date 30 June 2007. No extensions will be granted.

Kindly send completed applications to your Regional Office (details on pg. 10)

W&RSETA Date Stamp

SETA Office Use

Captured by:................................

Date:...

Approved by:...............................

Date:...

TABLE OF CONTENTS

Section 1:	
1.1 SDF Details	3
1.2 Company Details	4
1.3 Company Contact Person (Other than SDF)	4
1.4 Confirmation of Banking Details	5
Section 2:	
2.1 Annual Training Report	6
2.2 Current Employment Profile and Needs Training	7
Section 3:	
3.1 Declaration by Employer	8
3.2 Confirmation	9
Appendix A: Contact Details for W&RSETA	10
Appendix B: Checklist for SDF and SETA	11

SECTION 1

1.1 SDF DETAILS

Please confirm your details to ensure that our database can be updated

Title _____   Surname _____

First Name _____   Initials _____

Gender   Male ☐   Population Group   African ☐   Disability Status ☐
(for statistical   *(for statistical*   *(for statistical*
purposes only) Female ☐   *purposes only)* Coloured ☐   *purposes only, please*
                                                                          tick if applicable)
                                          Indian/Asian ☐

                                                White ☐

Current Occupation _____

Cell Phone Number   Postal Address

_____   _____

Telephone Number (work)   _____

_____

Fax Number (work)   City & Province   Postal Code _____

_____   _____

E-mail Address _____

ID Number _____

(Compulsory – needed for verification purposes)

Acting in capacity of:

Company SDF   ☐

Independent SDF   ☐

1.2   COMPANY DETAILS

> **Please confirm your details to ensure that our database can be updated**

Company Name _____

Skills Development Levy (SDL) number _____

SIC Code _____

Annual Payroll   Above R500K [   ]   Below R500K [   ]

Physical Address

_____

_____

_____

City _____   Postal Code _____

Province _____

Telephone Number (work)   Fax Number (work)

_____   _____

Postal Address

_____

_____

City _____   Postal Code _____

1.3   COMPANY CONTACT PERSON (OTHER THAN SDF)

> **Please confirm your details to ensure that our database can be updated**

Title _____   Surname _____

First Name _____   Initials _____

Telephone Number (work) _____

Cell Number _____

Fax Number (work) _____

E-mail Address _____

1.4   CONFIRMATION OF BANKING DETAILS

Please confirm your details to ensure that our database can be updated.

Company Name _____

Address _____

_____

_____ Postal Code _____

Skills Development Levy (SDL) number _____

Details of Company/Entity bank account are as follows:

Name of Bank _____ Branch_____

Type of account *(please tick the applicable box)* ☐ Current   ☐ Savings

Branch Code _____   Account Number _____

Attach at least one of the following to confirm banking details

- Copy of cancelled cheque (preferable).
- A copy of an entity bank statement.
- See website for banking details criteria.

Please Note:

The Organisation's name, Bank account number, Branch code, etc. on the attached cancelled cheque, must be the same as the detail reflected in section above.

Payment instructions

To Whom It May Concern:

The Organisation hereby requests and authorises W&RSETA to pay any amounts, which may accrue to the credit of the Organisation's account with the mentioned bank. The Organisation understands that the credit transfers hereby authorised will be processed by computer through a system known as the "ACB ELECTRONIC TRANSFER SERVICES", and the Organisation also understands that an additional advice of payment will be printed on the Organisation's bank statement. The Organisation understands that a payment advice will be supplied via the Seta Management System (SMS) and which will indicate that funds are deposited into the Organisation's bank account.

Compiled by	Signature	Job Title	Date

Authorised by	Signature	Job Title	Date

Company/Entity Registration Number   Company/Entity VAT Registration Number

SECTION 2

2.1 ANNUAL TRAINING REPORT (1 APRIL 2006 – 31 MARCH 2007)

Please refer to SMME Grant Application Form 2006/2007 when completing this section. On this form only indicate the actual beneficiaries that received training in the financial year.

Occupational Group	African			Coloured			Indian/Asian			White			Training Completed
	M	F	D	M	F	D	M	F	D	M	F	D	
Senior Officials, Managers/Owner Managers													
Professionals													
Technicians & Associated Professionals													
Clerical and/or Administrative Workers													
Agricultural & Fishery Workers													
Service Workers													
Skilled Workers													
Plant/Machine Operators & Assemblers													
Labourers													
Casual/Temporary Workers													
Apprentices and Learnerships													
Total													

M – Male
F – Female
D – Person with disability

Disability definition: The Employment Equity Act of 1998 defines people with disabilities as 'people who have a long term or recurring physical or mental impairment that substantially limits their prospects of entry into or advancement in employment'. Physical impairments include hearing and visual impairments, paralysis, amputations and problems with internal organs. Mental impairment includes clinically defined mental and emotional illnesses and learning disabilities.

2.2 CURRENT EMPLOYMENT PROFILE AND TRAINING NEEDS (1 APRIL 2007 – 31 MARCH 2008)

Please indicate the number of people employed as per the table below and indicate planned training identified per occupational group.

Occupational Group	African			Coloured			Indian/Asian			White			Planned Training
	M	F	D	M	F	D	M	F	D	M	F	D	
Senior Officials, Managers/ Owner Managers													
Professionals													
Technicians & Associated Professionals													
Clerical and/or Administrative Workers													
Agricultural & Fishery Workers													
Service Workers													
Skilled Workers													
Plant/Machine Operators & Assemblers													
Labourers													
Casual/Temporary Workers													
Apprentices and Learnerships													
Total													

M – Male
F – Female
D – Person with disability

Disability definition: The Employment Equity Act of 1998 defines people with disabilities as 'people who have a long term or recurring physical or mental impairment that substantially limits their prospects of entry into or advancement in employment'. Physical impairments include hearing and visual impairments, paralysis, amputations and problems with internal organs. Mental impairment includes clinically defined mental and emotional illnesses and learning disabilities.

SECTION 3

3.1 DECLARATION BY EMPLOYER

This is to confirm that this organisation is up-to-date with levy payments to the Commissioner of the South African Revenue Services.

SARS
SDL Number

Name _____

Signature _____

Position in organisation _____   Date _____

Please Note:

It is a legal requirement that Grants may only be paid to organisations who are up-to-date with their Skills Development Levy Payments to SARS
(See Regulation No. 8627 Volume 500, 2 February 2007, 9(b) c)

3.2 CONFIRMATION (ATR 2006–2007 AND SMME GRANT APPLICATION 2007–2008)

SARS
SDL Number

Skills Development Facilitator

Name _____

Signature _____

Position in organisation _____

Date _____

Representative of Workforce (Duly elected by the Workforce)

Name _____

Signature _____

Position in organisation _____

Date _____

CEO/MD/HR Director

Name _____

Signature _____

Position in organisation _____

Date _____

Please Note:

- The above three signatures are a declaration by the organisation confirming the validity of the information in this document and the W&RSETA will not approve any grant payments to organisations without the original three signatures above.
- Please take note of the draft regulation (Regulation No. 8627, Volume 500, 2 February 2007, 9(b) e) whereby the SETA may require companies to complete a certain percentage of training in order to qualify for their Mandatory Grant. Pending the final Regulations as well as W&RSETA Board-approval, organisations will be informed and this requirement would then be effective on submission of the 2007/2008 ATR.

APPENDIX A - CONTACT DETAILS FOR W&rRSETA

It is important to note that the SETA will not be able to approve any Grant payments to organisations without the <u>original signed hard copies</u> of sections 1.4, 3.1 & 3.2

Please return the completed Workplace Skills Planning Grant to:

W&RSETA Head Office	Gauteng Office	Kwazulu Natal Office	Western Cape Office	Limpopo/Mpumalanga Office	Eastern Cape Office	Free State Office
PO Box 9809 Centurion 0046	PO Box 14780 Hatfield 0028	PO Box 18473 Dallbridge Durban, 4014	PO Box 13913 Mowbray 7705	PO Box 17717 Emalahleni 1035	Not yet available.	PO Box 1419 Bloemfontein 9300
W&RSETA House 224 Witch-Hazel Street, Highveld Techno Park Centurion	1267 Pretorius Street Hadefield Office Park Block B, Ground Floor Hatfield, Pretoria	Ground Floor Smart Xchange Building 5 Walnut Road Durban	Ground Floor Old Warehouse Building Black River Park Fir Road Observatory	64 Mandela Street Parkmed Building Office 202 Emalahleni 1035	Office No. 8 Malcomess Park Southernwood East London	Justitia Building Corner Aliwal and St Andrew Streets Bloemfontein 9300
Tel: (012) 676 9000 Fax: (012) 665 2559	Tel: (012) 430 4930 Fax: (012) 430 4935	Tel: (031) 333 8800 Fax: (031) 333 8815	Tel: (021) 442 6700 Fax: (021) 442 6777	Tel: (013) 690 1214 Fax: (013) 690 1190	Not yet available. Please contact H/O	Not yet available. Please contact H/O
skillsadmin@wrseta.org.za	wmkhombo@wrseta.org.za	bdlamini@wrseta.org.za	jedwards@wrseta.org.za	dnametsa@wrseta.org.za	joycem@wrseta.org.za	lmotshabi@wrseta.org.za

APPENDIX B – CHECKLIST FOR SDF AND SETA

Please note that the WSP / ATR should comply with the requirements below to qualify for approval and the subsequent payment of the Mandatory Grant to the company.

Section	Description	SDF Check √	SETA Check √
SDF Details	Name, ID.No. and Contact details must be completed.		
Company Details	All details to be completed.		
Company Contact Person	All details to be completed.		
Banking Details	If a cancelled cheque has been submitted previously and no changes have occurred it is not necessary to resubmit a cancelled cheque or to complete this section.		
Annual Training Report	Beneficiaries of training completed are recorded.		
Current Employment Profile & Training Needs	Total Permanent Staff complement of the organisation (Employees who fall under annual payroll) and Training Needs identified per Occupational Group.		
Declaration by Employer	Confirm that levy payments are up to date.		
Authorisation	All three signatures must be present.		

Appendix 4

National scarce skills by occupational categories, 2004-2009 (Department of Labour, 2004)

Main occupational category	Minor occupational category
Senior officials and management	Experienced and qualified managers: • Project managers • Sales and marketing managers • Financial managers • Business leadership • General managers • Entrepreneurship
Financial E-commerce specialists	Engineers, including: • Mining • Electronic project • Agriculture • Civil • Chemical • Design • Electrical • Nuclear • Mechanical • Clinical Financial specialists, including: • Chartered accountants • Financial/business analysts/ • Auditors consultants/advisers • Actuaries Researchers, including: • Marketing • Entrepreneurs • Surveyors
Technicians and associated professionals	• Insurance brokers • Buyers • Bookkeepers • Qualified ETD practitioners • Sales workers Technicians, including: • Clinical • Electrical • Phlebotomy • Electronic • Medical • Aircraft • Water • Mechanical • IT • Entrepreneurs
Clerks	• Debt collectors • Administrative clerks • Conveyance secretaries
Service/shop/market sales workers	• Qualified recruitment consultants • Sales personnel • Traffic officers • Fire fighters • Police officers
Skilled agricultural/ fishery workers	• Skilled horticultural workers • Maintenance personnel
Craft and related trade workers	• Electricians • Plumbers
Plant/machine operators	• Taxi drivers (code 10) • Plant operators • Machine operators

Glossary of terms

A

Ability: A basic capacity for performing a wide range of different tasks, acquiring knowledge or developing a skill.

Accelerated learning: An approach to training that relates to the process of creating and maintaining a psychologically positive learning state by enhancing people's self-esteem and encouraging confidence in their ability to learn and perform, thereby reducing mental barriers to learning and improving performance.

Accreditation: The certification, usually for a particular period of time, of an ETD provider as having the capacity to provide the particular training.

Action learning: A form of organisational and individual learning that is also cyclical and experiential in nature.

Adult learners: Employees who participate in ETD interventions and activities in an organisational context.

Affective outcome: A type of learning outcome that includes attitudes or beliefs that predispose a person to behave in a certain way.

Applied competence: The combination of a learner's foundational, practical and reflexive competence specified in outcomes-based learning programmes, skills programmes and qualifications.

Assessment: A structured process for obtaining evidence about a learner's competence to make a judgement of competence. Also, a process in which evidence is gathered and evaluated against agreed criteria to make a judgement of competence for developmental and/or recognition purposes.

Assessment activities: What a learner does or is involved in as a means of producing evidence, for example designing things, making things, repairing things, reporting on something, answering questions, solving problems, or demonstrating techniques.

Assessment criteria: Descriptions of the required type and quality of evidence against which learners are assessed. Assessment criteria indicate the evidence required to declare learners competent in each specific outcome. An assessor will assess learners' achievements against the assessment criteria and declare them competent or not yet competent.

Assessment design: The analysis of defined outcomes and criteria to produce a detailed description of how an assessment should take place, including all instructions and information regarding the assessment activities and assessment methods. The product of assessment design is an assessment guide.

Assessment evidence: The evidence collected from workplace performance, supplemented by other performance. This evidence is weighed up against the assessment criteria in the unit standard.

Assessment facilitator (also called evidence facilitator): A person who works within particular contexts, under supervision of registered assessors, to help learners gather, produce and organise evidence for assessment.

Assessment guide: A complete package based on a thorough analysis of specified outcomes and criteria, assessment requirements and a particular assessment context. Assessment guides are designed primarily for use by assessors to conduct an assessment (or possibly a series of related assessments) in terms of a significant and coherent outcome of learning, for example a unit standard or set of learning outcomes specified for a learning programme.

Assessment instruments: Those items that an assessor uses or a learner uses as part of the assessment, for example scenarios with questions, case studies, description of tasks to be performed, descriptions of role-play situations.

Assessment methods: Assessment methods relate to what an assessor does to gather and evaluate evidence. Assessment methods include observing learners, questioning learners, interviewing supervisors/colleagues/managers of learners, listening to learners, reviewing written material, testing products.

Assessment plan: A document compiled by an ETD practitioner/assessor that gives an overview of the time frames and responsibilities for assessment and moderation for the agreed delivery period.

Assessment process: The process of planning the assessment, preparing the learner for assessment, conducting the actual assessment, documenting the evidence, evaluating the evidence and making assessment judgements, providing feedback to the relevant parties and reviewing/evaluating the effectiveness of the assessment process.

Assessor: A qualified subject matter expert registered as an assessor who conducts the particular assessment.

Attitude: A mental state of readiness, organised through experience to behave in a characteristic way towards the object of the attitude.

Authentic assessment: The measurement of complex performances and higher-order thinking skills in real-life contexts. Authentic assessment requires learners to demonstrate complex tasks rather than individual skills practised in isolation.

Automaticity: Occurs when tasks can be performed with limited attention; likely to be developed when learners are given several extra learning opportunities even after they have demonstrated mastery of a task.

B

Behaviour: Activity directed at achieving something.

Behaviour modelling: Learning approach that consists of observing actual job incumbents that demonstrate positive modelling behaviours, rehearsing the behaviour using role-playing techniques, receiving feedback on the rehearsal, and finally trying out the behaviour on the job.

Behaviourist perspective: Approach developed by B.F. Skinner that places the emphasis for behaviour and directed activity on the environment rather than on any internal needs or instincts.

Belief: A conviction that something is true.

Bottom-line measure: Evaluation of a learning programme by determining if the organisation actually saved money or earned more money as a result of the training.

Business impact: a method of evaluating the effectiveness of training by determining whether the objectives and outcomes of the learning programme or ETD intervention were met.

C

Case study: A training technique in which employees usually in a group, are presented with a real or hypothetical workplace problem and are asked to propose the best solution.

Certification: On successful completion of a learning programme, skills programme or learnership, the learner is awarded a qualification in the form of a certificate, issued by the relevant ETQA.

Classroom climate: The shared perception of learners about the classroom environment, that is, how they think and feel they are being treated by the teacher. The classroom climate can range from a warm, welcoming and nurturing atmosphere to one that is characterised by coldness and indifference as evident in the behaviour displayed by the trainer.

Classroom environment: The conditions, circumstances, and influences surrounding and affecting the development and performance of learners. These include, for example, the physical conditions of the classroom, the trainer's physical appearance, body language, language patterns, behaviour and attitudes towards learners.

Classroom training: Training method in which the ETD practitioner/learning facilitator communicates through spoken words, audiovisual materials and group activities; also commonly used to efficiently present a large amount of information to learners.

Coaching: An approach to training referring to a one-to-one relationship between a manager and individual employee with the aim of developing or enhancing the employee's on-the-job performance.

Cognitive approaches: Cognitive theories that focus on how individuals process and interpret information.

Competencies: Typical behaviours (which include attitudes and beliefs, knowledge and skills) that individuals demonstrate when undertaking job-relevant tasks to produce job-related outcomes within a given organisational context. Competencies relate to specific descriptions of work tasks or job outputs that have to be achieved to demonstrate satisfactory job performance.

Compliance evaluation: A form of ETD evaluation that emphasises the organisation's compliance with international and national quality standards for outcomes-based ETD practices. Also known as a quality audit or evaluation.

Continued professional development: The further and ongoing ETD activities that a professional engages in to retain the level of expertise necessary for him or her to remain abreast of the development in the profession and to function at the level at which he or she is registered with a professional body.

Course: The content of the short learning programme whereby learners may progressively attain the applied knowledge, skills, and values described in the learning outcomes of the programme, and/or unit standards, and/or qualifications.

Credits: The credit value on a unit standard that indicates the notional hours or amount of time a learner will need to complete the learning programme. One credit equals 10 notional hours.

Criteria: The standards used to measure performance.

Criterion-referenced assessment: An assessment approach that focuses on assessing learners' achievements against a set of external criteria.

Critical cross-field outcomes: A set of 12 national outcomes recognised as the basis for the design of learning programmes, curricula and qualifications. These learning outcomes are relevant throughout life, not simply in employment and further learning.

Curriculum: The learning programme strategy or broad plan of action for achieving the learning programme objective (or unit standard's and qualification's purpose and outcomes) by enabling learners to master the programme's learning outcomes.

Curriculum strategy: A written description of the prescribed content (or embedded knowledge as described in the unit standard), the formative assessment activities, required learning support material and learning programme delivery strategy.

D

Data: A collection of information, often in the form of numerical measures of a group of people. Also sometimes used to refer to other kinds of raw material used in research such as a collection of texts or images.

Data collection tools: Instruments such as survey questionnaires, interviews, focus groups and organisational records, used to collect data from the respondents (learners/stakeholders) to measure the effectiveness and efficiency of a programme.

Development: A long-term change effort intended to broaden individuals through experience and to give them new insights about themselves and their organisation in a way that supports them in fulfilling their potential.

Diagnostic assessment: Testing of a learner's pre-knowledge, pre-skills, pre-attitudes/values before attending a learning programme.

Diagnostic evaluation: A form of ETD evaluation relevant to evaluating the effectiveness of the planning and design of a learning programme.

Distributed practice: An approach to training that gives learners rest intervals between practice sessions, which are spaced over a longer period of time.

E

Education: An intermediate-term change effort intended to prepare individuals for promotions (vertical career progression) or for enhanced technical abilities in their current jobs (horizontal career progression). Education is broader in scope than training and aims to develop individuals' knowledge, social understanding and skill and intellectual capacity.

Embedded knowledge: The knowledge learners need to know in order to show competence and achievement in the unit standard. Also, the knowledge learners will gain from the start to the end of the learning programme.

Emotional intelligence: An approach to intelligence which describes it in terms of the ability to perceive, to integrate, to understand and reflectively manage one's own and other people's feelings.

Employability: People's ability to gain access to, adjust to, and be productive in the workplace. Also, the set of traits and competencies that permit a person to meet the demands of the 21st century workplace.

ETD competency profile: A written description of the set of behaviours, knowledge, skills, values and attitudes instrumental to the delivery of desired ETD results or outcomes.

ETD evaluation: A set of planned, information-gathering and analytical activities undertaken by ETD practitioners to provide those responsible for the management of the strategic HRD effort with a satisfactory assessment of the effects, progress, quality and added value of ETD interventions.

ETD management: The ongoing managerial process of enhancing the ETD function's ability to ensure that its ETD practices, processes, services and products contribute to the overall HRD strategy and business results along with adding value for stakeholders.

ETD needs analysis: The systematic collection and evaluation of information to find out where there are gaps in the existing competence levels, skills, knowledge and attitudes of employees.

ETD practitioner: A competent, professionally qualified person that demonstrates the ability to perform a specific or relevant role in educating, training and developing learners within the context of an outcomes-based ETD system.

ETD provider: The place where theoretical knowledge and skills are obtained. ETD providers are organisations or individuals who provide learning (education, training and development) programmes, and include universities, universities of technology, private providers or organisations' in-house training facilities. In terms of the SAQA Act, ETD providers are bodies that deliver and manage the assessment of learning programmes, which culminate in specialised NQF standards or qualifications. An ETQA may accredit a provider that meets the specified criteria when an application is received.

ETD value proposition: A written description stating the proposed results and value that ETD practices, products and services intend to deliver to stakeholders. This usually includes a description of how the learning programme design, delivery and outcomes will add value for stakeholders and measurably contribute to business results.

Ethics: An individual's moral beliefs about what is right and wrong, or good and bad, providing a guide to his/her behaviour.

Ethical behaviour: Behaviour that is regarded as right and good in relation to behaviour in an organisational or professional context.

Ethical dilemmas: Situations that have the potential to result in a breach of acceptable behaviour.

ETQA: The national moderating bodies which monitor and audit learners' achievements in terms of national quality standards, unit standards and qualifications. Moderating bodies are those appointed to ensure that the process of assessment of outcomes described in the NQF standards and qualifications is fair, reliable and valid. An ETQA may not be a provider – its primary function is to assure the quality and assessment of registered standards and qualifications.

Evaluation: The process of determining the monetary worth of ETD interventions and making judgements about their compliance with quality standards and best practices. Also, the systematic collection of descriptive and judgemental information necessary to make effective decisions related to the selection, adoption, value and modification of various ETD activities.

Evaluation criteria: An approach to ETD evaluation which classifies the purpose of evaluation into broad categories or dimensions. Each of these dimensions has a number of criteria according to different evaluation levels, which are the standards or rules by which the dimensions can be judged (for example learning programme design, delivery, transfer of learning, impact, value-added, quality standards).

Evaluation dimensions: An approach to ETD evaluation which classifies the purpose of evaluation into broad categories or dimensions.

Evaluation levels: Levels of sophistication in evaluating the value added by training. As the degree of sophistication goes up, the value tends to increase with it (for example reaction, learning, job behaviour change, value-added impact, return on investment).

Evaluation models: Theoretical frameworks which indicate the practical utility of evaluation levels in determining the ETD evaluation dimensions and criteria to be measured.

Evaluation process: The steps involved in a formal, professionally carried-out evaluation of ETD interventions conducted in a planned and systematic manner, using valid and reliable data collection tools and methodology.

Evaluation sponsor: The person(s), group, or organisation that requests or requires the evaluation and provides the resources to conduct it.

Evaluative assessment: A post-assessment activity integrated in the overall assessment process to ensure the quality of the process.

Evaluative expertise: The ability to judge the quality of a performance in relation to specified criteria consistently, reliably and with insight. Evaluative expertise implies deep subject matter understanding and knowledge about the outcomes being assessed at a theoretical and practical level, but does not necessarily include practical ability in the outcome.

Evaluator: The person responsible for conducting evaluations in the organisation. In most instances this person is not a full-time evaluator, but rather has part-time evaluation responsibilities.

Evidence: Tangible proof produced by or about learners that can be perceived with the senses, bearing a direct relationship to defined learning outcomes and performance criteria, based on which judgements are made concerning the competence of learners. Evidence includes, for example, plans, reports, answers to questions, products, testimonials, certificates, descriptions of observed performances, peer review reports. This evidence is weighed up by an assessor against the assessment criteria in the unit standard to evaluate whether a learner has achieved the learning outcomes of a learning programme.

Experience: Direct participation in, or observation of events and activities that serve as a basis for knowledge.

Experiential learning: An approach to training that sees learning as a cyclical, dynamic and continuous process. It also underscores learning as an active process in which learners are not passive recipients of training but actively seek out opportunities to apply their behaviour in new situations.

Explicit knowledge: Knowledge which is quantifiable and hence easily transferred and reproduced.

Explicit learning: Learning that requires conscious and deliberate thought and effort such as memorising, problem solving and understanding.

F

Facilitation: The skill of interacting with learners to draw out their ideas and lead them to new ideas and understandings with the aim to help them achieve learning goals and outcomes. See also: learning facilitation

Facilitator/trainer guide: A complete package containing written descriptions of the learning programme strategy, the learning facilitation process and quality assurance aspects related to the programme design and delivery.

Feedback: Providing employees/learners with specific information about how well they are performing a task or series of tasks. Also, evaluative or corrective information transmitted to employees/learners about their attempts to achieve learning tasks and improve their job and/or learning performance.

Fidelity: The extent to which the task trained is similar to the task required on the job. It is important that training tasks have fidelity so that extra time and expense of overlearning in training can directly benefit performance on the job.

Formal learning: Learning experiences that occur in the context of formally organised learning programmes; can include classroom training or workplace training.

Formative assessment: The ongoing assessment that takes place throughout a period of learning and teaching. It provides the learner with opportunities to practise what has been learnt, with the intention of improving performance in the next assessment. These assessments are conducted to measure the rate of progress and performance toward achieving competence in an outcome or outcomes. Formative assessments help to make decisions on the readiness of the learner to do a summative assessment.

Formative evaluation: A form of ETD evaluation relevant to evaluating the effectiveness of the delivery phase of a learning programme for the purpose of guiding programme improvement.

Foundational competence: Learners' understanding of and demonstration of insight regarding the knowledge and thinking that underpins the actions taken.

G

Generational diversity: Important differences in values, aspirations, preferences and beliefs that characterise the silent generation, the baby boomers, Generation Xers and Millennials.

Gross Domestic Product: The total value of the country's annual output of goods and services.

H

Human capital approach: A recognition that the contribution made by human skills and knowledge to the production of goods and/or services is a vital ingredient of organisational success.

Human resource development (HRD): Organised learning experiences provided by employers within a specified period of time to bring about the possibility of performance improvement, personal growth and enhancement of employees' employability orientation in order to satisfy the current and future needs of the organisation.

Humanist perspective: An approach to adult learning which proposes that knowledge is a personal, subjective issue, not an external commodity waiting to be internalised through the absorption of content. A basic tenet is that individuals have a natural aptitude for learning and have control over their own learning processes and outcomes.

I

Implicit learning: The implicit knowledge that people use daily in most of what they do, but that they cannot describe.

Informal learning: Learning experiences that occur outside of formal learning programmes; can include specific job assignments, experiences and activities outside work.

Integrated assessment: A form of assessment which combines diagnostic, formative, summative and evaluative assessment in assessing learners' ability to combine key foundational, practical and reflexive competencies with some critical cross-field outcomes and apply these in a practical context or a defined purpose.

Intelligence: The ability to learn and adapt to an environment; often refers to general intellectual capacity, as opposed to cognitive or mental ability which often refers to more specific abilities such as memory or reasoning.

J

Job profile: A written summary of task, behaviour and competence requirements for a particular job.

K

Knowledge: An outcome of learning which refers to information, facts, opinions, theory arguments, concepts, and their interrelationship relevant to the required outcome, which an individual can demonstrate in the workplace. Also, the cognitive outcome of a learning programme which relates to the way in which people process information and attach sense and meaning to it.

Knowledge management: A process or practice of creating, acquiring, capturing, sharing or using knowledge to enhance learning and performance in the organisation.

Knowledge test: A test that measures the level of an employee's knowledge about a job-related topic or a test that measures the level of a learner's knowledge about a topic/subject.

L

Leading: Directing and coordinating task-relevant group activities.

Learner: Anyone who wants to gain a qualification or credits toward a qualification may apply for an existing learnership, qualification, skills or learning programme. An individual who is being assessed by an assessor, participates in a learning or skills programme, or ETD intervention.

Learner-centred approach: An approach to training that regards the learner as an active participant in the learning facilitation process. It therefore takes into consideration learners' characteristics, levels of competence and life worlds in the design and delivery of learning programmes.

Learner-centred delivery methods: An approach to training delivery whereby the trainer and learners have an interdependent relationship: both share experiences and information. The trainer fulfils the role of learning facilitator and learners take ownership of their learning as active participants in the learning process.

Learner profile: Written statements describing learners' characteristics, levels of competence, demographics, ETD needs and motivation for attending a learning programme.

Learnership: A structured learning programme that leads to a nationally recognised qualification on the NQF. It is an integrated, occupation-directed programme that combines learning at a training institution with practical, on-site experience and learning.

Learnership agreement: A legally binding document that must be signed by the employer, the ETD provider and the learner. The agreement outlines the rights and duties of the various parties and also specifies the termination date of the learnership, which is formally registered with the Department of Labour.

Learning: A relatively permanent change in behaviour or potential behaviour that results from the acquisition of knowledge and facts through study, being taught and experience.

Learning activities: The means ETD practitioners use to expose learners to the knowledge, skills, attitudes and behaviour they will need to master the learning outcomes. Also, what learners do or are involved in as a means to master new competencies.

Learning assumed to be in place: The learning assumed to be in place is the knowledge and skills that the learner is expected to have before starting the learning programme.

Learning content: The material that is to be learnt by the learners, together with the different ways in which the learning facilitator will convey it to the learners.

Learning facilitation: A learner-centred approach to training in which roadblocks to successful performance of learners are eliminated, adequate resources to enable the achievement of learning outcomes are provided and careful attention is paid to the needs and motivation of learners. See also: facilitation

Learning organisation: An organisation in which continuous learning, knowledge sharing and mastery orientation are emphasised.

Learning outcomes: The learning results learners have to demonstrate at the end of each learning and assessment activity.

Learning programme: A single course or combination of courses, modules or units of learning (learning materials combined with methodology) by which learners can achieve agreed learning outcomes spelt out in unit standards or qualifications. Also, the plan for implementing the curriculum (the specifics regarding the what, the when and the how of learning and assessment activities) which lead to learners' achievement of the programme's learning outcomes and/or the unit standard's and qualification's purpose and outcomes.

Learning programme objectives: The overall intention or purpose of the learning programme.

Learning programme delivery strategy: A written description of the learning facilitation mode (contact or distance learning for example), training methods, learning material, media, resources and equipment that will be used in the facilitation of the learning programme.

Learning programme strategy: A broad plan of action for curriculum design, learning and assessment activities, training methods and learning support materials per learning outcome, with a view to help learners achieve the learning outcomes and overall objective of the learning programme.

Learning styles: Learners' preferred way of learning.

Learning support materials: A complete package of learning resources designed to enable the achievement of learning outcomes (for example, learner manuals, handouts, books, PowerPoint slides, posters).

Lecture: An informative talk given before an audience or group of learners.

Level descriptors: Level descriptors define the level of complexity of a unit standard or learning programme and the level of achievement expected from an individual at each of the NQF levels.

Levy grants: If the employer meets certain conditions, like producing a workplace skills plan, the SETA will pay a certain percentage of the levy back to the employer in the form of a grant. See also: Skills Development Levies Act

Longitudinal evaluation: A form of ETD evaluation relevant to evaluating the effectiveness of the learning programme as a whole some time after its completion – three months, six months to a year (including its compliance with SAQA quality standards and long-term value added to the company's bottom line).

M

Massed practice: Conditions in which individuals practise a task continuously and without rest.

Mastery orientation: An orientation in which individuals are concerned with increasing their competence for the task at hand; they view errors and mistakes as part of the learning process.

Measurement: Assigning numbers to objects in a rule-like manner to represent quantities of an attribute that the object possesses.

Media: Means of communication to facilitate learning (for example, paper, DVDs, video, audiotapes, CD-ROMs, computers, overhead projectors, data projectors).

Mentoring: A learning facilitation approach focusing on providing support, advice and friendship to a younger, less experienced person.

Mode: The style or manner of learning facilitation or delivery (for example, learner-centred, classroom training, distance education).

Moderation: The process of monitoring and verifying assessment practices comply with quality requirements and that assessment decisions are consistently accurate. Also, the process that supports and evaluates the assessment environment, process and instruments (with a view to confirm the reliability and authenticity of assessment results and improving the quality of assessments and assessors).

Module: A self-contained unit of learning within a learning programme with its own set of learning outcomes and the learning and assessment activities that are linked to these.

N

National Qualifications Framework (NQF): The framework or set of principles and guidelines that provide a national vision and structure for the construction of a qualifications system.

National Skills Development Strategy: The national strategy for developing and uplifting the skills of the South African workforce by utilising the workplace as an active learning environment, promoting self-employment, and securing work opportunities for new entrants into the labour market through legislative and other initiatives.

National Standards Bodies (NSBs): The national bodies responsible for making sure that all standards and qualifications fit into the NQF levels in the 12 learning fields and keeping qualifications and unit standards up to date.

Needs analysis: See ETD needs analysis.

Notional hours: The amount of time a learner will need to complete the learning programme. See also: Credits

Norm-referenced assessment: An assessment approach that focuses on comparing a learner's performance with the performance of other learners.

O

Objective: Specific, short-term statements of results that should be achieved.

On-the-job training: Training that involves assigning learners to jobs and encouraging them to observe and learn from more experienced employees.

Organisational capability: The identity and reputation of the organisation characterised by its capacity to use resources, get things done, and behave in ways that accomplish goals in a competitive business environment.

Organisational needs analysis: See skills audit.

Organisational sustainability: The capability of the organisation to meet the needs of the present and achieving success today without compromising the ability of future generations to meet their own needs

Organising: Planning and arranging activities, people and resources in an orderly way.

Outcomes: An inclusive term, referring to everything that is learnt, including social and personal skills, the activities of learning how to learn, understanding concepts, acquiring knowledge, understanding methodologies, values and attitudes.

Outcomes-based assessment: Also known as authentic assessment, which concerns the measurement of complex performances and higher-order thinking skills in real-life contexts in relation to predetermined learning outcomes and performance criteria for various purposes, including further development and recognition of learning achievements.

Outcomes-based education and training (OBET): An ETD approach that focuses on what the learners need to achieve at the end of the learning process.

Overlearning: Practising a task even after it has been mastered to retain learning.

P

Part learning: Learning which occurs when subtasks are practised separately and later combined.

Performance: The demonstration of skills, knowledge, understanding and attitudes, and the ability to transfer these to new situations.

Performance appraisal: A review of the job-relevant strengths and weaknesses of an individual or a team in an organisation.

Performance orientation: An orientation in which individuals are concerned about doing well in training (achieving the learning outcomes) and being evaluated positively (being assessed as competent).

Person analysis: The process of identifying the employees who need training and determining the areas in which each individual needs to be trained.

Personal development plan: A written statement of the employee's knowledge and skills that must be developed, as well as how and when these will be developed and the person who will be responsible for ensuring that the development is implemented.

Physical fidelity: The extent to which the training task mirrors the physical features of the actual task.

Physical learning environment: The physical layout of the venue arranged to suit the various outcomes of the learning programme.

Portfolio of evidence: A carefully organised folder compiled by a learner (as candidate for assessment) that contains samples of the learner's work that serve as evidence of ability to demonstrate the competencies stipulated in the learning outcomes.

Portfolios provide evidence of a learner's knowledge, skills, attitudes and academic development that affords the ETD practitioner/assessor opportunities for formative and summative assessment.

Post-test: A measure of job performance or knowledge taken after a learning programme has been completed.

Practical competence: A learner's ability to consider a range of practical possibilities for action and make a decision about which to follow (also the ability to apply the newly acquired skills in the workplace or real-life situations).

Pre-test: A measure of job performance or knowledge taken before the implementation of a learning programme.

Procedural knowledge: Knowing how to perform a job or task; often developed through practice and experience.

Process guide: A written outline of the learning facilitation strategy which generally describes how the learning facilitator plans to present, manage and monitor the learning process and environment so that learners can be effectively and productively engaged in learning.

Programmed instruction: A training method in which learners learn information at their own pace.

Psychological fidelity: The extent to which the training task helps learners to develop the competencies (attitudes, knowledge, skills, abilities) and other characteristics that are necessary to perform the job.

Psychomotor abilities: The physical functions of movement, associated with coordination, dexterity and reaction time.

Q

Qualification: A planned combination of learning outcomes with a defined purpose or purposes, and which is intended to provide learners with applied competence and a basis for further learning. National qualifications are made up of unit standards or learning outcomes. A qualification consists of a cluster of unit standards. Learners can use unit standards in various qualifications depending on their applicability and rules of combination as defined by SAQA. A qualification is made up of a minimum of 120 credits.

Quality assurance: The process of ensuring that the degree of excellence specified is achieved. The national unit standards and regulation requirements specify these degrees of excellence.

Quality audit: See compliance evaluation.

Quality management: All activities of the overall management function that determine the quality policy, objectives, strategies, responsibilities and implementation of these by means of a combination of managerial processes.

R

Range statement: A guide to users of a unit standard that states the scope, context and level for the unit standard. It also describes the situations and circumstances in which the learner is expected to perform.

Recognition of prior learning (RPL): The comparison of the previous learning and experience of a learner against specified learning outcomes for the award of credits for a specified unit standard or qualification; access to further learning; recognition in terms of meeting minimum requirements for a specific job; placement at a particular level in an organisation; or advanced standing or status.

Reflexive competence: A learner's ability to integrate the acquired foundational and practical competencies with understanding and with an ability to adapt to change in unforeseen circumstances. Also, a learner's ability to reflect on his/her learning or performance and the ability to transfer the newly acquired competencies to different social and workplace contexts.

Reinforcement techniques: Training techniques that reward behaviour with the intent to motivate learners to repeat the behaviour.

Reliability: The extent to which scores obtained on a measure are reproducible in repeated administrations under similar measurement conditions

Results criteria: Measures of how well training outcomes can be related to organisational outcomes such as productivity gains, cost savings, error reductions or increased customer/stakeholder satisfaction.

Return on investment (ROI): The amount of money an organisation makes after subtracting the cost of training or other ETD and organisational interventions.

RPL assessment: The process of identifying a learner's knowledge and skills or what the learner knows and can do; matching a learner's skills, knowledge and experience to standards and the associated assessment criteria of a qualification; assessing a learner against these standards; and crediting a learner for skills, knowledge and experience built up through formal, informal and non-formal learning that occurred in the past.

S

SAQA: The statutory body responsible for overseeing the setting of standards and the auditing of the quality of education and training. The tasks of SAQA are to register qualifications and standards on the NQF; and to ensure that the education and training that is delivered helps learners to reach these qualifications and standards.

Sectoral needs analysis: The process of identifying key skills shortages and the assessment of the relative importance of the identified shortages to the sector as they relate to the national skills plan and strategy.

Sectoral skills plan: A plan which includes a profile (description) of a specific sector, including current education and training happening within the sector, factors affecting future changes, the employment and skills needs in the sector, a future vision, strategies to address the skills needs, success measures, resources required to achieve targets and methods for monitoring, reporting and evaluating progress.

Self-directed learning: A desire to set one's own pace, establish one's own structure, and keep open the option to revise a learning strategy

SETA: A body established under the Skills Development Act. Its main purpose is to establish and promote learnerships/skills programmes/learning programmes, approve workplace skills plans, allocate grants and monitor the quality of education and training in the sector.

Short course: A type of short learning programme through which a learner may or may not be awarded credits, depending on the purpose of the programme.

Short learning programme (also called short course): A series of structured learning activities or events that are intended to equip learners with the applied competence needed to fulfil a particular occupational role. Short learning programmes can either be based on unit standards, parts of unit standards or no unit standard. Learning programmes based on unit standards or parts of unit standards are credit bearing, implying learners' achievements/performance are assessed against the learning outcomes and associated assessment criteria.

Skills: Those aspects of behaviour that need to be performed to an acceptable level to ensure effective job performance. Also, proficiency to perform a particular task.

Skills audit: The process of analysing ETD needs at the organisational level with the aim to identify critical and scarce skills, and comparing these to the skills required by the organisation now and in the future so that the shortfall or surplus of key skills can be determined and addressed.

Skills development committee: The group of people representative of the various departments in the company that is involved in discussions around the workplace skills plan and the ETD plan and/or strategy.

Skills development facilitator: The person who advises and helps plan skills development for a workplace.

Skills Development Levies Act: The Skills Development Levies Act describes how money will be collected through levies paid by employers.

Skills programme: An occupation-based learning programme provided by an accredited ETD provider and, when completed, will constitute a credit towards a qualification registered on the NQF in terms of the Skills Development Act.

Skills upliftment: The enhancement of employees' applied competence in their jobs by improving their knowledge, skills, abilities and attitudes through formal education, skills training and continuous development initiatives.

Social learning theory: A cognitive theory that proposes that there are many ways to learn.

Specific outcomes: See unit standard specific outcomes.

Stakeholders: Those individuals, groups, or organisations that have a significant interest in how well a learning programme or ETD intervention functions.

Strategising: Planning, designing or mapping out activities to achieve aims, goals or objectives.

Summative assessment: A form of assessment usually conducted at the end of a learning programme. It is the final measure of what was learnt. Summative assessments should include formative assessment evaluations and a final overall assessment of whether learners have achieved the specified learning outcomes for the overall programme.

Summative evaluation: A form of ETD evaluation relevant to evaluating the effectiveness of the learning programme as a whole at its completion (including the achievement of objectives and outcomes, compliance with SAQA quality standards and value added to the company's bottom line).

T

Tacit knowledge: Knowledge concerned with understanding and application. Tacit knowledge is often combined with experience and interpretation and is therefore more difficult to harness and reproduce.

Talent pool: The existing human resources in a company whose specialist skills, expertise, experience, abilities and potential have been identified as a scarce and critical resource in helping the organisation sustain its capability and competitive edge.

Task analysis: The process which involves examining what employees must do to perform the job properly and helps to determine the content of a learning programme.

Trainer-centred delivery methods: An approach to training delivery whereby the trainer is regarded as an instructor and presenter who is responsible and accountable for what learners should learn, how and when they should learn it and if they have learned.

Training: A planned short-term change effort intended to modify competencies, attitudes and beliefs, knowledge or skill behaviour through learning experiences (such as formal learning programmes) to sustain employees' employability by helping them to achieve effective performance in an activity or range of activities.

Training cycle: The reiterative, scientific and systematic process of determining learners' training needs; designing learning programmes and materials; delivering training; assessing and moderating learners' achievements; and evaluating the effectiveness of learning programmes for continuous improvement initiatives.

Training delivery: A structured process characterised by an individual acting as a learning facilitator in accelerating and structuring learning through well-designed formal delivery methods.

Training methods: The techniques, methodology or approach ETD practitioners use to facilitate learning or deliver a learning programme.

Training needs analysis: See ETD needs analysis.

U

Unit standard: A registered statement of desired education and training outcomes and their associated assessment criteria, together with administrative and other information as specified by SAQA regulations. It describes the scope and context within which the learner's competence is assessed. The results, not the processes, of the learning are described in unit standards. Also the smallest independent part of a qualification that bears credits.

Unit standard field and sub-field: Indicate to which learning field and sub-field the unit standard is allocated.

Unit standard issue date: The date indicates the registration date of the unit standard by SAQA.

Unit standard level: Indicates the level of complexity required to achieve the unit standard as per the NQF levels.

Unit standard purpose: Describes the general skills a learner will have acquired upon completion of a learning programme based on the unit standard; states also for whom the unit standard is intended and the reasons for writing the unit standard.

Unit standard review date: Unit standards have a life span of three years. This date indicates when the unit standard will be up for review again.

Unit standard specific outcomes: Specific outcomes are competence outcomes that focus on learning and performance. They capture a specific skill, knowledge and attitude that a learner must demonstrate in the unit standard. These are outcomes that the learner works toward.

V

Validity: The extent to which the measuring instrument reflects the concept it is intended to measure.

Value-added evaluation: A form of ETD evaluation that addresses the organisation's bottom line and is conducted to measure the cost-effectiveness of ETD interventions.

Value-added measurement: The measurement and evaluation of changes in the ETD processes, outcomes (results) and their resulting value (impact) on the company's bottom-line.

W

Whole-brain learning: See accelerated learning.

Whole learning: Learning which occurs when the entire task is practised at once.

Workplace: The place of employment where workplace experience, training and development take place.

Workplace skills plan: A plan which supports the sector skills plan and company strategic HRD plan by describing what skills are needed by whom in the relevant workplace, how they will get the skills (ETD strategies), and how much it will cost.

References

Aamodt, M.G. (2007). *Industrial and Organisational Psychology.* London: Thomson.

Alliger, G.M., Tannenbaum, S.I., Bennett, W., Traver, H. & Shotland, A. (1997). A meta-analysis of the relations among training criteria. *Personnel Psychology 50*, 341-358.

Ashkanasy, N.M. & Daus, C.S. (2005). Rumors of the death of emotional intelligence in organizational behavior are vastly exaggerated. *Journal of Organizational Behavior*, 26: 441-452.

ASTD. (2006). *Bridging the skills gap.* Alexandria: ASTD Press.

ASTD. (2007). Trends in the latest state of HR & Training Industry report in S.A. *Newsletter*, March, 1.

Baruch, Y. (2004). *Managing careers: Theory and practice.* London: Prentice Hall.

Bash, L. (2003). *Adult learners in the academy.* Bolton, MA: Anker Publishing.

Bell, B.S. & Kozlowski, S.W.J. (2002). Adaptive guidance: Enhancing self-regulation, knowledge and performance in technology-based training. *Personnel Psychology*, 55, 267-306.

Bellis, I. (2001). *Skills Development – A practitioner's guide to SAQA, the NQF and the Skills Development Acts.* Knowres: Johannesburg.

Bennis, W. & Mische, M. (1995). *The 21st century organization: Reinventing through reengineering.* San Diego, CA: Pfeiffer.

Birkinshaw, J. (2000). Network relationships inside and outside the firm, and the development of capabilities. In J. Birkinshaw & P. Hagstrom (Eds.), *The flexible firm* (pp 3-17). Oxford: Oxford University Press.

Blanchard, P.N. & Thacker, J.W. (2004). *Effective training. Systems, strategies and practices.* Upper Saddle, River, NJ: Pearson Prentice Hall.

Blanchard, P.N. & Thacker, J.W. (2007). *Effective training: Systems. Strategies, and practices (3rd ed.).* Upper Saddle River: Pearson Prentice Hall.

Blanpain, R. (1997). Work in the 21st century. *Industrial Law Journal*, 18(2), 185-213.

Block, P. (2000). *Flawless consulting (2nd ed).* San Francisco: Jossey-Bass/Pfeiffer.

Brethower, K.S. & Springer, J. (1992). Exploring human possibilities. In H.D. Stolovitch & E.J. Keeps (Eds.). *Handbook of human performance technology* (pp 715-731). San Francisco: Jossey-Bass.

Brown, J. (2002). Training needs assessment: a must for developing an effective training programme. *Public personnel management*, 31(4), 569-578.

Buckingham, M. (1999). Clone free zone. *People Management*, 5(19), 592-595.

Buckley, R. & Caple, J. (2004). *The theory and practice of training (5th ed.).* London: Kogan Page.

Byars, L.L. & Rue, L.W. (2004). *Human resource management.* New York: McGraw-Hill.

Cameron, E. (1998). *Facilitation made easy.* London: Kogan Page.

Camp, R.R., Blanchard, P.N. & Huszczo, G.E. (1986). *Toward a more organizationally effective training strategy and practice.* Englewood Cliffs, NJ: Prentice-Hall.

Carnetti, D. (1995). *Identifying, developing and implementing key business management competencies in a change environment following a merger.* Paper presented at the 27th Annual Human Resource Management Conference, London, 11-12 April, organized by Management Center Europe.

Cascio, W.F. (2003). *Managing human resources.* New York: McGraw-Hill.

Cascio, W.F. & Aguinis, H. (2005). *Applied psychology in human resource management.* Upper Saddle River, NJ.: Pearson/Prentice Hall.

Cassidy, M.F. & Cassidy, M.M. (2006). Principles and practice of work-group performance. In J.A. Pershing. *Handbook of human performance technology: Principles, practices, and potential.* (3rd ed.). San Francisco: Pfeiffer.

Castley, R.J.O. (1996). The sectoral approach to the assessment of skills needs and training requirements, *International Journal of Manpower*, 17(1), 56-68.

Chang, R.Y. (1994). *Creating high-impact training.* London: Kogan Page Limited.

CIPD. (2007). *Identifying learning and training needs.* Retrieved from the World Wide Web on 16 March 2007, http://www.cipd.co.uk

Clement, F.J. (1992). Accelerated learning systems. In H.D. Stolovitch & E.J. Keeps (Eds.). *Handbook of human performance technology* (pp 528-548). San Francisco: Jossey-Bass.

Codrington, G. & Grant-Marshall, S. (2004). *Mind the gap!* Cape Town: Penguin Books.

Coetzee, M. (2004). *Empowering the skills development facilitator.* Randburg; Knowres.

Coetzee, M (2004). *Planning quality outcomes-based learning programmes.* Johannesburg: Knowres.

Coetzee, M. & Stone, K. (2004). *Learner support: Toward learning and development.* Randburg; Knowres.

Coetzee, M. (2006). *Short course in Skills Development Facilitation.* Pretoria: University of South Africa.

Coetzee, M. (2006a). *Handout notes on outcomes-based training design*: Masters workshop session. University of South Africa, Pretoria.

Coetzee, M. (2007). *Getting and keeping your accreditation: The quality assurance and assessment guide for education, training and development practitioners (2nd edition)*. Cape Town: Van Schaik.

Coetzee, M. (2007a). *Handout notes on outcomes-based learning facilitation*. University of South Africa, Pretoria.

Coetzee, M. & Jansen, C.A. (2007). *Emotional intelligence in the classroom: The secret of happy teachers*. Cape Town: Juta.

Coetzee, M. & Jansen, C.A. (2007a). Unpublished *Emotional intelligence in the classroom: Train the Teacher Manual*. Pretoria: University of South Africa.

Coetzee, M. & Roythorne-Jacobs, H. (2007). *Career counselling and guidance in the workplace: A manual for career practitioners*. Cape Town: Juta.

Coleman, M.E. (1992). Developing skills and enhancing professional competence. In H.D. stolovitch & E.J. Keeps (Eds.). *Handbook of human performance technology* (pp 634-648). San Francisco: Jossey-Bass.

Cook, S. (1994). *Training for empowerment*. Gower: Aldershot.

Cranton, P. (2006). *Understanding and promoting transformative learning: A guide for educators of adults. Second edition*. 2006. San Francisco, CA: John Wiley & Sons.

Daniels, G. (2002). The great skills grab, in the Supplement "Skills for Africa": *Mail & Guardian*, 18(37), 20–26 September: 1

Department of Education. (July, 24, 1997). *A programme for the transformation of Higher Education*. Pretoria. Retrieved June 23, 1999 from the World-Wide Web: <http://polity.org.za.govdocs/white.papers/highed.html>

Department of Education. (1997). *Education White Paper 3: A programme for the transformation of Higher Education*. Pretoria: Government Printer.

Department of Education. (1997). *The Higher Education Act, no 101*. Pretoria: Government Printer.

Department of Education. (1998). *Green Paper on further education and training: Preparing for the twenty-first century through education, training and work*. Retrieved July 26, 1999 from the World-Wide Web: <http://polity.org.za.govdocs/green.papers/furtheredgp.htm>

Department of Education. (1998). *The Employment Equity Act*. Pretoria: Government Printer.

Department of Education. (1998). The Skills Development Act. Pretoria: Government Printer.

Department of Education. (1998). *The Skills Development Act Regulations*. Pretoria: Government Printer.

Department of Labour. (2001). *Ensuring quality in education and training – the role of Education and Training Quality Assurance Bodies (ETQAs)*. Pretoria: Department of Labour.

Department of Labour, (2003). *Labour Market Review Report 2003*. Pretoria: Government Printer.

Department of Labour. (2004). *State of skills in South Africa*. Pretoria: Department of Labour.

Department of Labour, (2005). *Labour Market Review Report 2005*. Pretoria: Government Printer.

Department of National Education. (1995). *South African Qualifications Authority Act*. Pretoria: Government Printer.

Department of National Education. (1997). *Outcomes-based education in South Africa*. Pretoria: Government Printer.

Department of National Education. (1997). *Education White Paper 3: A programme for the transformation of Higher Education*. Pretoria: Government Printer.

DeRouin, R.E., Parrish, T.J. & Salas, E. (2005). *On-the-job training: A review for researchers and practitioners*. Poster session presented at the 20th annual conference of the Society for Industrial and Organisational Psychology, Los Angeles, CA.

Diamond, R.M. (1984). *A love affair with the brain*. Psychology Today, November, 62.

Dooley, K.E., Lindner, J.R. & Dooley, L.M. (2005). *Advanced methods in distance education*. 2005. Hershey, PA: Information Science Publishing.

Du Toit, J. (1998). *The structure of the South African economy*. Cape Town: Southern Africa.

Dyer, W.W. (1998). *Wisdom of the ages*. New York: Harper Collins.

Edwards, R. (1997). *Changing places: Flexibility, lifelong learning and a learning society*. London: Routledge.

Employment Equity Act, No 55 of 1998.

Erasmus, B.J. & Van Dyk, P.S. (1999). *Training Management in South Africa*. International Thompson Publishing: Johannesburg.

Erasmus, B.J. & van Dyk, P.S. (2003). *Training management in South Africa (3rd ed.)*. Cape Town: Oxford University Press, South Africa.

Erasmus, B.J., Loedolff, P.vZ., Mda, J. & Nel, P.S. (2006). *Managing training and development in South Africa. Fourth edition*. Cape Town: Oxford University Press, South Africa.

ETDP SETA. (2006). *Sector skills plan for the period 2005-2010*. Retrieved from the World Wide Web, http://www.etdpseta.org.za on 15 April 2007

Fitz-ens, J. (1995). *How to measure human resources management*. New York: McGraw-Hill.

Folscher, E. & Chonco, L. (2006). *Skills development practice made easy*. Johannesburg: Knowres.

Freiberg, J.H. & Driscoll, A. (1996). *Universal teaching strategies*. London: Allyn & Bacon.

Further Education and Training Act, No 98 of 1998.

Galbraith, M.W. (Editor). (1990). *Adult learning methods. A Guide for effective instruction.* Malabar, Florida: Krieger publishing.

Gardner, H. (1983). *Frames of mind.* New York: Basic Books.

Garger, E.M. (1999). Goodbye training, hello learning. *Workforce*, November, 35-42.

Geis, G.L. & Smith, M.E. (1992). The function of evaluation. In H.D. Stolovitch & E.J. Keeps (Eds.). *Handbook of human performance technology* (pp 130-150). San Francisco: Jossey-Bass.

Gibb, S.E. (2002). *Learning and development: Processes, practices and perspectives at work.* Houndmills: Palgrave Macmillan.

Gilmore, E. (2006). Using content analysis in human performance technology. In J.A. Pershing (ed.) *Handbook of human performance technology: Principles, practices and potential.* San Francisco: Pfeiffer.

Goldstein, L.I. (1986). *Training in Organizations: Needs Assessment, Development and Evaluation.* 2nd ed., Brooks Cole, Pacific Grove, CA.

Goldstein, I.L. & Ford, J.K. (2002). *Training in organisations: Needs assessment, development, and evaluation.* Belmont: Wordsworth.

Goleman, D. (2001). An EI-based theory of performance. In C. Cherniss & D. Goleman (Eds.), *The emotionally intelligent workplace* (p. 27). San Francisco: Jossey-Bass.

Goleman, D. (2002). *The new leaders.* Great Britain: Harvard Business School.

Gregory, G.H. (2005). *Differentiating instruction with style.* Thousand Oaks, California: Corwin Press.

Grobler, P.A., Wärnich, S., Carrell, M.R., Elbert, N.F. & Hatfield, R.D. (2006). *Human Resource Management in South Africa.* Cornwall: Thomson Learning.

Guba, E.G. & Lincoln, Y.S. (1989). *Fourth generation evaluation.* Newbury Park: Sage.

Gully, S.M., Payne, S.C., Koles, K.L. & Whiteman, J.K. (2002). The impact of error training and individual differences on training outcomes: An attribute treatment interaction perspective. *Journal of Applied Psychology*, 87, 143-155.

Gultig, L., Lubisi, C., Parker, B. & Wedekind, V. (1999). *Understand outcomes-based education, teaching and assessment in South Africa.* Cape Town: SA Institute for Distance Education and Oxford University Press.

Harrison, R. (2000). *Employee development.* London: Institute of Personnel and Development.

Hattingh, S. (2003). *Learnerships: A tool for improving workplace performance.* Knowres: Johannesburg.

Hattingh, S. & Smit, S. (2004). *Building learning organisations to enhance competitiveness.* Johannesburg: Knowres.

Higher Education Act 101 of 1997.

Higher Education Amendment Act 38 of 2003.

Human Resource Strategy for the Public Service 1997.

Ivancevich, J.M. & Matteson, M.T. (2000). *Organisational Behaviour and Management.* McGraw-Hill: Boston.

Jackson, S.F. & Addison, R.M. (1992). Planning and managing projects. In H.D. Stolovitch & E.J. Keeps (Eds.), *Handbook of Human Performance Technology* (pp. 66-76). San Francisco: Jossey-Bass.

Jacobs, R.L. (1992). Structured on-the-job training. In H.D. Stolovitch & E.J. Keeps (Eds.). *Handbook of human performance technology* (pp 499-512). San Francisco: Jossey-Bass.

Kanfer, R. & Kantrowitz, T.M. (2002). Emotion regulation: Command and control of emotion in work life. In R.G. Lord, R.J. Klimoski, & R. Kanfer (Eds.), *Emotions in the workplace: Understanding the structure and role of emotions in organizational behaviour* (pp 429-472). New York: Jossey-Bass.

Kaufman, R. & Watters, K. (1992). Challenges to human performance technology: Ethics, quality and professionalism. In H.D. Stolovitch & E.J. Keeps (Eds.). *Handbook of human performance technology* (pp 732-742). San Francisco: Jossey-Bass.

Killen, R. (2000). *Teaching strategies for outcomes-based education.* Cape Town: Juta.

Kinicki, A. & Kreitner, R. (2006). *Organisational behaviour: Key concepts, skills and best practices (3rd edition).* New York: McGraw-Hill.

Kirkpatrick, D.L. (1994). *Evaluating training programs – The four levels (2nd ed.).* San Francisco: Berrett-Koehler.

Knowles, M. (1972). *The modern practice of adult education: Andragogy versus pedagogy.* New York: Association Press.

Kohler, W. (1925). *The mentality of apes.* New York: Harcourt Brace Jovanovich.

Kolb, D.A. (1985). *Experiential learning: Experiences as the source of learning and development.* New York: Prentice Hall.

Kolb, D.A. & Fry, R. (1975). Towards an applied theory of experiential learning. In C.L. Cooper (Ed.), *Theories of group processes* (pp 33-57). Chichester: Wiley.

Koo, L.C. (1999). Learning action learning. *Journal of Workplace Learning*, 11(31, 89-94).

Laird, D. (1993). *Approaches to training and development (2nd ed.).* Reading: Addison-Wesley.

Lambert, D. & The Diagram Group. (1996). *Body*

language. London: Harper Collins.

Landy, F.J. & Conte, J.M. (2004). *Work in the 21st century: An introduction to Industrial and Organisational Psychology*. New York: McGraw-Hill.

Leatherman, D. (1990). *The training trilogy: Facilitation skills*. Amherst: Human Resource Development Press.

Lee, S.H. (2006). Constructing effective questionnaires. In J.A. Pershing (ed.) *Handbook of human performance technology: Principles, practices and potential*. San Francisco: Pfeiffer.

Lee-Davies, L. (2007). *Developing work and study skills*. London: Thomson.

Le Roux, C., Loedolff, P., Louw, W., Nel, J. & Roman, M. (2004). *Training and development*. Pretoria: University of South Africa.

Lei, D., Slocum, J.W. & Pitts, R.A. (1999). *Designing organisations for competitive advantage: The power of unlearning and learning*. Organisational Dynamics, (Winter), 24-38.

Lev, B. (2001). *Intangibles: Management, measurement and reporting*. Washington, DC.: Brookings Institution Press.

Locke, E.A. (2005). Why emotional intelligence is an invalid concept. *Journal of Organizational Behavior*, 26, 425-431.

Losey, M., Meisinger, S. & Ulrich, D. (Eds.). (2005). *The future of human resource management*. Hoboken, New Jersey: John Wiley & Sons.

Machin, M.A. (2002). Planning, managing and optimizing transfer of training. In K. Kraiger (Ed.), *Creating, implementing and managing effective training and development* (pp 263-301). San Francisco: Jossey-Bass.

MacLean, P. (1973). *A triune concept of the brain and behaviour*. Toronto: University of Toronto Press.

Maira, A. & Scott-Morgan, P. (1997). *The accelerating organisation: Embracing the human face of change*. New York: McGraw-Hill.

Mandell, B. & Pherwani, S. 2003. Relationship between emotional intelligence and transformational leadership style: A gender comparison. *Journal of Business and Psychology*, 17(3): 387-404.

Marchington, M. & Wilkinson, A. (2005). *Human Resource Management at Work*. London: CIPD.

Martin, J. (2005). *Organisational behaviour and management*. London: Thomson.

Mayer, J.D., Caruso, D.R., & Salovey, P. (1999). Emotional intelligence meets standards for traditional intelligence. *Intelligence*, 27: 267-298.

Mayer, J.D. & Salovey, P. (1993). The intelligence of emotional intelligence. *Intelligence*, Vol. 17: 433-442.

Mayer, J.D. & Salovey, P. (1997). What is emotional intelligence: Implications for educators. In

P. Salovey & D. Sluyter (Eds.), *Emotional development, emotional literacy, and emotional intelligence: Educational implications* (pp. 3-31). New York: Basic Books.

McGhan, B. (1994). The possible outcomes of outcomes-based education. *Educational Leadership*, 51, 70-72.

Merriam, S.B. (2004). The changing landscape of adult learning theory. *Review of adult learning and literacy*, 4, 199-220.

Merriam, S.B. (2004). The changing landscape of adult learning theory. *Review of adult learning and literacy*, 4, 199-220.

Meyer, M., Mabaso, J., Lancaster, K. & Nenungwi, L. (2004). *ETD practices in South Africa*. Durban: LexisNexis Butterworths.

Michalak, D.F. & Yager, E.I.G. (1979). *Making the training process work*. New York: Harper and Roe.

Ministerial Committee for Development Work on the NQF. (1996). *Discussion document: lifelong learning through a national qualifications framework*. Pretoria: Department of Education.

Molenda, M. & Russell, J.D. (2006). Instruction as an intervention. In J.A. Pershing (ed.) *Handbook of human performance technology: Principles, practices and potential*. San Francisco: Pfeiffer.

Nadler, L. (1982). *Designing training programmes: The critical events model*. Reading: Addison Wesley.

National Education Policy Act, No 27 of 1996.

National Training Board. (1998). *Education, training and development practices project: An indigenous model for progression paths, qualifications and standards within the National Qualifications Framework*. Pretoria: Department of Labour.

Neidorf, R. (2006). *Teach beyond your reach*. Medford, NJ: Information today, Inc.

Newstrom, J.W. & Lengnick-Hall, M.L. (1991). *One size does not fit all*. Training and Development, 45(6), 43-46, 48.

Nonaka, I. & Takeuchi, H. (1995). *The knowledge creating company*. New York: Oxford University Press.

Ornstein, R. (1977). *The education of the intuitive mode: The psychology of consciousness*. San Diego, Calif.: Harcourt Brace Jovanovich.

Padayachee, S. (1998). EE" does not equal "AA" but the Employment Equity Bill still boggles. *People Dynamics*, 16(5), 54-55.

Palmer, R. (2002). *Training with the midas touch*. London: Kogan Page.

Paris, S.G. & Ayres, L.R. (1994). *Becoming reflective students and teachers with portfolios and authentic assessment*. Washington DC: American Psychological Association.

Patrick, J. (1992). *Training Research and Practice*.

Harcourt Brace Jovanovich, London and San Diego, CA.

Pershing, J.L. (2006). Interviewing to analyze and evaluate human performance technology. In J.A. Pershing (ed.) *Handbook of human performance technology: Principles, practices and potential*. San Francisco: Pfeiffer.

Pershing, J.A.; Scott, S.J. & Rowe, D.T. (2006). Observation methods for human performance technology. In J.A. Pershing (ed.) *Handbook of human performance technology: Principles, practices and potential*. San Francisco: Pfeiffer.

Philips, J.J. (1994). *Measuring ROI: Progress, trends and strategies*. ASTD Press.

Phillips, J.J., Phillips, P.P. & Hodges, T.K. (2004). *Make training evaluation work*. Alexandria: ASTD Press.

Piaget, J. (1926). *The language and thought of the child*. New York: Harcourt Brace Jovanovich.

Prinsloo, P. (2007). *Handout notes on NQF level descriptors*: Workshop session conducted in March 2007 at the University of South Africa, Pretoria.

Rae, L. (1994). *How to design and introduce training and development programmes*. London: McGraw-Hill.

Reid, G. (2005). *Learning styles and inclusion*. London: Paul Chapman Publishing.

Reynolds, J., Caley, L. & Mason, R. (2002). *How do people learn?* London: CIPD.

Robinson, I. (2006). *Human Resource Management in Organisations*. London: CIPD.

Robinson, D.G. & Robinson, J.C. (1989). *Training for impact: How to link training to business needs and measure the results*. San Francisco: Jossey-Bass.

Rogers, C. (1969). *Freedom to learn*. Ohio: Merrill.

Rogers, C. & Freiberg, H.J. (1994). *Freedom to learn*. New York: Maxwell Macmillan International.

Rollinson, D. (2005). *Organisational behaviour and analysis: An integrated approach*. London: Prentice-Hall.

Roscoe, J. (1995). Analysis of organizational training needs, in Truelove, S. (Ed.). *The Handbook of Training and Development, 2nd ed.*, Basil Blackwell, Oxford.

Rossett, A. (1992). Analysis of human performance problems. In H.D. Stolovitch & E.J. Keeps (Eds.). *Handbook of human performance technology* (pp 97-113). San Francisco: Jossey-Bass.

Rossi, P.H., Freeman, H.E. & Lipsey, M.W. (1999). *Evaluation: A systematic approach*. Thousand Oaks: Sage.

Rothwell, W.J. & Kazanas, H.C. (1994). *Human resource development: A strategic approach*. Massachusetts: HRD Press.

Rothwell, W.J. & Sredl, H.J. (1992). *The ASTD guide to professional roles and competencies: Volume 1:* Amherst: ASTD Press.

Rothwell, W.J., Sullivan, R. & McLean, G.N. (1995). *Practicing Organisation Development: A guide for consultants*. Johannesburg: Pfeiffer & Co.

Salas, E., Burke, S.C. & Cannon-Bowers, J.A. (2002). What we know about designing and delivering team training: Tips and guidelines. In K. Kraiger (Ed.), *Creating, implementing and managing effective training and development* (pp 234-259). San Francisco: Jossey-Bass.

Salovey, P. & Mayer, J.D. (1990). *Emotional intelligence. Imagination, Cognition, and Personality*, 9, 185-211.

Sanchez, R. (1995). Strategic flexibility in product competition. *Strategic Management Journal*, 16, 135-139.

SAQA. (1999). *Criteria and guidelines for ETQAs*. Pretoria: SAQA.

SAQA. (2000). *The National Qualifications Framework: An Overview*. Pretoria: SAQA.

SAQA. (2000a). *The National Qualifications Framework and Quality Assurance*. Pretoria: SAQA.

SAQA. (2000b). *Quality Management Systems of ETQAs*. Pretoria: SAQA.

SAQA. (2000c). *NQF and Standard Setting*. Pretoria: SAQA.

SAQA. (2001). *Guidelines for the assessment of NQF registered unit standards and qualifications*. Pretoria: SAQA.

SAQA. (2001a). *Criteria and guidelines for ETQAs*. Pretoria: SAQA.

SAQA. (2001b). *Criteria and guidelines for Providers*. Pretoria: SAQA.

SAQA (2001c). *Quality management systems for education and training providers*. Pretoria: SAQA.

SAQA. (2001d). *Criteria and guidelines for the registration of assessors*. Pretoria:SAQA.

SAQA. (2004). *Criteria and guidelines for short courses and skills programmes*. Pretoria: SAQA.

SAQA. (2005). *Guidelines for integrated assessment*. Pretoria: SAQA.

SAQA. (2007). *Unit Standard: Bachelor-Occupationally Directed Education, Training and Development Practices (US ID: 50330)*. Retrieved from the World Wide Web on 19 February 2007, http://regqs.saqa.org.za

Schacht, N. (2002). Blended learning. *E-learning*, May, 34-35.

Schunk, D.H. (2004). *Learning theories: an educational perspective. Fourth edition*. Upper Saddle River, New Jersey: Pearson Prentice Hall.

SGB (Assessors). (2000). *Unit Standards for Assessment and Moderation*. Pretoria: SAQA.

SGB (ETD: Adult Learning – ABET). (2000). *Qualifications and Unit Standards for Adult*

Basic Education and Training (ABET) Practitioners. Pretoria: UNISA ABET Institute.

SGB (Occupation-directed ETD). (2000). *Standards and Qualifications for Occupation-directed Education, Training and Development Practitioners*. Pretoria: SAQA.

Sink, D.L. (1992). Success strategies for the human performance technologist. In H.D. Stolovitch & E.J. Keeps (Eds.). *Handbook of human performance technology* (pp 564-575). San Francisco: Jossey-Bass.

Skills Development Act, No 97 of 1998.

Skills Development Levies Act, 1999.

Smith, M.E. & Geis, G.L. (1992). Planning an evaluation study. In: H. Stolovitch & E.J. Keeps (Eds.). *Handbook of human performance and technology* (pp. 151-166). San Francisco: Jossey-Bass.

South African Qualifications Authority Act, No 58 of 1995

Sperry, R.W. (1974). Lateral specialisation in the surgically separated hemispheres. In *The Neurosciences Third Study Program*. Cambridge, Mass.: MIT Press.

Stevenson, R.J. & Palmer, J.A. (1994). *Learning: Principles, processes and practices*. New York: Cassell Educational Limited.

Stewart, J. (2002). Employee development. In J. Leopold (Ed.), *Human Resources in Organisations*. Harlow, FT: Prentice Hall.

Steyn, G.M. & Van Niekerk, E.J. (2002). *Human Resource Management in Education*. Pretoria: University of South Africa Press.

Stolovitch, H.D. & Keeps, E.J. (1992). *Handbook of Human Performance Technology: A comprehensive guide for analysing and solving performance problems in organisations*. San Francisco: Jossey-Bass Publishers.

Strong, L. & Vorwerk, C. (2001). *Developing learning materials and resources for workplace learning*. Randburg: Knowres.

Swanepoel, B., Erasmus, B., Van Wyk, H. & Schenk, H. (2003). *Human resource management*. Juta: Cape Town.

Swanson, R.A. (1994). *Analysis for improving performance: Tools for diagnosing organisations & documenting workplace expertise*. Thousand Oaks: Sage

Swart, J., Mann, C., Brown, S. & Price, A. (2005). *Human resource development: Strategy and tactics*. Oxford: Elsevier Butterworth-Heinemann.

Technikon SA. (2000). *Get Active; Writing Outcomes-based Learner-centred Study Materials*. Roodepoort: TSA.

The National Skills Development Strategy. (2005). Pretoria: Department of Labour.

Thorne, K. & MacHray, A. (2000). *World class training*. London: Kogan Page.

Telela, P. (2004). In McGrath, S., Badroodien, A., Krrak, A. & Unwin, L. (Eds.). *Shifting understanding of skills in South Africa: Overcoming the historical imprint of a low skills regime*. Department of Labour, Pretoria.

Tennant, M. (2006). *Psychology and adult learning*. Third edition. New York: Routledge.

Terre Blanche, K. & Durrheim, K. (eds.). (1999). *Research in practice: Applied methods for the social sciences*. Cape Town: University of Cape Town Press.

Thiagarajan, S. (1992). Small-group activities. In H.D. Stolovitch & E.J. Keeps (Eds.). *Handbook of human performance technology* (pp 412-430). San Francisco: Jossey-Bass.

Towler, A.J. & Dipboye, R.L. (2001). Effects of trainer expressiveness, organization, and trainee goal orientation on training outcomes. *Journal of Applied Psychology*, 86, 664-637.

Ulrich, D. & Brockbank, W. (2005). The *HR value proposition*. Boston, Massachusetts: Harvard Business School.

Van der Horst, H. & McDonald, R. (1997). *Outcomes-based education: A teacher's manual*. Pretoria: Kagiso Publishers.

Van Dam, K. (2004). Antecedents and consequences of employability orientation. *European Journal of Work and Organizational Psychology*, 13(1), 29-51.

Van Dyk, P.S., Nel, P.S., Loedolff, P.vZ., & Haasbroek, G.D. (1997). *Training Management: A multidisciplinary approach to human resources development in Southern Africa*. Western Cape: International Thomson Publishing SA (Pty) Ltd.

Viviers, A.M., Vosloo, S.E., Ras, C. & Nöthling, M. (2000). *Human capacity development*. Pretoria: University of South Africa.

Ward, J. & LaBranche, G.A. (2003). Blended learning: The convergence of E-Learning and meetings. *Franchising World*, May/June, 22-23.

Westgaard, O. (1992). Standards and ethics for practitioners. In H.D. Stolovitch & E.J. Keeps (Eds.). *Handbook of human performance technology* (pp 576-585). San Francisco: Jossey-Bass.

Whetton, D.A. & Cameron, K.S. (2002). Developing management skills. New Jersey: Prentice-Hall.

Whitehead, M. (1999). Collection Time. *People Management*, 28 October: 68-71.

Wolmarans, S. (2004). *Heart Currency: Advanced Emotional Competencies Series*. Johannesburg: Learning Link International.

Yelon, S.L. (1992). Classroom instruction. In H.D. Stolovitch & E.J. Keeps (Eds.). *Handbook of human performance technology* (pp 383-413). San Francisco: Jossey-Bass.

Index

ABET 7–8, 12, 15
Absenteeism 195
Abstract conceptualisation 61
Abstract/random learning style 63
Abstract/sequential learning style 63
Accelerated learning 66
Accreditation 28–29, 315–318
  application for 28
  benefits of 27–28
  categories of 29
  criteria, SAQA 315–318
  models of 29
Accreditation of provider, see Provider
  accreditation
Action learning 65
Active experimentation 61
Active practice 204–205
Adaptive guidance 207
Adult learners 55
Adult learning centres 12
Affective domain 134, 136, 137, 139
Agenda 182–183
American Society for Training and
  Development (ASTD) 335
Analytical learner 64
Andragogy 56, 177
Annual training report 34, 37, 38
Applied Competence, see Competence
Apprenticeship 40, 41, 175
Assessment and moderation 214–246
Assessment documents 238–239
Assessment guide 232–233
Assessment instruments 223–228
  uses of 226–227
Assessment methods 223–228
  uses of 224–225
Assessment process 228–242
  evaluation by candidate 242
  review of 241–242
Assessment
  conduct of 235–237
  consistency of 240
  criteria 24, 129
  diagnostic, 218, 219
  evaluative 221–222
  formative 219–220, 221
  input-based 218
  integrative 222–223

  moderation of 242–245
  outcomes-based 214
  planning of 228–233
  portfolio 225
  preparation of learner for 233–234
  principles of 236–237
  purposes of 214–215
  role players in 215–216
  RPL 227–228
  summative 221
  types of 218–219
Assessor competence 216–217
Assumed learning 203
Attitudes 48
Authenticity declaration 235–236
Automaticity 65

Banking operations 107
Batho Pele principle 86–87
BBBEE 10
Behaviour
  change in 186–187, 207
  dysfunctional 194
  emotionally intelligent 194
  evaluation 270
  problem195–196
Behaviourist theories 56, 57
Bias, in performance appraisal 104
Bill of Rights 217–218
Blended learning methods 173
Body language 192–195
  meanings of 193
  negative 192
  positive 192

Camping gear, case study 114
CCFO 20–22, 24, 132, 138, 139
Chalkboard 172
Change through learning 50, 266, 268
Classroom training 167–173, 202–206,
  180–187
  advantages 167
  learning support materials for 170
  limitations of 167
  management of 207–209
  methods of 168–170
  principles of 202–206
  selection of 168–170

Coaching, and mentoring 64–65, 175
Cognitive domain 134, 135, 137, 139
Cognitive theories 56, 57–59
Common sense learner 64
Community development projects 39
Competence 48, 94, 97 110, 263
Competence charts 108–109
Competence
  applied 22
  core 87
  cross-functional 110, 111
  foundational 18, 22, 97, 155
  practical 18–19, 22, 97, 155
  professional 110, 111
  reflexive 19, 22, 97, 155
Competitive advantage 297
Conceptual principles 52
Concrete experiences 61
Concrete/random learning style 63
Concrete/sequential learning style 63
Confidentiality 103
Contact learning 154
Content
  essential 203
  sequencing of 143–144
  sources of 140
  types of 140
Continued professional development 336,
  342–345
Control group 279
Core skills 87
Cost
  input analysis of 267
  per learner 267
  per unit of training 266–267
Course outline 141–142
Course planning, checklists 151, 152
Credibility
  challenges to 195
  establishing 179
Credit management 107
Credits 22, 24
Critical cross-field outcomes, see CCFO
Critical incidents 104
Critical skills 12, 13, 34
Curriculum design 122–125, 154–155
Customer requirements, alignment with 297
Customer service development 290–291

Data analysis 113, 280
Data collection 108
  by interview 276

by observation 277
by organisational records 277–278
by questionnaires 275–276
cycle 112
tools of 275, 278
Delivery, as part of ETD management 304
Demographics of employees 93
Department of Education 14
Design down, deliver up approach 123, 125
Development planning 113
Development through learning 49–50
Developmental outcomes 21
Diamond's regenerative brain theory 67
Direct instruction 167
Disabilities, workers with 5
Discretionary funds 11
Distraction in the classroom 196
Distributed practice 66
Diversity training, case study 346
Dynamic learner 64

Education and training quality assurance
  bodies, see ETQA
Education level 93
EE 7, 10, 37, 291
Effective learning 168–169
  conditions for 168
Effectiveness of ETD, criteria for 298
e-learning 174
Eli Lilly, case study 292
Emotions and classroom atmosphere
  158–160
Empathy 70
Employability, enhancing of 291
Employee performance 6
Employee statistics 89
Employee status 94
Employment equity, see EE
Environmental analysis as part of ETD
  management 305
Equal opportunity 20
ETD management 290–323
  evaluation as part of 304, 310–311, 312,
    319
  functions of 307–313
  key functions of 311–312
  organising resources of 308, 311, 319,
    320
  priorities of 290
  process of 303–307
  reasons for failure of 312
  resources for 307–308

ETD practitioners
  challenges for 347
  characteristics of 331–333
  competency of 333–335
  core skills of 334–335
  education and training of 335–341
  ethical issues of 345–346
  networking of 343
  qualifications of 336
  roles of 328–331
  self-assessment for 337–341
ETD priorities 290–291
ETD providers, recognition of 29–30
ETD, challenge 4
ETD, key points of 3
ETD, needs of 123, 124
Ethical issues in ETD 113, 345–346
Ethics declaration 235–236
ETQA 14
  functions of 27
  types of 28
Evaluation, 113
  criteria 262, 275
  dimensions 275
  forms 150, 151
  models 269–273
  of ETD 250, 251–254, 310–311, 312, 319
  of ETD, advantages of 251
  report 281
  results 280–282
  compliance 256, 257–262
  diagnostic 251, 252, 253
  factors that discourage 282–284
  focus of 253
  formal 256
  formative 251, 252, 253, 254
  integrated 256
  learning 270
  longitudinal 251, 252–253
  management of 254
  peer 256
  process of 273–282
  reaction 269–270
  results 270–271
  stakeholders in 254–257
  summative 251, 252–253, 255–256
  timing of 253
  value-added 256, 262–269
  value-added, levels of 268–269
Evaluation plan, drawing up of 278–279
Evidence
  direct 237, 138

documenting of 237–240
evaluation of 239–240
gathering of 237–240
historical 238
indirect 237, 138
of application 239
of knowledge 239
of understanding 239
supplementary 237
VACS analysis of 239
Experience level of learners 54–55
Experiential learning 60–61
Extended public works programme 12

Feedback 81–82, 98, 113, 142, 178, 180,
  191–192, 205–206, 240–241
  360-degree system 98
  contract 191
  giving 192
  positive 180, 240–241
  receiving 192
Fidelity
  physical 65
  psychological 65
Flexibility 178
Flip charts 172
Foundational competence, see Competence
Friendly helper 71
Further education and training, (FET) 15,
  16

Gardner's eight intelligences, see
  Intelligence
General Education and Training (GET) 15,
  16
Generation
  Xers 146–147, 190
  boomer 146, 190
  millennial 14, 190
  silent 146, 190
Generations 190
  characteristics of 146–147
  needs of different 145
Generic skills 88
Goal setting 205
Grants 11–13, 36–37
  BEE 11
  discretionary 11, 13, 36, 37
  mandatory 36, 37
  new venture creation 12
  work experience 12
Gregorc's learning styles 63

Ground rules, establishing of 183
Group dynamics 189
Group work 60
Guba and Lincoln's 4th generation
   evaluation 272–273
Gym equipment, case study 114

Handouts 150, 171
Higher education and training (HET) 16
Hippocampus 67
HRD 48
   committee 106
   policies 106
   procedures 106
HRDS 90, 299–302
   as part of ETD management 303
   forces affecting 303
Human capital, development of 291–292
Human resource development strategy, see
   HRDS
Human resource development, see HRD
Humanist perspectives on learning 56, 60

Imaginative learner 64
Impact, of ETD 263, 266, 268
   measurement of 268
Improvement plan, example of 318–319
Incentivised training 11
Informal sector support 12
Information processing 58
Inputs, as element of QA 315
Institute of sectoral or occupation
   excellence 13
Intelligence 68–72
   analytical 69, 72
   bodily or kinaesthetic 68, 72
   creative 69, 72
   emotional 69, 72
   Gardner's eight 68–69
   interpersonal 69, 72
   intrapersonal 69, 72
   linguistic or verbal 68, 72
   logical or mathematical 68
   musical or rhythmic 68, 72
   naturalist 68
   practical 69, 72
   spatial or visual 68, 72
   stimulation of 72
   Sternberg's three 69
Internet-based training 174

JC Penny, case study 294

Job rotation 175

Kirkpatrick's taxonomy of ETD evaluation
   269–271
Knowledge 49
   application of 180
   management of 292–294
   tests 103
   conceptual 52
   embedded 24, 129
   skills, attitudes and other behaviour 95
Kolb and Fry's learning style inventory 62
Kolb's learning cycle 61

Labour market 5
Labour Market Review Report 8–9
Labour market skills profile of 5
Labour-intensive 4
Language, of learners 217
Languages, official 217
Leadership as part of ETD management
   309, 311, 319
Learner support 156
Learner-centred approach 60, 121, 183
Learners
   background of 84
   characteristics of 54
   rights and needs of 177, 217–218
Learners' profile analysis 125–127
Learnership 39–42 175
   agreements 40
   requirements 41
   vs apprenticeship 41–42
   vs skills programmes 42
Learning activities
   design of 144–145
   examples of 145
Learning content, determining of 139
Learning context 59
Learning contracts 195
Learning environment 180–205
   conducive 196–202
   emotional 196–199
   physical 199
Learning facilitation 176–180, 182, 185,
   188–196
   collaborative 179
   effective 179
   elements of 185
   process of 188–196
Learning facilitator 56, 140, 152–153, 166
   ability of 140

guide 157–160
Learning materials, effective 151, 152
Learning organisation, characteristics of 292–294
Learning outcomes 124, 128, 131–134, 142, 143
  classifying of 134
  formulating of 131
Learning programme 25, 123–125, 128, 153–156, 263–264
  design 263–264
  strategy 125, 153, 156
  vs short course 25
  curriculum of 123–125
  delivery strategy of 154
  objectives of 128
Learning resources, examples of 141
Learning styles 62–64
Learning support materials 149, 170, 203
Learning
  approaches to 60–61
  barriers to 53
  explicit 50–53
  implicit 50
  nature of 50
  principles of 65–66
  theories of 56–60
  transfer of 263
Left brain 66–67
Levy grants 36–37
Levy payments 35–36
Levy payments, claiming back of 36
Lifelong learning 23, 55–56
Limbic system 67
Listening skills 178
Logical thinker 71

Mammalian brain 67
Massed practice 66
Mastery orientation 54
McCarthy's 4MAT model 63–64
Meaningfulness, of topic 203
Memorising 50–51
Mentoring and coaching 64–65, 175
Modelling, as teaching method 204
Moderation and assessment, see Assessment
Moderation system 242–245
  components of 243
  extent of 243
  functions of 243
  management of 242–243

materials for 243
methods of 243–244
personnel 243
timing of 243
Moderation, tools of 244–245
Modules 123, 150

Nadler's model of evaluation 271–272
National Education Policy Act 14
National learner record database 15, 40
National Qualification Framework, see NQF
National scarce skills guide 87
National skills authority 31
National skills development strategy, see NSDS
National skills fund, see NSF
National standards body, see NSB
Needs analysis 77, 78
  as part of ETD management, 303
  by individual interviews 103
  quality checklist 115
  system 106
  implementation phase of 112–113
  levels of 85–102
  methods of 102–105
  national 85
  organisational 85, 87–95
  proactive 89
  process 105–115
  purpose of 80–85
  reactive 80
  sectoral 85, 86–87
  training 90
Negative comments, dealing with 195
Neocortex 67
Neomammalian brain 67
Non-critical atmosphere 198
Non-verbal communication 192–195
Novelty 203–204
NQF 13, 15–20, 23
NQF as QA for ETD management 313–323
NQF, current 16
NQF, level descriptors of 18–19
NQF, principles of 19–20
NQF, proposed new 17
NSB 26
NSB, functions of 26
NSDS 3, 7–13, 336
  mission of 9
  objectives of 10–13
  principles of 9
  success indicators of 10–13

vision of 9
NSF 8, 11, 35–36
NSF top-up funding 37

OBET 20–21, 119–163
Observation 103
Observational learning 59
On-the-job training 175
Organisational
    capability 294–296
    effectiveness 295
    flexibility 294–296
    goals 87
    outputs 264
    sustainability 295
Orientation of learners 182
Outcomes 23
Outcomes based education and training,
    see OBET
Outcomes
    as element of QA 315
    critical cross-field, see CCFO
    developmental 21
    of ETD, see change
    specific 129
Overhead transparencies 171
Overlearning 65

Participation, lack of 196
Participative process 56
Pattern recognition 58
People development 157–158
Performance appraisal 104, 175
Performance discrepancy 82–83
Performance gap 83
Performance orientation 54
Performance problems 81–83
    causes of 81
    solutions for 81–83
Person analysis 85, 98–102
Personal development plans 98–102, 104
Personal growth 6
Personnel budget 11
Phillips' ROI model 271
Pilot learning programme 252
Post office, case study 293–294
Post-class intervention 187
PowerPoint 170–171
Practical competence, see Competence
Practice 65, 142
Pre-class intervention 181–182
Pre-course learning 154

Presentation skills 180
Prioritisation matrix 91
Problem solving 51–52
Process, as element of QA 315
Professional
    associations 335, 342
    competence, see Competence
    development 297
Programmed instruction 173
Project skills plans 39
Provider accreditation 27–30
    application for 28
    benefits of 27–28
    categories of 29
    models of 29
Providers, recognition of 29–30
Psychomotor domain 134, 136, 137, 139
Public service departments 35
Public service training 299–300
Punctuality 195

QA 242, 260–261
    as part of ETD management 309–310,
    312, 313–323
    bodies 26
    checklist for learning programme
    161–162, 320–323
    documentation 160–162
    critical points of 315
    elements of 314–315
    NQF 257–258
Qualification, definition of 24, 25
Qualifications 22–25
    components of 25
Quality assurance, see QA
Quality improvement 290
Questioning skills 178
Questionnaires 102–103
    for data collection, see Data collection
    design of 109–111
    guidelines for 276
Questions, guidelines for 191

Range statement 24, 130
Readiness to learn 54
Recognition of prior learning, see RPL
Reflective observation 61
Reflexive Competence, see Competence
Reflexive learning 154
Reinforcement 57
Reptilian brain 67
Research questions, formulation of 275

Results, organisational 263–265
    intangible 264–265
    tangible 264
Return on Investment, see ROI
Reward 57
Right brain 67
Right skilling 78
Role modelling 59
Role play 59, 148
RPL 20, 22, 84–85

SABPP 335
SABPP, ethical principles of 345–346
SABPP, levels of professional registration 336
SAQA Act 14–20, 22
SAQA
    assessment policies 259
    learner policies 259
    management systems 258, 259
    programme delivery 259
    quality requirements 258–259
    review mechanisms 258
    staff policies 259
    structures 15
Scarce skills 87
Schedule of learning 182–183
SDA 3, 14, 30–34, 37, 40
    structures of 30–34
SDF 38–39, 88, 90
    role of 38–39
SDLA 14, 30, 34–39
Seating layout 200–202
Sector skills plan 33
Self-assessment 101–102
Self-awareness 70
Self-directed learning 55
Self-evaluation 98, 256, 322
Self-management 207
    emotional 70
Self-study materials 150
SETAs 12, 31–33
    governing board 32
    functions of 32
    list of 32–33
SGB 25, 26
Short learning programme 42, 119–163
Short term memory 58
Skills 49
Skills analysis 87
Skills audit 87, 90, 93–94
Skills development 4

Skills Development Act, see SDA
Skills development committees 38
Skills development fund, see SDF
Skills development legislation 14
Skills development levy fund, see SDLF
Skills gap 4, 78
Skills gap analysis 88
Skills gap analysis as part of ETD management 303, 306
Skills matrix 89, 92
Skills planning 93
Skills programmes, characteristics of 42–43
Skills shortage 87
Skills tests 103
Skills upliftment 6, 7
Social development initiatives 12, 91
Social learning theories 56, 59–61
South African Board for Personnel Practice, see SABPP
South African Qualifications Authority, see SAQA
South African Revenue Services 35–36
Special needs, learners with 323
Split-brain theory 66–67
Sports equipment, case study 114
Stakeholders 272, 296
Stakeholders, identification of 274
Standards 98
Standards generating body, see SGB
Status of trainers 300
Sternberg's three intelligences, see Intelligence
Strategic skills planning process 94
Strategising, as part of ETD management 307–308, 311, 319
Strong achiever 71

Talent pool 87–88
Task analysis 85, 95–97
Task clusters 95
Team training 176
Technological change 6, 290
Technology 4, 93
Time management 178
Train operator, case study, 95
Trainer guide 152–153
Training acceleration 10
Training boards 39
Training committee 38, 106
Training cycle 48, 78, 79, 166, 188–189, 214, 250

Training delivery 165–173 264
  methods of 166–173
Training environment checklist 202
Training intervention 91
Training methods 147–149
Training needs matrix 91
Training 48, 148, 174–175, 266
  definition of 48
  measures of 266
  near-the-job 175
  orientation 175
  sensitivity 148
  technology-based 148, 174
  workplace methods 175
Transfer of learning 206–207
Triune brain theory 67–68

Umalusi 28
Understanding, as part of learning 52
Understudy assignments 175
Unit standards 18–19, 20, 22–24 124,
  128–130, 154
  alignment of 154
  elements of 23–24

level of complexity of 18–19
US social security, case study 306

VACS analysis, see evidence
Value added, measuring of 265–268
Value chain 266
Value proposition, 296–298, 303, 307, 311,
  319
Videos 172–173
Virtual university, case study 294

Whiteboard 172
Whole brain learning 67
Whole vs part learning 66
WIFI Corporation, case study 283
Workbooks 150
Working memory 51
Workplace skills development committee,
  see WSDC
Workplace skills plan, see WSP
WSDC 88, 91
WSP 10, 34, 37, 38, 88, 90, 304
  as part of ETD management 304

NOTES

NOTES